CONTEMPORARY CRIMINAL JUSTICE

Edited by
HARRY W. MORE, JR.
and
RICHARD CHANG

JUSTICE SYSTEMS DEVELOPMENT, INC.

San Jose

© 1974, by Justice Systems Development, Inc.
All rights reserved. Published 1974.

ISBN: 0-914526-00-6

Library of Congress Catalog Card Number: 74-77186

Published by Justice Systems Development, Inc.
P.O. Box 24649, San Jose, California   95154

Printed in the United States of America

CONTRIBUTING ARTICLES
(Reprinted with permission of the author and/or the publisher)

American Bar Association, Institute of Judicial Administration, *The Urban Police Function*, New York, The American Bar Association, 1972, pp. 47-71.

Advisory Committee on Intergovernmental Relations, *State-Local Relations in the Criminal Justice System*, Washington, Advisory Commission on Intergovernmental Relations, 1971, pp. 261-271.

Egon Bittner, *The Functions of the Police in Modern Society*, National Institute of Mental Health, Washington, U.S. Government Printing Office, 1972, pp. 48-62.

Daniel J. Freed, "The Nonsystem of Criminal Justice," National Commission on the Causes and Prevention of Violence, *Law and Order Reconsidered*, Washington, U.S. Government Printing Office, 1969, pp. 265-284.

Ernest C. Friesen, Jr., "Future Roles of Judges, Prosecutors and Defenders," *Future Roles of Criminal Justice Personnel: Position Papers*, Project STAR, American Justice Institute, Marina del Rey, California, 1972, pp. 1-13.

Daniel Glaser, "Changes in Corrections During the Next Twenty Years," *Future Roles of Crimnal Justice Personnel: Position Papers*, Project STAR, American Justice Institute, Marina del Rey, California, 1971, pp. 1-62.

Robert E. Keldgord, *Coordinated California Corrections: The System*, Sacramento, Board of Corrections, State of California, 1971, pp. 23-54.

Harry W. More, "Disparity in the System," *Administration of Justice Journal*, Vol. 1, No. 2, 1974, pp. 33-39.

Edward Peoples, *Why We Are Failing to Recycle Our Most Valuable Resource—Human Beings*, Paper presented at the Congress of the National Recreation and Park Association, October, 1972.

President's Commission on Law Enforcement and the Administration of Justice, *The Challenge of Crime in a Free Society*, Washington, U.S. Government Printing Office, 1967, pp. 128-141.

Clarence Schrag, *Crime and Justice: American Style*, National Institute of Mental Health, Washington, U.S. Government Printing Office, 1971, pp. 157-186.

CONTEMPORARY CRIMINAL JUSTICE

Daniel P. Stang, "The Police and Their Problems," National Commission on the Causes and Prevention of Violence, *Law and Order Reconsidered*, Washington, U.S. Government Printing Office, 1969, pp. 285-308.

Judith Toth, "Citizen Involvement in Law Enforcement," National Commission on the Causes and Prevention of Violence, *Law and Order Reconsidered*, Washington, U.S. Government Printing Office, 1969, pp. 411-426.

James Q. Wilson, "The Future Policeman," *Future Roles of Criminal Justice Personnel: Position Papers*, Project STAR, American Justice Institute, Marina del Rey, California, 1971, pp. 1-28.

PREFACE

Conflict and disparity in our system of criminal justice is clearly evident. This has been readily apparent to all "justice actors," but for the most part, the public has been ignorant of the conflict between the sub-systems of justice.

It has only been in recent years that this topic has received in-depth consideration.

In spite of the lofty principles propounded in the Bill of Rights, the system presents numerous obstacles to effective crime control, and it sometimes threatens the very ideals it was designed to preserve and promote. There is evidence that instead of preventing crime, the system of justice—as it is now embodied in our police, courts, and correctional agencies—is a significant factor in crime causation.

In theory the system operates under a few clear and simple precepts, of which the following are fair examples. All law violations are to be reported to the police. The reports are investigated, and if there is sufficient evidence the offender is arrested. Whenever an arrest is warranted there should be a court conviction. Conviction is followed by an appropriate punishment which, in turn, should serve as a deterrent against further offenses.

According to this model the case of an offender progresses by highly visible procedures from arrest to conviction to punishment. There is little opportunity for officials to exercise discretion and their decisions are presumably founded on conclusive information. Public participation is assured by the requirement that a jury of peers determine if the evidence warrants conviction, leaving the judge's decision regarding an appropriate punishment as the main point of discretionary authority.

In practice, however, the cycle of arrest to conviction to punishment is more the exception than the rule. Most offenses remain unreported. Many of those reported cannot be investigated. The lack of sufficient police personnel is the most obvious reason for this. In addition, the investigated cases are often screened to avoid the filing of official charges if conviction seems improbable. Moreover, our overcrowded court calendars encourage both prosecution and defense to engage in "bargaining justice" aimed at sparing the time and cost of a trial. Frequently this results in a plea of guilty to reduced charges or in outright dismissal. Even after conviction, most offenders receive fines, probation, or jail sentences instead of imprisonment in state or federal institutions. The unavoidable conclusion is that our police, court, and institutional resources are too limited to sustain the arrest to conviction to punishment model, even if that were the desired course of action.

To illustrate, in a recent year for which detailed estimates are available, approximately 2,800,000 major felonies—including murder, robbery, aggravated assault, burglary, grand larceny, and auto theft—were reported to the police. These reports resulted in 727,000 arrests, with the juvenile courts assuming jurisdiction over 260,000 of the individuals arrested. Among the remaining 467,000 cases arrested, more than 60 percent had their charges reduced or terminated, leaving 177,000 individuals who were formally accused in court as initially charged by the police. Of these, about 160,000 were found guilty by plea or court verdict and sentenced: 63,000 received felony commitments to correctional institutions; 35,000 were confined in jails or other local facilities; 56,000 were placed on probation; and 6,000 were given fines or unsupervised sentences.

The best estimate, then, is that there was one felony commitment for every 45 major offenses reported, or—if fines, probation, and jail terms are included—one application of court sanctions for every 17 offenses. While this estimate excludes the cases handled by juvenile courts—which cannot result in criminal convictions anyway—and fails to consider adequately the fact that a single offender can be responsible for several reported violations, it nevertheless suggests the extent to which the arrest to conviction to punishment model is circumvented in current practice.

The topics selected for inclusion in the text identify the major conflicts within the system and numerous recommendations for resolution of the conflict.

We wish to express our appreciation to the authors and publishers who so graciously granted permission to reprint their work. In addition, we would like to dedicate this book to our wives, Ginger and Mary.

Harry W. More, Jr.
Richard Chang

CONTENTS

II. THE FUNCTIONS OF THE POLICE IN MODERN SOCIETY

III. THE URBAN POLICE FUNCTION

IV. THE FUTURE POLICEMAN

PART 3. THE COURTS

I. CRIMINAL COURTS

II. ADJUDICATION AND THE COURTS

III. FUTURE ROLES OF JUDGES, PROSECUTORS AND DEFENDERS

PART 4. CORRECTIONS

I. CORRECTIONS AS A SYSTEM

II. CHANGES IN CORRECTIONS DURING THE NEXT TWENTY YEARS

PART 1

THE JUSTICE SYSTEM

The system of criminal justice America uses to deal with those crimes it cannot prevent and those criminals it cannot deter is not a monolithic, or even a consistent, system. It was not designed or built in one piece at one time. Its philosophic core is that a person may be punished by the government if, and only if, it has been proved by an impartial and deliberate process that he has violated a specific law. Around that core layer upon layer of institutions and procedures, some carefully constructed and some improvised, some inspired by principle and some by expediency, have accumulated. Parts of the system—magistrates' courts, trial by jury, bail—are of great antiquity. Other parts—juvenile courts, probation and parole, professional policemen—are relatively new. The entire system represents an adaptation of the English common law to America's peculiar structure of government, which allows each local community to construct institutions that fill its special needs. Every village, town, county, city, and state has its own criminal justice system, and there is a federal one as well. All of them operate somewhat alike. No two of them operate precisely alike.[1]

Any criminal justice system is an apparatus that society uses to enforce the standards of conduct necessary to protect individuals and the community. It operates by apprehending, prosecuting, convicting, and sentencing those members of the community who violate the basic rules of group existence. The action taken against lawbreakers is designed to serve three purposes beyond the immediately punitive one. It removes dangerous people from the community, it deters others from criminal behavior; and it gives society an opportunity to attempt to transform lawbreakers into law-abiding citizens. What most significantly distinguishes the system of one country from that of another is the extent and the form of the protections it offers individuals in the process of determining guilt and imposing punishment. Our system of justice deliberately sacrifices much in efficiency and even in effectiveness in order to preserve local autonomy and to protect the individual. Sometimes it may seem to sacrifice too much. For example, the American system was not designed with Cosa Nostra-type criminal organizations in mind, and it has been notably unsuccessful to date in preventing such organizations from preying on society.

3

The criminal justice system has three separately organized parts—the police, the courts, and corrections—and each has distinct tasks. However, these parts are by no means independent of each other. What each one does and how it does it has a direct effect on the work of the others. The courts must deal, and can only deal, with those whom the police arrest; the business of corrections is with those delivered to it by the courts. How successfully corrections reforms convicts determines whether they will once again become police business and influences the sentences the judges pass; police activities are subject to court scrutiny and are often determined by court decision. And so reforming or reorganizing any part or procedure of the system changes other parts or procedures. Furthermore, the criminal process, the method by which the system deals with individual cases, is not a hodgepodge of random actions. It is rather a continuum—an orderly progression of events—some of which, though of great importance, occur out of public view.

What has evidently happened is that the transformation of America from a relatively relaxed rural society into a tumultuous urban one has presented the criminal justice system in the cities with a volume of cases too large to handle by traditional methods. One result of heavy caseloads is highly visible in city courts, which process many cases with excessive haste and many others with excessive slowness. In the interest both of effectiveness and of fairness to individuals, justice should be swift and certain; too often in city courts today it is, instead, hasty or faltering. Invisibly, the pressure of numbers has effected a series of adventitious changes in the criminal process. Informal shortcuts have been used. The decision making process has often become routinized. Throughout the system, the importance of individual judgment and discretion, as distinguished from stated rules and procedures, has increased. In effect, much decision making is being done on an administrative rather than on a judicial basis. Thus, an examination of how the criminal justice system works and a consideration of the changes needed to make it more effective and fair must focus on the extent to which invisible, administrative procedures depart from visible, traditional ones, and on the desirability of that departure.

At the very beginning of the process—or, more properly, before the process begins at all—something happens that is scarcely discussed in lawbooks and is seldom recognized by the public: law enforcement policy is made by the policeman. For policemen cannot and do not arrest all the offenders they encounter. It is doubtful that they arrest most of them. A criminal code, in practice, is not a set of specific instructions to policemen but a more or less rough map of the territory in which policemen work. How an individual policeman moves around that territory depends largely on his personal discretion.

That a policeman's duties compel him to exercise personal discretion many times every day is evident. Crime does not look the same on the street as it does in a legislative chamber. How much noise or profanity makes conduct "disorderly" within the meaning of the law? When must a quarrel be treated as a criminal assault: at the first threat or at the first shove or at the first blow, or after blood is drawn, or when a serious injury is inflicted? How suspicious must conduct be before there is "probable cause," the constitutional basis for an arrest? Every policeman, however complete or sketchy his education, is an interpreter of the law.

Every policeman, too, is an arbiter of social values, for he meets situation after situation in which invoking criminal sanctions is a questionable line of action. It is obvious that a boy throwing rocks at a school's windows is committing the statutory offense of vandalism, but it is often not at all obvious whether a policeman will better serve the interests of the community and of the boy by taking the boy home to his parents or by arresting him. Who are the boy's parents? Can they control him; Is he a frequent offender who has responded badly to leniency? Is vandalism so epidemic in the neighborhood that he should be made a cautionary example? With juveniles especially, the police exercise great discretion.

Finally, the manner in which a policeman works is influenced by practical matters: the legal strength of the available evidence, the willingness of victims to press charges and of witnesses to testify, the temper of the community, and the time and information at the policeman's disposal. Much is at stake in how the policeman exercises this discretion. If he judges conduct not suspicious enough to justify intervention, the chance to prevent a robbery, rape, or murder may be lost. If he overestimates the seriousness of a situation or his actions are controlled by panic or prejudice, he may hurt or kill someone unnecessarily. His actions may even touch off a riot.

In direct contrast to the policeman, the magistrate before whom a suspect is first brought usually exercises less discretion than the law allows him. He is entitled to inquire into the facts of the case, and into whether there are grounds for holding the accused. He seldom does. He seldom can. The more promptly an arrested suspect is brought into magistrate's court, the less likelihood there is that much information about the arrest other than the arresting officer's statement will be available to the magistrate. Moreover many magistrates, especially in big cities, have such congested calendars that it is almost impossible for them to subject any case, except an extraordinary one, to prolonged scrutiny.

In practice the most important things, by far, that a magistrate does, are to set the amount of a defendant's bail and in some jurisdictions to appoint counsel. Too seldom does either action get the careful attention it deserves. In many cases the magistrate accepts a waiver of counsel without insuring that the suspect knows the significance of legal representation.

Bail is a device to free an untried defendant and at the same time make sure he appears for trial. That is the sole stated legal purpose in America. The Eighth Amendment to the Constitution declares that it must not be "excessive." Appellate courts have declared that not just the seriousness of the charge against the defendant; but the suspect's personal, family, and employment situation, as they bear on the likelihood of his appearance; must be weighed before the amount of his bail is fixed. Yet more magistrates than not set bail according to standard rates: so and so many dollars for such and such an offense.

The persistence of money bail can best be explained not by its stated purpose but by the belief of police, prosecutors, and courts that the best way to keep a defendant from committing more crimes before trial is to set bail so high that he cannot obtain his release.

The key administrative officer in the processing of cases is the prosecutor. Theoretically the examination of the evidence against a defendant by a judge at a preliminary hearing, and its reexamination by a grand jury, are important parts of the process. Practically they seldom are because a prosecutor rarely has any difficulty in making a prima facie case against a defendant. In fact most defendants waive their rights to preliminary hearings and much more often than not grand juries indict precisely as prosecutors ask. The prosecutor wields almost undisputed sway over the pretrial progress of most cases. He decides whether to press a case or drop it. He determines the specific charge against a defendant. When the charge is reduced, as it is in as many as two-thirds of all cases in some cities, the prosecutor is usually the official who reduces it.

In the informal, noncriminal, nonadversary juvenile justice system there are no "magistrates" or "prosecutors" or "charges," or, in most instances, "defense counsel." An arrested youth is brought before an intake officer who is likely to be a social worker or, in smaller communities, a judge. On the basis of an informal inquiry into the facts and circumstances that led to the arrest, and of an interview with the youth himself, the intake officer or the judge decides whether or not a case should be the subject of formal court proceedings. If he decides it should be, he draws up a petition, describing the case. In very few places is bail a part of the juvenile system; a youth whose case is referred to court is either sent home with orders to reappear on a certain date, or remanded to custody. This decision, too, is made by the screening official. Thus, though these officials work in a quite different environment and according to quite different procedures from magistrates and prosecutors, they in fact exercise the same kind of discretionary control over what happens before the facts of a case are adjudicated.

When a prosecutor reduces a charge it is ordinarily because there has been "plea bargaining" between him and a defense attorney. The issue at stake is how much the prosecutor will reduce his original charge or how lenient a sentence he will recommend, in return for a plea of guilt. There is no way of judging how many bargains reflect the prosecutor's belief that a lesser charge or sentence is justified and how many result from the fact that there may be in the system at any one time, ten times as many cases as there are prosecutors or judges or courtrooms to handle them, should every one come to trial. In form, a plea bargain can be anything from a series of careful conferences to hurried consultation in a courthouse corridor. In content it can be anything from a conscientious exploration of the facts and dispositional alternatives available and appropriate to a defendant, to a perfunctory deal. If the interests of a defendant are to be properly protected while his fate is being thus invisibly determined, he obviously needs just as good legal representation as the kind he needs at a public trial. Whether or not plea bargaining is a fair and effective method of disposing of criminal cases depends heavily on whether or not defendants are provided with competent and conscientious counsel, during early stages of the criminal process.

Plea bargaining is not only an invisible procedure but, in some jurisdictions, a theoretically unsanctioned one. In order to satisfy the court record, a defendant, his attorney, and the prosecutor will at the time of sentencing often ritually state to a judge that no bargain has been made. Plea bargaining may be a useful procedure, especially in congested urban jurisdictions, but neither the dignity of the law, nor the quality of justice, nor the protection of society from dangerous criminals is enhanced by its being conducted covertly.

In a juvenile system there is, of course, no plea bargaining in the sense described above. However, the entire juvenile process can involve extra-judicial negotiations about disposition. Furthermore, the entire juvenile process is by design invisible. Though intended to be helpful, the authority exercised often is coercive; juveniles, no less than adults, may need representation by counsel.

An enormously consequential kind of decision is the sentencing decision of a judge. The law recognizes the importance of fitting sentences to individual defendants by giving judges, in most instances, considerable latitude. For example the recently adopted New York Penal Code, which went into effect in the fall of 1967, empowers a judge to impose upon a man convicted of armed robbery, any sentence between a 5-year term of probation and a 25-year term in prison. Even when a judge has presided over a trial during which the facts of a case have been carefully set forth and has been given a probation report that carefully discusses a defendant's character, background, and problems, he cannot find it easy to choose a sentence. In perhaps nine-tenths of all cases there is no trial; the defendants are self-confessedly guilt.

In the lower or misdemeanor courts, the courts that process most criminal cases, probation reports are a rarity. Under such circumstances judges have little to go on and many sentences are bound to be based on conjecture or intuition. When a sentence is part of a plea bargain, which an overworked judge ratifies perfunctorily, it may not even be his conjecture or intuition on which the sentence is based, but a prosecutor's or a defense counsel's. But perhaps the greatest lack judges suffer from when they pass sentence, is not time or information, but correctional alternatives. Some lower courts do not have any probation officers, and in almost every court the caseloads of probation officers are so heavy that a sentence of probation means, in fact, releasing an offender into the community with almost no supervision. Few states have a sufficient variety of correctional institutions or treatment programs to inspire judges with the confidence that sentences will lead to rehabilitation.

The correctional apparatus to which guilty defendants are delivered is in every respect the most isolated part of the criminal justice system. Much of it is physically isolated; its institutions usually have thick walls and locked doors, and often they are situated in rural areas, remote from the courts where the institutions' inmates were tried and from the communities where they lived. The correctional apparatus is isolated in the sense that its officials do not have everyday working relationships with officials from the system's other branches, like those that commonly exist between policemen and prosecutors, or prosecutors and judges. It is isolated in the sense that what it does with, to, or for the people under its supervision is seldom governed by any but the most broadly written statutes, and is almost never scrutinized by appellate courts. Finally, it is isolated from the public partly by its invisibility and physical remoteness; partly by the inherent lack of drama in most of its activities, but perhaps most importantly by the fact that the correctional apparatus is often used—or misused—by both the criminal justice system and the public as a rug under which disturbing problems and people can be swept.

The most striking fact about the correctional apparatus today is that, although the rehabilitation of criminals is presumably its major purpose, the custody of criminals is actually its major task. On any given day there are well over a million people being "corrected" in America, two-thirds of them on probation or parole and one-third of them in prisons or jails. However, prisons and jails are where four-fifths of correctional money is spent and where nine-tenths of correctional employees work. Furthermore, fewer than one-fifth of the people who work in state prisons and local jails have jobs that are not essentially either custodial or administrative in character. Many jails have nothing but custodial and administrative personnel. Of course many jails are crowded with defendants who have not been able to furnish bail and who are not considered by the law to be appropriate objects of rehabilitation because it has not yet been determined that they are criminals who need it.

What this emphasis on custody means in practice is that the enormous potential of the correctional apparatus for making creative decisions about its treatment of convicts is largely unfulfilled. This is true not only of offenders in custody but of offenders on probation and parole. Most authorities agree that while probationers and parolees need varying degrees and kinds of supervision, an average of no more than 35 cases per officer is necessary for effective attention; 97 percent of all officers handling adults have larger caseloads than that. In the juvenile correctional system the situation is somewhat better. Juvenile institutions, which typically are training schools, have a higher proportion of treatment personnel and juvenile probation and parole officers generally have lighter caseloads. However, these comparatively rich resources are very far from being sufficiently rich.

Except for sentencing, no decision in the criminal process has more impact on the convicted offender than the parole decision, which determines how much of his maximum sentence a prisoner must serve. This again is an invisible administrative decision that is seldom open to attack or subject to review. It is made by parole board members who are often political appointees. Many are skilled and conscientious, but they generally are able to spend no more than a few minutes on a case. Parole decisions that are made in haste and on the basis of insufficient information, in the absence of parole machinery that can provide good supervision, are necessarily imperfect decisions. And since there is virtually no appeal from them, they can be made arbitrarily or discriminatorily. Just as carefully formulated and clearly stated law enforcement policies would help policemen, charge policies would help prosecutors and sentencing policies would help judges, so parole policies would help parole boards perform their delicate and important duties.

In sum, America's system of crimnal justice is overcrowded and overworked, undermanned, underfinanced, and very often misunderstood. It needs more information and more knowledge. It needs more technical resources. It needs more public support. It needs the help of community programs and institutions in dealing with offenders and potential offenders. It needs, above all, the willingness to re-examine old ways of doing things, to reform itself, to experiment, to run risks, to dare. It needs vision.

Notes

1. President's Commission on Law Enforcement and the Administration of Justice, *The Challenge of Crime in a Free Society.* Washington, U.S. Government Printing Office, 1967, pp. 7-12.

I. THE NON-SYSTEM OF CRIMINAL JUSTICE

SOURCE: Daniel J. Freed, "The Non-system of Criminal Justice," National Commission on the Causes and Prevention of Violence, *Law and Order Reconsidered*, Washington, U.S. Government Printing Office, 1969, pp. 265-284.

Despite broad agreement that crime is increasing faster than the ability of most cities to cope with it, deep division prevails among those who prescribe anticrime remedies. Energy that ought to be devoted to action programs to reduce crime, is being poured instead into words—into an escalating conflict between proponents of the hard line and of the soft line. Political campaigns, legislative hearings and curt arguments find intelligent law enforcement officers handcuffed or brutal; Should we support or reform the local police? Should prosecution policy be tough or selective? Should prison sentences be long or flexible?

While to an informed observer the answers to such questions are complex, a multitude of persons holding positions of authority or power behave as if they were simple. Instead of seeking the very large common ground on which the hard line and the soft line converge, law enforcement "experts" have shown an increasing tendency to identify symbolic issues, such as Supreme Court decisions, civilian review boards, capital punishment and preventive detention, as if they held the keys to the crime problem.

The anger with which such issues have been debated in recent years has contributed little to public confidence, to the safety of streets or to the effectiveness of criminal procedures. It has, however, caused actual reform in the institutions of public order and justice to lag far behind the excellent recommendations of three presidential crime commissions (National, D.C., and Civil Disorders) which have reported since the end of 1966.

If the sad record of the 1960's and early 1970's is to be bettered as law enforcement and criminal justice face the challenge of the future, consideration must be given to three questions:

(1) What does a typical criminal justice system look like today?
(2) How well is that system integrated into the program of cities for meeting the problems of urban inadequacy?
(3) What new directions should comprehensive reform of the criminal justice system take?

The responses set forth below sketch a profile of today's criminal justice process and suggest some of the ingredients for its improvement.

§ 1.2   The system: theory vs. practice

Our society has commissioned its police to patrol the streets, prevent crime, arrest suspected criminals, and "enforce the law." It has established courts to conduct trials of accused offenders, sentence those who are found guilty and "do justice." It has created a correctional process consisting of prisons to punish convicted persons and programs to rehabilitate and supervise them so that they might become useful citizens.

It is commonly assumed that these three components—law enforcement (police, sheriffs, marshals), the judicial process (judges, prosecutors, defense lawyers) and corrections (prison officials, probation and parole officers)—add up to a "system" of criminal justice. The system, however, is a myth.

A system implies some unity of purpose and organized inter-relationship among component parts. In the typical American city and state, and under federal jurisdiction as well, no such relationship exists. There is, instead, a resonably well-defined criminal process, a continuum through which each accused offender may pass: from the hands of the police, to the jurisdiction of the courts, behind the walls of a prison, then back onto the street. The inefficiency, fallout, and failure of purpose during this process is notorious.

The dismal crime control record to date is well know. According to the 1967 report of the President's Commission on Law Enforcement and Administration of Justice, well over half of all crimes are never reported to the police. Of those which are, fewer than one-quarter are cleared by arrest. Nearly half of all arrests result in the dismissal of charges. Of the balance, well over 90 percent are resolved by a plea of guilt. The proportion of cases which actually go to trial is tiny, representing less than 1 percent of all crimes committed. A large portion of those convicted are sentenced to jails or penal institutions; the balance are released under probation supervision.

Nearly everyone who goes to prison is eventually released, often under parole supervision. Between two-fifths and two-thirds of all releasees are sooner or later arrested and convicted again, thereby joining the population of repeater criminals we call recidivists.

Nearly every official and agency participating in the criminal process is frustrated by some aspect of its ineffectiveness, its unfairness or both. At the same time, nearly every participant group itself is the target of criticism by others in the process.

Upon reflection, this turmoil is not surprising. Each participant sees the commission of crime and the procedures of justice from a different perspective. His daily experience and his set of values as to what effectiveness requires and what fairness requires are therefore likely to be different. As a result, the mission and priorities of a system of criminal justice will in all likelihood be defined differently by a policeman, a trial judge, a prosecutor, a defense attorney, a correctional administrator, an appellate tribunal, a slum dweller and a resident of the suburbs.

In the mosaic of discontent which pervades the criminal process, public officials and institutions, bound together with private persons in the cause of reducing crime, each sees his own special mission being undercut by the cross-purpose, frailties or malfunctions of others. As they find their places along the spectrum between the intense concern with victims at one end, and total preoccupation with reforming convicted lawbreakers at the other, so do they find their daily perceptions of justice varying or in conflict. The conflicts in turn are intensified by the fact that each part of the criminal process in most cities is over-loaded and undermanned, and most of its personnel underpaid and inadequately trained.

Under such circumstances it is hardly surprising to find, in most cities, not a smooth functioning "system" of criminal justice but a fragmented and often hostile amalgamation of criminal justice agencies. To the extent they are concerned about other parts of the "system," police view courts as the enemy. Judges often find law enforcement officers themselves violating the law. Both see correctional programs as largely a failure. Many defendants perceive all three as paying only lip service to individual rights.

Mechanisms for introducing some sense of harmony into the system are seldom utilized. Judges, police administrators and prison officials hardly ever confer on common problems. Sentencing institutes and familiarization prison visits for judges are the exception rather than the rule. Neither prosecuting nor defense attorneys receive training in corrections upon which to base intelligent sentencing recommendations.

Nearly every part of the criminal process is run with public funds by persons employed as officers of justice to serve the same community. Yet every agency in the criminal process in a sense competes with every other in the quest for tax dollars. Isolation or antagonism rather than mutual support, tends to characterize their intertwined operations. And even when cooperative efforts develop, the press usually features the friction, and often aggravates it.

One might expect the field to be flooded with systems analysts, management consultants and publicly-imposed measures of organization and administration in order to introduce order and coordination into this criminal justice chaos. It is not.

A recognized profession of criminal justice system administrators does not exist today. In fact, most of the sub-systems are poorly run. For example, court administrators are rare, and court management by trained professionals is a concept that is taking hold very slowly.

The bail "system," which should involve coordination among at least a half dozen agencies, is presided over by no one. Few cities have neutral bail agencies to furnish bail-setting magistrates with reliable background data on defendants. Prosecutors usually ignore community ties and factors other than the criminal charge and the accused's criminal record in recommending bail. Defense lawyers rarely explore nonmonetary release conditions in cases involving impecunious clients. Detention reports on persons held long periods in jail prior to trial are rarely acted on by courts, and bail review for detainees is rarely requested. Enforcement of bail restrictions and forfeitures of bond for bailjumpers are unusual. Bail bondsmen go unregulated.

Effective police administration is hard to find. The great majority of police agencies are headed by chiefs who started as patrolmen and rose through the ranks, whose higher education is scanty, whose training in modern management techniques, finance, personnel, communications and community relations is limited, and whose isolation is profound. Lateral entry of police administrators from other departments or outside sources is usually prohibited by antiquated Civil Service concepts.

Apart from lack of leadership, the process of crime control in most cities has no central collection and analysis of criminal justice information. It has no focal point for formulating a cohesive crime budget based on system needs rather than individual agency requests.

It has no mechanism for planning, initiating or evaluating systemwide programs, or for setting priorities. It has no specialized staff to keep the mayor or other head of government regularly informed of the problems and progress of public safety and justice. Crime receives high-level attention only as a short-term reaction to crisis. An effective system does not exist.

This bleak picture should not obscure occasional bright spots. Within recent years, scattered about the country, some promising developments have appeared: innovations have been introduced, new leadership has emerged, modern facilities have been built, a systems approach has been tried. While the impact has been small, hopes have been raised. States here and cities there have shown that crime control and justice can be improved. The question is whether isolated reforms can grow into a pattern.

§ *1.3　Criminal sanctions as a solution to urban problems*

The internal disorganization of the criminal justice system is not its only handicap. Even if it functioned like a well-oiled machine, it would—without other changes—probably fail to achieve either a substantial reduction in most categories of conduct now labelled as crime, or a material increase in public respect for law.

The likelihood of failure is promoted by two traditional features of criminal law administration: (1) the criminal sanction applies by statute to much more human behavior than it can realistically control, and (2) the criminal process operates too largely in isolation from other programs aimed at the breeding grounds of antisocial behavior. Until the target conduct of criminal penalties can be narrowed and the myth of full enforcement dispelled, and until crime reduction is perceived as requiring better education, housing, health and employment opportunities for would-be offenders, the criminal process will continue to suffer from demands that it accomplish more than is possible with less help than is indispensable to success.

The case for limiting the use of the criminal sanction has been advanced most effectively by Professor Sanford Kadish in his Annals article on The Crisis of Overcriminalization (1967) and by Professor Herbert L. Packer in The Limits of The Criminal Sanction (1968). For present purposes, their relevant point is that the demands made upon the police, the courts and the penal process, far exceed the capacity of these organizations collectively to investigate, apprehend, prosecute, adjudicate and correct individual behavior.

The overload means that full enforcement, speedy trial, fair procedure and effective sentencing have become slogans rather than facts. The crimes of violence society fears most—murder, forcible rape, robber, assault—are currently processed through many of the same channels as are social actions which injure third parties least; e.g., prostitution, homosexuality, intoxication, gambling, marijuana use, vagrancy, and other minor offenses. The disabling impact on law enforcement is suggested by the fact that the police are overloaded with minor cases at a time when their clearance rate for serious crimes in virtually every city is less than 25 percent.

Without condoning conduct which offends prevailing moral standards, a community could undoubtedly act more expeditiously and effectively against violent invasions of person and property if fewer of its law enforcement resources were detoured into crime objectives of low priority. Finding alternative ways of handling low priority offenses would make particular sense in the case of conduct which is extremely difficult to detect (because it occurs voluntarily and often inside private homes), produces no injury to another person, and offers little likelihood of deterrence or cure even if criminal penalties are imposed. The sporadic and discriminatory enforcement, the charges of abuse of police discretion, the assembly-line justice and the ineffective sanctions which characterize most of the present effort to deal with these lesser offenses tends to perpetuate cynicism and disrespect for law.

The search for nonpenal techniques to control behavior involving consenting parties should be viewed not as a soft approach to lesser offenses, but as a realistic route to meaningful sanctions against crimes that injure society the most. Some forms of conduct should probably be eliminated entirely from regulation by statute. Some, like intoxication, should be dealt with through voluntary health reforms, such as those being pioneered by the Manhattan Bowery Project. Others, like traffic infractions, might be transferred to an administrative or regulatory process, as California and New York have done. But until the wide range of behavior now subject to arrest, trial and sentencing is materially reduced, the police, courts and prisons are likely to remain overwhelmed and underachieving.

§ 1.4　Relationship to civil programs

Just as the conduct amenable to criminal sanctions needs to be narrowed, so should the range of community-based programs tied to the criminal process be broadened. Education, job training, medical care and shelter are needed at least as much by juveniles and adults charged with crime as by their counterparts in the deprived community who have not been so charged. The criminal justice process cannot continue to function in isolation from the more affirmative social programs for improving individual lives. The objective of integrating criminal and noncriminal programs is easy to advocate but difficult to achieve.

For example, a major goal of an offender's contact with the criminal process is said to be corrective—rehabilitation followed by reintegration into the community, with enhanced respect for law. Yet the opposite is often true: the typical prison experience is degrading, conviction records create a lasting stigma, decent job opportunities upon release are rare, voting rights are abridged, military service options are curtailed, family life disruptions are likely to be serious, and the outlook of most ex-convicts is bleak. The expectation of the community, that released offenders will be "corrected" is matched by outdated laws and community responses which tend strongly to defeat those expectation.

This unfortunate pattern is not confined to the handling of convicted offenders. The odds are high that unconvicted persons will encounter similar, and sometimes greater, constraints. Cities are full of people who have been arrested but not convicted, and who nevertheless served time in jail and were stigmatized in other seriously disabling ways.

Thus, local facilities in which arrested persons are detained prior to conviction are typically worse, in terms of overcrowding and deterioration, than the prisons to which convicted offenders are sentenced. Accused first offenders are mixed indiscriminately with hardened recidivists. The opportunities for recreation, job training or treatment of a nonpunitive character are almost nil.

If released, a person's arrest record alone becomes a substantial liability. In many segments of a community, the difference between arrest status and that of conviction is indiscriminately regarded as a technicality.

In its present state of disrepair, the criminal process—when it operates alone—at best performs a holding function. This function may provide society respite when a serious offender with a long record and minimal prospect of improvement is identified. In such cases, denial of release for as long as the law allows may seem reasonable, even though almost all convicts are eventually released.

In nearly every case, however, a city candid about its own criminal justice deficiencies needs to ask whether full enforcement aimed at detention, prosecution and imprisonment, will in the long run reduce or reinforce criminality.

The traditional assumption has been that punishment will reduce crime. In attempting to separate myth from reality, however, it is worth noting that experienced judges have resorted increasingly in recent years to various forms of post-conviction probation. They have done so after weighing the possibilities for rehabilitation if the offender is so released against the usually disastrous prognosis which would accompany his incarceration. It is a painful choice, little understood by the public. But the decision to seek correction of an offender in the community reflects less a compassionate attitude toward law-breakers: more a hardheaded recognition, based on data, that long-term public safety has a better chance of being protected.

The alternatives are no longer simply prison or outright release. Integrating the criminal process with community programs requires closely supervised forms of release: daytime work release, release in the custody of reliable counselors, prerelease guidance centers, alcoholism and narcotic treatment centers, halfway houses.

Community-based programs will, of course, fail equally with prisons if the resources and attitudes which accompany them are no better. Identifying the offender's needs in terms of education, job training, employment, family aid, hospitalization and shelter, and providing for them, must be seen as inuring to society's benefit as well as his own.

The stage at which these services are furnished should whenever possible be advanced from after conviction to after arrest. Voluntary correctional programs should be offered without a prior finding of guilt. As urged by the National Crime Commission, accused offenders should be routed away from the criminal process at the earliest stage that vindication of the community's interest permits.

Most such efforts will tend to reduce the cost of criminal

prosecution by eliminating it when it is not needed, and to increase the speed and firmness of prosecution for hardened offenders for whom no meaningful alternative exists. Public funds thus diverted from the revolving door functions of imprisonment, warehousing, degradation and contamination can be invested instead in community programs where the crime reduction payoff is higher.

§ 1.5   Guidelines for reform

Against this background of the criminal justice nonsystem, and unrealistic expectations as to what its sanctions can achieve, emerged the 1967 Report of the President's Commission on Law Enforcement and Administration of Justice and the 1968 Omnibus Crime Control and Safe Streets Act. In theory, the 1968 legislation provided the framework and the funds for massive federal grants to the states with which the comprehensive and detailed recommendations of the President's Commission could be implemented. In fact, early performance has been handicapped by unrealistic deadlines, inadequate funds and a shortage of experienced manpower to convey a criminal justice system approach to the states.

During the first year since its launching, the federal program to assist states and cities in dealing with crime has come under attack from several sources, e.g., the Conference of Mayors, the National League of Cities, the National Urban Coalition. Instead of emphasizing federal leadership to guide the development of sound criminal justice systems at the local level, as originally proposed by the President's Commission, the Act has assigned the leadership role in distributing block grants and guiding their application to the states. State planning groups have failed in many instances to represent the full range of citizen as well as official interests in crime control. Friction has erupted between cities and their state governments over the question whether funds should be allocated on the basis of population or crime rate. Agencies of the criminal process have tended to plan their own individual programs by themselves. Crime control has continued to remain isolated from social programs aimed at employment, education, housing and health. Outside expertise to augment local planners has remained scarce. The consequence, in many instances, has been pedestrian state plans.

Unless some new ingredients are added, deficiencies such as these foreshadow the channeling of massive federal funds into old programs, and into higher salaries for old-line personnel. They will thereby tend to reinforce rather than reform the inadquate criminal justice institutions and to perpetuate the polarized attitudes which exist today.

These are, of course, no short cuts to the reduction of crime. More money and personnel, new equipment and revised procedures will all be essential to the goal. Yet without new organizations and relationships to help spend money wisely and use personnel well, history suggests that significant changes are unlikely.

Reform in the criminal field has a long record of excellent recommendations never carried out. A substantial portion of the National Crime Commission's proposals in 1967 are, for example, remarkably similar to those urged by the Wickersham Commission established by President Hoover 37 years earlier. Despite that Commission's equally impressive documentation, conservatism and presidential prestige, little follow-through was mounted. Experience with commissions at the state and local levels shows similar results. Library shelves are crowded with reports on police inadequacy, court chaos and prison disgrace, and reform proposals which never produced effective action.

Moreover, money poured into the crime problem does not by itself buy crime reduction. Wealthy states and localities which have spent vast sums for crime control have become no more noticeably crime-free than jurisdictions which haven't. The District of Columbia, with a superb crime commission report, constant oversight by Congress and federal money close by, has failed to achieve anything resembling what two Presidents have called a model system of criminal justice.

This pattern suggests the existence of substantial built-in obstacles to change. It suggests that unless much more attention is spotlighted on the inability and unwillingness of present crime control systems to effectuate reform, new money may go down old drains. Vexing problems of politics, organization and leadership underlie the maintenance of the status quo and need to be faced up to directly.

In the search for new approaches to the implementation of crime commission recommendations, two promising but comparatively untried strategies have been suggested by recent experience on the frontiers of criminal justice in several cities: (1) a program to coordinate public criminal justice agencies more effectively, and to link them to companion social programs, by placing them under the supervision of a new high-level criminal justice staff or agency; and (2) a program to develop private citizen participation as an integral operating component, rather than a conversational adjunct, of criminal reform. The success of citizen participation will in many ways be dependent on the establishment of a central criminal justice office.

§ *1.6* *The criminal justice agency*

The pervasive fragmentation of police, court and correctional agencies suggests that some catalyst is needed to bring them together. An assumption that public agencies will operate consistently can no longer suffice as a substitute for deliberate action to make it happen in real life. Arrested offenders—the common target or client of criminal justice agencies—afford their only continuous link today.

Periodic crime commissions—which study these agencies, file reports and then disappear—are valuable, but they are too transient for the catalyst role. A law enforcement council—consisting of chief judges and agency heads who meet periodically—will likely constitute little more than another committee of overcommitted officials.

A full-time criminal justice office should be considered basic to the formation of a criminal justice system. Its optimum form and its location in the bureaucracy need to be developed through experimentation.

The function could be vested in a criminal justice assistant to the mayor or county executive, with staff relationships to executive agencies, and liaison with the courts, the bar and the community. Or it could be established as a new agency, a ministry of justice, possessing authority under the direction of a high ranking official of local government (e.g., Director of Public Safety or Criminal Justice Administrator) to oversee and coordinate the police, prosecutorial and correctional functions. Special kinds of administrative ties to the courts and the public defender office would have to be evolved to avoid undermining the essential independence of the judiciary and the adversary role of the defense.

The establishment of a new office or agency should not be permitted to disparage or overwhelm the diversity of values and perspectives which are essential to preserve in the separate agencies of a criminal justice system. Otherwise, a single official—oriented too heavily toward law enforcement or toward individual rights—might seriously disturb the balance of an entire system. The appointment of a carefully representative criminal justice advisory council, composed of key public officials and knowledgeable private citizens can help guard against this danger as well as promote the broad interests of reform.

Whatever the form of the new agency, its basic purposes would be to allocate resources, to introduce innovation within as well as among the constituent agencies so as to improve the fair and effective processing of cases and to develop understanding and respect among the component parts of the system. For example:

> It would develop a system of budgeting for crime which takes account of the interrelated needs and imbalances among individual agencies and jurisdictions;
>
> It would initiate a criminal justice information system which, as an adjunct to personnel, budgeting and legislative decisions, would embrace not simply crime reports (as is typical today), but arrests, reduction of charges, convictions, sentences, recidivism, court backlogs, detention populations, crime prevention measures, and other data essential to an informed process;
>
> It would perform a mediating and liaison role in respect to the many overlap functions of the criminal process, e.g., development of programs to reduce police waiting time in court, to enlist prosecutors and defense attorneys in cooperative efforts to expedite trials, to bring correctional inputs to bear on initial decisions whether to prosecute, to improve relations between criminal justice agencies and the community;
>
> It would perform or sponsor systems analyses and periodic evaluations of agency programs, and encourage innovations and pilot projects which might not otherwise have a chance in a tradition-oriented system;
>
> It would develop minimum standards of performance, new incentives and exchange programs for police, court and correctional personnel.

Most of all, the comprehensive grasp of the system by an experienced criminal justice staff would facilitate informed executive, judicial and legislative judgments on priorities. It would enable wise planning and action by the city with funds received from the Law Enforcement Assistance Administration and the state. It would help decide, for example, whether the new budget should cover:

> A modern diagnostic and detention center to replace the jail, or 1000 policemen;

Additional judges and prosecutors, or a prior management survey of the courts;

A computerized information system or a roving leader program for juveniles;

New courtrooms or a half-dozen halfway houses.

For a full-time well-staffed criminal justice office to be successful, it must achieve a balanced perspective within its own ranks on the problems of public safety and justice. Practical experience in law enforcement, in the assertion of individual rights, and in the efficiency and effectiveness of programs must be represented in the staff as well as in the advisory council.

The transition from today's chaotic process to a well-run system will not be easy. Most troublesome is the fact that the criminal process does not operate within neat political boundaries. Police departments are often funded at the city level; county and state police and sheriffs must also be taken into account. Judges are sometimes appointed, sometimes elected, and different courts are answerable to local, county and state constituencies. Correctional functions are a conglomerate of local and county jails, and county and state prisons. Probation systems are sometimes administered by the courts, sometimes by an executive agency. Prosecutors may be appointed or elected, from all three levels of government. Defense lawyers usually come from the private sector but are increasingly being augmented by public defender agencies.

Reform will be difficult even within a single jurisdiction, where political control of criminal justice agencies is traditionally loose. Many mayors have difficulty with the concept of the police department as a subordinate agency. "Keep the politics out of policing" has become a watchword often used by inbred police departments to resist the recruitment of new leadership from outside police civil service rosters. By deferring more to police chiefs than to the heads of other critical city agencies, mayors avoid making crime their own problem. At the same time, the police themselves have avoided responsibility for crime control, especially in recent years, by attributing the increase in crime to Supreme Court decisions.

If this confusing pattern makes the creation, location, staffing and political viability of a criminal justice office difficult, it also symbolizes why little semblance of a system exists today. Fragmentation is in many ways inherent in the antiquated structure of local government. The challenge of crime poses a high priority inducement to reallocate political power and make government more effective.

An adequately staffed criminal justice office will be more than most cities can currently afford. Its need is not presently seen as high on their priority lists. To encourage the development of such offices, the Violence Commission should recommend aid to cities or counties submitting suitable plans for structuring and staffing them. Caution will have to be exercised to avoid funding new operations which are systemwide in appearance but prosecutorial in purpose. Some commitment should be required to assure the recruitment of a balanced staff. The applicant's plan should also spell out in detail the contemplated relationship between the proposed office and the relevant governmental structure of the city, county and state.

§ 1.7   Private citizen involvement

Government programs for the control of crime are unlikely to succeed all alone. Informed private citizens, playing a variety of roles, can make a decisive difference in the prevention, detection and prosecution of crime, the fair administration of justice, and the restoration of offenders to the community.

Each function is being grossly underplayed today. New citizen-based mechanisms are needed at the national and local levels to spearhead greater participation by individuals and in groups.

Constructive citizen action on the local level can be a powerful force for criminal justice reform. There are simply too many important aspects of the private citizen's duty to expect local government to solve the crime problem by itself.

The private role begins with each citizen responding individually when called: reporting crime, appearing as a witness, serving as a juror, hiring the ex-offender. The prevailing low level of performance in most of these areas is exemplified by the finding of the President's Commission on Law Enforcement and Administration of Justice that more than half of all crimes are never reported; by the widespread refusal of citizens to "become involved"; by the frequent failures of victims to prosecute, or to continue to show up in court despite seemingly endless court delays; and by rampant refusal of employers, public and private, to employ persons with criminal records.

Beyond individual action the private role requires group participation. By and large, citizens fearful of crime are uninformed about the problems of criminal justice administration. They are too often unread in the literature of crime commissions, uninvolved in efforts to improve the system, and overloaded with myths and scapegoats. All too many citizens continue to advocate simple solutions to complex crime problems. Those who dig deeply almost always change their minds.

The myths can be erased but only by firsthand involvement in the process of reform. New York City has established a Criminal Justice Coordinating Council to tie private business, labor, education, religion and other citizen interests to public officials in tackling specific crime control projects. In narcotics, alcoholism, burglary prevention, court delay, police manpower utilization, offender employment and other areas, teams of public and private persons—aided by full-time private staff from the Vera Institute of Justice—work together, analyzing the facts, planning for change, and overseeing reform. The coordinatining council idea is catching on elsewhere.

Royal Oak, Mich., and Denver, Colo., have seen groups of private citizens develop one to one programs through which a private person helps a misdemeanor offender or a juvenile delinquent make his way back into law abiding community life.

Washington, D.C., has produced Bonabond, Inc.—an organization run by ex-offenders to help other ex-offenders in trouble.

In a host of cities, local chapters of national organizations like the Lawyers Committee for Civil Rights Under Law, the Urban League, the Urban Coalition, the National Council on Crime and Delinquency, the League of Women Voters, and the American Friends Service Committee, have launched programs to improve jails and prisons, juvenile courts, offender employment, police recruitment and crime prevention, plan emergency justice procedures, etc.

As such local efforts multiply, several elements critical to their success or failure, and their overall impact on law and justice in the community, emerge: e.g. full-time staffing, adequate funding, long-term continuity, involvement in a spectrum of criminal justice system problems, and frequent evaluation of progress.

Perhaps the most successful of private organizations in attacking a broad range of crime control problems through a public-private partnership is New York City's Vera Institute of Justice. Its unique role in cooperation with the office of the mayor, the police, the courts and corrections has developed over eight years. Its non-bureaucratic approach has permitted it to test new programs, through experiments and pilot projects, in a way no public agency would likely find successful. Its core funding is entirely private; its individual project financing comes from a wide range of federal, state and private sources.

The philosophy and technique, which characterize the Vera operations, have been summarized by its Director, Herbert J. Sturz:

It has often been said that public institutions are inherently resistent to change—particularly to change proposed by a private outside organization. Vera has not found this to be the case in New York City. We received support from Mayor Wagner when we began the Manhattan Bail Project. We have had support from Mayor Lindsay for our more recent projects. The agencies with which we have dealt have acknowledged the need for change, and they have been, for the most part, hospitable to new ideas and, to some extent, experimentation.

Many irritants in the system arise from the lack of coordination among agencies. The principal mechanism for dealing with a problem which cuts across agency lines—the interdepartmental committee and the task force—have been largely unsuccessful. A neutral private agency, such as Vera, can successfully bring together several agencies in a joint innovative program or experiment. Perhaps because we are not part of the bureaucratic machinery, we pose little threat to existing agencies and carry with us no residue of past misunderstandings. Also, bringing about the required cooperation is our business and not an extra duty imposed on a crowded schedule.

In addition, Vera can intercede with the city's power structure; we are not bound by chains of command. We do not seek reform by exposing inefficiency or injustice, by leveling indictments, or by public confrontation with line agencies. Too often, this approach hardens opposition to change or at best leaves the kind and quality of change to the agency under attack. And we have found that, although preliminary fact-finding is necessary as a prelude to experimentation, a study alone is seldom effective in bringing about change. In the criminal process Vera has used the pilot project to advantage.

Small test programs can usually be mounted inexpensively; specialists can be brought in ad hoc; red tape can be bypassed; relatively quick results can be expected. Since no new agency, bureau, or division is created, a project can be easily dismantled if it proves ineffective, without diastrous results politically or financially, and even in failure it may provide useful information. If the project proves worthwhile, the city can take it on as a permanent fixture, and the private planning group can move on to a new area.

It is my belief that this action-oriented intervention approach, which Vera has tried with some success in New York City, can be useful in other cities provided that certain conditions can be met. Among them are: (1) that funding, at least for a core staff, be available over a two or three year period from the private sector (money for specific projects can be raised from city, state and federal sources); (2) that the new institute be system-oriented as well as client-oriented and should quickly establish in the community the principle that the two are not mutually exclusive; (3) that the first couple of projects show visible results within a year; (4) that the people who run the institute are content to stay in the background and give credit to those within the system.

The Vera experience should be tried elsewhere. The federal government should join the private sources to provide the funds for spurring the establishment of similar institutes in other urban centers. A major task of the proposed NCJCC should be to help localities develop such private catalysts for change.

The mechanisms suggested here could go a long way toward reversing the picture of a criminal justice nonsystem falling apart at the seams. Money in vast sums is the other part of the lifeblood of a functioning system. The injection of federal funds into state crime control programs has been an important step in the right direction. Much more money must be channeled, and must reach down into the cities, if action to reduce crime is to make a difference. Much more money must be injected into research, development and pilot projects, if the outdated techniques of yesterday are to be converted into an effective criminal process tomorrow.

Until these impediments are remedied, and until staffed organizations—public and private—are developed to assure wise investment and monitoring of new funds, crime control will continue to be a high priority campaign fought with bold words but no system.

II. DISPARITY IN THE SYSTEM

SOURCE: Harry W. More, "Disparity in the System," *Administration of Justice Journal*, Volume 1, No. 2, 1974, pp. 33-39.

The American justice system functions as a social mechanism for maintaining ordered liberty in our society. It is the primary governmental instrument for insuring the equitable implementation of juristic policy essential and fundamental to the perpetuation of a democratic society.

The justice system responds to the seriousness of deviate behavior in our society as a diffused and stratified entity. The system (non-system) has reacted to the complexities of the crime problem and its increasing sophistication through a negative congruence pattern. The conflict created by the adversative posture of the system demands an acceptance of responsibility for concerted reasoning about the competing goal structure of the primary elements of the criminal justice system.

The substantive conditions and realistic circumstances that have resulted in non-continuity and a lack of cohesiveness in the system must receive more than ideational consideration. The democratic process of our nation demands an emblematic response to the moral aspirations of social justice for all. It is a mandate which must be met by an accurate appraisal of needs and a correctional response leading to system conflict resolution.

Basic to our society is the concept of liberty under law; each citizen has the inalienable right to demand equal protection under the law.

The achievement of justice is difficult to assess. The scales of justice must be balanced between the rights of the individual and the rights of society. Needless to say, history suggests that the balance shifts very slowly in reaction to societal and political demands.

The romanticist who is the champion of human rights immediately comes into conflict with the pragmatist who is concerned about the state. The individuals who prescribe one political tendency attack the establishment for its failure to acknowledge the rights of the individual and the persons who embody the belief that the state is pre-eminent, attack the establishment for failing to protect society.

With relative ease the concept of justice becomes a political issue.

The logical positivists marshal their forces on one side in support of the government and the emotional humanists conjure up lucid descriptions of dooms day in terms of their view of individual rights. In most instances the most accurate appraisal ignores the extremes and attempts to accommodate the conflicting views.

In recent years the term crime and the means of insuring its control has become a political issue transcending the total political spectrum from local to national levels. Mayoralty and gubernatorial candidates have assumed office with a pledge to make the streets safe. The achievement of this goal has been lost in political rhetoric, but it has proven to be a basic issue to which many voters respond. At the national level the subject of crime has become an important aspect of party platforms. The Democratic party in 1972 emphasized the need for protection of all people without undermining fundamental liberties. It further called for the cessation of "law and order" as justification for repression and political persecution. While platforms are seldom implemented, the above clearly illustrates that crime has serious emotional and political implications.

In our culture the phrase "political crimes" is of recent origin. A term long associated with governments that have exercised the forcible suppression of opposition it seems strange to many Americans that a term such as political persecution should be applied to our governmental system. The fact that it is considered by some to be politically significant during a presidential campaign does not legitimize its claim. In fact, based upon recent acquittals of a prominent black communist and numerous anti-war advocates, it is becoming increasingly clear that such polemics are based upon few facts and limited judgments. The present criticisms directed against the justice system are submerged in conflicting and tacit presuppositions demanding a stoical examination rather than an intricate response.

The justice system is a legal construct of man, consequentially it is not a perfect system, but it has served our nation well and has become one of the dominant stabilizing institutions. The foundation for our justice system is a highly structured and formalized legal philosophy. Contemporary American society has evolved to the point where the formal legal institutions and procedures occupy a pre-eminent position in the preservation of social order. As our society has been revolutionized by change and become increasingly complex and pluralistic, the influence of traditional stabilizing institutions such as family, church and community has waned, and rule making institutions have assumed increasing importance.

The concept of acceptance of rules based upon legitimacy is termed the "rule of law." It describes the willingness of a people to accept and order their behavior according to the rules and procedures that are prescribed by political and social institutions.[1]

The enforcement of the laws is the function of the justice system and that system must generate and sustain a position of legitimacy. Ordered liberty demands a new system of criminal justice effectively controlling deviant behavior in a manner that insures equal protection under the law.

System legitimacy can only be attained if there is a concerted effort to maintain a reasonable balance between the collective need and individual rights. Under our concept of government there must be a pervasive mission guiding the actions of all criminal justice personnel. This mission is best defined as "justice." The most illustrious and inspiring definition of "justice" was included in the Justinian code by Roman Lawyers: "justice is the constant and perpetual will or rendering to each his right . . . "[2]

The concept of justice has long been the subject of discussion by scholars, philosophers and theologians. Although it is a universal concept and an ideal, there are a multiplicity of definitions and interpretations. What is of concern is the implementation of the concept; it should not be lost in repetative rhetoric.

A contemporary philosopher defines justice in three parts, according to the three theories of justice: "justice is . . . conformity to law; doing what is useful for the social good; and rendering to each what is his own or due by right."[3]

This combined definition encompasses the positive law, social, and natural right theories of justice. It is a definition that meets the needs of a dynamic and changing society.

Justice as a mission of America's criminal justice system should be the philosophical foundation for each component of the system. Each justice actor should direct his or her total action toward the attainment of absolute justice. In each conflict with the law justice must be tempered in terms of equity. Each human action or reaction resulting in an infraction of the law must be analyzed and legal sanctions applied in the interests of justice.

It is essential to identify and analyze the factors that have a direct relationship to the effectiveness of the criminal justice system. The parameters of this system encompass the totality of justice official-dom from the detection phase to the correctional process. It is a common structure established by the people to deal with crime either through its prevention or the arrest of an offender.

When an infraction of the law occurs, a policeman finds, if he can, the probable offender, arrests him and brings him promptly before a magistrate. If the offense is minor, the magistrate disposes of it forthwith; if it is serious, he holds the defendant for further action and admits him to bail. The case then is turned over to a prosecuting attorney who charges the defendant with a specific statutory crime. This charge is subject to review by a judge at a preliminary hearing of the evidence and in many places—if the offense charged is a felony—by a grand jury that can dismiss the charge or affirm it by delivering it to a judge in the form of an indictment. If the defendant pleads "not guilty" to the charge he comes to trial; the facts of his case are marshaled by prosecuting and defense attorneys and presented, under the supervision of a judge, through witnesses, to a jury. If the jury finds the defendant guilty, he is sentenced by the judge to a term of probation, under which he is permitted to live in the community as long as he behaves himself or to a term in prison, where a systematic attempt to convert him into a law-abiding citizen is made.[4]

The simplistic process described above is implemented by three major components of the justice system: law enforcement, judicial, and corrections. It is a system whose development has closely paralleled that of other governmental institutions and because of our federalized constitutional democracy it has developed into a non-homogenious, multi-layered, institution.

§ 1.8　Adversative structure

The American system of criminal justice was an accomodation of the English common law to our type of government. This has allowed each state, and for the most part the majority of local communities, to interpret and identify their own institutional needs. Local autonomy and the strong fortress of "home rule" has allowed every burrough, township, town, city, county or state to establish its own system of criminal justice. In addition, there is a separate federal justice system. Some of the units of local government have a carefully constructed system while others have come into existence as a result of political manipulation. The diversity of origin is also represented operationally and the intricate characteristics of the system prove to be as puzzling and unfathomable to the accused as well as the general public. In reality this system is not a system for it does not have the qualities or the properties of a system.

The magnitude and the complexity of the system serves to create tensions resulting in a negative congruence pattern. The structure of the system constantly reinforces this pattern. Each element of the system functions essentially in structural isolation, with the primary unifying force being the processing of the accused through the intricate labyrinth of justice. Even this process provides for limited reduction of dispersion, for the accused is processed through each segment of the system in order to comply with minimal procedural requirements rather than the unifying concept of "justice."

Intra-agency controls are truly minimal. The district attorney influences the police by determining the specific disposition of individual cases which in turn affects arrest procedures and the processing of evidence. Through this process the district attorney influences the number and type of cases coming before the court and, consequently, the potential number of offenders who enter the correctional sub-system.

The courts exercise a strong influence over the criminal process through decisions regarding rules of evidence as they relate primarily to arrest, search, and seizure. Case decisions of this nature have a direct effect on law enforcement agencies. For instance, the U.S. Supreme Court in numerous landmark decisions has extended, through the appropriate amendment to the constitution, nationwide standards for police performance of specific functions as they related to the rights of an accused.

The courts have expressed their concern for the rights of prisoners, in recent years, consequently correctional agencies have had to alter their rules and procedures affecting the rights of inmates and parolees.

The controls exerted by one element of the system over the other are clearly criminal process oriented and have limited impact in terms of affecting the overall administration of other justice agencies. In fact, the controls essential to the establishment of a true system of criminal justice are absent. The isolation and genuine independence of the component of the system has fostered an adversative structure that reinforces indecisiveness. The system is formless, fluid and highly fragmented. Except for the thin thread of commonality, that of the criminal process, it is an absolute non-system.

§ 1.9 Rigid boundaries

The rigidity of boundaries of the elements of the justice system is of historical significance. It stems from a number of variables including tradition, federalism, the adversary aspects of criminal law, and intra-agency conflict. "The police see crime in the raw." They are exposed firsthand to the agony of victims, the danger of the streets, the violence of lawbreakers. A major task of the police officer is to track down and arrest persons who have committed serious crimes. It is often discouraging for such an officer to see courts promptly release defendants on bail, or prosecutors reduce charges in order to induce pleas of guilty to lesser offenses, or judges exclude incriminating evidence, or parole officers accept supervision of released prisoners but check on them only a few minutes each month.

Yet the police themselves are often seen by others as contributing to the failure of the system. They are the target of charges of ineptness, discourtesy, brutality, sleeping on duty, illegal searches. They are increasingly attacked by large segments of the community as being insensitive to the feelings and needs of the citizens they are employed to serve.

Trial judges tend to see crime from a more remote and neutral position. They see facts in dispute and two sides to each issue. They may sit long hours on the bench in an effort to adjudicate cases with dignity and dispatch, only to find counsel unprepared, or weak cases presented, or witnesses missing, or warrants unserved, or bail restrictions unenforced. They find sentencing to be the most difficult of their tasks, yet presentence information is scanty and dispositional alternatives are all too often thwarted by the unavailability of adequate facilities.

Yet criminal courts themselves are often poorly managed and severely criticized. They are seriously backlogged. All too many judges are perceived as being inconsiderate of waiting parties, police officers and citizen witnesses. Throughout the country, lower criminal courts tend to be operated more like turnstiles than tribunals.

Corrections officials enter the crime picture long after the offense and deal only with defendants. Their job is to maintain secure custody and design programs which prepare individual prisoners for a successful return to society. They are discouraged when they encounter convicted persons whose sentences are either inadequate or excessive. They are frustrated by legislatures which curtail the flexibility of sentences and which fail to appropriate necessary funds. They are dismayed at police officers who harass parolees, or at a community which fails to provide jobs or refuses to build halfway houses for ex-offenders.

Yet jails are notoriously ill-managed. Sadistic guards are not uncommon. Homosexual assaults among inmates are widely tolerated. Prison work usually bears little relationship to employment opportunities outside. Persons jailed to await trial are typically treated worse than sentenced offenders. Correctional administrators are often said to be presiding over schools in crime.''[5]

This failure to control crime and the inadequacies of the system serves to intensify the conflict between the components of the system and reinforces the boundaries. Each agency identifies and circumscribes its functional areas as it is subjected to criticism from other agencies and the community. Intensified criticism engenders a hostile response and as the justice actors close ranks within an agency the psychological and physical barriers become increasingly insurmountable.

Such a sequestering act mandates operational isolation and fragmentation. As the components of the system internalize the conflict becomes supervenient as exemplified by the statement of some police officials that the courts have "handcuffed" them, showing undue concern for the rights of the offender. Conflict of this nature should not be minimized for it augments the tendencies to reinforce agency boundaries.

Conflict is not only a matter of component isolation, but has been evident in jurisdictional disputes of law enforcement agencies. Most of these have been caused by our federalized system of government.

Federal, state, county and local law enforcement agencies have limited involvement or have refused to cooperate in areas of dual jurisdiction. Information (and in some instances evidence) has been withheld from other law enforcement agencies. Jealousy, rivalry, and invidious action on the part of individual law enforcement agencies resulted, in some instances, in delayed or denied "justice." It has also intensified the boundaries between some law enforcement agencies where a fluid and highly penetrable boundary is essential.

Inter-agency conflict between functional units of some law enforcement agencies such as patrol and detective has resulted in division and divisiveness to the point where these units function as separate agencies with clearly discernible boundaries. Fortunately the agencies suffering from this malady are few, but it does serve to illustrate the lack of clarity, substance and direction apparent in the law enforcement component of the justice system.

The field of corrections exhibits the same disparity where the boundaries essential to the security of personnel conflicts with the resocialization mode of other correctional actors. Furthermore, probation officers view the other segments of the correctional components with disdain and the interaction between juvenile probation, adult probation, parole and institutions is minimal. Contemporary corrections is viewed as a continuing process in the treatment of an offender, but in actuality there are distinct and clearly identifiable sub-components, each of which have differing objectives and fairly distinct functional boundaries. These barriers are educational, philosophical, and political realities that serve to identify a distinct boundary of isolation.

A concern for organizational statics is easily understandable and to a certain degree, essential because justice organizations compete for manpower and resources within an uncertain environment. Recurring disintegrative pressures from the environment constantly reinforce agency boundaries as the organizations strive for stability. Each justice agency develops a social structure, traditions, customs, and a culture which serve as organizational stabilizers and reinforcers of a closed system with impermeable boundaries.

Boundaries are essential to the functioning of justice agencies because they serve the positive function of identifying areas of responsibility. They allow for a division of authority and the implementation of unity of purpose. Boundaries provide for the processes of planning, organizing, coordinating and budgeting.

Identifiable parameters allow for concerted organizational response to routine and crisis situations or problems. Specialization is enhanced and organizational objectives can be specified within the legal and administrative limits of the agency.

Boundaries provide for structural entities and functional referents which circumscribe the total activities of an agency and identify guideposts for justice personnel. Boundary definition, as indicated, has many positive characteristics, but rigid and impenetrable boundaries of the components of the justice system have been instrumental in the creation and perpetuation of a non-system.

§ 1.10   Ideological conflict

Serious justice theorists focus their attention on a theory of applied justice that can be roughly divided into three broad areas identified as the conservative, the liberal and the radical. These dominant categories can be traced throughout the history of administration of justice in the United States. While the theories clearly are not mutually exclusive and at times even overlap, it is possible to identify justice actors or theorists who have significantly contributed to one of the categories.

The conservative concept of applied justice has dominated America since its establishment and has based its philosophical underpinnings on a combination of religious, moralistic, and legal authority. Extensive institutionalization of the offender, harsh treatment, and the paramount need for protecting society has characterized its application of justice.

Liberalism which has dominated American political theory since the times of our founding fathers has, since the turn of this century, played an increasingly important part in justice administration. The basis of this ideology is the belief that the individuals secular destiny can be steadily improved by improving the justice system, and the total environment. The individual, under this ideology, is viewed as a product of the function of his natural and social conditions. Improvement of the social conditions is perceived as the modal response to improvement of the individual. As a victim of the situation, the environmentalist presupposes the need for social justice and consequently has had considerable impact on this philosophical position.

The radicals differ from both the liberals and the conservatives in that their finalized conceptualizations are closer to the liberals, yet the more immediate pragmatic goals are based on perspectives held by the conservatives. The revolutionaries share the liberal's belief that the individual can be responsive to change, but they believe that this can only be achieved by a holocaustic restructuring of the justice system as it is and as it has been since the beginning of this nation.

The radicals have made it abundantly clear that they reject the totality of the justice process. For the most part they display the classical characteristics of political revolutionary movements in terms of strategy, tactics, structural response and philosophy. The participants of this movement advocate dysfunctional individual action and group activities with considerable impact on the justice system, but their pervasive solutions remain suspect in many quarters.

The criminal justice apparatus, racked by criticism and being the recipient of its share of the shock of cultural change has clearly been affected by its critics. Notwithstanding, it has been relatively effective in rejecting the challenge from within and without, but at the same time the justice systems posture has been modified by the revisionists.

The slippage in the American justice apparatus is readily apparent, but its institutions must continue to function if society is to continue to exist. Conflict resolution is essential and the hiatus between the protection of society and the safeguarding of individual liberty must be narrowed not on the basis of special irresponsibility but upon that of civil responsibility.

The challenge of justice ordering in our society has been made behind the walls of our prisons and on the streets of our cities. It has been a most formidable challenge and it should be responded to in terms of a careful assessment of efficiency and effectiveness of the justice apparatus.

A democracy must allow for a degree of violence and dissent. It should allow for and accept doubt as to the stability and viability of our social ordering mechanism. The values of the revisionists should serve as a catalyst for a constant and continuing evaluation of policy, procedures and programs. At the same time, the justice system must develop its capacity for conflict management as a means of containing and limiting disruption.

A balance of power must be maintained between those who demand stability at any cost and those who believe that catastrophic restructuring is the order of the day.

§ 1.11 Change

Criminal justice agencies must be able to adapt to meet the changing demands of their constituencies. None of these organizations can afford the luxuries of complacency, immobility, and the status quo. Each one is faced with intense pressures to alter their approaches to law enforcement and criminal justice. There is no question that change and adaptability have become requirements for organizational viability in the criminal justice field.[6]

Yet change is no simple process. It requires a meshing of the social and technical structures within an agency. It requires a continuing process of problem assessment, solution development, and implementation. It often requires a fracturing of some change-resistant traditions, changes required so that further change is possible. In short, it needs the development of an agency capability for change.

In many cases, an agency's capabilities for change will have to be developed. In other cases, the capacity may exist without being part of a formal organizational system for encouraging change.

Change must be consciously encouraged if it is to be carried out on a continuing basis. Agencies must develop an ability to recognize needs for change and consider the consequences of any specific change both for themselves and for those they serve.

Once a need has been assessed and a solution developed and considered, the change must be made into a reality through implementation. Success in implementing change requires that the agency both be adaptable and be known as adaptable through its commitment to change when needed; these become essentials in situations where constant change exists and continuing adaptiveness is required.

During implementation, evaluation of the success of the change must occur to insure that the effort continues on target. If the project is not succeeding, the evaluation should point to modifications designed to achieve success. Evaluation offers the lessons of experience to those in a planning capacity to improve their future planning efforts.

The transfer aspect of the process of change is important for two reasons: It provides potential solutions for agency problems. It offers assistance to agencies in establishing an adaptive approach to change. Therefore, transfer rests on the planning, implementation, and evaluation of change. It also serves as a basis for planning and solution development.

This is not to suggest that all change is good. In fact, it may be bad. The criterion for judgment is how well the change solves the problem faced by the agency. With the adaptive approach to planning, implementation, evaluation and transfer, the agency minimizes the possibility of accepting an inappropriate solution.

The consequences of a change will often extend beyond the boundaries of the host agency. When they do, the parties affected by the change must themselves be included in its planning and implementation. This involvement is required because, while these parties are being affected by the change, they are also influencing it. Involvement requires identification of the affected parties and strategies for their inclusion.

The form of a strategy must depend on the character of the parties affected and the nature of the change. Involvement of community organizations will require an approach different from the involvement of a prosecutor's or probation office.

The most effective general strategy, yet the most difficult to implement, is one of continuing involvement. This strategy includes the identification of the set of significant relationships with other agencies, organizations, and segments of the public. Once these relationships have been identified, linkages need to be established that enable communication and cooperation among the agency, and those affected by the change. These linkages need to be specifically designed, recognizing the qualities of the parties involved and the kinds of communication and cooperation desired.

Change, through its very meaning, affects or acts on something. A change in one justice agency often affects other. The community served by the agency may also be affected by the change. It is hard to think of any organizations less autonomous than those in the criminal justice field. Not only are they related to one another by the flows of criminal offenders, but each is itself embedded in a context of clients, public opinion, community pressures, and governmental authority. In other words, each criminal justice agency is likely to be dependent on any number of other organizations for support. This support would include the budgetary and financial resources received from a governmental funding source. It would also include approval or disapproval from community or governmental sources of the activities, plans, or role of the agency. Each agency needs to protect its ties to these diverse influence groups. These ties both define and limit an agency's activities; if the agency oversteps the limits, the result is a failure in satisfying the public for whom the agency exists.

Change within a police department, therefore, may become something that cannot be considered without understanding its interrelationships with other agencies or social forces. For instance, in a police agency the administrators may not be able to institute a change without considering its effects on government, it will require the support of the mayor or council to obtain the resources needed to support the change. Since the change may influence working relationships between the police department and the prosecutor's office, the courts, and the public defender, their cooperation may be required if the change is to succeed. Finally, if the change will alter the kind of service given the victim, offender, or general community, then the agency may have to work to obtain the support of the relevant community organizations. A lack of consideration of any or all of these relationships could dampen or even end a significant and important response to a problem faced by the agency.

Notes

1. National Commission on the Causes and Prevention of Violence, *Law and Order Reconsidered* (Washington: U.S. Government Printing Office, 1969), pp. 3-8.

2. Otto A. Bird, *The Idea of Justice* (New York: Frederick A. Praeger, Publishers, 1967), p. 122.

3. *Op. cit.*, p. 164.

4. Advisory Commission on Intergovernmental Relations, *State-Local Relations in the Criminal Justice System* (Washington: U.S. Government Printing Office, August, 1971), p. 67.

5. Daniel J. Freed, "The Nonsystem of Criminal Justice," National Commission on the Causes and Prevention of Crime, *op. cit*, pp. 367-377.

6. National Advisory Commission on Criminal Justice Standards and Goals, *Criminal Justice System* (Washington: U.S. Government Printing Office, 1973), pp. 207-210.

PART 2

THE POLICE

IV.   THE FUTURE POLICEMAN

§ 2.1 Introduction

The attitudes of the American people toward the police service often are inconsistent. The police are appreciated when they are needed but are often feared because they represent authority.[1] They are ridiculed in the low humor of situation comedies, and idealized in police television drama. In some cases, political ideology dictates attitudes of respect or hatred toward the police. Only rarely is the real nature of the police service broadcast; rarely is the man inside the uniform known, or his true role appraised. Yet, his role is critical. Every day of his professional life he is met with conflicts and situations that are too painful or too frightening for many Americans to confront.

There is no confusion about one point. When faced with trouble, Americans expect quick police response; when victimized, they want—and expect—the services of a professional.

The inconsistency of public support for the police service often causes feelings of discouragement among policemen. Yet many of the more vocal and least informed critics are those who rely heavily on their police to provide a secure place to live.

The police in the United States are not separate from the people. They draw their authority from the will and consent of the people, and they recruit their officers from them. The police are the instrument of the people to achieve and maintain order; their efforts are founded on principles of public service and ultimate responsibility to the public.

To a police officer, public service is more than a vague concept. When people need help, it is to a police officer that they are most likely to turn. He responds—immediately—without first ascertaining the status of the person in need. It does not matter if that person is rich or poor; he need not meet complicated criteria to qualify as a recipient of aid or as a potential client.

Police officers are decision makers. A decision—whether to arrest, to make a referral, to seek prosecution or to use force—has a profound effect on those a police officer serves. Most of these decisions must be made within the span of a few moments and within the physical context of the most aggravated social problems. Yet, the police officer is just as accountable for these

43

decisions as the judge or corrections official is for decisions deliberated for months.

The role the police officer plays in society is a difficult one; he must clearly understand complex social relationships to be effective. He is not only a part of the community he serves, and a part of the government that provides his formal base of authority, he is also a part of the criminal justice system that determines what course society will pursue to deter lawbreakers or rehabilitate offenders in the interest of public order.

Although the police service is a formal element of local government, it is responsible to the people in a more direct way. The specific goals and priorities which the police establish within the limits of their legislatively granted authority are determined to a large extent by community desires. These desires are transmitted to the police through the community and the governing body of the jurisdiction in which the police operate. For example, elements of the community might urge increased patrols around schools, stricter enforcement of parking regulations in congested areas, or reduced enforcement activities against violations of certain crimes. The priorities established by police agencies in such cases are often influenced more by the wishes of those policed than by any other consideration. The police officer is accountable to the people for his decisions and the consequences. The success of his mission depends to a great extent on the support of the people.

In the exercise of its police power, government enacts laws designed to protect the health, welfare, and morals of its citizens. Under this nation's form of government, police power is exercised by the states and their political subdivisions in the promulgation of laws and regulations concerning building and safety, zoning, health, noise and distrubance, disorderly conduct, and traffic regulations. Repeated and willful violation of these regulations is generally considered criminal conduct.

Each state has developed a comprehensive criminal code defining crimes and providing punishments. Responsibility for the enforcement of these laws, however, has been largely delegated to local government.

Although local government provides many services, the police are its most visible representatives. Because they are the agents of government who are most frequently in contact with the public, and because they are accessible around-the-clock, police are often contacted regarding services provided by other municipal, county, state and federal agencies.

Often the public does not differentiate between various elements of local government. An irate citizen is simply concerned that he is not receiving a service to which he feels entitled. If he is bewildered by the profusion of government divisions, he turns to the one most familiar and most recognizable—the police. Because their service to the citizen affects his respect for government in general and the police in particular, police should respond as helpfully as possible, even if the matter is outside their immediate jurisdiction.

Through the identification and arrest of a suspected offender, the police initiate the criminal justice process. The individual's guilt or innocence is then determined in the courts. If the individual is found guilty, an attempt is made to rehabilitate him through a corrections process that may include probation, confinement, parole, or any combination of these.

While each of the elements of the criminal justice system is organizationally separate, these elements are functionally interrelated. In most cases, for example, the police act before the other elements of the system. The subsequent release of an otherwise guilty person from custody because a court found the evidence necessary for his conviction to be unlawfully seized, the reluctance of a prosecutor to present a case for court determination, or the failure of corrections to reform a convict prior to his release, have a direct effect upon the manner and conditions in which the police must perform their tasks.

A very high percentage of police work is done in direct reponse to citizen complaints. This underlines the frequently unrecognized fact that members of the public are an integral part of the criminal justice system; in fact, the success of the system depends more on citizen participation than on any other single factor.

The police are the criminal justice element in closest contact with the public—as a result, they are often blamed for failures in other parts of the system. In like manner, public confidence in the criminal justice system depends to a large extent on the trust that the people have in their police.

The police, the criminal justice system, and government in general could not control crime without the cooperation of a substantial portion of the people. In the absence of public support, there would be little that an army could not do better than the police.

Currently, the relationship in most communities between the police and the public is not entirely satisfactory. Members of the public frequently do not notify the police of situations that require enforcement or preventive action. Often, they avoid involvement in averting or interfering with criminal conduct, and many are suspicious of the police, the criminal justice system, and the entire political process.

During the 20 years following World War II, the police became increasingly isolated from their communities. Reasons for this isolation include urbanization, rapidly changing social conditions, greater demands for police services, increased reliance by the police on motorized patrol, police efforts to professionalize, and reduced police contact with noncriminal elements of society. These factors, combined with public apathy, caused many police agencies to attempt to combat rising crime without actively involving their communities in their efforts.

Due in large part to the widespread riots in the sixties, and the report of the President's Commission on Law Enforcement and Administration of Justice many police agencies reassessed their role and made changes that resulted in greater community involvement in crime control. Police agencies throughout the nation have significantly improved their ability to deal with crime and disorder. They have also taken great strides in reponding to the demands of their communities for greater service involvement and responsiveness. Perhaps more than any other institution, the police have advanced their ability to cope with rapidly changing social conditions.

In less than 10 years, the nature of debate in the police service has changed. The question is "How should we be involved in them?" As is usual during any time of great change, experimentation has resulted in both success and failure.

In attempting to reduce tension and improve their relationships with the public, the police have experimented with innovative programs. In some communities policemen wear blazers instead of the traditional military-type uniform, operate storefront offices, discuss local problems at neighborhood "coffee klatches," and engage in "rap sessions" with juveniles.

Inside and outside the service, there is little agreement on the role of the police. While one citizen group demands more non-enforcement programs, another demands that police devote all resources to direct protection and vigorous enforcement. Lack of manpower and fiscal resources has caused delay or abandonment of many programs to improve police-community relations, and the police have had to assign priorities to the delivery of direct protection services.

There have been drastic changes in the police service during the past 40 years. Striving for greater efficiency, the police service evolved away from the concept of the cop on the beat of the 1940's to the idea of a more mechanized police service in the 1950's. Yet, in this process, police officers often became anonymous. Confronted with civil turmoil in the 1960's, the police responded too slowly and too impersonally to suit many. The police service in the 1970's is aware that it must have greater support from prosecutors, courts, corrections agencies, and the people they serve if crime is to be curbed.

The President's Commission on Law Enforcement and Administration of Justice recognized many of the problems the police service faced. It described problems and revealed specific conditions that worked to inhibit the effective operation of the police and the criminal justice system. Yet, its direct impact upon the reduction of crime and the system which it sought to improve remains uncertain.

American culture combines factors that contribute to crime and disorder. Widely varying beliefs and changing life styles mark the structure of this complex and competitive society. Extremes in ideals, emotions, and conduct are trademarks of life in the United States.

Americans are, nevertheless, regulated by a far-reaching and detailed collection of federal, state, and local laws. But the maintenance of order cannot be accomplished through the enforcement of laws by the police alone. Abraham Lincoln urged every American to share responsibility for maintaining order when he said:

Let every American, every lover of liberty swear never to violate in the
least particular, the laws of the country and never to tolerate their
violation by others. Let every man remember that to violate the law is to
tear the character of his own and his children's liberty. Let reverence for
the laws be breathed by every American mother to the baby . . . on her
lap. Let it be written in primers and spelling books. Let it be preached
from the pulpit, proclaimed in legislative halls and enforced in courts of
justice. And in short let reverence for the law become the *political religion*
of the nation . . . .

A team effort between the community and the police is needed to
roll back crime. The most efficiently administered police agency will
falter unless the community it serves genuinely supports it.
Conversely, a supportive community, intensely interested in reducing
crime, will be ineffective if the police agency is complacent or
incompetent. Vigorous cooperation is necessary.

The need for change must be acknowledged before change can be
made. The events of the last decade point to greater support for the
police, and greater police response to the needs of the people.
Americans are encouraging new ideas and are receptive to new
approaches in police service. The seventies should mark an era of
change.

Notes

1. National Advisory Commission on Criminal Justice Standards and Goals,
Police, Washington: U.S. Government Printing Office, 1973, pp. 1-11.

I. THE POLICE AND THEIR PROBLEMS

SOURCE: Daniel P. Stang, "The Police and Their Problems," National
Commission on the Causes and Prevention of Violence, Law and Order
Reconsidered, Washington, U.S. Government Printing Office, 1969, pp.
285-308.

In society's day-to-day efforts to protect its citizens from the
suffering, fear, and property loss produced by crime and the
threat of crime, the policeman occupies the front line. It is he
who directly confronts criminal situations, and it is to him that
the public looks for personal safety. The freedom of Americans
to walk their streets and be secure in their homes—in fact, to do
what they want when they want—depends to a great extent on
their policemen.[1]

There is little question that during the past decade of turbulent social change, our nation's policemen have not been able to escape from the front lines. More than that, they are called upon to fight against one side one day and then for it the next day. The same policeman who on a Wednesday is mobilized to help control a blazing ghetto riot and arrest throngs of looters may by week's end find himself assigned to keep traffic clear from the parade route being followed by hundreds of blacks conducting an anti-poverty march.

In fact, the very same policeman may on a Saturday rescue a hippie college student victimized by a gang of motorcyclists, and by the next Monday be summoned to the campus to assist University officials in re-capturing a building held by stone-throwing, epithet-screaming student dissidents. The same policeman in the morning may be called "soft and ineffective" by our "forgotten man" and "fascist pig" by a young revolutionary in the afternoon. How our nation's police are able to fulfill such drastically conflicting roles without lapsing into an anomic stupor[2] is perhaps the best measure of the degree to which the policeman is in fact a professional.

What is the policeman's job? Who and what is he supposed to protect? How can he most effectively execute his responsibilities? What are his problems and how can these problems be solved? These are the questions we address in this section.

§ 2.2 Duties of the police

Police responsibilities fall into three broad categories.[3] First, they are called upon to "keep the peace." This peace-keeping duty is a broad and most important mandate which involves the protection of lives and rights ranging from handling street corner brawls to the settlement of violent family disputes. In a word, it means maintaining public safety.

Secondly, the police have a duty to provide services which range from bestowing menial courtesies to the protection of public and private property. This responsibility is the one that many police officers complain about the most but, nevertheless, are called upon to perform the most frequently. In fulfilling these obligations, a policeman "recovers stolen property, directs traffic, provides emergency medical aid, gets cats out of trees, checks on the homes of families on vacation, and helps little old ladies who have locked themselves out of their apartments."[4]

The third major police responsibility, which many policemen and a considerable segment of the public feel should be the exclusive police responsibility, is that of combating crime by enforcing the rule of law. Execution of this task involves what is called police operations and this ranges from preparing stakeouts to arresting suspects.

That policemen have difficulty assigning priorities to these sometimes conflicting responsibilities is one major operating limitation the police have recently had to endure.[5] There are, however, other important limitations imposed on the police to which we shall briefly refer before returning to the crucial subject of conflicting police roles.

Among these, special attention must be given to manpower deficiencies, inadequate financing, and frictions with courts and other governmental agencies.

§ 2.3 Manpower limitations

According to the President's Crime Commission, there are approximately 420,000 policemen in the United States.[6] Yet most police departments are under-manned, thus spreading the existing complement of police personnel much too thin. This manpower supply has been further depleted by more generous holiday, vacation and sick-leave policies, reduced weekly work-hours, increased specialization, continued use of police personnel to perform a heavier burden of clerical, technical and service activities more suitable for civilian employees. The manpower problem is further exacerbated by difficulties in recruiting, especially recruitment among minority groups; resignations of experienced police officers; early retirements; overly rigid restrictions on manpower distribution and assignment; and the dissipation of police-man-hours in nonproductive or minimally productive activity. This latter category involves, in part, hours spent waiting to be called as a witness, writing out multiple copies of reports, assignment to fixed posts of questionable utility, being forced to provide special escort services, and other irritating and time consuming chores. Nor is the available manpower scientifically allocated either in terms of ratios of police to population (which range from fewer than 1:1000 to more than 4:1000) or in terms of crime incidence, traffic volume, calls for police services or other meaningful indices of demands for more effective policing.

This inadequacy is magnified by reports that newly recruited officers are less well-educated than veteran officers, that they are being assigned to full police patrol duty without completing the prescribed training; that morale is low and supervision lax;[7] and that advanced in-service and refresher training to keep them abreast of legal, social, and technological changes is inadequate.[8]

§ 2.4   Financial limitations

In the most affluent nation in world history, our total expenditures for police (federal, state, and local, including sheriffs and such *ad hoc* police agencies as the New York City Transit Police, Port of New York Authority Police, park police, Capitol Police, and other full-time enforcement personnel) approximated $3 billion. Most commentators consider this amount inadequate in light of current recruitment problems, resignations, early retirement difficulties, and widespread police "moonlighting" with its negative effects on police alertness and departmental sick-leave rates.

Inadequate police budgets, too, have made it difficult or impossible in many jurisdictions to construct needed modern headquarters facilities, to provide decentralized substations in areas of demonstrated need, to modernize communications systems, to install improved traffic control devices, to acquire computers and other advanced management and operations control "hardware," to finance pilot projects and demonstrations and to recruit at highly-paid specialist levels the qualified personnel, all of which are essential to the implementation of the recommendations of the President's Commission on Law Enforcement and Administration of Justice and of the National Advisory Commission on Civil Disorders.

Police costs in the United States have been traditionally a local burden ... a burden which many local jurisdictions are no longer able to support if fully effective law enforcement is to be achieved. Certainly the funds now being provided by Congress through the Law Enforcement Assistance Administration of the Department of Justice to support police planning, training, and research will prove of some assistance in easing the budgetary limitations under which many law enforcement units are presently operating.

§ 2.5   Police conflicts with other criminal justice agencies

The police establishment is only one of the agencies constituting the criminal justice system. By the very nature of the criminal justice system, the police are required to cooperate with the other agencies, including the prosecutors, the courts, the jails and correctional institutions. In many locations, however, there is neither formal nor informal machinery for cross-professional dialogue between the police and the representatives of the other agencies involved in criminal justice administration or policy-making, so that minor irritations and misunderstandings often cumulate into major bureaucratic conflicts. The failure to involve the courts, prosecutors, and corrections officials in the training of police, the failure to involve police in the orientation of newly-chosen judges and prosecutors and in the training curricula for newly appointed probation and parole officers, and the even more general failure to consult police in the planning stages of executive and legislative decision-making in areas which may directly or indirectly affect their responsibilities or operations—all further compound this already difficult situation.

In recent years the courts in particular have become more and more the target of severe police criticism. Police problems involving the courts arise at three levels: (1) Procedural requirements which result in the loss of many hundreds of thousands of police man-hours annually and resistance to changes in traditional practices (e.g., central booking, computerized dockets, the impanelling of additional grand juries, and such apparently simple courtesies as moving cases involving police witness to the top of the calendar or the taking of police testimony in pre-trial proceedings): (2) allegedly improper dispositions of cases both at preliminary hearings and arraignments and after trial (e.g., dismissal of charges and release of persons arrested for serious crimes, speedy setting of low bail or release on personal recognizance of offenders police believe dangerous and likely to commit additional crimes or granting probation to dangerous and persistent offenders where probation supervision is inadequate); and (3) constitutional limitations on police tactics and procedures both in general law enforcement and specifically in the area of criminal investigation (e.g., the decisions of the Supreme

Court which have forced the police to be more careful in the conduct of searches and seizures, and in warning suspects of their constitutional rights against compulsory self-incrimination).

The question of court-imposed constitutional limitations on police practices is especially sensitive. Whether these restrictions on traditional police practices have actually reduced police effectiveness is a matter of some controversy even among police and prosecutors; but a significant consensus among police officers of all ranks in every part of the country interprets these decisions as favoring the criminal and as deliberately and perversely hampering, indeed punishing, the police.

One police spokesman has stated:

> It would appear that the primary purpose of the police establishment has been overlooked in the tendency of our courts and the other officers of the judicial process to free the most heinous of criminals because of legalistic errors by law enforcement officers . . . . To allow criminals to go free because of legalistic error turns our judicial process into a game and makes mockery of our supposedly sophisticated society . . . . From the police standpoint, one of the very real dangers is that decisions from the courts are breeding indecision and uncertainty in the individual police officer. The inevitable result is that the policeman's duty has become so diffused that it is difficult for him to carry out his responsibilities.[9]

Another observer stated even more dramatically that, "The courts must not terrorize peace officers by putting them in fear of violating the law themselves."[10] Views of this kind are set forth repeatedly in articles and comments in such respected police professional periodicals as *The Police Chief, Law and Order* and *Police*.

Police in general also have little confidence in the ability of jails and prisons to reform or rehabilitate convicted offenders. This is not surprising, of course, for this view is shared, if perhaps for different reasons, by the great majority of American criminologists and even by residents of our so-called "correctional system." This lack of confidence in institutional rehabilitation programs underlies the strong police opposition to the parole system and the somewhat less aggressive opposition to work release, school release, and prisoner furlough programs, open institutions, and halfway houses. There is a rather generalized feeling among large segments of the police that potentially dangerous offenders are released far too often on low bail, or their own recognizance or following conviction far too soon by parole boards; that these paroled offenders are frequently inadequately supervised by unqualified parole officers with excessive case-load responsibilities; and that they commit new and serious crimes thus adding additional burdens of investigation and apprehension to already overburdened police agencies.

Police in some jurisdictions have encountered difficulties in their relationships with the executive and legislative branches of government. These difficulties range from the irritation of requests for special treatment for favored traffic offenders and detail of police personnel to jobs as chauffeur and doorman in the Mayor's office to outside interference in internal personnel matters such as assignments and promotions and in general policy matters such as enforcement strategies and operational tactics.

Legislatures too have been criticized by police for failure to appropriate sufficient funds to provide adequate law enforcement for repeated investigations and inquiries which contribute to a negative police image; for penal law and criminal procedure changes which reduce penalties, make parole easier, or impose new restrictions on police efforts; and for failure to protect the police from changes in their working conditions which police feel deleterious to their welfare.

§ 2.6 Police role conflicts

As we stated earlier, perhaps the most important source of police frustration, and the most severe limitation under which they operate, is the conflicting roles and demands involved in the order maintenance, community service, and crime-fighting responsibilities of the police. Here both the individual police officer and the police community as a whole find not only inconsistent public expectations and public reactions, but also inner conflict growing out of the interaction of the policeman's values, customs, and traditions with his intimate experience with the criminal element of the population. The policeman lives on the grinding edge of social conflict, without a well-defined, well-understood notion of what he is supposed to be doing there.

Police involvement in order maintenance situations such as family disputes, tavern brawls, disorderly teenage loitering in the streets, quarrels between neighbors, and the like inevitably produces role conflict. One party is likely to feel harassed, outraged or neglected.

The police officer quite frequently has no clear legal standard to apply—or one that, if applied, would produce an obviously unjust result. The victim is often as blameworthy as the perpetrator, often the parties really want him only to "do something" that will "settle things" rather than make an arrest. Should an arrest be demanded, he is in many jurisdictions foreclosed from complying since the misdemeanor complained of was not committed in his presence, and the vociferously compaining victim or witness is unwilling to sign entirely on his own discretion and judgement.[11]

Oftentimes the policeman is forced to arrest persons for violations of law he does not believe are fair. But more often, he sees the fear and the pain and the damage that crime causes, and he feels that criminals are getting away with too much. This frustration mounts each time he arrives at the scene of a recently-reported crime to discover the offender has escaped. He finds justification for his contempt for the "criminal element" when he reads of public approval of night-stick justice techniques.

Police in the United States are for the most part white, upwardly mobile lower middle-class, conservative in ideology and resistant to change. In most areas of the country, even where segregation has been legally eliminated for long periods, they are likely to have grown up without any significant contact with little or no experience of the realities of ghetto life. They tend to share the attitudes, biases and prejudices of the larger community, among which is likely to be a fear and distrust of Negroes and other minority groups.

Appointed to the police force and brought into day-to-day contact with what is to him an alien way of life, the young police officer experiences what behavioral scientists refer to as "cultural shock." His latent negative attitudes are reinforced by the aggressive and militant hostility which greets him even when he is attempting to perform, to the best of his ability, a community service or order maintenance function, or is attempting to apprehend a criminal whose victim has been a member of the minority community.

Negative responses to minorities and to non-conforming groups such as "hippies," campus militants, antiwar demonstrators, and the new breed of "revolutionaries," are also reinforced by the socialization process which transforms the new recruit into a member of the police community. Not only during the formal training process but in the everyday contacts with his fellow officers and his participation with them in both on-duty activity and off-duty socializing tend to mutually reinforce the police ideology, the closed-ranks defensiveness, which separates "we" who are on the side of law, order, morality and right from "they" who are immoral, criminal, delinquent, idle, lazy, dirty, shiftless or different.

Efforts to bridge the gap between the police and some segments of the community have proved only minimally successful.[12] The realities of police confrontation with these "undesirable elements," whether on occasions of episodic violence or, more importantly, when a police officer is killed or seriously injured as a result of minority group militance, tend to offset the gains made by efforts directed toward improving police attitudes and police-community relationships.

§ 2.7 Police ineffectiveness

The cumulative result of the many limitations and frustrations described above is an evident inability of the police, as presently organized, manned, financed, equipped and led, to meet effectively all of the demands and expectations placed on them by the public. These inadequacies are evidenced in their inability to prevent crime, their declining record in solving crimes known to them; their sluggish response to and indifferent investigation of all but major crimes or those involving important persons, businesses, or institutions.[13] Particularly evident is an inability to deal effectively with crime in minority-populated ghettoes—for reasons which involve minority group attitudes and noncooperation as importantly as police attitudes, facilities and efficiency.

Various analyses of police confrontations with minority and protest groups have identified 'over-response,' inadequate crowd control training, poor planning, failures in supervision and leadership, as well as the residual hostility of the police to the minorities and nonconformists involved, their suspicion of dissent, and their disagreement with the demonstrators on the substantive issues as causative factors.[14] Nor have these analyses neglected to underline the difficult conditions to which the police have been subjected: the provocations, verbal and physical, to which they were subjected by participants in demonstrations;[15] and at least in some instances the distorted or at least unbalanced coverage by news media.[16] That at least some participants in many of these conflict episodes wanted to provoke a police over-response may be true—but that individual police officers, and sometimes apparently whole police units, cooperated enthusiastically with their plans is equally obvious.[17]

That the police and major elements of the public are becoming more polarized is well established.[18] This polarization is intensified by police frustrations growing out of what they perceive as the public's unreasonable expectations of them and even more unreasonable limitations imposed on them, the growing militancy of minority and dissident groups, their strategy of confrontation, and the vicious cycle of police over-response. These factors often are aggravated by new and highly publicized charges of police brutality and derogatory attitudes toward minority groups, which attract new sympathizers from previously moderate or non-activist segments of the population and often tend to encourage reactive ghetto counter-violence.

§ 2.8 Police politicization

Recently, the police have begun to realize that acting exclusively as individuals in attempting to deal with their role, conflicts, frustrations and limitations has failed to pay dividends. Thus, as is the case with other newly self-aware special interest groups in our society, the police have begun to enter active politics on a much larger scale.

Police participation in the political process in America has traditionally been limited and local: limited to securing favorable legislation as to pensions, working conditions and pay rates,[19] with occasional lobbying for or against proposals to abolish the death penalty, legalize gambling, or raise the age of juvenile court jurisdiction—and local in the sense that it invariably involved approaches by the locally organized police to municipal authorities or at most to the state legislator representing the district. Occasionally charges would be made of more active police involvement in local campaigns, but there was a consensus even among the police that they, like the military, should abstain from active, overt participation in politics. Various police departments incorporated in their police regulations stringent rules prohibiting political activity other than voting.

In the past decade, largely as a result of efforts to raise police pay scales to a parity with those of skilled workmen, more militant police associations—some trade-union affiliated, others in loose state and national affiliations—escalated their pressure tactics so that job action, "blue-flu," and even threatened police strikes became commonplace in police-municipality salary disputes.[20]

The major impetus to police politicization, however, was without doubt the attempt to impose a civilian review apparatus to adjudicate complaints against police officers by aggrieved citizens and attempts of citizen groups to restrict police use of firearms. The proposals for civilian review boards were fought in the communications media, in the courts, in the legislature, and finally in a popular referendum in New York City in which the police won a resounding victory after a campaign which did much to further polarize the dissident minorities. The victory convinced many in the police community of the desirability of abandoning the internecine battles which had divided them and reduced their political effectiveness in the past.

The future of expended police participation in politics is not entirely clear at present. Certainly there has been important police support for conservative, even radical right, candidates in recent national and local elections, and there are signs that police officials are finding increasing opportunities as successful political candidates.

But the police have not had an unbroken record of political successes. In a recent legislative session in Albany, a bill abolishing the fifty-eight year old three-platoon system passed by a near unanimous vote, despite strong opposition by the united police pressure groups. Whether activities such as aroused police officers seeking the removal of a judge in Detroit, or an equally agressive organization (the Law Enforcement group in New York City) seeking to monitor the conduct of judges and their case dispositions will be widely and successfully imitated cannot be predicted at this time.

What is clear, however, is that a politicized police force united and well financed and perhaps closely allied to conservative political and social forces in the community, poses a problem for those interested in preserving internal democracy and insuring domestic tranquility. As the only lawfully armed force within the community, and possessed by the nature of their duties and responsibilities of unique authority and powers over their fellow citizens (including access to derogatory information, potential for discriminatory enforcement of the laws against their opponents, licensing and inspection functions), the united incursion of the police into active politics must be regarded with some trepidation.

More and more, the police community perceives itself as a minority group, disadvantaged and discriminated against, surrounded by, servicing, and protecting a public, which is at best apathetic or unaware of the frustrations and limitations imposed on the police; and at worst, unsympathetic or hostile. The dynamics of this self-perception, assuming a continuation or possible escalation of the external aggravants (verbal and physical abuse of the police; more stringent judicial and legislative restrictions; budgetary difficulties), involve reinforced defensive group solidarity, intensified feelings of alienation and polarization, and a magnified and increasingly aggressive militancy in reaction and response to those individuals, groups and institutions (social and governmental) perceived as inimical—an action-reaction pattern which, unfortunately, will inevitably be replicated within the aggrieved and dissident communities.

There are two areas of police-public confrontations in which changes in police policy and practice can lead to a reduction of friction and restoration of public respect for the police which the police themselves feel to be so sorely lacking. The first involves highly visible police relationships with the public, often involving the combined presence of great numbers of police and the public at the same time and place. The second is the less visible contact of the police with the public and usually involves ordinary relationships between individual police officers and individual members of the public.

§ 2.9   The police and political violence

The police often believe that ideological and political conflicts like the Chicago convention demonstrations involve clashes between good, upright and honest groups of citizens on the one hand and bad, lawless and deceitful troublemakers on the other. In fact, however, these great struggles between large groups of the public more clearly involve political differences than they do questions of criminal behavior. Often the "good, upright and honest" citizens are better characterized simply as conservative elements of the population who are resisting the demands of other factions seeking social, political, or economic benefits at the direct expense of the conservative groups.

Unfortunately, these conflicts involving demonstrations, mass protests, and strikes by the dissidents often involve violence and the call-up of the police for front-line duty. The police, instead of taking a neutral position in attempting to restore order during these primarily political clases, often tend to become participants in the clash on the side of the conservative elements and against the dissident elements.[21] The dissidents quickly recognize the active participation of the police in siding with the "enemy" and then begin to concentrate their attacks, both verbal and physical, more directly on the police than on the groups whose interests the police are supposedly protecting. The cycle becomes vicious and the ultimate loser is always the police.

This recurring phenomenon continues and the conservative-reformist clashes, entailing the victimization of the police, between management and labor of the 1930's; between the landowners and the migrant farm workers in California of the late 1930's and early 1940's; between the small town or rural white southern population— and the civil rights workers and Southern blacks of the early 1960's; between the urban governments, employers, landlords, and business establishments—and the anti-poverty and black power advocates of the middle to late 1960's. On each of these battlefields some of the police have unnecessarily taken sides and have become the target of violence.

In the Washington counter-inaugural demonstration, it was shown that when the police, through disciplined supervision, refrain from taking sides and steadfastly remain neutral in the face of a political demonstration that is perhaps distasteful to most of them personally, physical injuries and the destruction of property are minimized and the police emerge as widely respected umpires and peace-keepers. Thus, with respect to political differences between elements of the population in these socially troubled times, police leadership must decline invitations to take sides and to refrain from engaging in unnecessary fights. Only in this way can the police surely reemerge as the respected keepers of the peace—the principle duty of their worthy profession.

§ 2.10 The patrolman and the people

The second area of police-public confrontation in which there has been a loss of respect for the police is the routine day-to-day encounters between individual police officers and members of minority groups. These encounters form the crux of what is commonly referred to as the "police-community relations problem."

The problem manifests itself particularly in the inner city.

The crowded center city is where crime rates are the highest, where the black minority has experienced the catharsis of bloody, blazing riots, and is now struggling to develop a new and proud identity. The people no longer doubt that they are entitled to be treated with respect and dignity, and often militantly demand it. They are aspiring for the social and material benefits that they have been so long without. Hopes are high, but the results have not yet begun to materialize substantially. Houses and apartments are still over-crowded, too cold in the winter, and unbearably hot in the summer. Homes still are often without fathers. Mothers still are searching for the wherewithal to purchase the next meal. Children of all ages are out on the street and in the alleys.

They see the very visible white man who, for years, has owned the corner grocery stores. He still tells them to get out if they are not going to buy anything. But he's scared of them now and they know it. So they goad him, throw his merchandise around and sometimes steal it if they think they can do so without getting caught. The grocer calls the police.

The police arrive in a radio-dispatched squad car with red lights flashing. The young candy theives have made a clean getaway. Their friends, however, are still on the street. The policemen talk with the grocer then return to the street to question the kids. The kids are amused and enjoy the excitement. "No," they did not see anybody leave the store. The policemen know otherwise and in frustration they ask, "What are you kids doing here?" "Nothing," is the answer. "Then you better move on or we're gonna lock you up," the kids are told. Reluctantly they make feeble efforts to obey. The police get back into their squad car and start to drive off. Ten seconds later they hear the kids' jeers and laughter.

Night falls. More of the older kids are now seen on the street corners "shucking and jiving." Others dance or feign boxing matches.

In the homes the fights begin. Sometimes it is between man and woman; sometimes between teenage child and an aunt or grandmother. The police are called again. The people on the street watch as the squad car arrives. The police go inside; they hear shouting. The accusations begin. The police explain that in order for them to arrest anybody, the complainant is going to have to go down to the D.A.'s office and sign a complaint. "Just lock the 'so and so' up," is the response. The police do the best they can to quiet things down, then leave. Nobody is satisfied. As the squad car pulls away from the curb, the kids jeer again.

Later in the evening the same policemen see a loud street corner disturbance involving about a dozen young men. The policemen are now a little more weary. In another half hour their tour will be finished.

They get out of the car and ask, "What's going on?" Two of the young men continue to swing at one another. "Alright, break it up!," a policman orders. One of the two stops swinging. The other, apparently intoxicated,

continues to brawl. The policemen get gruff. "I said, 'knock it off'!,"
barks the policeman. The young fighter utters a profane epithet followed
by, "Honky cop." More people gather around.

One of the policemen responds, "Buddy, you're coming down to the
stationhouse. We're gonna lock you up." The policemen reach for his
arms. He kicks, swings his fists, and continues to yell "Honky cop!" The
two policemen slam him up against the squad car, handcuff him, pat him
down and shove him into the back seat. The crowd is sullen. Fists are
clenched and teeth are gritted. One of the policemen says, "Move on. We
don't want any more trouble out of you people tonight." The policemen
get back into the squad car and drive off. The still undispersed crowd
mutters words of hatred.

These are ordinary events in the average day of a policeman
assigned a squad car beat in the center city. There is no love lost
between the police and the center city residents. The residents,
whether they be black, Puerto Rican, Mexican, of any other minority
group, or just plain hippies, see the police as bullies, unfair, stupid,
rude, and brutal—a symbol of "Whitey's power." The police, in turn,
see the minority groups as hostile, dirty, lazy, undisciplined,
dishonest, immoral, and worst of all, disrespectful of the "badge"
they try to represent.

"In the old days," the police say, "colored people would move on if you
told them to. Now they don't. They just give you a bunch of crap."

On a wooden fence in the center city there are new epigrams scrawled
in crayon. They read 'Black Power!,' "Say it now and say it loud—I am
black and I am proud!," "Kill a pig."

§ 2.11   Improving police-community relations

The police are, indeed, prejudiced against minorities. And the
minority groups are equally prejudiced against the police. The
prejudice on both sides is not without some foundation. The views of
each side toward the other are constantly being reinforced and have
become self-fulfilling prophesies. Doing something about this problem is what is called "improving police-community relations."

The need to improve police-community relations has existed and
been recognized for decades. Local, state and federal commissions
have written hundreds of pages about it. Police experts and
academics have written books about it.[22] Public officials, including
police chiefs, have made speeches about it. Civil rights leaders have
conducted demonstrations concerning it. All agree that something

should be done. Recommendations have been made by the score. The most frequently made suggestions—many of them worthwhile—include:

Extending human-relations training of recruits and officers;

Creating or enlarging police-community relations units within police departments;

Starting precinct and city-wide citizen advisory committees, including minority leaders, to meet with the police;

Developing programs to educate the public about the police, such as visits of school children to precinct stations, lectures by police officers to adults or youth groups, and school courses concerning police work;

Running recruitment campaigns aimed at members of minority groups;

Ending discrimination within police departments, such as that relating to promotions, and integration of patrols;

Issuing orders banning use of abusive words or excessive force by police officers; and

Developing procedures to handle citizen complaints within the police department which are fair and designed to impose real discipline.[23]

Other recommendations have included the suggestion that the police be disarmed or at least that each police department adopt a strict firearms use policy. Some have suggested that the police discontinue wearing military-type uniforms and instead don more friendly working garb, such as blazers and slacks. Still others have encouraged the adoption of psychological pre-and post-recruitment tests designed to identify for "weeding-out" purposes the bullies and misfits. More extreme suggestions have been made to the effect that all the "bully cops" be fired or retired and that college graduate, social science majors be hired to replace them. Some have suggested either neighborhood control of the police or that neighborhoods desiring it police themselves and that regular policemen not be permitted to enter such areas.

Although some of these ideas have been adopted by some police departments in whole, or in part, in even the most progressive police departments the problem of police-community relations have been undertaken merely as "programs," minor changes in the police department's organizational structure, or as public relations efforts.

To produce effective results, efforts at improving police-community relations require modification of the underlying context of attitudes stemming from the everyday contacts between the policeman on the beat and the people he normally deals with. The individual patrolman must recognize that for some time to come he will be viewed by members of the center city community not as an individual but as an oppressive symbol of the dominant white society. Of course, no community believes that "all cops are bad," and when a police officer treats people with consistent fairness, he will tend to gain a reputation for being "a good cop." But the depth of hostility between the police and the ghetto resident means that the policeman will have to persist in his efforts to be "a good cop" without any significant rewards in terms of appreciation from the community he serves.

On the other hand, the inner-city community, and particularly its leaders, must recognize that policemen cannot be converted into social workers who operate on the assumption that felons are morally innocent products of a criminogenic environment. More importantly, members of the center city community must recognize not only the inevitability, but the desirability, of the policeman's primary identity as a member of the "thin blue line." A policeman's over identity with the community and a non-identity with "the force" tends to destroy a policeman's effectiveness both in the eyes of the community, and of his peers and superiors on the force. Just as members of the military think of themselves as "the military" as opposed to "the civilians," police officers, too, will continue to think of themselves primarily as policemen. Thus, instead of attempting to destroy this "we-they" identity it should be capitalized upon and used to maximum advantage.

It is true that the "we-they" identity of the police has undesirable aspects to it, especially an apparent need to be tougher than "they." It is also true, however, that this toughness (or at least a confidence in a superior toughness) lies at the very foundation of a policeman's ability to arrest a violently resisting suspect who is 6 inches taller and 75 pounds heavier than he, or to calm an unruly group of aggressive teenagers. The problem is how to shape the "we-they" identity so that the end result will not lessen the policman's ability to apprehend criminals and maintain order, yet at the same time not destroy the policeman's desire or ability to interact on a humane, civil basis with the community.

We do not accept the views of some critics that the problem is a dilemma, the solution to which is impossible without changing the very nature of the policeman's role. Scores of interviews with the police themselves have convinced us otherwise (although we do believe that the present service-providing function of the police can be shifted in part to civilians and citizen auxiliaries).

When we asked various policemen what they thought the main advantage was in being police officers as contrasted to most other occupations, most replied, first, that it was the superior ability to understand people and how they behave that was afforded them by constant exposure to all segments of the public. Secondly, the majority answered that it was the ability to "keep a cool head" under stress, danger, and provocation. A black policeman, asked why he decided to become a police officer, gave us this answer:

> Man, when I was a little kid I thought cops were God. I lived in the ghetto and I saw drunks, addicts, cuttings, shooting, and husbands hitting wives and kids fighting on street corners and other bad scenes everyday.
>
> Somebody always called the police. The police arrived in the middle of the hassle and were always cool and always got on top of the problem fast. If they could break it up by quiet mouthing it they would. If they had to bust somebody they did it quick and were gone. Whatever it was, they arrived on the scene, got with it fast, stopped the trouble and split—always with a cool head. I figured that was smooth and so I decided when I was a kid I wanted to be a policeman and do the same thing.

Understanding and coolheadedness—these qualities represent the very essence of a "good cop." These are the traits most required by the patrolman in the performance of his peace-keeping function. If these two qualities can be developed in more of our policemen, it will do much to alleviate tensions between the police and the community.

The breeding ground of community resentment of the police is principally at the patrolman level, not at the command level. When patrolmen fail to show understanding, i.e., act insensitively, and fail to maintain coolheadedness, i.e., loose control and act intemperately, the community becomes incensed. The state of police-community relations is basically the result of everyday contacts of the community with the patrolmen, not the chiefs. The problem of police-community relations is thus one of ascertaining how to encourage understanding and discourage insensitivity in the patrolman—how to encourage coolheadedness and discourage losing control or "blowing one's cool."

The yardstick for testing the application of a mature, sensitive understanding and coolheadedness is often (once deciding that intervention is necessary) how quickly and quietly a patrolman can restore calm without having to make an arrest. This is what 'good cops' are made of. This is what constitutes "good police work." This is what breeds community respect for the police.

One of the major problems with the present system of policing is that of convincing patrolmen that when they perform their *peacekeeping* duties well, they are rendering a service no less valuable to the community than when they perform their *law-enforcement* function. Presently the rewards to a patrolman who is an effective peace-keeper at best, are slight. His promotion in rank is seldom the result of a good record at peacekeeping. This situation should be changed and greater recognition accorded to the effective peacekeeper as well as to the effective crime-fighter. (Properly trained sergeants and lieutenants who demand compliance with departmental policy can also ensure remarkable results.)

As Professor Wilson has noted:

> The central problem of the patrolman, and thus the police, is to maintain order and to reduce, to the limited extent possible, the opportunities for crimes.[24]
>
> A police department that places order maintenance uppermost in its priorities will judge patrolmen ... by their ability to keep the peace on their beat. This will require, in turn, that sergeants and other supervisory personnel concern themselves more with how the patrolmen function in family fights, teenage disturbances, street corner brawls, and civil disorders, and less with how well they take reports at burglary scenes or how many traffic tickets they issue during a tour of duty. Order maintenance also requires that the police have available a wider range of options for handling disorder than is afforded by the choice between making an arrest and doing nothing. Detoxification centers should be available as alternative to jail for drunks. Family-service units should be formed which can immediately assist patrolmen handling domestic quarrels, provide community-service information, answer complaints, and deal with neighborhood tensions and rumors.[25]

Some police departments are already making notable progress along these lines. Under a federal grant, the New York City Police Department has formed a "Family Crisis Intervention Unit" consisting of 18 highly trained officers to handle inter-family assaults and violence in West Harlem. Although it is estimated that as much as 40 percent of police injuries stem from family complaint calls, these crisis unit officers have not received any injuries in 15 months. Moreover, in the 1,120 family crises in which they have intervened, there has not been a single homicide among the families. At the root of this project is a recognition that specialized peacekeeping training pays off.

Police departments throughout the country are beginning to conduct what is referred to as "provocation training." These projects range from training involving crowd control to handling of street corner disturbances. Provocation training entails, in part, staging the kind of provocation which police offenders may expect to face on the job. The trainees are taunted by instructors who call them names, use obscene gestures, and generally imitate the kinds of abuse policemen may expect to face in the conduct of their assigned responsibilities. The purpose of this specialized training is to develop and maintain coolheadedness under extreme provocation.

Other projects being conducted by large city police departments involve efforts to establish closer links between patrolmen and the neighborhoods or communities they serve. The advantage of establishing firmer ties with the community is that it increases a police officer's capacity to make reliable judgments about the character, motives, intentions and future actions of those among whom they keep the peace. As Professor Wilson has suggested, "The officer's ability to make such judgments is improved by increasing his familiarity with and involvement in the neighborhood he patrols, even to the extent of having him live there. The better he knows his beat, the more he can rely on judgments of character . . . ."[26] One method being used by several police departments in achieving this end is through a return to the foot-beat policeman. Most cities which have increased the number of foot-beat patrolmen have used them as a supplement to squad-car or motorcycle beats, thus preserving the mobility inherent in the latter technique. Other police departments have been experimenting with motorscooters in combination with foot-beat patrols.

Another notable example of a departments's attempt to bridge the gap between the police and the community is the model precinct project being conducted by the Washington, D.C. Metropolitan Police. This project involves the creation of neighborhood centers, staffed around the clock by resident civilians as well as police officers. The police teams working out of the centers are assigned for long periods of time to work in the neighborhoods covered by the centers' jurisdiction. Instead of being spread thin, they have an opportunity to get to know families, youth on the street, house-holders, and proprietors of businesses much more intimately. With a narrower area of patrol responsibility, the possibilities for positive, interested, and friendly contact among police and citizens is greatly improved.

The resident civilian workers, employed and trained by agencies such as welfare and legal aid, provide assistance to citizens referred by police on patrol, as well as to those who walk in off the street. These civilian positions help relate police peacekeeping to other activities of a positive help-giving nature, and to provide avenues by which civilians from the neighborhood can formally assist in keeping the peace (and perhaps later enter into careers in law enforcement or allied fields).

§ 2.12 Minority recruitment

One fundamentally important method by which the police can improve their relations with the public is through increased recruit-ment of minority group policemen. The absence of many minority group policemen in our Nation's center city areas has been a source of community hostility for many years.

Minority recruitment efforts by police departments was surveyed in several large cities and it was found that a rising percentage of minority policemen were being recruited each year, the ratio of white to minority group policemen on any force never approximated the ratio of white to minority citizens in any given city's total population.

Many of the cities reported stepped up recruiting campaigns for minority group policemen. We inquired about the relative lack of success of such campaigns. One police chief answered:

> The problem as we see it is twofold: (1) in today's labor market there is full employment and special efforts are being directed toward the Negro community by private industry in an effort to attract qualified applicants. These companies are able to offer outstanding starting salaries and numerous fringe benefits that place police departments in a competitive disadvantage; (2) several of our Negro applicants have expressed the opinion that many segments of the Negro community regard Negro

officers as "Uncle Toms" and enforcers of a white man's justice and are therefore hesitant to apply with a police department. Also we have not been entirely pleased with our efforts in the Negro community. Organizations such as the Urban League and the NAACP have not been able to refer many applicants to the department.

There are other problems too. Although we found that in terms of percentages more minority group recruits succeeded in graduating from police training school than did white policemen, more minority applicants failed the original entrance examination that did whites. We do not feel that these failures were "arranged" by prejudiced police officials. The failures seem to us to reflect the tragedy of the ghetto schools' failure to educate its students.

The police are caught in a bind. Law enforcement consultants, Presidential and state crime commissions constantly urge that recruitment standards be upgraded. The result is that many applicants for police work who have attended ghetto schools simply are not intellectually equipped to pass the entrance examinations. If more minority policemen are to be recruited, accommodations must be found for the disparities in public school education.

Some police departments have been making commendable efforts toward achieving such an accommodation. The Atlanta Police Department reported to us that during the summer months it employed 50 "Community Service Officers" between the ages of 17 and 21. These young men are recruited from the heart of the ghetto and are furnished police uniforms and equipment (except firearms). Their work is largely in the ghetto and has resulted in a betterment of police community relations. The Chief of Police reported to us that most of them returned to school in October to finish their education and "we are convinced that eventually we will get at least 40 good patrolmen out of this group."

Other cities have shown similar good faith through special recruitment campaigns by sound truck, neighborhood centers, newspaper, TV, radio and billboard advertisements. More efforts of these kinds are needed if minority group policemen are to have an equal opportunity to demonstrate an ability to serve the community in the interest of keeping the peace.

§ 2.13　Conclusion

That the policemen of our country are both criticized and

misunderstood by large and diverse elements of the population is becoming increasingly clear. That these diverse elements make inconsistent and contradictory demands on the police is also clear. As a result of being thus criticized and misunderstood, and being called upon to perform inconsistent and contradictory services in the front lines of our disturbed and often violent urban society, the policeman is becoming more confused not only about what his function is, but also about what it should be.

Besides lacking the financial, manpower and technological resources necessary to respond adequately to the many demands made of them, the police also lack a coherent sense of what direction their changing mission must take. Our police consequently are becoming more alienated from many factions of the pluralistic society which it is their duty to protect. The police have thus begun to fight back, not only as individuals with threats and counter-violence, but also as an increasingly organized group doing combat in the political arena.

How are we to bring the police and the diverse groups they serve back together again? With regard to the police taking sides in primarily political struggles, bitter past experience, at least, dictates that the abstention of the professional is the wisest choice. As to day-to-day contact between the police and the citizenry, there must be renewed attention to the peace-keeping role of the patrolman on the beat, which entails in part increased efforts to develop in the patrolman the understanding and coolheadedness which that vital role demands. Despite the depth of the hostility which exists between the police and some of the communities they serve, we believe that a "good cop" can still be a good friend to all of our people. Better training, supervision, and recognition, together with more effective minority group recruitment, are needed if our hopes of producing police excellence are to materialize.

Notes

1. President's Commission on Law Enforcement and Administration of Justice, *Challenge of Crime in a Free Society*, Washington, D.C.: Government Printing Office, 1967, p. 92.

2. See Arthur Niederfhoffer, *Beyond the Shield: The Police in Urban Society*, Garden City, N.Y.: Doubleday, 1967, pp. 95-108.

3. See, generally, O.W. Wilson, *Municipal Police Administration*, 1961; Bruce J. Terris, "The Role of the Police," Volume 374, *Annals* pp. 58-69, 1967.

4. James Q. Wilson, *Varieties of Police Behavior,* Cambridge: Harvard University Press, 1968, p. 4.

5. See Paul Chevigny, *Police Power; Police Abuses in New York City,* New York: Pantheon Books, 1969.

6. The Challenge of Crime in a Free Society, *op. cit.,* p. 91.

7. The National Commission on the Causes and Prevention of Violence, *The Politics of Protest,* Washington D.C., Government Printing Office, 1969, pp. 192-194.

8. Challenge of Crime in a Free Society, *Ibid.,* p. 113. See also James Q. Wilson, "Police Morale, Reform and Citizen Respect: The Chicago Case," in *The Police: Six Sociological Essays,* pp. 137-162.

9. Quinn Tamm, "Police Must Be More Free," *Violence In The Streets,* Shalom Endelman, ed., Chicago: Quadrangle Books, 1968.

10. *Ibid.*

11. *Wilson,* pp. 83-139.

12. Such efforts include human relations courses, police-community councils, recruitment of minority group policemen, advanced educational opportunities, and civilian complaint mechanisms.

13. John Guidici, "Police Response to Crimes of Violence," a paper submitted to the Task Force, pp. 1-14.

14. See Report of the *National Advisory Commission on Civil Disorders,* Washington, D.C.: Government Printing Office, 1968, and Chevigny, supra note 5, pp. 161-179.

15. See *Rights in Conflict,* a special report to this Commission by Daniel Walker, Director of the Chicago Study Team.

16. *Guidici,* pp. 7-8.

17. See *Rights in Conflict.*

18. See, *The Politics of Protest,* and *Shoot-Out in Cleveland* and *Miami Report,* two investigative reports submitted to the Commission.

19. Wilson, p. 248.

20. Chevigny, pp. 51-83.

21. See Rights in Conflict, *op. cit.*

22. See Edwards, *The Police On The Urban Frontier,* 1967; One Year Later, Washington, D.C. Urban America, Inc., and The Urban Coalition, 1969; Reiss, "Police Brutality—Answer to Key Questions," *Transaction,* July/August 1, 1968, p. 10.

23. Terris, *op. cit.,* p. 58.

24. Wilson, *op. cit.,* p. 58.

25. James Q. Wilson, Dilemmas of Police Administration, *Public Administration Review,* Sept./Oct. 1, 1968, pp., 407, 412, 413.

26. Wilson, Varieties of Police Behavior, *op. cit.,* p. 291.

II. THE FUNCTIONS OF THE POLICE IN MODERN SOCIETY

SOURCE: Egon Bittner, *The Functions of the Police in Modern Society*, National Institute of Mental Health, Washington, U.S. Government Printing Office, 1972, pp. 48-62.

In his assessment of the police, Bruce Smith wrote in 1940 that, in spite of the still rather bleak picture, "the lessons of history lean to the favorable side."[1] He pointed to the fact that the then existing police forces had moved a long way from the past associated with the notorious names of Vidocq and Jonathan Wild,[2] and he suggested that the uninterrupted progress justifies the expectation of further change for the better. It is fair to say that this hope has been vindicated by the events of the past 30 years. American police departments of today differ by a wide margin of improvement from those Smith studied in the late 1930's. The once endemic features of wanton brutality, corruption, and sloth have been reduced to a level of sporadic incidence, and their surviving vestiges have been denounced by even generally uncritical police apologists. Indeed, police reform, once a cause espoused exclusively by spokesmen from outside the law enforcement camp, has become an internal goal, actively sought and implemented by leading police officials.

§ 2.14 Introduction

Despite these widely acknowledged advances, however, the police continue to project as bad an image today as they have in the past.[3] In fact, the voices of criticism seem to have increased. The traditional critics have been joined by academic scholars and by some highly placed judges. Certain segments of American society, notably the ethnic minorities and the young people, who have only recently acquired a voice in public debate, express generally hostile attitudes toward the police. At the same time, news about rising crime rates and widely disseminated accounts about public disorders—ranging from peaceful protest to violent rebellion—contribute to the feeling that the police are not adequately prepared to face the tasks that confront them. As a result of all of this, the police problem has moved into the forefront of public attention, creating conditions in which highly consequential and long range decisions are apt to be formulated.

§ *2.15*   *The police and "war on crime"*

Mr. Justic Reid of the United States Supreme Court once drew attention to the dangers inherent in the tendency to develop maxims of judgment and conduct from figures of speech. The matter of his concern was the proverbial "wall between church and state" and the confusion of logic resulting from this metaphor.[4] Needless to say, the warning fell on deaf ears because the intent of rhetoric is to appeal to associations that are established below the level of rational discourse and to evoke responses that would ordinarily not issue from sober analysis. The use of imagery in public debate is, of course, not simply a regrettable state of affairs, conflicting with a more composed attitude. In mobilizing sentiment and support for causes, an aptly chosen phrase may do the work of a thousand good reasons. Regrettable is only the total abdication of the supervisory role of rational scrutiny over the flight of the imagination which sometimes feeds on its own popular appeal.

A figure of speech that has recently gained a good deal of currency is the "war on crime." The intended import of the expression is quite clear. It is supposed to indicate that the community is seriously imperiled by forces bent on its destruction and it calls for the mounting of efforts that have claims on all available resources to defeat the peril. The rhetorical shift from "crime control" to "war on crime" signifies the transition from a routine concern to a state of emergency. We no longer face losses of one kind or another from the depredations of criminals; we are in imminent danger of losing everything! The perception of such is held up as a realistic possibility there is no need to show its impending certainty nor to estimate its likelihood with precision. It matters little that the metaphor, like many metaphors, contains a contradiction in terms. For in truth a community can no more wage war on its internal ills than an organism can "wage war" against its own constitutional weaknesses. Though it may seem paradoxical on first glance, the existence of crime in society is like the existence of organic malfunction, a normal aspect of human life.[5] Both are properly subject to vigilant control. But the conceit that they can be ultimately vanquished, which is the implicit objective of war, involves a particularly trivial kind of utopian dreaming. Out of control malfunction and crime could posssibly overcome life, but control can never succeed in more than keeping them to a level appropriate to the prevailing form of human life. But vigilance waxes and wanes; to insure that it does not fall below a level of minimally necessary tension it must be fed a diet of rhetorical illuminations.

The recognition of the positive role of rhetorical figures of speech in public life also forces the realization that their effects are not easily confined. Insofar as they involve exaggeration, they appear to sanction more than calculating advocates intend. Worse yet, they project unrealistic hopes. The expression "war on crime," not only implicitly extends the stamp of legitimacy to methods that would not be acceptable on moral and legal grounds, but it also encompasses the impossible. Professor Harold Lasswell observed long ago that under certain demands "police action ... becomes military action, requiring for efficiency a will to ruthlessness which cannot, in fact, be mobilized in the situation."[6]

Lasswell's formulation, though exhaustively correct as stated, requires some elaborations to fully grasp its import. The "situation" to which he refers is never definable solely in terms of those forms of disorder and crime the police face. Instead, it always encompasses the whole range of interlocking relations to other aspects of life in which these targets of police action are located and from which they cannot be extricated. Thus, the absence of the "will to ruthlessness" is not predicated on tender and charitable sentiments towards offenders, but on devotion to the principle that dealing with them must not be allowed to affect adversely the context in which offenses are located. The price we are prepared to pay to defeat crime and disorder does not include visiting incidental suffering on innocents. Not to observe this stricture would turn crime control into a hand-maiden of crime. Second, the "will to ruthlessness" involves not only attitudes toward the adversary but also the organization of the struggle against him. It is characteristic of the posture of the military establishment that it is as unsparing of its own as it is of the enemy. Its ferocity in engagement is preceded by a

ferocity in preparedness, achieved by means of an unapolo-
getically depersonalizing discipline among the ranks. Though one
could conceivably organize police forces along such lines, the
result would bear no resemblance to the institution as it exists.
Finally, the "ruthlessness" of the military enterprise is a matter
of coldly calculated expediency. It is deliberately produced and
maintained with full regard to the exigencies of warfare against
an alien enemy. To be sure, its maintenance involves appeals to
spontaneous sentiments of manliness and patriotism but these
feelings must not be allowed to escape the harness of strategy.
The objectives and strategies involved in fighting off internal
attacks are, however, different from those related to confronting
an external foe, and while "ruthlessness" is the method of choice
in the latter, it is not in the former. In sum, Lasswell is not
overly sanguine about the capacity of policemen to be as
unscrupulously belligerent against criminals as soldiers are against
alien enemies. He only denies the structural feasibility of the
approach.

Professor Allan Silver argues the same point even more force-
fully in proposing that "the replacement of intermittent military
intervention in a largely unpoliced society by continuous professional bureaucratic policing meant that the benefits of police
organization—continual pervasive moral display and lower long
classes—absolutely required the moral cooperation of civil society.
He recognizes and emphasizes that the police, like the military,
are instituted for purely coercive tasks. But he also makes it
clear that the police have radically different organizational needs
from the objectives of military victory, on the one hand, and
from "the penetration and continual presence of central political
authority through daily life" on the other hand.[7] To cite one
more authority, Professor Morris Janowitz pointed out that even
when the tasks of policing are taken over by the military establishment it involves a reorientation of their normal posture. "The
constabulary function as applied to urban violence emphasizes a
fully alert force committed to a minimum resort to force and
concerned with the development and maintenance of conditions
for viable democratic institutions."[8]

Though it may seem like quibbling about words whether one
calls the concerns of the police with lawlessness and disorder an

effort to control them or war against them, the ambiguities of expression are symptomatic of deeper confusion. While most informed observers will readily agree that there is a difference between the military and the police they would also adhere to the view that the police are in some sense a quasi-military establishment. What the qualification "quasi" is supposed to mean is, however, not clear. In some countries with national police forces, notably in certain western European states, the problem is solved by maintaining parallel organizations, one with a distinctly military cast and the other free of constraints of military organization.[9] Something like this situation is also evident in the United States where some aspects of policing sometimes devolve on the National Guard. Contrary to the situation prevailing in European states, the National Guard is, however, not continually available. Consequently, American police forces have broader responsibilities than the civilian police forces of France, Spain, or Italy. In an apparent effort to meet these responsibilities, our police are more generally militarized than is the case elsewhere. This causes profound organizational problems. On the one hand, the military model does seem to furnish a form of control and supervision that helps to overcome laxness and corruption where it exists. On the other hand, the core of the police mandate is profoundly incompatible with the military posture. On balance, the military-bureaucratic organization of the police is a serious handicap.

§ 2.16 *The quasi-military organization of the police*

The conception of the police as a quasi-military institution with a war-like mission plays an important part in the structuring of police work in modern American departments. The merits of this conception have never been demonstrated or even argued explicitly. Instead, most authors who make reference to it take it for granted or are critical only of those aspects of it, especially its punitive orientation, that are subject of aspersion even in the military establishment itself.[10] The treatment the topic receives in the Task Force Report on the Police of the President's Commission on Law Enforcement and Administration of Justice is representative of this approach. The authors note that "like all military and semi-military organizations, a police agency is governed in its internal management by a large number of standard operating procedures."[11]   This observation is accompanied by remarks indicating that the existence of elaborate codes governing the conduct of policemen relative to intra-departmental demands stands in stark contrast to the virtual absence of formulated directives concerning the handling of police problems in the community. The imbalance between proliferation of internal regulation and the neglect of regulations relative to procedures employed in the field leads to the inference that the existing codes must be supplemented by substantive instructions and standards in the latter area. The question whether such an expansion of regulation might not result in a code consisting of incompatible elements is not considered. Instead, it is implicitly assumed that policemen can be instructed how to deal with citizens by regulations that will not affect the existing system of internal disciplinary control.

The lack of appreciation for the possibility that the developments of professional discretionary methods for crime control and peace-keeping may conflict with the enforcement of bureaucratic-military regulations is not merely a naive oversight; more likely, it represents an instance of wishful thinking. For the military model is immensely attractive to police planners, and not without reason. In the first place, there exist some apparent analogies between the military and the police and it does not seem to be wholly unwarranted to expect methods of internal organization that work in one context to work also in the other. Both institutions are instruments of force and for both institutions the occasions for using force are unpredictably distributed. Thus, the personnel in each must be kept in a highly disciplined state of alert perparedness. The formalism that characterizes military organization, the insistence on rules and regulations, on spit and polish, on obedience to superiors, and so on, constitute a permanent rehearsal for "the real thing." What sorts of rules and regulations exist in such a setting are in some ways less important than that there be plenty of them and the personnel be continually aware that they can be harshly called to account for disobeying them.[12]   Second, American police departments have been, for the greater part of their history, the football of local politics, and became tainted with sloth and corruption at least partly for this reason. Police reform was literally forced to resort to formidable means of internal discipline to dislodge undesirable attitudes and influences, and the military model seemed to serve such purposes admirably. In fact, it is no exaggeration to say that through the 1950's and 1960's the movement to "professionalize" the police concentrated almost exclusively on efforts to eliminate political and venal corruption by means of introducing traits of military discipline. And it must be ackowledged that some American police chiefs, notably the late William Parker of Los Angeles, have achieved truly remarkable results in this respect. The leading aspiration of this reform was to replace the tragicomic figure of the "flatfoot cop on the take" by cadres of personally incorruptible snappy operatives working under the command of bureaucrats-in-uniform. There is little doubt that these reforms succeeded in bringing some semblance of order into many chaotic departments and that in these depart-ments "going by the book" acquired some real meaning.

Finally, the police adopted the military method because they could not avail themselves of any other options to secure internal discipline. For all its effectiveness, the military method is organiza-tionally primitive. At least, the standard part of the method can be well enough approximated with a modicum of administrative sophistication. Moreover, since most of the men who go into police work have some military experience, they need not go to outside resources to obtain help in building a quasi-military order. This is important because a century of experience taught American police forces that outside intervention into their affairs—known as the "shake-up"—was almost always politically inspired. Because the suspicion of high-level chicanery is still very much alive, and not without reasons, the police is the only large scale institution in our society that has not benefited from advances in management science. In the absence of lateral recruitment into supervisory positions and developed technical staff skills, changes had to be achieved mainly by means of rigid enforcement of regulations of internal procedure and by emphasizing external trappings of discipline. In a situation where something had to be done, with little to do it with, this was not mean accomplishment.[13]

Ackowledging that the introduction of methods of military-bureaucratic discipline was not without some justification, and conceding that it helped in eliminating certain gross inadequacies, does not mean, however, that the approach was beneficial in larger and longer range terms. Even where the cure succeeded in suppressing many of the diseases of earlier times, it brought forth obstacles of its own to the development of a model of a professional police role, if by professional role is meant that practice must involve technical skill and fiduciary trust in the practitioner's exercise of discretion. The reason for this is simple. While in early police departments there existed virtually no standards of correct procedure at all and no inducement to do well—since rewards were scant and distributed along lines of personal favoritism—one can now distinguish between good and bad officers, and engaging in what is now defined as correct conduct does carry significant rewards. But since the established standards and the rewards for good behavior relate almost entirely to matters connected with internal discipline, the judgments that are passed have virtually nothing to do with the work of the policeman in the community, with one significant exception. That is, the claims for recognition that have always been denied to the policeman are now respected, but recognition is given for doing well in the department, not outside where all the real duties are located.

The maintenance of organizational stability and staff morale require that praise and reward, as well as condemnation and punishment, be distributed methodically, i.e., predictably in accordance with explicit rules. Correspondingly, it is exceedingly difficult to assign debits and credits for performances that are not set forth in the regulations, it does not furnish his superior a basis for judging him.[14] At the same time, there are no strongly compelling reasons for the policeman to do well in ways that do not count in terms of official occupational criteria of value. The greater the weight placed on compliance with internal departmental regulation, the less free is the superior in censoring unregulated work practices he disapproves of, and in rewarding those he admires, for fear that he might jeopardize the loyalty of officers who do well on all scores that officially count—that is, those who present a neat appearance, who conform punctually to bureaucratic routine, who are visibly on the place of their assignment, and so on. In short, those who make life easier for the superior, who in turn is restricted to supervising just those things. In fact, the practical economy of supervisory control requires that the proliferation of intradepartmental restriction be accompanied by increases in license in areas of behavior in unregulated areas. Thus, one who is judged to be a good officer in terms of internal, military-bureaucratic codes will not even be questioned about his conduct outside of it. The message is quite plain: the development of resolutely careful work methods in the community may be nice, but it gets you nowhere!

There is one important exception to the priority of intradepartmental quasi-military discipline in the judging of the performances of policemen. Police departments have to produce visible results of their work. The most visible results are arrested persons who keep the courts busy. This demand naturally devolves on individual officers. The question about the expected contribution of individual policemen to the statistical total of crimes cleared, summonses delivered, and arrests made is a matter of heated controversy. The problem is usually addressed as to whether or not there exist quotas officers must meet. Of course, the question can always be so framed that one can answer it truthfully either way.[15] But more fundamentally it is quite clear that individual policemen must contribute to the sum total of visible results, unless they have some special excuse, such as being assigned to a desk job. Moreover, how could any police superior under present conditions of supervision ever know whether the men assigned to the traffic division or to the vice squad are on the job at all, if they did not produce their normal share of citations or arrests?

Clearly, therefore, there is added to the occupational relevance of the military-bureaucratic discipline the demand to produce results.[16] While the emphasis on stringent internal regulation, taken alone, merely discourages the elaboration of careful approaches to work tasks, it exercises in combination with production demands a truly pernicious influence on the nature of police work. There are several reasons for this but the most important is based on the following consideration. Though the explicit departmental regulations contain little more than pious sermonizing about police dealings with citizens, whether they be offenders, an unruly crowd, quarreling spouses, accident victims, or what not, it is possible that a policeman could, despite his discretionary freedom, act in some such way as to actually come into conflict with some stated rule, even though the rule is not topically relevant to the situation at hand. Since he knows that his conduct will be judged solely with respect to this point he must be attuned to it, avoiding the violation even if that involves choosing a course of action that is specifically wrong with respect to the realities of the problem. For example, it is far from unusual that officers decide whether to make an arrest or not on the basis of their desire to live within departmental regulation rather than on the merits of the case at hand. In these situations the military-bureaucratic discipline regulates procedure speciously; it does not provide that in such-and-such a situation such-and-such a course of action is indicated. On the contrary, the regulations are typically silent about such matters; but in insisting on specific ways for officers to keep their noses clean they limit the possibilities of desirable intervention and they encourage transgression. Thus, it has been reported that in the New York Police Department, known for its stringently punitive discipline, officers who violate some official rules of deportment while dealing with citizens simply arrest potential complainants, knowing the complaints of persons charged with crimes are given no credence. Incongruously, while in New York the Police Department is much more likely to discipline an officer for brutalizing a citizen than elsewhere, it in fact rarely gets a chance to do it. For whenever there is a situation in which it is possible that an officer could have an infraction entered in his record, an infraction against an explicit regulation, he will redefine it into an instance of police work that is not regulated. Thus, while citizens everywhere run the risk of receiving a beating when they anger a policeman, in New York they run the added risk of being charged with a crime they did not commit, simply because its officers must keep their records clean.[17]

As long as there are two forms of accounting, one that is explicit and continually audited (internal discipline), and another that is devoid of rules and rarely looked into (dealings with citizens), it must be expected that keeping a positive balance in the first might encourage playing loose with the second. The likelihood of this increases proportionately to pressures to produce. Since it is not enough that policemen be obedient soldier-bureaucrats, but must, to insure favorable consideration for advancement, contribute to the arrest total, they will naturally try to meet this demand in ways that will keep them out of trouble. Thus, to secure the promotion from the uniformed patrol to the detective bureau, which is highly valued and not determined by civil service examinations, officers feel impelled to engage in actions that furnish opportunities for conspicuous display of aggressiveness. John McNamara illustrates this tactic by quoting a dramatic expression of cynicism, "If you want to get 'out of the bag' into the 'bureau' shoot somebody."[18] Leaving the exaggeration aside, there is little doubt that emphasis on military-bureaucratic control rewards the appearance of staying out of troubles as far as internal regulations are concerned, combined with strenuous efforts to make "good pinches," i.e., arrests that contain, or can be managed to appear to contain, elements of physical danger. Every officer knows that he will never receive a citation for avoiding a fight but only for prevailing in a fight at the risk of his own safety. Perhaps there is nothing wrong with that rule. But there is surely something wrong with a system in which the combined demands for strict compliance with departmental regulation and for vigorously productive law enforcement can be met simultaneously by displacing the onus of the operatives' own misconduct on citizens. This tends to be the case in departments characterized by strong militaristic-bureaucratic discipline where officers do not merely transgress to make "good pinches," but make "good pinches" to conceal their transgressions.[19]

No matter how elaborate and no matter how stringently enforced codes of internal regulations are, they do not impinge on all segments of police departments with equal force. By and large the highly visible uniformed patrol is exposed to far greater disciplinary pressures than personnel in the detective bureaus, which Arthur Niederhoffer aptly described as "mock bureaucracies."[20] While this situation is viewed as unavoidable, because the conduct of detectives cannot be as closely scrutinized as the conduct of patrolmen, and necessary because detectives need more freedom than patrolmen,[21] it tends to demean uniformed assignments. Because patrolmen perceive military discipline as degrading, ornery, and unjust, the only motive they have for doing well—which, of course, involves, among others, the devious practices we have just described—is to get out of the uniformed assignments.[22] Thus the uniformed patrol suffers from a constant drain of ambitious and enterprising men, leaving it generally understaffed and, incidentally, overstaffed with men who are regarded as unsuitable for more demanding tasks. Though by no means all competent personnel take advantage of opportunities to leave the patrol for the detective bureaus, those who remain are dispirited by the conditions under which they are obliged to work and by the invidiously low level of prestige connected with their performance.[23] In consequence the outwardly snappy appearance of the patrol hides a great deal of discontent, demoralization, and marginal work quality.

Another complex of mischievous consequences arising out of the military bureaucracy relates to the paradoxical fact that while this kind of discipline ordinarily strengthens command authority it has the opposite effect in police departments. This effect is insidious rather than apparent. Because police superiors do not direct the activity of officers in any important sense they are perceived as mere disciplinarians.[24] Not only are they not actually available to give help, advice, and direction in the handling of difficult work problems, but such a role cannot even be projected for them. Contrary to the army officer who is expected to lead his men into battle—even though he may never have a chance to do it—the analogously ranked police official is someone who can only do a great deal *to* his subordinates and very little *for* them. For this reason supervisory personnel are often viewed by the line personnel with distrust and even contempt.[25] It must be understood that his character of command in police departments is not due solely to its administrative incompetence. It is exceedingly rare that a ranking police officer can take positive charge of police action, and even in the cases where this is possible, his power to determine the course of action is limited to giving the most general kinds of directions.[26] But like all superiors, police superiors, do depend on the good will of the subordinates, if only to protect their own employees interests within the institution. Thus, they are forced to resort to the only means available to insure a modicum of loyalty, namely, covering mistakes. The more blatantly an officer's transgression violates an explicit departmental regulation the less likely it is that his superior will be able to conceal it. Therefore, to be helpful, as they must try to be, superiors must confine themselves to white-washing bad practices involving relatively unregulated conduct, that is, those dealings with citizens that lead up to arrests. In other words, to gain compliance with explicit regulations, where failings could be acutely embarrassing, command must yield in unregulated or little regulated areas of practice. It is almost as if patrolmen were told, "Don't let anyone catch you sleeping on the job; if they do I'll get it in the neck and you will too. So, please, keep walking; in return I'll cover for you if you make a false arrest." Superiors, needless to say, do not speak in such terms. They probably do not even communicate the message covertly. Indeed, it is quite likely that most police officials would honestly view the suggestion with contempt. But this is the way things work out and the more a department is organized along military-bureaucratic lines the more likely it is that they will work out this way. Naturally, the situation is not conducive to the development of relations of genuine trust, respect, and loyalty.

Finally, emphasis on elaborate codes of internal regulation of a military kind tends to subvert police training, at least wherever this training is administered in departments, as is commonly the case. In the very best existing training programs instruction consists of three parts. There are some lectures concerning criminology, criminal law, human relations, mental health, etc., given by visiting social scientists and lawyers. The second part consists largely of homilies about the social importance and dignity of police work, which emphasize that the occupation makes the highest demands on integrity, wisdom, and courage. The third part, to which the bulk of instructional time is devoted, relates to the teaching of departmental regulation. Since this is the only practical part of the course of instruction, it is abundantly clear that the overall purpose of the training is to turn tyros into compliant soldier-bureaucrats rather than competent practitioners of the craft of peacekeeping and crime control.[27] But since there exist no direct relation between knowing the regulations and maintaining the appearance of complying with them, the first thing graduates learn on their first assignment is that they must forget everything they have been taught in the academy. The immediate effect of the "reality shock" is a massive increase in the attitude of cynicism among first year policemen, not surprisingly since their introduction to the occupation was not only inadequate as far as their work duties are concerned, but also misleading.[28]

It could be said, of course, that the argument proposed thus far merely shows that efforts to professionalize police work by means of importing traits of outward military discipline is apt to create tendencies to displace misconduct into unregulated areas because the pertinent regulations have not yet been formulated. In time, these areas too will come under the scope of the existing discipline. It is our view that it is exceedingly unlikely that this development will take place. The charting of realistic methods of peacekeeping and crime control is profoundly incompatible with the style of current regulations of internal discipline. One simply cannot bring under the same system of control rules relating to dress and bureaucratic formalities, on the one hand, and norms governing the discretionary process of handling an instance of disorderly conduct on the streets, on the other. Emphasis on the first defeats care for the other. This does not imply that all presently existing regulations must be rescinded to encourage a methodical approach to police work tasks. Quite the contrary, the majority of present expectations will probably retain value in any alternative system of control. But their relevance, mode of presentation, and enforcement will have to be made subsidiary to a system of procedure that charts professionally responsible decisionmaking under conditions of uncertainty. In simplest terms, if policemen can be induced to face problems in the community and to deal with citizens in ways that meet at once criteria of purposeful efficiency and will correspond to the expectations of the kind public trust commonly associated with the exercise of professional expertise, then there will be no need to treat them like soldier-bureaucrats. Correspondingly, as long as policemen will be treated like soldier-bureaucrats, they cannot be expected to develop professional acumen, nor value its possession.

It must be said, however, that the true professionalization of police work, in and of itself, is no weapon against sloth and corruption, no more than in the case of medicine, the ministry, law, teaching, and social work. That is, the professionalization of police work still leaves open the matter of its control. But if we are not willing to settle for having physicians who are merely honest, and who would frankly admit that in curing diseases and dealing with patients they have to rely entirely on "playing by ear," it is difficult to see why we would devote all our energies to trying to make the police honest without any concern whatever for whether or not they know, in a technical sense, how to do what they are supposed to do. Some people say it is foolish to demand technical proficiency and professional ethics where none exists. This view is certainly premature and probably wrong. We know far too little about the way police work is actually done to say with assurance that what we desire does not exist. What we know is that policemen have not written any scholarly tracts about it. We also know that presently good and bad work practices are not distinguishable, or, more precisely, are not distinguished. Worst of all, we have good reasons to suspect that if some men are possessed by and act with professional acumen, they might possibly find it wiser to keep it to themselves lest they will be found to be in conflict with some departmental regulation. The pending task, therefore, has less to do with putting external resources of scholarship at the disposal of the *police departments,* than with discovering those good qualities of police work that already exist in the skills of *individual practitioners.* It is not enough to discover them, however, they must be liberated and allowed to take their proper place in the scheme of police organization. By making the possession and use of such skills the controlling consideration in the distribution of rewards, we will have a beginning of a professional system for controlling police practices. The prospect of such a control is in strict competition with presently existing methods of military-bureaucratic regulation.[29]

Notes

1. Bruce Smith, *Police Systems in the United States,* New York: Harper & Row, 1960, second rev. ed., p. 3.

2. For descriptions of early European police practices, see Patrick Pringle, *The Thief-Takers,* London: Museum Press, 1958 and P.J. Stead, *Vidocq, London: Staples Press, 1958.* Early American urban police is described in Roger Lane, *Policing the City: Boston 1822-1885,* Cambridge, Mass.: Harvard University Press, 1967; and in the literature cited therein.

3. J.Q. Wilson cites evidence that improvement undertaken under the leadership of America's foremost police reformer, O.W. Wilson, did not result in better public attitudes; see his "Police Morale, Reform and Citizen Respect: The Chicago Case," in D.J. Bordua (ed.), *The Police: Six Sociological Essays,* New York: John Wiley & Sons, 1967, pp. 137-162.

4. M. DeWolfe Howe, *The Garden and the Wilderness: Religion and Government in American Constitutional History,* Chicago: University of Chicago Press, 1965, p. 1.

5. The argument about the "normalcy" of crime and other forms of social pathology is contained in Emile Durkheim, *The Rules of Socialogical Method,* Chicago: University of Chicago Press, 1938, chap. 3.

6. H.D. Lasswell, *World Politics and Personal Insecurity,* Glencoe, Illinois Free Press, 1950, p. 228.

7. Silver, *op. cit.,* pp. 12-14.

8. Morris Janowitz, *Social Control of Escalated Riots,* Chicago: University of Chicago Center for Policy Studies, 1968, p. 8. For a general discussion of the concept of the military constabulary see his *The Professional Soldier: Political and Social Portrait,* New York: Free Press of Glencoe, 1960, pp. 417-440. Some armed forces appear to exist solely for constabulary purposes; a case in point is the Irish army; see J.A. Jackson, "The Irish Army and the Development of the Constabulary Concept," paper presented to the Sixth World Congress of Sociology, September 1966, mimeo.

9. P.J. Stead, "The Police of France," *Medico-Legal Journal,* Volume 33, 1965, pp. 3-11.

10. Recently some authors have expressed doubts about the merits of organizing the police along military lines. Wilson takes issue with Smith's assertion that the police have "disciplinary requirements of a quasi-military body." *Op. cit.,* p. 79. Similarly, A.J. Reiss and D.J. Bordua have questioned the adequacy of the idea of the police as a military organization; see "Environment and Organization: A Perspective on the Police," in Bordua (ed.), *op. cit.,* p. 16.

11. Task Force Report: Police, *op. cit.,* p. 16.

12. The tendency of police departments to adopt outward military rigidities has been frequently emphasized; see *Task Force Report: Police,* p. 29; J.D. Lohman and G.E. Misner, *The Police and the Community,* A Report prepared for the President's Commission on Law Enforcement and Administration of Justice, Washington, D.C.: U.S. Government Printing Office, 1966, Vol. I, p. 152, Vol. II, p. 196; Banton reports that American police chiefs admire Scottish officers who "bare themselves well, and were smartly and uniformly dressed," *op. cit.,* p. 123.

13. In addition to the rigors of outward discipline, military establishments also rely on "command charisma," a feature observed in American police departments by D.J. Bordua and A.J. Reiss; see their "Command, Control and Charisma: Reflections on Police Bureaucracy," *American Journal of Sociology,* Volume 72, 1966, pp. 68-76. The term indicates a leadership principle in which subordinates are moved to obedience by a high regard for, and trust in, the person in command.

14. See Task Force Report: Police, *op. cit.,* p. 20; Goldstein, *op. cit.,* p. 162; and Wilson, *op cit.,* p. 16.

15. Niederhoffer, *op. cit.,* pp. 68-69.

16. The most illuminating and extensive discussion of pressures to produce is contained in Skolnick, *op. cit.,* pp. 164-181.

17. Paul Chevigny explains that New York policemen sometimes rebut allegations of brutality by maintaining that they are obviously fabrications since the complainant would have been arrested had the officer laid hands on him. Chevigny reports numerous instances of arrests following altercations with citizens which were ineptly or deviously provoked by policemen, and he comments, "Many lawyers think it a triumph for a felony to be reduced to a mere offence, but the truth is that it requires only two simple ingredients: guiltless clients and infinite patience," *Police Power: Police Abuses in New York City,* New York: Pantheon Books, 1969, p. 167.

18. J.H. McNamara, "Uncertainties in Police Work: The Relevance of Police Recruits' Background and Training," in Bordua (ed.) *op. cit.,* pp. 163-252.

19. McNamara cites the following case at p. 171, *ibid.;* "a patrolman directing traffic in the middle of an intersection . . . patrolman fired his revolver and hit an automobile whose driver had not heeded the officer's hand signals. The driver immediately pulled over to the side of the street and stopped the car. The officer realized the inappropriateness of his action and began to wonder what he might offer as an explanation to his supervisor and to the citizen. The

patrolman reported that his anxiety was dissipated shortly upon finding that the driver of the car was a person convicted of a number of crimes. The reader should understand that departmental policy did not specify that any person convicted of crimes in New York City thereby became a target for police pistol practice." Nevertheless, as the officer's feeling of relief indicates, the transgression was apparently construable as an instance of aggressive crime control.

20. Niederhoffer, *op. cit.*, p. 85.

21. Wilson notes, however, that this view is probably mistaken. The patrolman deals with matters that are ill defined and ambiguously emergent, while detectives deal with more precisely defined crimes and only after they have been committed; *op. cit.*, pp. 8-9.

22. "A high arrest record reinforces the cynicism that inspired it in the first place, while often establishing a policeman's reputation for initiative and efficiency. His superiors recommend him for assignment to the detective division. This route to promotion appeals to many young policemen who have little hope of passing a written competitive test for promotion, and impels many of them to adopt cynicism as a rational and functional way to advancement." Niederhoffer, *op. cit.*, pp. 76-77.

23. "At present the principal rewards are promotion, which takes a patrolman off the street, or reassignment to a detective or specialized unit, which takes him out of order maintenance altogether; not surprisingly, patrolmen wanting more pay or status tend to do those things . . . that will earn them those rewards." Wilson, *op. cit.*, pp. 292-293.

24. On the pervasiveness of purely punitive discipline, see McNamara, *op. cit.*, pp. 178-183. Wilson reports that regulations are so framed that they do not instruct but "give the brass plenty of rope with which to hang us."

25. McNamara, *op. cit.*, pp. 187-188, reports attitudes of patrolmen towards their superiors and concludes, "Regardless of their accuracy, these assertions strongly support the feeling that the 'bosses' of the department do not deserve the respect which the organization requires or demands."

26. Banton views the absence of instructions and supervision as a main characteristic distinguishing American police from their British counterpart, *op. cit.*, pp. 115-116. The absence of supervision is frequently noted; see McNamara, *op. cit.*, p. 183; and Task Force Report: The Police, *op. cit.*, pp. 28-52.

27. McNamara speaks about the dilemma, "whether to emphasize training strategies aimed at the development of self-directed and autonomous personnel or to emphsize strategies aimed at developing personnel over whom the organization can readily exercise control. It appears that the second strategy is the one most often emphasized," *op. cit.*, p. 251. Niederhoffer similarly states that, "At the Academy he (the recruit) masters and simultaneously succumbs to, the web of protocol and ceremony that characterizes any quasi-military hierarchy," *op. cit.*, p. 45.

28. Niederhoffer, *ibid.*, speaks about the "reality shock" and documents the rapid rise of synicism among first year policemen; see especially p. 239.

29. The competitive nature of ideals of military discipline and methodical discretion has been noted in a survey of the Boston police department undertaken in 1934; "Too often the military aspect of organization pushes the essentially individual character of police work into the background," cited in Task Force Report: Police, *op. cit.*, p. 136.

III.   THE URBAN POLICE FUNCTION

SOURCE: American Bar Association, Institute of Judicial Administration, *The Urban Police Function*, New York, The American Bar Association, 1972, pp. 47-71.

Municipal police agencies are responsible for performing a wide range of tasks, only part of which relate specifically to criminal law enforcement. These tasks are typically performed not out of any continuing community assessment of what it would like its police to achieve, but rather, generally reflect ad hoc judgments by the police of what they should be doing. In many ways, this is understandable since much of police work necessarily must involve reacting to situations as they arise. On the other hand, there is a need to determine more precisely what the police should be trying to achieve, how the police should react to various situations, and what priorities should govern police intervention.[1]

Instead of responding to any community planning governing overall police direction, the police more commonly react to a number of factors from different sources which influence or appear to influence their involvement or degree of involvement in meeting numerous government or community needs. Before identifying and characterizing the various objectives to which the police appear to be committed, it is worthwhile to assess what factors either affect police involvement or give the perception of directing police activities. There are five principal factors to be considered, subsequently.

§ 2.17　Broad legislative mandates to the police

An examination of the statutes of the various states and the charters and ordinances of a random sampling of cities reveals that the duties of municipal police agencies, to the extent that they are spelled out statutorily, are typically defined in various combinations of the following terms: "to enforce the law"; "to maintain the peace"; "to protect persons and property"; "to preserve order"; and "to prevent crime." Typical of the statutory language is that contained in Tennessee law:

> It shall be the duty of the chief of police and the members of the police force to preserve order in the city, protect the inhabitants and property owners therein from violence, crime and all criminal acts, prevent the commission of crime, violations of law and of the city ordinances, and perform a general police duty . . . .[2]

City charters and ordinances tend to be much more comprehensive and much more specific. New York City's charter provides:

> The police department and force shall have the power and it shall be duty to preserve the public peace, prevent crime, detect and arrest offenders, suppress riots, mobs and insurrections, disperse unlawful or dangerous assemblages and assemblages which obstruct the free passage of public streets, sidewalks, parks and places; protect the rights of persons and property, guard the public health, preserve order at elections and all public meetings and assemblages; subject to the provisions of law and the rules and regulations of the commissioner of traffic, regulate, direct, control, and restrict the movement of vehicular and pedestrian traffic for the facilitation of traffic and the convenience of the public as well as the proper protection of human life and health; remove all nuisances in the public streets, parks and places; arrest all street mendicants and beggars; provide proper police attendance at fires; inspect and observe all places of public amusement, all places of business having excise or other licenses to carry on any business; enforce and prevent the violation of all laws and ordinances in force in the city; and for these purposes to arrest all persons guilty of violating any law or ordinance for the suppression or punishment of crimes or offenses.[3]

The broad and ambiguous language used in the statues and charters provides a foundation for much of what the police do, but it provides little basis for deciding on the propriety of some specific aspects of police operations, and it provides no basis for setting priorities between and among different objectives when one or more conflict.

Although police functioning in many of the areas identified above is not explicitly authorized by legislative bodies, there is indirect authority for much of what the police do in these areas by virtue of their ultimate responsibility for enforcing the criminal law. Thus, while statutes may not be explicit in imposing a positive responsibility upon the police for protecting constitutional rights, the kind of conduct that is typically disruptive of constitutional rights usually constitutes a criminal offense. This then provides the police with a basis for their action against those responsible for the disruption.

§ 2.18   The authority of the police to use force lawfully

It is obvious that the police, invested with certain statutory authority, are viewed as the primary coercive force in our society. Contributing to this image is their authority to arrest, to detain, to search and to prosecute—but perhaps most fundamentally their authority to use physical force in doing so. Professor Egon Bittner states that the capacity of the police "to use coercive force lends thematic unity to all police activity in the same sense in which, let us say, the capacity to cure illness lends unity to everything that is ordinarily done in the field of medical practice."[4] Bittner further notes:

> Whatever the substance of the task at hand, whether it involves protection against an undesired imposition, caring for those who cannot care for themselves, attempting to solve a crime, helping to save a life, abating a nuisance, or settling an explosive dispute, police intervention means above all making use of the capacity and authority to overpower resistance to an attempted solution in the native habitat of the problem.[5]

The police are not explicitly authorized to use force in each of the situations cited. But a general awareness that the police have the authority to use force in some situations is sufficient to give each police officer an aura of authority that, in turn, results in a willingness on the part of most citizens to respond to his requests and his orders.

The fact that all police officers in this country are armed and are authorized to make use of deadly force results in our looking to the police to handle those situations in which a life is endangered by the threat of force. And since this represents the ultimate in potentially-dangerous situations, the police naturally come to be viewed as especially qualified to handle less dangerous situations as well. Thus, the presence of any possibility of physical harm (ranging from concern over the actions of a person known to have access to a weapon all the way to concern over the unknown, such as mysterious noises heard in the middle of the night) is likely to result in the police being summoned.

Although the police possess this special authority to use force, it is often not necessary to utilize this capacity in achieving many of the police objectives. This was also noted by Professor Bittner:

> It must be emphasized, however, that the conception of the centrality of the capacity to use force in the police role does not entail the conclusion that the ordinary occupational routines consist of the actual exercise of this capacity. It is very likely, though we lack information on this point, that the actual use of physical coercion and restraint is rare for all policemen and that many policemen are virtually never in the position of having to resort to it.[6]

But again, as Bittner points out, "What matters is that police procedure is defined by the feature that it may not be opposed in its course, and that force can be used if it is opposed."[7]

§ 2.19   The investigative ability of the police

Much of policing and much of government's overall needs involve getting at the facts—especially for purposes of detecting and identifying persons who engage in prohibited behavior. Of all the skills that police officers possess, the capacity to sift through complex situations in order to establish and verify facts is among the most important. That ability is required not only in situations in which a crime is alleged to have occurred, but also in a myriad of everyday occurrences in which, although something appears awry, there is no way of predicting the exact nature of the situations. Because of this special ability, it is to the police that the public turns not only when there are outward signs of the unusual, but also when only further inquiry will establish whether there is actually a need for assistance or intervention.

§ 2.20   The twenty-four-hour availability of the police

The police are generally recognized as the only governmental or private agency that operates twenty-four hours a day, seven days a week, and that has the capacity through its strategically-dispersed personnel to respond quickly to wide-ranging requests for assistance. Round-the-clock availability takes on special importance when one recognizes that many of the governmental and private agencies providing social services are closed and their personnel are unavailable when the need for such services is the greatest. When situations reach crisis proportions during these hours, requiring assistance or intervention (e.g., an injury, the absence of heat, a quarrel, etc.), it is to the police that citizens usually turn. This is especially true in large urban areas where, lacking family ties and suffering the anonymity common to such areas, residents frequently do not have a circle of relatives or friends to call upon in time of need. Much of what the police do has accrued to the police because of their twenty-four-hour availability.

§ 2.21   Community pressures on the police

In the absence of any clear legislative or other form of mandate, the specific nature of the goals which the police seek to achieve in their efforts to maintain order is, in large measure, the result of the array of pressures that have been exerted upon them over the years. Police administrators are under constant pressure to provide additional services or to increase both the quantity and the quality of services currently being rendered. All areas of a community typically want more of a police presence than they are receiving. A serious crime that occurs in an area normally free of major crime typically results in an intensification of demands for additional police protection. Additionally, special interest groups compete for available police resources. Commercial interests, for example, typically want more time devoted to checking on the security of their establishments; insurance firms want more time devoted to activities that will reduce their losses, such as traffic safety and the solving of burglaries; and specially-organized citizen groups want more time devoted to such concerns as pornography, venereal disease communicated through prostitution, and the sale of narcotics to minors.

Some such pressures, as for example those which emanate from a community subjected to a particularly heinous crime, are temporary—lessening with the passage of time. Others carry sufficient weight and are of such a recurring nature as to have a permanent impact upon the allocation of available resources. The failure of most police agencies to develop administrative procedures that routinely subject these operations to systematic review has often resulted in a high priority continuing to be attached to a specific activity long after the need for the activity disappears.

By design, most police time is devoted to patrol activities. Patrol consists in part of merely making the presence of a police officer known within a community. But while from the administrative standpoint the officer on patrol is viewed as not only fully occupied, but profitably engaged, large segments of the citizenry and many other municipal officials view the officer as idle pending his next assignment. This widespread impression that the police have considerable "time on their hands" has, in the past, led to their being identified as the logical agency to which miscellaneous chores could be assigned. This is especially true with regard to assignments which can be assumed without significantly detracting from the effectiveness of patrol.

Whether or not the police respond to community pressures is determined in large measure by a police department's self-concept of its role. This is especially true with regard to the handling of those matters viewed as "social problems," for it is generally assumed by police officers that such problems require the attention of a "social worker." "Social work," in turn, is generally thought of as involving a commitment to working with individuals on a continuing basis and employing a "permissive" approach which many police see as being inconsistent with efforts at achieving effective control.[8] On the other hand, there are indications that the police want very much to be viewed in a helping role and therefore welcome the opportunity to perform those functions that require speed, courage, and resourcefulness.

§ 2.22   *Major current responsibilities of police*

In assessing appropriate objectives and priorities for police service, local communities should initially recognize that most police agencies are currently given responsibility, by design or default:

(1) to identify criminal offenders and criminal activity and, where appropriate, to apprehend offenders and participate in subsequent court proceedings;
(2) to reduce the opportunities for the commission of some crimes through preventive patrol and other measures;
(3) to aid individuals who are in danger of physical harm;
(4) to protect constitutional guarantees;
(5) to facilitate the movement of people and vehicles;
(6) to assist those who cannot care for themselves;
(7) to resolve conflict;
(8) to identify problems that are potentially serious law enforcement or governmental problems;
(9) to create and maintain a feeling of security in the community;
(10) to provide other services on an emergency basis.

In examining each of the objectives toward which the police work, an effort is made here to identify the specific nature of the activities in which the police engage and to establish the basis, if any, for police involvement.

§ 2.23   —*To identify criminal offenders and criminal activity and, where appropriate, to apprehend offenders and participate in subsequent court proceedings*

The most traditional goal of the police—constituting what many would argue is their primary contribution to community order—is the control of conduct that is legislatively prohibited. For the most part, this consists of identifying those thought to be guilty of having committed a criminal offense and subsequently proceeding against them. The investigative process typically involves the gathering of information from victims and witnesses, the collection and analysis of physical evidence, and the relating of the results of these and other inquiries to one or more individuals identified as likely to have committed the offense.

Police activity in this area takes three forms. The bulk of what police do is aimed at identifying offenders in response to reports received by the police indicating that a crime has been committed. (The extent to which crime is reported to the police varies a great deal from one community to another, depending upon a wide range of factors. Indications are that the actual amount of crime is several times that reported.)[9] The police response to a report of a crime will vary a great deal from one community to another, and also within a single community. In large cities, where the volume of criminal activity is high, police may be selective in determining whether or not to investigate a reported crime. This is especially true with regard to minor offenses—in particular those for which there is very little likelihood that the police will be able to establish the identity of the offender.

Secondly, there are those aspects of police work that are aimed at identifying offenses in the process of their being committed. Thus, while police patrol activities are primarily intended to dissuade persons from committing crimes, they are also intended to discover crimes in progress. Officers on patrol—especially in the larger cities—may have occasion to come upon individuals stealing a vehicle, staging a robbery, or breaking into a home or a commercial establishment. In addition, police officers pursuing some other police goal, such as in aiding a drunk or in facilitating the movement of traffic, may have occasion to discover the presence of a concealed weapon or of burglary tools. The extent to which the police identify criminal acts subject to their view depends almost entirely upon the amount and intensity of police patrol.

Finally, there is a whole range of criminal activity which, unlike a single isolated incident such as a homicide, a rape, or a robbery, can continue for long periods of time without surfacing. This is true, for example, with regard to most forms of organized crime, fraudulent business practices, and thefts perpetrated by professional criminals. The lack of disclosure, in such instances, is attributable either to the fact that the victim is not aware he is being victimized or has not yet learned of his losses; or to the fact that the offense is of a consensual nature—there being no victim. While it is commonly assumed that the police have an obligation to take the initiative in attempting to ferret out all criminal activity, they do so in practice on a highly selective basis. Thus, as to certain types of crime, they may make no effort. They may investigate other forms of criminal activity only upon complaint. And, as to still others, they may go so far as to establish a special unit to probe, test, and otherwise seek to uncover evidence of wrongdoing. Illustrative of the latter are units assigned to the investigation of gambling, narcotics, prostitution, confidence games, pickpocketing, shoplifting, and professional burglaries. It is apparent that the decision on the part of the police as to whether to investigate a specific form of criminal activity is an extremely important administrative decision that has not received careful attention in the past.

Most statutory provisions relating to the police role in controlling crime speak of their responsibility to "enforce the law." They do not address themselves, in any detail, to the role of the police in investigating reports of criminal activity and in ferreting out criminal activity. Thus, while the police are commonly mandated to enforce the law, there is some ambiguity as to their responsibility for investigating that which is reported to them and for seeking out evidence of criminal activity.

§ 2.24   —To reduce the opportunities for the commission of some crimes through preventive patrol and other measures

From the very beginnings of the police service in England, emphasis was placed upon the role of the police in preventing crime. Sir Charles Rowan, the first commissioner of the Metropolitan Police, in speaking of prevention, said: "To this great end every effort of the Police is to be directed. The security of person and property, the preservation of the public tranquility and all the other objects of a Police Establishment will thus be better effected than by the *detection and punishment* of the offender after he has succeeded in committing the crime . . ."[10] Police administrators in this country continue to characterize prevention as their primary goal. Assigning highest priority to preventive activities has a strong appeal in that it lends a positive note to what the police do, drawing public attention away from the somewhat negative image of the police as being exclusively oriented toward the catching and punishing of wrong-doers, and it reflects a degree of enlightenment in that it commits police to the more efficient concept of preventing trouble before it occurs.

The primary method that the police depend on for preventing crime implements the very elementary concept that a person contemplating a criminal act will not commit it if he can be convinced that he will be identified or apprehended in the process. As a result, most police efforts have been directed at making their presence felt to the maximum degree through unpredictable, conspicuous patrol—seeking thereby to create an impression of police omnipresence. In the course of their patrol activities, police identify and correct conditions, such as open premises, that increase the opportunity for criminal activity and also check out suspicious circumstances and persons.[11]

There is a widespread feeling among police administrators that what the police do in their patrol activities constitutes the most important and most potentially-effective response that police can make to the crime problem. Police administrators are constantly seeking to devote more of their resources to patrol. But, at the same time, there is a growing awareness that relatively little is known regarding the value of police patrol as a deterrent to crime.

The President's Commission on Law Enforcement and Administration of Justice noted that resources and talent for proper research have not been devoted in any great extent to discovering and analyzing the relationship between police patrol and deterrence and that there have been few scientifically controlled experiments concerning deterrent effects of various patrol techniques.[12] It is clear, however, that whatever impact patrol activity has is limited to certain types of crimes that occur on the streets. A patrolling police officer, for example, is not likely to deter crimes of the kind that most commonly occur in private premises, nor is he likely to interfere with the carefully-planned offenses of the professional criminal. It has never been doubted that the presence of a police officer at a given spot will deter the commission of a crime in the immediate area within view of the officer. But it is obviously not economically feasible to consider such a plan for policing, nor is it likely that citizens would desire to have a police presence in the numbers that would be required for such coverage. There have been a number of dramatic highly-publicized experiments in which areas have been blanketed with police officers, but these have proved little more than the obvious—that the presence of a police officer will deter crimes in the immediate area subject to his view.

All of these considerations force recognition of the limited capacity of the police to perform in a preventive role and—more basically force a renewed awareness that, while the police may reduce the opportunity for the commission of a crime, their efforts do not begin to affect the deep-rooted causes of crime. Yet, despite this limited capacity, the public continues to expect the police to prevent all crime and the police tend to continue to commit themselves to the same goal. This is most clearly reflected in the practice of using crime statistics as a measure of police effective-ness—the police being held accountable for increases in reported crime and being credited when a reduction occurs. Holding the police responsible in this manner for achieving a goal that is so obviously impossible of achievement has a terribly disruptive influence upon rational plans for improving police service. It is for this reason that police activities aimed at preventing crime have, for purposes of this study, been categorized under the more modest and more accurate label of contributing toward reducing the opportunities for the commission of a crime.

If the goal of the police in the preventive area is more narrowly defined, it is easier to see how the police can in realistic fashion make significant efforts toward reaching it. For example, Edward Davis, the Chief of the Los Angeles Police Department, recently attempted to place the preventive role of the police in clearer perspective in describing professional police principles:

> Now the police themselves cannot prevent crime . . . However, the police play a major role as the catalytic agent in society to assist the process of "feeding back" to the rest of society information on what is happening in terms of crime and disorder. No one else can perform this function but the police. No one else is in contact with crime and disorder in its totality. No one else has the machinery or perception or access to the basic facts as do the police.
>
> The police cannot prevent the development of criminality in any individual. However, through a feedback process, information on crime can be passed to social institutions which may hopefully generate programs to prevent criminality of individuals in the future.[13]

Illustrative of other types of programs which police have undertaken with increasing frequency in recent years are those designed to educate the public on ways in which the public can, through simple measures, reduce the likelihood of their homes being burglarized, their cars being stolen, or their persons being robbed. Advice has been spread through the use of brochures, billboards, and consulta-tions with those who have been the victims of crime. Police administrators, as a group, have gone further. They have, for example, prevailed upon car manufacturers to construct an ignition mechanism that makes theft more difficult. There is reason to believe that considerably more progress could be made in reducing the opportunities for crime by making greater use of the knowledge of experienced police personnel in the planning of urban renewal areas, new public housing, and new schools, parks, and recreational facilities.[14]

§ 2.25 —To aid individuals who are in danger of physical harm

The role of the police in coming to the aid of a person subjected to a criminal attack is an objective of police operations quite apart from their role in identifying and possibly apprehending the offender. Thus, for example, in considering the importance of speed on the part of the police in responding to reports of serious criminal activity, it is possible to weigh separately its value for purposes of identifying and apprehending the person alleged to have committed an offense and its value in providing assistance and protection to a victim being held, for example, at knife point.

But police concern for protecting people from physical harm commonly extends beyond simply those incidents in which the threatened harm is the result of a criminal attack. Thus, in carrying out the common statutory and charter mandate to protect persons, police see themselves, for example, as having an obligation to roust individuals from a burning building, to rescue a person who is drowning, and to come to the aid of a person attacked by a dog. As the President's Crime Commission observed, "it is natural to interpret the police role of 'protection' as meaning protection not only against crime but against other hazards, accidents or even discomforts of life."[15]

The priority to be attached to this goal in competition with other goals that the police are committed to achieving has been the subject of great interest in the past several years because of the injuries and deaths that have occurred in connection with major disorders. Until recently, the issue arose most commonly in those situations in which the police resorted to the use of deadly force or engaged in a high-speed chase. Both situations illustrate the need for providing the police with a clearer policy decision on the extent to which their obligation to minimize the likelihood of physical harm should be the overriding concern when it conflicts with their efforts to suppress riots, to identify criminal activity, or to resolve conflict.

In the above situations, the conflict between objectives occurs in the handling of a single incident. But the problem of priorities arises in a broader context as well—where the competition is not between different objectives in a single incident, but for allocation of a proportion of total police resources. How much police manpower should be devoted to protecting specific individuals in the community who feel endangered? What responsibility, if any, does a police agency have, for example, to protect a small merchant or a taxi-driver from repeated robberies? What responsibility is there for protecting a citizen who, as a result of his private business affairs, indicates that he has been threatened with physical harm—or the wife who lives in fear of being attacked by her estranged spouse? In the most recent case in which the responsibility of the police under such circumstances was litigated, the New York Court of Appeals held, in a tort action, that a municipality, although obligated to provide police protection to the public, was not liable for its failure to provide police protection for an individual.[16] But it is apparent that a finding that there is no tort liability does not provide an adequate basis for the police to make the kind of decisions that they are called upon to make in responding to reports that a life has been threatened. Community expectations in this area of police activity are much broader than this narrow interpretation of police liability.

§ 2.26   —Protect constitutional guarantees

Because so much of the attention in policing has been focused upon the processing of alleged offenders, there is a tendency on the part of police personnel to view the Constitution primarily in negative terms as the source of numerous limitations and controls upon their authority and their actions. Events of the past several years, however, have made it clear that the police cannot afford to limit their concern for constitutional guarantees to the various safeguards in the processing of alleged offenders. Police have become increasingly involved in protecting the right of citizens to live where they choose to live, to attend school where they are entitled to do so, to assemble, to demonstrate, and to speak out freely. The need for responding to these situations has created an awareness that the police have a much broader and, in many respects, a much more affirmative role in taking positive action to protect the constitutional rights of all citizens.

Policemen, as public officers, take an oath committing themselves to uphold the Constitution of the United States and the Constitution and laws of the state in which they are employed. What this means in practice—and particularly in the controversial area of free speech and assembly—is not always easy to determine. For example, it is clear that the police may not deprive people of their rights to free speech or assembly by the arbitrary denial of parade and rally permits nor by the unreasonable refusal to make areas available for the exercise of such rights. It is not so clear to what extent the police are obligated to protect speakers and marchers from interference from private persons. The constitutional right of free speech is the right to be free from restriction of that right by state action. It is possible that in a given situation the failure of the police to do anything at all to protect an unpopular speaker would constitute state action denying the exercise of such rights.

Nor is it always clear how the police should resolve the conflict between their duty to protect free speech and their responsibility to maintain the peace and to protect the public's right to free access.

Decisions by the courts that there ordinarily cannot be a prior restraint (as by denying a permit to speak) make it the on-the-spot decision of the police officer whether to maintain order or to protect free speech when emergencies arise.

A speaker with a permit may go beyond bounds and incite violence, or a mob may undertake to break up an authorized and properly conducted meeting. In either case, the policeman on the spot must make the judgment as to what measures will most likely avoid violent disorders.[17]

Some would argue that the conflict should be resolved by balancing the importance of the interests involved with the proviso that the police may not substitute "uncontrolled official suppression of the speaker ... for the duty to maintain order."[18] Another argument is that priority over other interests must be given to the constitutional right of free speech. According to the late justice Black, who espoused this position, this would mean that, in practice, the threat of individuals to assault a speaker does not justify suppression of the speech when there are "obvious alternative methods of preserving public order." "If, in the name of preserving order, (the police) ever can interfere with a lawful public speaker, they first must make all reasonable efforts to protect him."[19]

Yet the specific nature of the police authority in such cases is rarely spelled out. Although some states[20] define the intentional breaking up of a lawful meeting as a misdemeanor, in most states the only bases for making arrests are the disorderly conduct and trespass statutes.[21]

Interference with the police and other public officials when they are exercising their duty to protect constitutional rights is actionable in the federal courts. Thus, in *Brewer v. Hoxie School District No. 46*,[22] the court enjoined the defendants from interfering with the exercise of the school board's duty to operate its schools on a desegregated basis. The school board members had taken oaths to "support the Constitution of the United States." As a consequence, the court held:

> The members of the school board are under a duty to obey the Constitution ... They are bound by oath or affirmation to support it and are mindful of their obligation. It follows as a necessary corollary that they have a federal right to be free from direct and deliberate interference with the performance of the constitutionally imposed duty.[23]

Unfortunately, this case leaves unanswered many questions, as do the earlier cases discussed. Do the police have the authority to use force, including arrest, where necessary to protect constitutional rights quite apart from the question of whether the arrested person's conduct is criminal? What kind of interference should speakers be protected against? Physical attacks certainly, but what about mere heckling? It is evident that there is a need to spell out the authority and responsibility of the police more clearly so that the current uncertainty is eliminated.

§ 2.27   —*To facilitate the movement of people and vehicles*

Life throughout this country—and especially in urban areas—is heavily dependent upon the free movement of people and vehicles. The police, over the years, have assumed a major share of the responsibility for achieving and maintaining the high degree of order that is necessary to make the free movement of people and vehicles possible. The typical police agency enforces all traffic regulations; investigates traffic accidents; directs traffic in congested areas; guides children across busy streets; enforces parking restrictions; promotes traffic safety; controls crowds; and prevents the blockage of sidewalks, streets, and other public ways. Exact figures are unavailable, but all indications are that a substantial proportion of all police resources are devoted to these activities.[24]

Most firmly established is the police role in regulating vehicular traffic. State statutes are very detailed and specific in setting down the rules of the road. And they are usually explicit in making it the duty of police officers to enforce the rules and to direct traffic within their respective jurisdictions. The authority of the officer is commonly supported by a specific statutory provision in the traffic code that makes it a violation to refuse to comply with his lawful orders, signals, or directions.

Implied in the objective of facilitating the movement of people is a concern for their safety. This concern accounts for the fact that most police agencies go substantially beyond their legislative responsibilities in the traffic field—engaging in extensive efforts to prevent accidents by conducting driver training programs, by teaching traffic safety in the schools, and by issuing advice and warnings to drivers and pedestrians against whom they have no intention of bringing charges.

Another aspect of police activity aimed at facilitating the movement of people is that involved in the control of crowds. The actions of police officers at large events, such as athletic contests, parades, and performances of various kinds, are commonly recognized to be in the interests of all of those present, and as a result, police instructions and requests are not likely to be challenged. A different situation arises, of course, if a conflict develops between segments of a large crowd or if a group of people block the use of a thoroughfare to others or deny them access to a structure or facility. The responsibility of the police in such situations shifts from that of facilitating the movement of people to the suppressing of a disorder.

§ 2.28   —*To assist those who cannot care for themselves*

Much of policing consists of providing care and assistance to those who cannot care for themselves because of their age, their state of health, or the influences which they come under—the young and the old, the physically disabled, the mentally ill and retarded, those who are intoxicated by alcohol, and those who are addicted to drugs.

As to some of the categories of individuals who cannot care for themselves (e.g., the drunk, the narcotic addict, the mentally ill person who attempts to commit suicide), police involvement may come about because the behavior is commonly defined as constituting a criminal offense. There has been a great deal of interest,

scholarly debate, and litigation in recent years over the propriety of
dealing with such behavior problems by means of the criminal justice
system.[25]

Among the major values commonly cited by those advocating the
removal of the criminal sanction from such forms of behavior is the
claim that the change would take the police out of the business of
having to relate to such individuals. But this reflects an erroneous
belief—widely held—that the police function consists of enforcing the
criminal law. Police are involved—and are likely to continue to be
involved—with individuals of the type identified above quite apart
from whether the activity in which the individuals are engaged is
defined as criminal. It seems inevitable—absent other provisions—that
the public will continue to look toward government and especially
toward the police to aid the drunk who is in danger of freezing to
death if left unattended; the narcotic addict who engages in bizarre
behavior in a public gathering; or a person poised atop a bridge,
threatening to jump.

Separating police responsibilities from decisions regarding the use
of the criminal sanction, however, does not mean that the outcome
of the current debate will have no implications for the police. To the
contrary, the implications will be far reaching, for, as is indicated
below, the only current legal basis for much of what the police do in
aiding individuals who cannot care for themselves is derived from
their authority to enforce the criminal law. Eliminating the criminal
sanctions would make more apparent the need for establishing a
clearer base for police functioning in this area. More specifically,
assuming the need for some form of governmental intervention, it
would require augmenting the single means currently available to the
police for providing assistance, i.e., arrest, detention, and criminal
prosecution.

§ 2.29   —To resolve conflict

A number of recent studies have pointed up what has long been
obvious to patrolmen—that much of what they do involves resolving
conflicts.[26] Among the specific types of conflict commonly confronted by the police are those involving husband and wife;
neighbors; landlords and tenants; and businessmen and their customers.

The tendency on the part of the police has generally been to view such conflicts as being of a petty nature and as constituting a nuisance to the police. Indeed, in many jurisdictions, requests for police assistance in resolving minor conflicts are commonly referred to as "nuisance calls." More recently, there has been a tendency to view police activities in this area as falling under the umbrella of maintaining order or, by virtue of the fact that the incidents commonly involve situations that have the potential for escalating into assaultive conduct, to view police efforts to cope with them as constituting an effective means by which the police can help prevent crime. The volume of police work in this area and the problems in developing an adequate police response suggest that there is merit in considering the police role in resolving conflict as a distinctive goal.

More recently, attention has been drawn to the unique opportunities that the police have to contribute to the order of the community by resolving intergroup conflict. In an effort to minimize outbreaks of violence, many police departments—especially in the larger cities—have undertaken to maintain continual contact with militant groups and with parties in conflict with each other—with the objective of resolving clashes before they involve physical confrontations. Thus, police personnel assigned as liaison officers or as "human relations" officers have, for example, taken the initiative in bringing neighborhood residents and school officials together; have arranged for meetings between black-dominated unions and white-dominated union management; and have worked out peace treaties between rival gangs. At least one community (Dayton, Ohio) has decided to advance its work in this area through the formation of a broadly-conceived program of involvement on the part of the police with the community and through the fielding of a "community conflict management team."

As a matter of law or public policy, there is very little basis for police doing anything with regard to a conflict that comes to their attention other than make a determination as to whether a law has been violated and to effect an arrest if such is the case. In practice, the police order people to be quiet, order them to separate, threaten criminal prosecution, and, in a variety of other ways, exhort feuding parties to settle their differences without resorting to violence. Persuasive arguments have been made for greater involvement on the part of the police in responding to the need for mediation in interpersonal and intergroup disputes. There is a very positive ring to such proposals, characterized as they are by an effort to provide assistance to those in need of help. The nature of the role urged upon the police, however, is a very fragile one, involving as it does intervention by one clothed with rather awesome powers, and raises a number of potential problems that should receive careful attention.

§ 2.30 —*To identify problems that are potentially serious law enforcement or governmental problems*

By virtue of the fact that police are the "foot soldiers" of municipal government, they have occasion to see various indications of failures in the provision of municipal government services and to identify problems in need of attention. It is not uncommon to find that a state legislature or a city council has made the reporting of such conditions a responsibility of the police. Thus, the Nebraska Legislature, for example, has provided:

> It shall be the duty of policemen to make a daily report to the chief of police of . . . any lamps that may be broken or out of repair . . . any defect in any sidewalk, street, alley . . . ice, dangerous obstructions . . . disagreeable odors . . . .[27]

Police literature also recognizes this activity. O.W. Wilson, for example, notes:

> The patrolman is the ultimate in the decentralization of municipal service. . . .Services which the police may perform for other departments include searching for and eliminating fire and health hazards, such as accumulations of trash, weed-covered lots, garbage unsanitarily housed, foodstuffs unhygienically displayed for sale; discovering and reporting street lights not burning and broken water mains; checking on building permits and occupation licenses; observing and reporting safety hazards for which other departments have some responsibility, such as defective sidewalks and streets.[28]

The disorders of the past several years have resulted in new importance being attached to the role of the police in identifying problems plaguing the community. In an effort to reduce the dissatisfaction with governmental services that has been a major factor contributing toward the outbreaks of violence, the police in many cities have undertaken to channel complaints to appropriate governmental agencies. In St. Louis and Baltimore, for example, police man "storefront" offices to facilitate receipt and follow-up of such complaints. In some communities, the police have gone beyond the channeling function—actually taking the initiative in ferreting out situations that require attention and identifying policies and practices of other governmental agencies which are in need of correction. Thus, some police departments have pressed other municipal agencies to extend the operational hours of swimming pools on hot nights, to provide more adequate playground facilities, and to turn on fire hydrants for recreational purposes.

In still a further extension of this role, it has been urged that police administrators, given their knowledge of the problems of the community, undertake a more active role in support of legislation and other means for relieving some of the major underlying problems that give rise to matters of concern to the police, such as poverty and discrimination.[29]

§ 2.31   —To create and maintain a feeling of security in the community

There is a purpose in much of what the police do in making their presence felt in the community that is quite apart from its value in deterring behavior defined as criminal. While rarely articulated, it seems obvious that police have assumed the responsibility for creating a sense of security in the community—for helping to create an atmosphere that makes it possible for people, exercising reasonable care and precaution, to carry on their ordinary, daily activities with the expectation that they will not be endangered, interfered with, or subjected to criminal attack.

A number of recent studies have indicated that the fear of crime is as much of a problem as crime itself.[30] This being the case, it can be argued that, while the deterrent value of police patrol activities may be questionable, a police presence in the community in itself has a positive value as a means of giving citizens the minimal feeling of security and safety that is necessary if they are to enjoy freedom of movement.

Admittedly, there is an illusory quality in this form of security, in that the actual potential of the police to guarantee the safety of residents—their persons and their property—is far less than is suggested by the presence of police personnel. But few doubt the value in generating the illusion.

The distinction drawn here between police efforts to reduce the opportunity for criminal actions and police efforts aimed at creating a feeling of security is of importance in determining the allocation of police personnel and in deciding upon police operating policies. The most cursory analysis of the current assignment of police officers in some of our largest cities will indicate that their assignment rarely contributes toward the reduction of crime—although this is the avowed purpose in having them spend their time in the way in which they do. This does not mean that their time is wasted. But it does mean that if the objective in such assignments is more realistically defined as contributing toward the creation of a feeling of security in the community, the priorities in police activity can be better evaluated.

§ 2.32 —To promote and preserve civil order

The wave of large-scale civil disorders that has occurred in the past several years has made the control of rioting one of the paramount concerns of the police. Originally a large-city problem, the spread of confrontation and violence from the ghettos of the large cities to smaller communities and to college campuses has led to the involvement, if only under the provisions of mutual-aid pacts, of police officers from even the most rural of jurisdictions. The use of military personnel to aid the police, once viewed as a measure of last resort, has become widely accepted.

While the duties of the police in the handling of a civil disturbance continue to be viewed as extraordinary, they are in fact, from the historical standpoint, among their most firmly established responsibilities. The modern police force, in the sense of a single organization of salaried personnel having city-wide jurisdiction and full-time responsibility for the general enforcement of the law, came into being largely in response to the need for controlling major disorders. The informal arrangements for policing by the citizenry that were in effect in England prior to 1820, having been found inadequate for coping with large-scale conflicts, increased reliance being placed upon the militia. Reactions to the repressive tactics employed by the military in turn led to proposals for the establishment of a full-time police force that would be committed to a restrained use of both authority and force and that would see its prime function as forestalling both crime and riots. Somewhat the same sequence of events occurred in this country. The Charlestown Convent burning, the attack on William Garrison, the Broad Street riots in Boston, the three-month-long native American riots of 1844, the Negro riots in Philadelphia, and large-scale rioting in New York brought home to municipal officials the ineffectiveness of their own peace-keeping forces and the disadvantages in utilizing military force in putting down disorders.[31]

There is generally no lack of clarity in the statutory basis for police actions in civil disorders. Typical is the Wisconsin provisions that makes it the duty of all sheriffs and their undersheriffs to "quiet and suppress all affrays, routs, riots, unlawful assemblies and insurrections."[32] The Wisconsin statute defining unlawful assemblies also incorporates a provision that makes explicit the duty of all police officers to "suppress unlawful assemblies."[33] Approximately half of the states require the police to disperse an unlawful assembly; all states authorize them to do so.

§ 2.33   —To provide other services on an emergency basis

Every society has need for some source to which people can turn in dire emergencies when persons to whom they might otherwise turn are unavailable. It is the police who have come to fill this need—and it can be argued that filling the need constitutes a contribution toward the maintenance of community order.

Police become involved in administering first aid, in locating emergency shelter, in extinguishing minor fires, and in catching rabid animals because they are the only employees of municipal government who are on the streets twenty-four hours a day, seven days a week, capable of responding quickly to a range of calls for assistance. In larger jurisdictions, where the volume of such incidents warrants them, alternative arrangements are sometimes made whereby other governmental agencies or private organizations fill these needs. For the police to respond to requests of this kind—in large volume and on a routine basis over a long period of time—can become burdensome. It nevertheless must be recognized that there is a basic instinct in all able-bodied men to want to be helpful when an emergency presents itself—and police are no exception. Various arrangements may come into being by which the volume of emergency services provided by the police is reduced, but it is unlikely that the police will remain aloof from situations where they can be helpful and it is equally unlikely that the police will be relieved of their standing as the agency one turns to as a last resort.

Notes

1. The ABA Standards are printed in 17 volumes. They may be ordered from ABA Circulation Dept., 1155 E. 60th St., Chicago, Ill. 60637. Cost is $3.25 for a single volume; $38 for a set of 17 volumes; $2.25 ea. for bulk orders of 10-24 of the same title, or $1.75 ea. for 25 or more of same title.

2. Tennessee Code Annotated, 6-2129, 1971.

3. New York City Charter, 435a, 1963.

4. Egon Bittner, *The Functions of the Police in Modern Society*, Volume 42, National Institute of Mental Health, Public Health Service Publication No. 2059, November 1970.

5. *Ibid.*, p. 40.

6. *Ibid.*, p. 41.

7. *Ibid.*

8. This view appears to be attributable, in large measure, to the fact that the police see themselves as the last resort to whom people turn when all other forms of control fail. Thus, Egon Bittner, in his study of the police handling of skid-row problems, quotes a police officer as saying, "I can't be soft like a social worker because unlike him I cannot call the cops when things go wrong. I am the cops!" Bittner, "The Police on Skid-row: A Study of Peace Keeping," *American Sociological Review*, Volume 32 pp. 699, 709, 1967.

9. See President's Commission on Law Enforcement and the Administration of Justice, *The Challenge of Crime in a Free Society*, Washington, Government Printing Office, 1967, pp. 20-22.

10. C. Rowan, Handbook of General Instructions, quoted in C. Reith, *A New Study of Police History*, 1956.

11. For a description of patrol activities as taught to the police, see G. O'Connor and C. Vanderbosch, *The Patrol Operation*, Washington, International Association of Chief's of Police, 1967.

12. The Challenge of Crime, *op. cit.*, p. 96.

13. Davis, "Professional Police Principles," *Federal Probation*, Volume 35, 29 March, 1971.

14. The Challenge of Crime, *op. cit.*, p. 98.

15. *Ibid.*, p. 97.

16. Riss v. City of New york, 22 N.Y. 2d 579, 240 N.E. 2d 860, 293 N.Y.S. 2d 897, 1968. A city may, however, be liable under special circumstances such as those in which the police undertake responsibilities to particular persons, Schuster v. City of New York, 5N.Y. 2d 75, 154 N.E. 2d 534, 180 N.Y.S. 2d 265, 1958, or those in which the city is undertaking a proprietary or special function such as the operation of a rapid transit line, a hospital, or a housing project Bass v. City of New York, 61 Misc. 2d 465, 305 N.Y.S. 2d 801 Superior Court, 1969.

17. Kunz v. New York, 340 U.S. 290, 313, 1951.

18. Niemetko v. Maryland, 340 U.S. 268, 288-289, 1951.

19. Feiner v. New York, 340 U.S. 315, 326 1951.

20. See, California Penal Code § 403, 1970: "Every person who without authority of law, willfully disturbs or breaks up any assembly or meeting, not

unlawful in its character . . . is guilty of a misdemeanor."

21. There currently is pending in the United States Senate a bill that would make it unlawful to interfere in any way with any person's exercise of his constitutional rights of religion, speech, press, assembly, or petition and that would provide for appropriate relief through civil actions under federal jurisdiction. See S.397, 91st Congress, 2d Session (June 16, 1970). For a critical analysis of this proposed legislation, see Report on the First Amendment Freedoms Act, 26 The Record of the Ass'n of the Bar of the City of New York 312, April 1970.

22. 238 f. 2d 91, 8th Cir. 1956.

23. *Ibid.*, p. 99.

24. Some percentage breakdowns which support this view can be found in Bercal, "Calls for Police Assistance." *American Behavioral Scientist,* Volume 13, p. 681, 1970.

25. See, e.g., H. Packer, *The Limits of the Criminal Sanction,* 1968; Robinson v. California, 370 U.S. 660, 1962; Easter v. District of Columbia, 361 F. 2d 50 D.C. Cir. 1966; Powell v. Texas, 392 U.S. 514, 1968, For a classic treatment of the problem from the police standpoint, now somewhat dated, see A. Vollmer, *The Police and Modern Society,* 1936. More recently, broader questions have been raised regarding not only the appropriateness of any form of governmental effort to protect an individual from himself.

26. See, in particular, Cumming, Cumming, & Edell, "Policeman as Philosopher, Guide and Friend," *Social Problems* Volume 12, p. 276, 1965; Parnas, "The Police Response to the Domestic Distrubance," 1967 *Wis. L. Rev.* 914; National Institute of Law Enforcement and Criminal Justice, *Training Police as Specialists in Family Crisis Intervention,* Washington: Government Printing Office, 1970.

27. Neb. Rev. Stat., 14-607, 1962.

28. O.W. Wilson, *Police Administration,* New York: McGraw Hill, 2nd Edition, 1962.

29. Task Force Report: *The Police,* Washington D.C.: U.S. Government Printing Office, 1967, pg. 163.

30. See *Challenge of Crime,* supra note 9, pg. 50; and McIntyre, Public Attitudes Toward Crime and Law Enforcement, *Annals,* Volume 374, pg. 34, 1967.

31. For a comprehensive picture of the development of early police forces in this country, see S.D. Bacon, *The Early Development of American Municipal Police,* unpublished Ph.D. thesis, Yale University, 1939; R. Lane, *Policing the City—Boston,* 1822-1885, 1967; J. Richardson, *The New York Police: Colonial Times to 1901,* 1970.

32. Wisconsin Statutes § 59.24 (1), 1969.

33. Wisconsin Statutes § 947,06 (1), 1969.

IV. THE FUTURE POLICEMAN

SOURCE: James Q. Wilson, "The Future Policeman," *Future Roles of Criminal Justice Personnel: Position Papers,* Project STAR, American Justice Institute, Marina del Rey, California, 1971, pp. 1-28.

To make a reasonable guess as to how police officers will be expected to behave over the next twenty or so years, one must first have some understanding of what aspect, if any, of the police role is subject to change. That question is not answered by banal statements that "society is undergoing rapid change" or "the police officer must respond to new challenges." In some sense, of course, both those statements are true; indeed, they are almost tautologies. But society may "change" in the sense of getting richer or poorer, larger or smaller, more integrated or less integrated, isolationist or internationalist, without any of the essential tasks of the police patrolman changing in the slightest. And the "new challenges" to which the officer must respond may be peripheral to his role and thus his response to them, while perhaps important psychologically to him or symbolically to society as a whole, may not alter in any significant way how he performs his central tasks. As with most weighty matters, one is here confronted with contradictory aphorisms: if one philosopher could say that "all is flux," another could respond, "plus *ça change plus c'est la même chose."*

In general, one would expect that change would be most evident in the secondary relationships among persons (i.e., in their participation in large organizations, the mass media of communication, the world of fashion and entertainment) and least evident in their primary relationships (i.e., familial, peer group, neighborhood, and personal concerns). The former are subject to the deliberate acts of large institutions; the latter are shaped by the spontaneous and informal interactions among individuals. Ferdinand Tönnies applied the term *Gesellschaft* (roughly, "society") to the former relationships and explained them as emerging from the exercise of "natural will" (*Wesenwille*); he gave the term *Gemeinschaft* (roughly, "community") to the latter and explained them as arising out of the exercise of "rational choice" (*Kurwille*). Insofar as a person participates in contractual relationships or large-scale social institutions that are created to achieve specific ends, he will find his role and the nature of his tasks subject to change; insofar as he participates in communal, primary relationships, expectations about his behavior will change much more slowly, if at all.

Obviously, each social form partakes of some features of the other and each affects the development of the other. No social institution is wholly rationalized in part because each contains important communal elements (e.g., a factory or office has within it informal work groups) and no communal order is entirely unaffected by the behavior of rational social elements (e.g., the family structure slowly changes from extended to nuclear as work opportunities expand and specialized institutions emerge to care for the sick and the elderly). While recognizing that the distinction is over-simplified and to a degree abstract, it is still useful to attempt to locate various social roles in either the communal or social/contractual order so as to form some crude idea of the extent to which each role is likely to undergo rapid change.

One of the interesting features of the role of police patrolman is that it combines elements of the communal and the social/contractual. The patrolman is a member of a large bureaucratic organization in which relationships are defined by rule; he is paid a regular salary in exchange for stated hours of work; he must undergo formal training; he is subject to formal disciplinary actions; and in his everyday tasks he is guided by a set of written laws. If this were all there were to his role, he would be pre-eminently a member of a rationalized social order whose behavior could and would be modified as the institution developed. But the patrolman's essential task is not defined by any of these institutional relationships, but rather by his relationship with small groups of citizens experiencing anxiety, fear, or anger about vital personal and familial concerns. Some of these concerns are those of a victim who has experienced a loss, assault, or a threat; others are those of a disputant who disagrees with a relative or neighbor about what is orderly, fair, or right; still others are those of a group challenging the propriety and legitimacy of a public action. The patrolman's role, as I have described it elsewhere, is one in which "subprofessionals, working alone, exercise wide discretion in matters of utmost importance (life and death, honor and dishonor) in an environment that is apprehensive and perhaps hostile."[1] Those matters with which the police role deals are not likely to change rapidly: men and women will continue to value their property and their privacy, to have differing standards of public and private virtue, and to disagree with many government decisions. Whoever responds to the distress or manages the disputes of these people will of necessity have to take many, if not most, of his cues as to proper action from the immediate circumstances of excited demands of individuals and primary groups.

Over *very* long time periods, of course, the primary relationships with which police patrolmen deal will change, perhaps profoundly. Personal liberty, economic opportunity, and the division of labor have substituted the extended for the nuclear family, and thus weakened (or so it is believed) the informal constraints and sanctions of family life and led to a greater reliance of formal social controls. The shift in this century from a population with relatively little formal education to one in which the great majority of citizens have a high school diploma and the enormous increase in the size of the middle class (however defined) has helped foster a greater level of civility with respect to many face-to-face relationships (perfunctory politeness is more common, barroom and alley brawls are less common) and simultaneously has stimulated a greater level of stridency in many collective acts (ideology has been reinjected into politics and more persons "know their rights" and are willing to assert them). And to take an obvious case, blacks are no longer passive or deferential: they demand fair treatment and black leaders, though almost invariably middle-class, feel obliged to speak and act to some degree in the language and according to the expectations of their lower- and working-class audience.

But except for the fairly recent and seemingly sudden mobilization of black and youth politics, the changes in the class structure of society, and the accompanying changes in the manner of social intercourse, have been, and will continue to be, gradual. Life-styles change more slowly than income. On the other hand, the big-city patrolman is likely to believe that these changes are occurring faster than in fact they are because persons seeking to maintain or acquire a middle-class life-style move out of the central city, leaving behind those who either cannot move or who do not wish to move, and the latter inevitably includes an increasingly large proportion of persons who value a lower-class life-style. The policeman in the central city will encounter in his daily rounds ever larger numbers of non-upwardly-mobile or even downwardly-mobile persons. Thus it is that, while society is becoming more middle-class and (with respect to at least many of its interrelationships) more civil, the patrolman believes it is becoming more lower-class and less civil. When a patrolman says that the people he meets today on his beat are, compared to those he once met, less respectful of authority, more assertive of their rights, and less constrained by familial norms, he is probably correct. When he generalizes those changes to society as a whole, he is probably not correct.

But though the central-city policeman must deal with a population that consumes police services at a higher rate than before and do so under conditions that place his actions under more critical scrutiny than ever before, it is not clear that the nature of the circumstances that require his intervention have altered: loss, fear, and conflict are and will continue to be his daily preoccupations.

The area in which great and rapid changes will be attempted is not to be found in the communal aspects of the patrolman's role but in the organizational and legal context in which that role is embedded. The police organization is now and will continue to be caught up, in varying degrees, with many of the same forces that have been at work in almost all large organizations in our society—the effort to decentralize, to humanize, and to rationalize the structure and procedures of the police bureaucracy, and to apply rationalistic and utilitarian, as opposed to moralistic and ethical criteria, to the substance of the criminal law. Utilitarianism and human self-actualization are the ruling motives of the contemporary reform impulse. Their meaning is not always fully understood, their justification is rarely based on serious philosophical considerations, and the two concepts are at some points in conflict (utilitarianism, seeking the best results for society as a whole, may require that a large organization be created to serve a particualr end; self-actualization, seeking what is best for a particular individual, may require that organizational constraints be lifted and even organization itself destroyed). They are nonetheless powerfully influential goals. These issues can be made clearer by considering in more detail proposed changes in the structural and legal aspects of police work.

§ 2.34   *Possible social-structural changes in police role*

§ 2.35   *—Legal*

There is little reason to suppose that the proposals heard in recent

years for the "decriminalization" of various forms of behavior will
abate and good reason to believe that the isolated changes that have
already occurred will become widespread. Various kinds of gambling
have been legalized in several states, and more states are considering
taking similar steps. Public intoxication may well cease being a
"crime" and thus cease being grounds for a lawful arrest. The
prospects for decriminalizing the use of various drugs and narcotics
are less clear: pressure to legalize the use of marijuana, or at least to
reduce substantially the penalties for its use, is likely to increase;
pressure to maintain and perhaps intensify penalties for the use of
drugs with known harmful effects (such as LSD) will probably
continue. The legal management of heroin and of its chemical
substitutes, such as methadone, will remain a complex and emotional
issue, with increased use of substitutes, perhaps some cautious
experimentation with heroin maintenance programs, but no major
change in the legal status of heroin sale or use. The sale and
distribution of obscene materials, now utterly permissive, may well
be contracted slightly by tightened legal restraints and increased
demands for police action, but it is not likely that we will see a
return to the time when indecency was forbidden and the trade in
pornography was almost entirely underground. There is as yet
relatively little demand for decriminalizing prostitution, though the
semi-legal status of that industry in Nevada may stimulate an interest
in similar experiments elsewhere. What is perhaps more likely,
because there is a readily available model to copy, is a move toward
the British pattern of regulation in which soliciting, pimping, and
brothels are prohibited but prostitution as such is not. The laws
prohibiting "unnatural" sexual acts among consenting adults will
probably either disappear or fall almost entirely into disuse.

If some behavior may be decriminalized, other kinds may be
criminalized. Drunk driving, already an offense, is likely to become a
more serious one as the effort mounts to reduce highway fatalities.
Though the failure to wear a helmet while riding a motorcycle or a
seat belt while driving a car harms no one but the careless victim, we
are likely to see increased efforts to pass laws that attempt to protect
people from themselves and thus increased demands that the police
penalize persons who refuse to protect themselves.

§ 2.36 —*Organizational*

Experiments with redistributing authority in the police department and redefining the patrolman's tasks will continue. The lesson learned by many police administrators during the 1960's was that order maintenance and service provision are as important, or more important, than law enforcement; that the earlier emphasis on centralized command systems and patrol mobility reduced the contact the officer had with the neighborhood and the individual citizen; and that "community relations," somehow defined, is an important part of their task. During the 1970's we shall no doubt witness continued efforts to implement changes based on these views: greater decentralization, more precinct or "store-front" police headquarters, more community relations meetings and councils, and increased efforts to assign officers in teams to areas for which they will have continuing responsibility.

In addition, efforts will continue to redefine the task of the patrolman. One such effort might be called, to borrow a term from industrial psychology, "job enlargement." the Patrolman would, in this plan, be given wider responsibilities and greater formal discretion. He would do follow-up investigations as well as make on-the-spot reports; he would visit with residents as well as respond to calls for service; and he would handle some tasks—such as juvenile work, narcotics investigation, or community relations—formerly assigned to specialists.

In addition, we will surely see further efforts to involve the community in some way in police matters in several (but not all) cities. Typically, such involvement in the past has taken the form of monthly meetings and consultative councils. In a few cases, such as Dayton, Ohio, attempts have been made to provide the council with significant powers, and in other cases (such as Berkeley, California) political campaigns have been waged to put some or all of the police services under the complete control of neighborhood governing boards. Such a complete devolution of authority is not likely to occur, but the scope of the consultative bodies may broaden and their representation expand. One obvious change, arising out of the decentralized "team policing" concept, is to assign beat patrolmen (rather than command or staff officers from headquarters) as police members of the councils.

Finally, efforts will no doubt continue to develop new techniques for providing traditional patrol services. The Family Crisis Intervention Unit developed by the New York City Police Department under the guidance of Dr. Morton Bard is the best known example. Specially-selected officers given special training are assigned the task of handling disputatious or problem families in a conciliatory manner and referring them to appropriate city agencies. The Unit is being emulated in other cities though it is not clear it is being institutionalized in New York.

§ 2.37 —Personnel

Two efforts will continue to dominate police personnel recruitment and selection: the first to "upgrade" the caliber of regular police officers (by increased educational requirements, for example), the second to attract officer recruits who are ethnically more representative of the communities they serve. The latter goal will be served both by new measures to recruit black and Spanish-speaking officers in cities with significant numbers of such residents and by programs designed to bring "para-professional" personnel into police work in such roles as cadets, community service officers, and police aides. Several departments are endeavoring both to increase the number of minority group officers and to experiment with the use of para-professionals and many report difficulties, especially in minority recruitment. The difficulties will remain, but will be overcome— partly because the demand for such changes will continue, partly because the successes of a few departments will provide a model for other departments, and partly because once change has progressed beyond a certain point (for example, once a certain percentage of black officers has been hired) further success becomes easier (in this case, potential black recruits will no longer suspect they are unwelcome on the force). The use of civilians and para-professionals will also continue for the same reason it is continuing in the medical profession—such as personnel are cheaper than fully-trained personnel but can do many tasks as well. Should the wage differential vanish or become trivial, the pressures for using sworn officers for all police tasks will again become dominant.

§ 2.38 —Political

The police chief, and indeed the entire command structure, will experience a continued effort to place important constraints on his freedom of action. Political leadership in city hall (the mayor, the city manager, local criminal justice coordinating councils) will continue to express a more active concern with police deployment, manpower levels, and planning than has been customary in the past. Now that local elective officials, liberal as well as conservative, have discovered that their constituents demand greater public safety, the police department will no longer be entirely free to run itself. At the same time, militant police unionism will grow, thereby placing an internal constraint on departmental policy. Large cities that do not have police unions (under whatever name) will get them; those that do have them will probably grant them, sooner or later, quasi-official bargaining status; and the unions themselves will broaden their interests beyond merely wage and benefit matters to include a number of aspects of substantive police policy. In this they will be little different from other organizations of municipal employees, at least in the larger cities. In virtually every large governmental bureaucracy, the employees eventually organize in an effort to control, or at least powerfully influence, the agency's personnel system and thus to reduce administrative discretion over hiring, promoting, and firing.

§ 2.39   Some consequences of these structural changes

No one can know how these various legal, organizational personnel, and political changes will in time affect any given police department, to say nothing of departments generally. One cannot even be confident that efforts at change will continue in the directions now evident. Police reform has gone, after all, through several phases. During the 1930's, 1940's, and 1950's, there was a more or less continuous effort to see the problems of police corruption and political "interference" in police affairs as the paramount issues. Certainly those were the major problems in the view of the Wickersham Commission, as they were (along with the problem of police personnel quality) in the writings of August Vollmer, the dean of police modernization in this country. Concurrently with these concerns, but in time becoming a virtually separate (or at least distinctive) reform impulse, was the effort to apply what were traditionally regarded as the canons of correct management to police work: centralization of authority, clear lines of command, the separation of line and staff functions, the importance of formal training, and the development of systematic and impartial record and information systems. By the end of the

1960's, however, this view of sound administration was giving way to a different model that emphasized human relations over command authority, decentralization over centralization, job enlargement over job specialization, and the "de-militarization" of the police.

Concomitant with those changes in reform strategy have been changes in the reform goal. During the first two phases, crime prevention and criminal apprehension were assumed to be the paramount objectives; thus both anti-corruption and police reorganization compaigns were based on the view that dishonesty and inefficiency impeded crime prevention. With the arrival of the human relations/community relations approach, there has been a noticeable decrease in emphasis on crime prevention and criminal apprehension—the current reformers believe either that there is little the police can do about the crime rate, or that efforts to combat crime cannot succeed without there being highly-motivated officers operating in a sympathetic or at least cooperative community.

Since the pattern of change has itself changed, there is no logical reason to assume that the present pattern will endure. There are some reasons, however, to suppose that it is more than a passing fancy. Perhaps the most important is the fact that almost every large institution in our society has experienced for prolonged periods pressures to change in precisely these directions. Private industry, government agencies, hospitals, and educational institutions have all been shaped by both the demands for greater productivity and efficiency *and* the demand for improved human relations with the reconciliation of these demands occurring under the suspicious eyes of union and professional organizations. What is happening to police organization is not strikingly different from what has happened in other organizational contexts.

The problem for the police, and for many other government agencies, is that no one has devised as yet an adequate means to assess the consequences of *any* major organizational change whether directed at the objectives of efficiency, humanity, community relations, or improved manpower. This being the case, very few proposed changes are likely, for some time to come, to be defensible on the grounds of the relationship between their demonstrated benefits and known costs. Accordingly, changes will be selected on grounds of their *a priori* appeal, informed by an awareness of the mood of the times, and judged (at least until some way is found of providing better judgments) by some combination of political feasibility and command intuition. Until evaluative techniques have been developed and their use accepted, the case for or against any particular change is not likely to withstand close critical scrutiny. Thus, the changes being proposed now, like the ones proposed in earlier periods, are likely to be responsive to mood rather than of efficacy.

Since these changes, as shall be indicated below, are to some extent inconsistent with each other, the absence of a reliable and widely accepted standard for testing them will probably lead to a hit-or-miss, start-and-stop style of police reform. The need to make a change for the sake of change, coupled with the need to distinguish oneself from one's predecessor as chief and to meet political criticisms, will lead to the adoption, over the next decade, of many partially incompatible programs, a few of which will become controversial and thus stopped or modified, others of which will prove unimportant and disappear from sight, and some of which will endure but with uncertain consequences. Consider three potential contradictions in police reorganization:

§ *2.40   —Decentralization vs. centralization*

The demand for patrol strategies that are more responsive to neighborhood concerns will lead to continuing by team policing, beat-commander systems, store-front police offices, and community councils. This trend will be re-enforced by the awareness among administrators of the service and information-gathering function of the patrolman. At the same time, crisis events will lead to renewed efforts to centralize authority in the department in order to deal with public demands that corruption be eliminated, that particularly heinous crimes be stopped, or that civil disorders be managed. To break up corruption, patrolmen will be reassigned (thus reducing neighborhood contact) and the authority of local commanders curtailed (at least temporarily); to meet the public concern over street crime, patrolmen will be periodically instructed to "crack down" (by making more traffic and street stops, carrying out more field interrogations, and generally "showing the flag"). Some will be redeployed from their neighborhoods to high crime areas and others will find their neighborhood role overlaid by saturation patrol carried out by centrally-controlled units. The conflict between centralization and decentralization is inherent in the police function, and cannot permanently be resolved in favor of either strategy to the exclusion of the other. That there is such a conflict does not mean that police administrators cannot achieve at least a partial reconciliation by, for example, centralizing some patrol functions or units and decentralizing others. But whatever balance is achieved will be a temporary one, because the administrator must repond to demands for riot control as well as personal service, for law enforcement as well as order maintenance, and for ending corruption as well as widening discretion.

§ 2.41   Job enlargement vs. job specialization

Enlarging the job of the patrolman is currently much in vogue for reasons of both morale and effectiveness. Reversing the past tendency to take away from the patrolman various tasks and give them to specialized units (detectives, juvenile officers, community relations specialists, narcotics investigators) should have, in the view of many, the effect of making the patrolman's tasks personally more satisfying and organizationally more effective. The officer will have a wider range of duties, greater freedom in scheduling his own time, and accordingly higher morale; at the same time, he will be able to carry out follow-up investigations on the spot and provide more services to the citizen and provide them without the interruptions arising from other radio calls. Theoretically, there is much that is attractive about this conception of the patrolman's role, but as yet there is little evidence that the theory works. Studies in industry have already shown that there is no clear relationship either between job enlargement and worker satisfaction or between satisfaction and worker productivity.[2] It is entirely possible that many patrolmen may prefer functioning solely as a report-taker and crook-catcher and that the service and investigatory duties being assigned them will prove burdensome and unwelcome. It is also possible that the generalist patrolman will be no more effective, and perhaps less effective, than the specialized detective in making arrests and clearing crimes. Finally, it may turn out that the services many citizens require can only be provided by specialized units. Family crisis intervention, for example, can in principle be provided by specialized units or by beat patrolmen who have received specialized training. There is some evidence that the specialized-unit strategy works; there is as yet no comparable evidence that attempting to make every patrolman a part-time manager of family crises will work. It may well be that job enlargement will prove to be the optimal way of defining the patrolman's tasks; it is equally likely that the demand for specialized services can only be met with specialized units. Furthermore, we may discover that a patrol task definition that is appropriate for a middle-income suburban community is not appropriate for a lower-income, inner-city area. Until these issues are settled by evaluated experiments, we are likely to see further efforts at *both* enlargement and specialization, even in the same department.

§ 2.42   —*Upgraded vs. representative personnel systems*

Most police administrators publicly agree that it is important to recruit both better qualified and more representative officers. Privately, some will confess that they suspect these objectives are in conflict. Size requirements must be lowered to ensure an adequate supply of Puerto Rican officers, yet some administrators believe that smaller officers have a less commanding presence, and accordingly greater difficulty in asserting their authority, than larger ones. Educational requirements are being increased in some departments, but this may well reduce significantly the supply of potential black officers, either because there are proportionately fewer blacks enrolled in colleges or because a black with substantial college experience has better opportunities open to him than those afforded by police work. Intelligence testing of recruits is a controversial subject; part of the controversy arises from the fact, privately admitted but publicly denied, that in certain departments blacks are allowed to pass various tests with lower scores than those of whites. A final decision on suitability for patrol work is then made after the completion of police academy training or during the probationary period. The strategy may result in no dimunition in the quality of police manpower, but it is not likely to result in its appreciable enhancement if one believes that what these tests measure has any bearing on the capacity to perform police tasks. And that of course is the issue: no one has established what personal qualities are required for, or at least positively correlated with, optimal patrol performance. At command levels, the relationships between intelligence or formal education on the one hand and staff abilities on the other may be easier to observe, but it is important to keep separate in our minds what we require of recruits to enable them to perform patrol tasks and what we require of them to enable them to succeed in promotional competitions and command and staff responsibilities. In theory at least, many of the latter needs could be met by lateral entry, in-service training, or post-entry higher education. The conflict between the apparent demands of an "upgraded" patrol force and a representative one are likely to endure for some time, particularly since widely accepted measures of patrol effectiveness are likely to be slow in coming. Perhaps as important, even if intelligence, or college schooling, or particular personality traits are shown to be positively associated with effectiveness, it is not clear that there is any feasible combination of working conditions and money benefits that will induce large numbers of persons possessing these traits to apply for police work.

§ 2.43   The enduring features of police patrol

In many departments, the formal definition of the patrol tasks, the quality of the patrol recruit, and the organizational and legal context in which the officer functions will change marginally. I contend they will not change fundamentally or in ways that profoundly alter the nature of the patrol tasks or the way it is routinely performed. The essential elements of the patrolman's role are not defined by legal codes or the organizational directives, but by the relationship between a frightened, aggrieved, or angry citizen and a particular man in uniform. Over time, the nature of this relationship will alter as the social class (income, schooling, and life styles) of the participants in it change, but such changes cannot be measured in years but only in generations.

Further more, the differences in the emerging police organization as experienced by the patrolman or the citizen will be marginal because such changes as can be made will meet powerful sources of resistance. One is to be found in the growing constraints on the freedom of action of the police administrator arising out of political supervision and police unionism, another in the unresolved contradictions that exist, as the previous section has indicated, in the proposed changes themselves.

The most rapid changes will occur in those communities in which the resistance is minimal or the contradictions most easily overcome. Relatively homogeneous communities will express clearer preferences for a certain style of policing than will heterogenous ones. Middle-class communities will have fewer order maintenance problems than working- or lower-class ones, and thus fewer sources of police-citizen conflict. New communities will have greater opportunities for experimentation than old ones. But even in these places, it remains to be seen whether these changes affect the inner realities or only the outward appearances of police work.

If this view of patrol work is correct, then the most important implication is that police personnel and training systems must emphasize the performance of the patrol task as it is now understood and not as it may become. Unfortunately, recruits are selected and trained in ways that often bear little relationship to their inevitable responsibilities. Though I am not aware of any survey that bears directly on this point, most training programs I have observed emphasize the memorization of legal codes and departmental rules more than the development of skills at manageing social conflict. And familiarization with the law (which is of course important) is done inefficiently (by lectures) rather than efficiently (by programmed, individualized instruction). Furthermore, the precinct or station-house socialization process that occurs after the recruit leaves the academy probably fails to re-enforce the desirable aspects of recruit training and may in fact lead the recruit to believe that his formal training can be discredited or ignored.

It is easy to misunderstand the problem. What is necessary is *not* to replace training for police work with training for social work, *not* to separate order-maintenance and law-enforcement responsibilities, *not* to substitute "human relations skills" for the ability to make an arrest or take charge of a situation. The debate over the role of the patrolman has tended to obscure the fact that the patrolman does all of these things most of the time—though the law-enforcement, order-maintenance, and service-provision aspects of his task can be analytically distinguished, concretely they are thoroughly intermixed. Even in a routine law enforcement situation (for example, arresting a fleeing purse snatcher), how the officer deals with the victim and the onlookers at the scene is often as important as how he handles the suspect. The victim and onlookers, after all, are potential witnesses who may have to testify in court; assuring their cooperation is as necessary as catching the person against whom they will testify. The argument about whether "cops" should be turned into "social workers" is a false one for it implies that society can exercise some meaningful choice over the role the patrolman should play. Except at the margin, it cannot; what it can do is attempt to prepare officers for the complex role they now play.

Furthermore, the patrolman can no more be a "social worker" than he can be a "cop." Unlike the former, he wears a uniform, carries a gun, is a symbol of authority, and must often use force; unlike the latter, he rarely can make a "clean" arrest of a solitary felon—such arrests as he makes are typically of a misdemeanant, they frequently take place in a social situation, and they often involve controversial standards of public propriety and order (as in arrests for disorderly conduct).

The legal code is not irrelevant to performing in this role, but neither does it always provide an unambiguous cue as to the correct course of action. And even when it does provide such a cue, the other elements of the situation (for example, challenges to the officer's authority or self-respect) may obscure that cue.

A recruitment program must have the tested capacity to identify persons who:

(1) can handle calmly challenges to their self-respect and manhood;
(2) are able to tolerate ambiguous situations;
(3) have the physical capacity to subdue persons;
(4) are able to accept responsibility for the consequences of their own actions;
(5) can understand and apply legal concepts in concrete situations.

A training program should develop each of the above abilities by means of instruction in situations that simulate as far as possible real-world conditions. The object should be to develop an inner sense of competence and self-assurance so that, under conditions of stress, conflict, and uncertainty, the officer is capable of responding flexibly and in a relatively dispassionate manner rather than rigidly, emotionally, or defensively. These objectives will not be attained by simply multiplying courses that, *seriatim*, take up the law, departmental rules, unarmed combat, and "human relations." There is, of course, a growing awareness of the social and psychological aspects of police work, but lectures on such topics and the scrutiny of texts that urge the reader to become aware of how others perceive him are hardly adequate.

To use an analogy, a football team cannot be trained by having its members memorize the playbook, learn how to put on their uniforms, work out on tackling dummies, and study the rules of the game. The team must in addition practice together, experience physical conflict, hear the crowd noises, and make mistakes that can be corrected. Training for police work is even harder, since so little of it is a team effort.

The training conditions must be designed to place officers in situations of stress and conflict in which they must manage their own behavior and that of others in a manner consistent with (but rarely determined by) legal standards. Generating such situations in the classroom is not simple but the efforts of some departments have shown that it can be done in ways that lead the students involved to experience genuine emotions, lose their tempers, and feel threatened.[3] By observing the behavior of others and by hearing comments on their own behavior in these situations, the recruit can better learn what he can expect from others and (most importantly) from himself in real-life situations. If a way can also be found to continue this process of self-awareness and supervised behavior after being assigned to his first patrol duty, the patrolman's training can be made continuous rather than (as is now the case) sharply segmented into (often inconsistent) "academy" phase and "street" phase.

In sum, the future patrol tasks will be much like the present ones. There will be unplanned near-term changes (with the rise and fall of protest movements and collective disorders), some planned near-term changes (with alterations in the criminal law, changed deployment tactics, and new directives about priority targets for investigation), and perhaps fundamental long-term changes (with modifications of the class structure of society). The near-term changes, while important in their own right, will not affect importantly the routine patrol tasks; the long-term changes may have a great effect on police roles, but they are still too distant and uncertain to be the basis for present-day planning. The men recruited for patrol work, as least in the larger cities, will be drawn from much the same backgrounds as present-day recruits—they will come from working-class and lower-middle-class families, will be men of average to slightly better than average intelligence, and will be highly sensitive to ethnic and racial differences in our society. Some, perhaps many, will have higher levels of schooling (perhaps a year or two of post-high school experience) but it is not yet clear that this will affect markedly the way in which they will perceive or perform their tasks. For the next two decades at least, the central task of police administrators with respect to recruit personnel will be to devise ways of improving (and getting civil service systems to accept) selection standards and of reshaping training programs in order to develop the ability of men to handle complex, stressful, dangerous, and conflict-laden situations in ways that serve both law-enforcement and order-maintenance objectives.

Notes

1. James Q. Wilson, *Varieties of Police Behavior* (Cambridge: Harvard University Press, 1968), p. 30.

2. A useful summary of the inconclusive state of the evidence on the relationship between job enlargement and either morale or productivity is Charles L. Hulin and Milton R. Blood, "Job Enlargement, Individual Differences, and Worker Responses" in L.L. Cummings and W.E. Scott, *Readings in Organizational Behavior and Human Performance* (Homewood, Ill.: Irwin Co., 1969), pp. 377-393. The weak evidence between morale and productivity is discussed in the same book in the article by Arthur H. Brayfield and Walter H. Crockett (pp. 268-283) and in Victor H. Vroom, *Work and Motivation* (New York: Wiley, 1964).

3. Without wishing to endorse it without qualification, the Applied Psychology Workshop of the Chicago Police Department's Police Academy is an example of the kind of training experience I suspect will prove valuable.

PART 3

THE COURTS

131

III.   FUTURE ROLES OF JUDGES, PROSECUTORS AND DEFENDERS

§ 3.1 Introduction

The crime problem is likely to grow rather than diminish in the coming decades. By the year 2000 the population of the United States is expected to increase by 50 percent. This increase will mean a corresponding increase in the amount of crime. Increased social change, moreover, is likely to contribute to national instability—and more crime—during the next 30 years. Technological advances and rapid urbanization also will heighten the vulnerability of our society to criminal activity, making the act of the offender more harmful to personal and social interests and the offender more likely to escape apprehension.

These worsening crime trends have generated mounting dissatisfaction with America's system of criminal justice. While all components of the system have been criticized, it is becoming apparent that, as the Nation's crime-consciousness grows, the role of the courts in crime control is becoming the center of controversy.[1]

The court system in the United States is in serious difficulty. There are too many defendants for the existing system to handle effectively and efficiently. Backlogs are enormous; workloads are increasing. The entire court system is underfinanced. The crisis in the court system was highlighted by the National Conference on the Judiciary, held in Williamsburg in March 1971, which brought together the President, the Chief Justice of the United States, and the Attorney General, along with the chief justices of nearly all the States, in the interest of judical reform. The consensus statement adopted at that conference makes it clear that the courts are appropriately the subject of close scrutiny in the fight against crime.

The crisis in the courts has not escaped the attention of the general public. Critical discussions of court processing of defendants have appeared in the news media with distressing frequency. Citizens—as victims, witnesses, defendants, or jurors—experience delay, inconvenience, and confusion. These personal experiences contribute to an undercurrent of popular dissatisfaction that is undermining the public's respect for the American court system.

Perhaps the most significant source of dissatisfaction with the courts' role in crime control, however, is the personnel directly involved in the criminal justice system. Attacks upon the courts by criminal justice practitioners are increasing. Judges, prosecutors, defenders, juries, and police officials are among the most vocal critics. Former Police Commissioner Patrick Murphy of New York City, for example, called the entire criminal judicial system lax, unjust, and inefficient, and said it must accept a share of the blame for increasing crime.

These concerns are not new. The courts have been criticized institutions of governance throughout American history. Trial delay, rules of evidence, selection of judges, sentencing practices, due process guarantees, and other issues have generated persistent questions about the courts' performance in criminal cases.

Despite this continual concern, however, the court system in the United States has proven relatively resistant to change, particularly in its structure and processes. There are many reasons for this, primarily the local character of court organization, the independent status of the judiciary, and the conservative character of traditional judicial responsibilities.

Developments in recent years suggest that this institutional intransigeance has ended. A new sense of urgency has triggered a number of attempts to improve the criminal justice performance of the courts.

The President of the United States, the Chief Justice and several members of the U.S. Supreme Court, other federal judges, members of state and local judiciaries, and prominent members of the bar and the educational community have argued that the courts are in serious difficulty and have called for basic reforms.

These concerns, moreover, are being translated into action. A number of major improvement projects have gotten under way—more in the past decade than perhaps during the preceding 178 years of United States history.

Some of the more ambitious and important projects have been undertaken by such groups as the American Bar Association, the American Bar Foundation, the American Judicature Society, the American Law Institute, the Institute for Court Management, the Institute of Judicial Administration, the Advisory Commission on Intergovernmental Relations, the Law Enforcement Assistance Administration and participating state and local planning agencies, the National College of the State Judiciary, the Federal Judicial Center, the National Center for State Courts, the National Council on Crime and Delinquency, the Vera Institue of Justice, the National

District Attorney's Association, The National College of District Attorneys, the National College of Juvenile Court Judges, the National Legal Aid and Defenders Association, numerous research centers sponsored by universities and private organizations such as the Ford Foundations, and several major commissions such as the President's Commission on Law Enforcement and Administration of Justice.

However, these projects have not solved the problems underlying the inadequate performance by courts in the fight against crime. Despite efforts by many concerned people, the problem still remains a major one.

Only a small percentage of cases that go through all or part of the court process involves the full litigation to which much of the formal law addresses itself and which is embodied in the traditional image of criminal trial. In this traditional situation, the judicial role—whether exercised by a jury or by a trial judge—is to make all of the important decisions involved in the processing of the case. But seldom does reality correspond to this model.

Rather, the judicial role often is to receive, to approve, or to review a decision arrived at by other participants in the process—prosecutors, defense counsel, the defendant, probation officers, mental health agency personnel, or some combination of these. Judicial in this context, usually will mean the trial judge subject to review by higher courts, because in most cases the defendent will have waived his right to jury trial. But where the prosecutor decides not to screen a defendant out of the system and the defendant then invokes his right to a trial by jury, the jury, in effect, reviews the prosecutor's determination that the defendant can be found guilty and should be convicted.

Limited use of the full trial procedure is not only inevitable but desirable. Not all cases present issues best solved by traditional full-scale litigation, and such litigation often involves costs to the public and the defendant—both in terms of financial outlay and emotional strain—that are best avoided if possible. It must also be recognized, however, that extensive use of informal processes creates a dual danger.

First, public interest in the most efficient use of the criminal justice system to reduce crime may not be well served. The wastefulness and inefficiency of decisions may be obscured by informality and may become a pattern of an almost institutional nature. The informality of those procedures minimizes the likelihood that they will be scrutinized for efficiency and economy.

The second danger affects those processed by the system. Each person accused of a crime, whether guilty or not, has a legitimate interest in being treated fairly and, if guilty, in a manner most likely to permit his reintegration into the community as a law-abiding citizen, without sacrificing other objectives of the criminal justice system such as deterence. The informality of many processes creates dangers to those interests as well as to those of the general public.

Those who criticize the informal administrative processing of criminal defendants do so primarily because the administrative procedure involves numerous discretionary decisions made by the various participants in the process, especially the prosecutor. It is this discretionary nature of administrative processing—and the actual or potential abuse of the power to make discretionary decisions—that needs attention.

There are two approaches to the problem. First, emphasis should be placed on minimizing the adverse effects of discretion by structuring the making of discretionary decisions.[2]

One means of structuring is to raise the visibility of discretionary decisionmaking. Discretionary decisions involved in the administrative processing of criminal defendants are ones of low visibility— that is, they are seldom seen by observers of the system or, in many cases, by the participants themselves. As a result, it is difficult to determine what decisions are being made as well as why they are being made.

Where possible and desirable, the visibility of administrative processing of criminal defendants should be raised by requiring that rules for such decisionmaking be formulated, written down, and publicized. In addition, the reasons for making particular decisions should be articulated and recorded. If this is done, the substance of discretionary decisions and the process by which they are made will become apparent. This will permit an evaluation of the general operation of the administrative process, not only by outsiders but most importantly by the participants themselves, such as prosecutors.

Once existing practice is better understood, corrective action may be taken. Corrective action often will be taken by the participants themselves, and outside interference will not be necessary. The administrative procedures established for raising the visibility of the process also will make corrective action more palatable and will ease the task of insuring that reforms are effective.

Raising the visibility of the administrative processes also will make it easier to correct any specific abuses of the exercise of discretionary power. If general rules are articulated and the reasons for particular decisions recorded, a person being processed through the system is in a better position to establish that he was the victim of an unfair administrative decision. In many cases, this greater ease of establishing an abuse of discretion will enable defendants to obtain redress from within the system itself, as by informally appealing an improper decision to a senior member of the prosecutor's staff. Again, outside interference will not be necessary.

Another method of structuring discretion in the administrative processing of criminal defendants is the development of informal procedures. Too often American law has assumed erroneously that the only alternative to a completely informal and unstructured process is a highly formalized proceeding based upon the model of the criminal trial.

Procedures can be developed that provide some formality and structure for the making of a particular decision but that are much less formal than those involved in the formal trial of a criminal case.

A second approach to preventing abuse of discretion in informal processing of criminal cases is judicial review of discretionary decisions. Such review need not involve a complete reevaluation by a judge of the appropriateness of a discretionary decision. Review could be limited here, as it is in other areas, to the determination of a reasonable basis for the decision; if a basis were found, the judge could not then find that another resolution would have been preferable. Even given the limited scope this review would take, it is generally considered to be ineffective as a means of controlling administrative discretion. In some areas—such as the administrative discretionary decision to permit a defendant to plead guilty to a lesser charge—judges may rely on review.

Recognizing that in most criminal cases judges and juries perform only the limited tasks described here does not depreciate the traditional notions of a criminal defendant's rights to a full and complete litigation of this case, with the burden upon the State to establish guilt. This opinion should always remain open to a defendant, and recognition of the fundamental principles of American jurisprudence rightfully demand this. It is recognized that, in most cases, neither the prosecution nor the defense will want the court to perform this function. They will prefer to have, in effect, an administrative disposition.

The propriety of relying in part upon administrative processes in the criminal justice system was recognized by the U.S. Supreme Court in Morrissey v. Brewer, 408 U.S. 471 (1972). Holding that a parolee whose parole is being revoked is entitled to due process of law, the Court stressed that due process did not necessarily mean the opportunity for a full judicial evaluation of the propriety of revocation. After stating that a parolee is entitled to a preliminary hearing to determine whether there is probable cause to believe that he has committed acts that constitute a violation of parole, the Court made clear that this hearing could be before a non-judicial administrative hearing officer who only need be someone other than the officer who made the decision to revoke the parole. Although the Court also held that a more extensive hearing was constitutionally required before formal revocation of parole, it made clear that due process required only that this be before "a 'neutral and detached' hearing body such as a traditional parole board, members of which need not be judicial officers or lawyers."

In both the preliminary hearing and the formal revocation procedure, however, the Court stressed the need for notice of the matters at issue, disclosure of the evidence relating to those issues, the opportunity to be heard, and formal statement of the reasons for the decision. This is, in essence, reliance upon administrative agencies for the bulk of the work in the parole revocation decision. Similar reliance upon similar agencies is appropriate in other facets of the criminal process, although the extent of such reliance may vary depending upon such factors as the mechanical feasibility of providing a more traditional judicial forum for resolution of the issue in the first instance, the complexity of the issues involved, and the significance of the resolution of the issue both for the defendant and for society as a whole.

A similar approach should be taken in those situations in which it is clear that the major initial decision will often be made by whether to screen a potential defendant out of the system, the decision whether to divert him into a noncriminal program, the decision to accept a plea of guilty in return for some concessions, and similar matters.

In concrete terms, it is urged that in some circumstances the responsibility for these decisions be identified and legitimated in nonjudicial agencies, that rules for the making of such decisions be articulated and publicized, that the agencies be given discretion for the making of such rules and for their application to particular cases, that the bases for particular decisions be articulated, and that the informal administrative processes function fairly and efficiently.

This position is viable for three reasons. The first is efficiency. In many cases, the administrative process, especially when conducted under judicial supervision, would be as fair as the traditional trial. It is also likely, however, to be less expensive in terms of time, personnel commitment, and emotional strain on the participants.

The second reason is flexibility. Whatever the benefits of the fully litigated case, the framework in which it must be conducted leads to a certain amount of inflexibility. In many cases, the formal rules of the litigated case are technicalities in the sense that they do little to achieve any better result in the particular case. The flexibility of the informal procedures frees the system from such rules, makes more alternatives available, and makes it easier to invoke them quickly. Thus, informal procedures provide the flexibility to adopt a resolution that best accommodates the sometimes competing interests of society and the defendant.

The third reason is fairness. Informality is to some extent inevitable. To ignore it means to fail to deal realistically with situations that create dangers of unequal treatment and injustice; the process remains partially hidden and hence subject to abuse. To attempt to structure informality moves toward minimizing the chances of unfairness without depriving the informal system of its advantages. Thus it realistically deals with the problems where they are inevitably going to exist.

Such an approach might well, in the long run, maximize judicial influence over the handling of criminal cases. Professors LaFave and Remington have asserted that this could be the case in regard to police control of law enforcement decisions:

> The alternative (to continuing to attempt to maximize direct judicial participation in the making of law enforcement decisions such as whether

to search) is to abandon the ideal of actual judicial participation in most of the important law enforcement decisions and to structure the system in a way which will give primary responsibility for these decisions to the police or prosecutor.

To suggest this alternative is not to say that judicial responsibility for insuring fairness in the law enforcement process should likewise be abandoned. Perhaps this responsibility can be better discharged if the judge is not viewed as a direct participant in the making of law enforcement decisions, but instead is seen as the person responsible for review of the policies, as is generally the courts' relationship with other administrative agencies. This might provide a more significant judicial control over law enforcement decisions, particularly if courts were systematically to require police to articulate their enforcement policy and practice relevant to the issue in the individual case. Both courts and police would thus be forced to consider the propriety of the general policies applicable in a particular case, instead of merely considering individual situations on an *ad hoc* basis.[3]

The argument is equally persuasive when applied to decisions of participants in the criminal justice system other than the police.

Not all of the problems related to the court's role in the criminal justice process can be dealt with in this manner. In many areas this report attacks issues at the more traditional level—by recommending changes in formal procedure, by urging additional facilities, and making other proposals for direct action on the part of the courts and the personnel involved. But wherever appropriate, the report stresses that the interest of all those concerned with the criminal justice system will be best served by recognizing that judges must and should often play a relatively limited role. It is in urging specific methods of developing this role of judges—and the appropriate roles of other participants in court processing, given this definition of the judge's role—that the report proposes a relatively uniform approach to improving the courts' role in combating crime.

The area of direct concern to the Courts Report is the court processing of persons accused of crime. This involves those steps beginning with the first appearance of an accused before a judicial officer and continuing through the affirmance of his conviction and sentence on review. But court processing is only one part of the three-component system of criminal justice, which consists of police and correctional agencies as well as the courts.

The interrelationship among the three components of the system is a complex one. Each may interact with both other components.

All such interaction takes place in a context in which all of the components are constantly interacting with the general public. This process can be visualized as three overlapping circles—representing the police, the courts, and corrections—within a larger circle—representing the general public.

The interaction among the components of the system and the relationships underlying it—the interfacing of the components—are often characterized by conflict and even hostility. In part, this is because of competition for attention and funds from outside the system. But it also is the result of viewing the common task of processing accused persons from different perspectives.

Police agencies focus upon the apprehension of offenders. Correctional agencies focus upon the modification of behavior of persons convicted of crime and, to some extent, upon the identification of persons who pose significant long-term danger to the community. The courts in part focus upon the mechanical process of determining guilt. In addition, the courts pursue other objectives, which often involve furthering interests other than prevention of crime. To some extent, this focus upon other objectives—such as insuring that even someone who is guilty is treated with respect and dignity—is inconsistent with the guilt-determining function. Courts also have assumed responsibility for insuring that the other components of the system protect or further these interests, sometimes in ways inconsistent with what the police or corrections officials see as their appropriate objectives.

Interface problems usually arise during court processing of alleged offenders. In part this is because courts, as the middle step in the process, provide the natural focal point for conflict. But the courts, more than the other components, have assumed a general supervisory role in the system, and it is often over this supervisory function that interface problems and conflicts arise.

There are two distinguishable types of interface problems. One interferes with the functioning of one or more of the components of the system.

The other type consists of matters that, despite the lack of any demonstrable impact upon the functioning of the other components of the system, are sources of irritation to some participants in the criminal justice process and may interfere with their ability or willingness to perform their functions.

Several of the informal aspects of court processing are areas of interface concern. Screening—the cessation of prosecution—often is resented by the police as unjustifiably negating their efforts. It also has implications for corrections, because screening an individual out of the system eliminates the possibility that correctional agencies can provide him with the services they can offer.

Much the same is true of diversion, the encouraging of an accused to participate in a noncriminal, rehabilitative program by suspending or dismissing formal proceedings. Police may view such action as unreasonable leniency. Correctional agencies may resent prosecutors, courts, and defense attorneys attempting to pressure a person into participating in a program they feel is not appropriate for him. For example, officials may think a narcotics user is not an appropriate subject for a corrections program and may resist efforts to have him incarcerated.

The plea bargaining process—or the negotiation of pleas of guilty—is one of the most serious interface problems. Police often view the result of such bargains as unjustified leniency, brought about by a prosecutor's permissiveness or his inefficiency in not being able to try all cases brought to him by the police. Correctional officials, on the other hand, may think that plea bargaining reinforces an offender's belief that he can manipulate the criminal justice system, thus minimizing his motivation to participate in correctional programs.

Formal trial of criminal cases also poses interface difficulties. The delay in processing cases is a source of irritation to police, who see offenders with pending trials, free and engaged in further illegal acts. During the trial itself, police officers often must participate in or be present for what they think are useless procedural steps. When rules are applied that further some interest other than the determination of guilt, police officers may think the system is being diverted from its appropriate course. Police also may feel that the quality of the prosecution is inadequate, and that their efforts are rendered useless by the lack of skill or effort on the part of prosecution attorneys.

Correctional officials may resent the delay formal processing often causes. The technicalities of litigation, like plea negotiations, may discourage an offender from attempting to change his lifestyle by reinforcing his belief that he can manipulate the system. Both police and corrections officials also may feel that justice is perverted by inappropriate defense tactics or an injudicious judge. On the other hand, correctional tasks may be rendered more difficult by the resentment of a convicted offender who believes that he did not receive adequate defense representation at his trial.

The disposition of an offender following formal conviction has similar potential impact upon police and correctional agencies. Police may feel that sentencing is too lenient. Corrections officials may feel that some sentences leave them insufficient flexibility. The sentence imposed affects the extent to which correctional authorities can institutionalize an offender, how long he can be institutionalized, at what point he can be released from institutionalization, and—if he is not institutionalized—what an offender can be required to do or to avoid while under community supervision. Sentencing may have an adverse impact on attitude; lack of sentencing uniformity, for example, is often cited as a source of offender resentment that makes the correctional task more difficult.

The review process has similar characteristics. Delay during appeal often means that institutionalization is delayed and the offender is given the opportunity to commit additional crimes. Correctional officials may think that an offender, who spends effort and time pursuing means of invalidating his conviction, is discouraged from facing the need to develop new patterns of behavior and consequently is less susceptible to correctional programs.

Some interface problems are inherent in the criminal justice system because of the different perspectives of the various components. There is no feasible way to abandon the adversary system, so court processing will remain a means by which a defendant can manipulate the system. Nor can—or should—the courts cease emphasizing the need to treat guilty persons with respect for their rights even at the expense of some accuracy. They also cannot give up responsibility for insuring that other components of the criminal justice system do the same. The courts must remain the ultimate forum in which an accused or convicted person may question the propriety of the way he is being handled and get a decision on his argument.

Notes

1. National Advisory Commission on Standard, and Goals, *Courts*, Washington: U.S. Government Printing Office, 1973, pp. 1-7.

2. See: Kenneth Davis, *Discretionary Justice, A Preliminary Inquiry*, Baton Rouge: Louisiana State University Press, 1969.

3. LaFave and Remington, Controlling the Police: The Judge's Role in Making and Reviewing Law Enforcement Decisions, 63 *Michigan Law Review*, 987, 1011, 1965.

I. CRIMINAL COURTS

SOURCE: President's Commission on Law Enforcement and the Administration
of Justice, *The Challenge of Crime in a Free Society*, Washington, U.S.
Government Printing Office, 1967, pp. 128-141.

In many big cities the congestion that produces both undue delay
and unseemly haste is vividly exemplified in the lower courts—the
courts that dispose of cases that are typically called "misdemeanors"
or "petty offenses," and that process the first stages of felony cases.
The importance of these courts in the prevention or deterrence of
crime is incalculably great, for these are the courts that process the
overwhelming majority of offenders. Although the offenses that are
the business of these lower courts may be "petty" in respect to the
amount of damage they do and the fear they inspire, their
implication can be great. Hardened habitual criminals do not
suddenly and unaccountably materialize. Most of them were
committed, and booked for small offenses before they began to
commit felonies. This does not suggest, of course, that everyone who
commits a small offense is likely to commit a big one.

The criminal justice system has a heavy responsibility, particularly
in cities where so many men are so nearly anonymous and where the
density of population and the aggravation of social problems produce
so much crime of all kinds, to seek to distinguish between those
offenders who are dangerous or potentially dangerous and those who
are not. It has an additional responsibility to prevent minor offenders
from developing into dangerous criminals. It is a responsibility that
the system is in some ways badly equipped to fulfill.

§ 3.2   The lower courts

The President's Commission was shocked by what it has seen in
some lower courts. It has seen cramped and noisy courtrooms,
undignified and perfunctory procedures, and badly trained personnel. It has seen dedicated people who are frustrated by huge
caseloads, by the lack of opportunity to examine cases carefully, and
by the impossibility of devising constructive solutions to the
problems of offenders. It has seen assembly line justice.

A central problem of many lower courts is the gross disparity
between the number of cases and the personnel and facilities
available to deal with them. For example, until legislation last year

increased the number of judges, the District of Columbia Court of General Sessions had four judges to process the preliminary stages of more than 1,500 felony cases, 7,500 serious misdemeanor cases, and 38,000 petty offenses and an equal number of traffic offenses per year. An inevitable consequence of volume that large, is the almost total preoccupation in such a court with the movement of cases. The calendar is long, speed often is substituted for care, and casually arranged out-of-court compromise too often is substituted for adjudication. Inadequate attention tends to be given to the individual defendant, whether in protecting his rights, sifting the facts at trial, deciding the social risk he presents, or determining how to deal with him after conviction. The frequent result is futility and failure. As Dean Edward Barrett recently observed:

> Wherever the visitor looks at the system, he finds great numbers of defendants being processed by harassed and overworked officials. Police have more cases than they can investigate. Prosecutors walk into courtrooms to try simple cases as they take their initial looks at the files. Defense lawyers appear having had no more than time for hasty conversations with their clients. Judges face long calendars with the certain knowledge that their calendars tomorrow and the next day will be, if anything, longer, and so there is no choice but to dispose of the cases.
>
> Suddenly it becomes clear that for most defendants in the criminal process, there is scant regard for them as individuals. They are numbers on dockets, faceless ones to be processed and sent on their way. The gap between the theory and the reality is enormous.
>
> Very little such observation of the administration of criminal justice in operation is required to reach the conclusion that it suffers from basic ills.

There are judges, prosecutors, defense attorneys, and other officers in the lower courts who are as capable in every respect as their counterparts in the more prestigious courts. The lower courts do not attract such persons with regularity, however. Judging in the lower courts is often an arduous, frustrating, and poorly paid job that wears down the judge. It is no wonder that in most localities judges in courts of general jurisdiction are more prominent members of the community and better qualified than their lower court couterparts. In some cities lower court judges are not even required to be lawyers.

In a number of jurisdictions the state is represented in the lower court not by the district attorney but by a special prosecutor or by a police officer. Part-time attorneys are sometimes used as prosecutors to supplement police officers. In jurisdictions where assistant district attorneys work in the lower courts, they usually are younger and less experienced men than the staff of the felony court. The shift of a prosecutor from a lower court to a felony trial court is generally regarded as a promotion. Movement back to the lower courts by experienced men is rare. As a result there often is inadequate early screening of cases that are inappropriate for prosecution, lack of preparation for trails or negotiated pleas, and little prosecutor control over the proceedings. These inadequacies add to the judge's burdens and increase the likelihood of inadequate attention by the judge to the processes of adjudication and the goals of disposition.

In many lower courts defense counsel do not regularly appear, and counsel is either not provided to a defendant who has no funds; or, if counsel is appointed, he is not compensated. In the "bullpens" where lower court defendants often await trial, some defense attorneys demand from a potential client the loose change in his pockets or the watch on his wrist as a condition of representing him. Attorneys of this kind operate on a mass production basis, relying on pleas of guilty to dispose of their caseload. They tend to be unprepared and to make little effort to protect their clients' interests. For all these shortcomings, however, these attorneys do fill a need; defendants probably are better off with this counsel than they would be if they were wholly unrepresented.

In most jurisdictions there is no probation service in the lower courts. Presentence investigations are rare, although the lower courts can and do impose sentences as long as several years' imprisonment. While jail sentences of 1, 2, or 3 months are very common, probation appears to be used less frequently than it is for presumably more serious offenses in the same jurisdictions.

Every day in large cities hundreds of persons, arrested for being drunk or disorderly, for vagrancy or petty gambling, for minor assaults or prostitution, are brought before the petty offense part of the lower courts. In some cities these defendants are stood in single file and paraded before the judge. In others, 40 or 50 or more people are brought before the bench as a group. Almost all plead guilty, and sentence is imposed in such terms as "30 days or $30." A large part of the jail population in many cities is made up of persons jailed in default of the payment of a fine. The offender subjected to this process emerges from it punished but unchanged. He returns to the streets, and it is likely that soon the cycle will be repeated in all its futility.

Those few cases in which the defendant demands a trial may be inordinately delayed by the unavailability of judges to try cases. One result of this can be that witnesses, who are grossly under-compensated at rates as low as 75 cents a day, become weary and disappear. The courthouse in which the lower court sits is likely to be old, dirty, and extremely overcrowded. Witnesses, policemen, lawyers, and defendants mill around halls and courtrooms. Office facilities for clerks and prosecutors are commonly inadequate.

Study commissions have pointed out the scandal of the lower criminal courts for over a century. More than 30 years ago the Wickersham Commission concluded that the best solution to the problem would be the abolition of these courts. While the grading of offenses as felonies, misdemeanors, and petty offenses is an appropriate way of setting punishments is dictated by history and constitutional provisions, and is necessary for such procedural purposes as grand jury indictment and jury trial, it is doubtful that separate judicial systems are needed to maintain these distinctions. A system that treats defendants who are charged with minor offenses with less dignity and consideration than it treats those who are charged with serious crimes, is hard to justify. The unification of these courts and services may provide a sound way to bring about long overdue improvement in the standards of the lower courts. Existing differences in punishment, right to grand jury indictment and jury trial, and the like, should be retained unchanged; but all criminal cases should be tried by judges of equal status under generally comparable procedures.

The rural counterpart of the lower criminal court is the justice of the peace, who continues to exercise at least some criminal jurisdiction in 35 states. In a majority of these states his compensation is fixed by a fee assessed against the parties. In at least three states justice of the peace receive a fee only if they convict a defendant and collect from him, a practice held unconstitutional 40 years ago by the Supreme Court. The dangers of the fee system are illustrated by reports that police receive kickbacks from justices of the peace for bringing cases to them. A justice who regularly rules for the defendant is likely to find that he does not receive cases or fees.

In more than 30 states justices of the peace are not required to be lawyers, and the incompetence with which many perform their judicial functions has long been reported.

In recent years a number of states have moved to reform the justices' courts. Illinois has abolished some 4,000 fee-system courts and replaced them with circuit courts aided by 207 salaried magistrates. In 1961 Connecticut and Maine replaced justices with professional judges. Delaware, Florida, and North Carolina have taken steps against the fee system. New York, Mississippi, and Iowa have sought to attack the problem by requiring justices to take training courses.

Careful consideration should be given to total abolition of these offices and the transfer of their functions to district or circuit judges who have full-time professional standing. In states where it is decided to retain the office, all justices of the peace should be placed under central state administration and supervision; they should be made accountable to a state judicial officer and be required to maintain records of their activities. Justices should be salaried and all fines and fees should go to the state treasury. The fee system should be replaced and local government foreclosed from considering criminal justice a prime source of revenue. All justices should be required to be fully trained in the law and in their duties, and their level of competence should be maintained by continuing training.

The large number of justices in many states impedes reform. In many places positions are unfilled or the incumbent is inactive and performs little judicial business. Where they are retained, states should substantially reduce the number of justices.

§ 3.3 The initial stages of a criminal case

The criminal process disposes of most of its cases without trial. The frequent use by policemen of their discretion not to arrest certain offenders is well known. Prosecutors exercise discretion in a similar fashion. They do not charge all arrested suspects, they frequently have wide choices of what offense they will charge, and they often move to dismiss charges they have already made. Beyond this the overwhelming majority of cases are disposed of by pleas of guilty. Often those pleas are the result of negotiations between prosecutors and defendants or their attorneys. Guilty pleas may be obtained in exchange for a reduction of charges or for agreed-upon sentencing recommendations. In many instances it is the prosecutor who, in effect, determines or heavily influences the sentence a defendant receives.

Much of the criminal process is administrative rather than judicial. There are good reasons for this. The most readily apparent is the enormous number of cases that come into the process, especially in the Nation's metropolitan areas. If a substantial percentage of them were not dropped or carried to negotiated conclusions administratively, justice would be not merely slowed down; it would be stopped. A second reason is that the facts in most cases are not in dispute. The suspect either clearly did or clearly did not do what he is accused of having done. In these cases a trial, which is a careful and expensive procedure for determining disputed facts, should not be needed.

Finally, subjecting all offenders to the full criminal process is inappropriate. It is inappropriate because, as already noted, the substantive criminal law is in many respects inappropriate. In defining crimes there is no way to avoid including some acts that fall near the line between legal and illegal conduct, thus including some offenders who violate the law under circumstances that do not seem to call for the invocation of criminal sanctions. It is inappropriate because placing a criminal stigma on an offender may in many instances make him more, rather than less likely to commit future crimes. It is inappropriate because effective correctional methods for reintegrating certain types of offenders into their communities often are either not avilable or are unknown. As Judge Charles Breitel has written:

> If every policeman, every prosecutor, every court, and every post-sentence agency performed his or its responsibility in strict accordance with rules of law, precisely and narrowly laid down, the criminal law would be ordered but intolerable.

Because many important decisions are, and must be, made in that part of the criminal process that is essentially administrative—outside the formal court procedures—it is essential that administrative procedures be visible and structured. Today many administrative decisions are made hastily and haphazardly. Most of them are made on the basis of insufficient information about the offense, the offender, his needs, or the community and correctional treatment programs that are available to him. They often are made invisibly, unguided by explicit statutes, judicial rules, or administrative policies, and are not subjected to public, or in most cases judicial, scrutiny.

When such decisions are made before the charge, defense counsel are seldom involved. When guilty pleas are negotiated, there is often a pretense in court that they have not been. There is no way of knowing how many decisions have been made accurately and how many inaccurately, how many dangerous offenders have been treated with excessive leniency, how many marginal ones with excessive harshness. Since these decisions are rarely arrived at on the basis of carefully worked-out policies or by the use of systematic procedures and are rarely reviewed more than perfunctorily after they have been made, it is surely safe to assume that many mistakes are made.

The wholly desirable objectives of early diversion of some cases from the criminal process, and disposition of many cases through a broader range of alternatives in the criminal process, can be reached fairly, efficiently and openly in the pretrial stage. Three particularly important events take place during the pretial stage: the conditions under which a defendant may be released pending trial are set by a magistrate; a specific charge against the defendant is made, usually by a prosecutor; and a plea of guilty or not guilty is entered by the defendant.

§ 3.4 —Pretrial release

One-half or more of the defendants who are brought into a police or magistrate's court are released or convicted and sentenced within 24 hours of their arrest. The cases of the remainder, including all those against whom the accusation of a serious crime can be maintained, await final disposition for days or weeks or sometimes months, depending on the prosecutor's caseload, the gravity and complexity of the case, and the condition of the calendar in the court that will hear it.

The magistrate is empowered to decide whether or not such defendants will be released pending trial. The importance of this decision to any defendant is obvious. A released defendant is one who can live with and support his family, maintain his ties to his community, and busy himself with his own defense by searching for witnesses and evidence and by keeping in close touch with his

lawyer. An imprisoned defendant is subjected to the squalor,
idleness, and possibly criminalizing effects of jail. He may be
confined for something he did not do; some jailed defendants are
ultimately acquitted. He may be confined while presumed innocent
only to be freed when found guilty; many jailed defendants, after
they have been convicted, are placed on probation rather than
imprisoned. The community also relies on the magistrate for
protection when he makes his decision about releasing a defendant.
If a released defendant fails to appear for trial, the law is flouted. If a
released defendant commits crimes, the community is endangered.

The device that is used in most magistrates' courts to resolve these
complicated issues is money bail in an amount fixed by the
magistrate; a defendant without access to that amount of money is
remanded to jail. The ordinary method defendants use to furnish bail
is to pay a fee, commonly from 5 to 10 percent of the full amount of
the bail, to a bail bondsman, who posts a bond for the full amount
with the court. By and large, money bail is an unfair and ineffective
device. Its glaring weakness is that it discriminates against poor
defendants, thus running directly counter to the law's avowed
purpose of treating all defendants equally. A study in New York,
where the bondsman's fee is 5 percent, showed that 25 percent of
arrested persons were unable to furnish bail of $500—i.e., raise $25;
45 percent failed at $1,500; 63 percent failed at $2,500. A massive
side effect of money bail is that it costs taxpayers millions of dollars
a year. A community spends from $3 to $9 a day to house, feed, and
guard a jailed defendant.

Beyond this, evaluating a defendant's reliability in terms of dollars
is so difficult that, perhaps inevitably, most jurisdictions have come
to use what might be called a standard crime-pricing system. On the
theory that the likelihood of a defendant's appearance depends on
the size of the penalty he faces and therefore on the seriousness of a
charge against him, bail rates are often preordained by station house
or judicial schedules: so and so many dollars for such and such a
crime. The effect of standard rates and their disparity from place to
place is to leave out of consideration not only the important
question of a defendant's financial means but also the equally
important ones of his background, character, and ties to the
community.

Although bail is recognized in the law solely as a method of insuring the defendant's appearance at trial; judges often use it as a way of keeping in jail, persons they fear will commit crimes if released before trial. In addition to its being of dubious legality, this procedure is ineffective in many instances. Professional criminals or members of organized criminal syndicates have little difficulty in posting bail, although, since crime is their way of life, they are clearly dangerous.

If a satisfactory solution could be found to the problem of the relatively small percentage of defendants who present a significant risk of flight or criminal conduct before trial, money bail can be totally discarded. Finding that solution is not easy. Empowering magistrates to jail defendants they believe to be dangerous might well create more of a problem than the imposition of money bail, in the light of the difficulty of predicting dangerousness. Such a system also might raise issues under state and federal constitutional grants of a right to bail, issues that have not been determined by the Supreme Court.

A partial solution for the problem would be to provide an accelerated trial process for presumably high-risk defendants. In Philadelphia, for example, a special calendar for defendants charged with crimes of violence has recently been set up; such defendants are to come to trial no more than 30 days after indictment. It is still too early to know whether and how much this lessens the likelihood that released defendants will commit dangerous acts, but other studies have shown that the risks are closely related to the length of time that elapses before trial. The use of conditions and restrictions short of detention to control potentially dangerous persons may provide an adequate and more clearly permissible approach and should be tried.

In any case, money bail should be imposed only when reasonable alternatives are not available. This presupposes an information-gathering technique that can promptly provide a magistrate with an array of facts about a defendant's history, circumstances, problems, and way of life. The Vera Institute of Justice in New York has been a pioneer in devising such a technique. The Institute prepared a short standard form on which pertinent facts about a defendant were entered. Employees of the criminal court's probation department now question defendants as they await their appearance before the judge, and fill out the form. Often they check by telephone the facts they are given with the defendant's family or neighbors or employer. The entire procedure can take as little as 20 minutes, and by the time the defendant makes his court appearance, the judge knows enough about him to make an informed decision about whether bail is appropriate or whether the defendant can be released on his own recognizance, that of a member of his family, or his lawyer's. Since the Vera Institute established this approach, more than a hundred other jurisdictions have adopted the same or similar techniques.

The Federal Bail Reform Act of 1966 may serve as a helpful guide for states considering comprehensive legislation. The act states a presumption in favor of the release of defendants upon their promise to return, or on an unsecured bond. Judges are authorized to place non-monetary conditions upon release, such as assigning the defendant to the custody of a person or organization to supervise him, restricting his travel, association or place of abode, or placing him in partial custody so that he may work during the day and be confined at night.

The act contemplates the gathering and consideration by the judge of information concerning the bail risk presented and provides rational standards against which the facts may be measured. Procedures are established for the speedy review and appeal of bail decisions. Special provisions for capital cases and bail for convicted persons pending appeal permit the judge to consider explicitly the dangerousness of the person in deciding whether to release the offender. The criminal penalties for a defendant's failure to appear also are strengthened by the act.

A number of recent projects have sought to gain the speedy release of arrested persons and, in limited classes of cases, to dispense with the arrest altogether by use of a summons or citation. Early release and summons projects reduce the time between arrest and release, avoiding the situation in some cities where several days may pass after arrest before a defendant gets before a judge who sets bail. Since 1964 the New York Police Department with the assistance of the Vera Institute of Justice has operated a stationhouse summons project for relatively minor criminal cases (simple assault, petty larceny, malicious mischief) which is to be expanded to major misdemeanors and some felonies.

This project, which has been followed in other cities, does not eliminate arrest. Rather, the arrested person is brought to the precinct station where, after identification, booking, search, questioning, and fingerprinting, his community ties are investigated, much as they might be for purposes of bail. If the defendant is found to be a good risk, the precinct officer is authorized to release him with a citation or summons directing him to appear in court at a later date. In addition to the advantages of bail reform, this procedure saves substantial police time and has shown economies in the operation of lockup and detention facilities.

Beyond stationhouse release there has been an effort to displace arrest in appropriate cases by greater use of summons or citations by police in the street. This procedure, now frequently used for traffic or administrative violations, has been expanded to certain minor offenses that do not call for booking and in-custody investigation. An experimental project in Contra Costa County, California suggests the potential of this procedure. Using a computer-based police identification network, an officer can find out in a minute or less whether the defendant is wanted for another crime, and he can decide on that basis whether to use summons rather than arrest for minor offenses. This procedure has permitted the broader use of the summons in cases of petty theft, breach of the peace, minor assault, and other offenses, when the defendant can properly identify himself.

§ 3.5 — The diversion of cases before charge

The limited statistics available indicate that approximately one-half of those arrested are dismissed by the police, a prosecutor, or a magistrate at an early stage of the case. Some of these persons are released because they did not commit the acts they were originally suspected of having committed, or cannot be proved to have committed them, or committed them on legally defensible grounds. The police can arrest on "probable cause," while conviction requires proof "beyond a reasonable doubt." Therefore, some justified arrests cannot lead to prosecution and conviction.

However, others who are released probably did commit the offenses for which they were arrested. In some instances offenders who could and should be convicted are released simply because of an overload of work, or inadequate investigation in the prosecutor's office. In other cases the police, or more often prosecutors, have exercised the discretion that is traditionally theirs to decline to

prosecute offenders whose conduct appears to deviate from patterns
of law-abiding conduct, or who present clear medical, mental, or
social problems that can be better dealt with outside the criminal
process than within it. First offenders are often dealt with in this
way. So are persons whose offenses arise from drinking or mental
problems, if the offenses are minor. So are many cases of assault or
theft within families or among friends, of passing checks with
insufficient funds, of shoplifting when restitution is made, of
statutory rape when both boy and girl are young, of automobile
theft by teenagers for the purpose of joyriding.

The exercise of discretion by prosecutors is necessary and
desirable. However, it has found that more often than not prosecutors exercise their discretion under circumstances and in ways that
make unwise decisions all too likely. The haste and tumult of the
lower courts in large cities have been described. In addition to having
generally unfavorable working conditions, prosecutors suffer from
several other handicaps.

One is the lack of sufficient information on which to base their
decisions. A prosecutor who bases his estimate on the provability of
a case on a one-page police report can easily dismiss strong cases and
press cases that ultimately prove to have little foundation. A
prosecutor with no background information about an offender can
easily mistake a dangerous person with a plausible manner or story
for a marginal offender. Or, in the absence of background information, he can operate on rule-of-thumb policies—for example, all
family assault cases should be dismissed, or all automobile theft cases
should be prosecuted. A prosecutor with little knowledge of the
treatment programs and facilities in the community can either
dismiss or prosecute a case that might better be referred to another
agency.

Another want, particularly felt by young, inexperienced assistants
in large offices, is the lack of clearly stated standards to guide them
in making decisions. Standards should pertain to such matters as the
circumstances that properly can be considered mitigating or aggravat-
ing, or the kinds of offenses that should be most vigorously
prosecuted in view of the community's law enforcement needs. In
large offices where no such standards are devised and communicated,
it is unlikely that assistants will charge or dismiss in the same
manner.

A third deterrent to the systematic making of charge decisions is the lack of established procedures for arriving at them. Procedures, in this sense, does not mean an elaborate and cumbersome apparatus for transacting business that should be done with a considerable amount of speed and informality. It means setting forth the separate steps that a prosecutor should take before making a charge decision, and indicating when he should take them. Clearly, before a prosecutor decides whether to charge or dismiss in any case that is not elementary, he should review the case file and discover whether there is sufficient evidence to justify a charge and whether more evidence and witnesses than the police have uncovered are available. He should confer with defense counsel in doubtful cases. Prosecutors often fail to do such things not so much because they lack time as because no one requires them to. Greater involvement of court probation departments and the availability of probation officers for consultation with the prosecutor and defense counsel at the stage of the proceedings could provide this link. When discretion not to charge is exercised in felony cases, the prosecutor's disposition of the case and the underlying reasons should be reduced to writing and filed with the court.

Prosecutors deal with many offenders who clearly need some kind of treatment or supervision, but for whom the full force of criminal sanctions is excessive; yet they usually lack alternatives other than charging or dismissing. In most localities programs and agencies that can provide such treatment and supervision are scarce or altogether lacking, and in many places where they exist, there are no regular procedures for the court, prosecutors, and defense counsel to take advantage of them.

Procedures are needed to identify and divert from the criminal process, mentally disordered or deficient persons. Not all members of this group are legally insane or incompetent to stand trial under traditional legal definitions. The question of how to treat such offenders cannot be satisfactorily resolved by recourse to the definitions of forensic psychiatry. While recognizing the importance of the long-standing controversies over the definitions of criminal responsibility, insanity, and competence to stand trial, they continue to defy easy resolution. It is more fruitful to discuss, not who can be tried and convicted as a matter of law, but how the officers of the administration of criminal justice should deal with people who present special needs and problems. In common prosecutorial practice this question is decided on the basis of the kind of correctional program that appears to be most appropriate for a particular offender. If an individual is to be given special therapeutic treatment, he should be diverted as soon as possible from the criminal process. Screening procedures capable of identifying mentally disordered or deficient offenders as early in the process as possible can be improved by training law enforcement and court officers by making specialized diagnostic referral services more readily available to the police and the courts.

In some communities a beginning has been made in providing alternatives other than charge or outright dismissal. In several cities the police or prosecutors conduct hearings at which the attempt is made to settle disputes, to arrange restitution or damages, to calm family quarrels, and to obtain promises to keep the peace in the future. In some places the judge participates in this process, and there are procedures to place defendants under informal probation supervision without conviction. The laws of at least five states and the provisions of the Model Sentencing Act specifically provide for such dispositions, and they appear to be used in other places without specific statutory authority.

Alternative ways of disposing of criminal cases that involve close supervision or institutional commitment without conviction, call for protections from their abuse, protections that should be roughly comparable to those of the criminal law. Experience with civil procedures for the commitment of the mentally ill, for so-called sexual psychopaths, and for similar groups demonstrates that there are dangers of such programs developing in ways potentially more oppressive than those foreclosed by the careful traditional protections of the criminal law. When the alternative noncriminal disposition involves institutionalization or prolonged or intrusive supervision of the offender in the community, the disposition should be reviewed by the court.

The effect of these recommendations might well be to alter the responsibilities of the prosecutor and defense counsel and require more effort on their part early in the case. But these procedures also would result in the early elimination of many cases from the process and thus relieve the system from some of its caseload burden without sacrificing the proper administration of justice. The additional investment of manpower and talent would not appear as great as that required to make existing practice work with equal effectiveness.

Of course, implementation of this recommendation is heavily dependent on the availability to the prosecutor, defense counsel, and the courts of adequate factual information on offenders and of appropriate facilities and programs in the community for the diagnosis and management of offenders who are diverted.

§ 3.6   —The negotiated plea of guilty

Most defendants who are convicted—as many as 90 percent in some jurisdictions—are not tried. They plead guilty, often as the result of negotiations about the charge or the sentence. It is almost impossible to generalize about the extent to which pleas are negotiated or about the ways in which they are negotiated, so much does practice vary from jurisdiction to jurisdiction. A plea negotiation can be, and often is in a minor case, a hurried conversation in the courthouse hallway. In grave cases it can be a series of elaborate conferences over the course of weeks in which facts are thoroughly discussed and alternatives carefully explored. Most often the negotiations are between a prosecutor and defense counsel, but sometimes a magistrate or a police officer or the defendant himself is involved. In some courts there are no plea negotiations at all. There almost never are negotiations in the cases of petty offenders. And, of course, many guilty pleas are not the result of negotiations. The two generalizations that can be made are that when plea negotiations are conducted, they usually are conducted informally and out of sight, and that the issue in a plea negotiation always is how much leniency an offender will be given in return for a plea of guilty.

Through his power over the charge the prosecutor has great influence on the sentence. Usually a prosecutor has considerable latitude as to what to charge. Some sets of facts can be characterized as either felonies or misdemeanors, or as crimes in the first, second, or third degree. Some defendants can with equal appropriateness be charged with one crime or with several related crimes. The forgery of the endorsement and the negotiation of a check may be charged as one offense; or the forging, uttering, and possession of the check may be charged as three distinct crimes. Misdemeanors typically carry lighter penalties than felonies, and misdemenants are typically sentenced by different judges than felons. The degree of a crime determines the maximum and sometimes the minimum penalty that can be imposed, and occasionally whether an offender may be granted probation or parole. If a defendant is convicted on more than one count, a judge can decide to have the sentences run concurrently or consecutively.

A distorting aspect of charge decisions is that the prosecutor, because of lack of information and contact with defense counsel before charge, may be under pressure to make the most serious possible charge. This leaves him freedom to reduce the charge later, if the facts are not as damning as they might be, and places him in an advantageous position for negotiating with defense counsel on a plea of guilty.

Beyond the prosecutor's influence on the sentence by his power over the charge, he is, in many courts, empowered or even required to make sentencing recommendations. Much more often than not such recommendations are given great weight by judges. Sometimes prosecutors are able to see to it that specific cases come before specific judges. Since some judges habitually sentence more leniently than others, this consideration can be an important factor in plea negotiations. In some cases there is a tacit or explicit agreement by the judge to the bargain, and in extreme cases the judge may participate in its negotiation.

The negotiated guilty plea serves important functions. As a practical matter, many courts could not sustain the burden of having to try all cases coming before them. The quality of justice in all cases would suffer if overloaded courts were faced with a great increase in the number of trials. Tremendous investments of time, talent, and money, all of which are in short supply and can be better used elsewhere, would be necessary if all cases were tried. It would be a serious mistake, however, to assume that the guilty plea is no more than a means of disposing of criminal cases at minimal cost. It relieves both the defendant and the prosecution of the inevitable risks and uncertainties of trial. It imports a degree of certainty and flexibility into a rigid, yet frequently erratic system. The guilty plea is used to mitigate the harshness of mandatory sentencing provisions and to fix a punishment that more accurately reflects the specific circumstances of the case than otherwise would be possible under inadequate penal codes. It is frequently called upon to serve important law enforcement needs by agreements through which leniency is exchanged for information, assistance, and testimony about other serious offenders.

At the same time the negotiated plea of guilty can be subject to serious abuses. In hard-pressed courts, where judges and prosecutors are unable to deal effectively with all cases presented to them, dangerous offenders may be able to manipulate the system to obtain unjustifiably lenient treatment. There are also real dangers that excessive rewards will be offered to induce pleas or that prosecutors will threaten to seek a harsh sentence if the defendant does not plead guilty. Such practices place unacceptable burdens on the defendant who legitimately insists upon his right to trial. They present the greatest potential abuse when the sentencing judge becomes involved in the process as a party to the negotiations, as in some places he does. Undoubtedly the Spiro Agnew (former Vice-President) case will go down in history as one of the most famous plea negotiations.

Plea negotiations can be conducted fairly and openly, can be consistent with sound law enforcement policy, and can bring a worthwhile flexibility to the disposition of offenders. But some courts are able to deal with their caseloads without reliance on guilty pleas, and in other courts, particularly single judge courts, it may not be feasible to introduce the safeguards that are necessary for the negotiated plea system to operate fairly and effectively. In many jurisdictions it is desirable for judges and prosecutors to reexamine existing practices.

Negotiations should be more careful and thorough, broader, and preferably held early in the proceedings. It does not contribute to the soundness of the practice when negotiations are held on the eve of trial or in the public atmosphere of the courtroom hallway.

Prosecutors should be available to defense counsel from the beginning of the case for the purpose of discussing the possibility of a disposition by plea of guilty. Except in the most petty cases, such discussion should be had with counsel rather than directly with the defendant. These discussions should thoroughly assess the facts underlying the prosecutions's case, consider information on the offender's background and correctional needs, and explore all available correctional alternatives as well as review the charge to which the plea will be entered. To a much greater extent than at present the facilities of the probation department and other referral and diagnostic services should be available to the parties. In some instances it may be desirable to have a full presentence report prepared so the negotiating parties as well as the reviewing judge can assess the agreed disposition, although in many cases less elaborate methods of factfinding should suffice. While the emphasis should be on correctional and law enforcement considerations, the prosecutor properly may take account of the defendant's cooperation, testimony against other criminals, and similar factors.

The defendant should be able to include in the discussions, and cover within the disposition, all specific crimes, charged or not, that could be charged within the jurisdiction of the court. This discussion should involve the full and frank exchange of information, and appropriate provision should be made to insure that a defendant's statements and information disclosed are not used against him in the event of a trial. Defense counsel should painstakingly explain to the defendant the terms of the agreement and the alternatives open to him.

An obvious problem is insuring that the defendant receives from the judge the sentence he has bargained for with the prosecutor. Under existing practice the fact that negotiations have occurred is commonly denied on the record, and so is the explicit or tacit expectation that the judge will impose the agreed punishment. It is undesirable that the agreed disposition should be openly acknowledged and fully presented to the judge for review before the plea is entered. A desirable change might be that before the plea is finally entered, the judge would indicate whether the disposition is acceptable to him and will be followed. Should the judge feel the need for more information or study, the plea may be entered conditionally, and if a more severe sentence is to be imposed, the defendant should have an opportunity to withdraw his plea.

Inevitably the judge plays a part in the negotiated guilty plea. His role is a delicate one, for it is important that he carefully examine the agreed disposition, and it is equally important that he not undermine his judicial role by becoming excessively involved in the negotiations themselves. The judge's function is to insure the appropriateness of the correctional disposition reached by the parties and to guard against any tendency of the prosecutor to overcharge or to be excessively lenient.

The judge should satisfy himself and insure that the record indicates that there is a factual basis for the plea, that the defendant understands the charge and the consequences of his plea, and where there has been an agreement on sentence that the agreed disposition appears within the reasonable range of sentencing appropriateness. In cases involving dangerous offenders or career criminals, the judge should be satisfied that the agreement adequately protects the public interest.

The judge should weigh the agreed disposition against standards similar to those that would be applied on imposition of sentence after a trial: The defendant's need for correctional treatment; the circumstances of the case; the defendant's cooperation; and the requirements of law enforcement. The court should be apprised of all information concerning the offense, including appropriate investigative reports, grand jury minutes, and all information and diagnostic reports concerning the offender. If the agreed sentence appears within the reasonable range of what would be an appropriate sentence after trial, it should satisfy the need to deal effectively with the serious offender, and at the same time not be an improper inducement to the defendant to surrender his right to a trial. The judge's role is not that of one of the parties to the negotiation, but that of an independent examiner to verify that the defendant's plea is the result of an intelligent and knowing choice and not based on misapprehension or the product of coercion.

Since this approach contemplates that the judge will assess and indicate acceptance of the agreement before the plea is entered, provision must be made for those cases in which he finds the agreement unacceptable and in which the case, therefore, is set for trial. In such instances the judge's participation as arbiter at the trial would be complicated by his participation during the plea proceedings and the knowledge he obtained then. Provision should be made that when a judge rejects an agreement, trial and all further proceedings in the case are referred, if possible, to another judge. The return of the parties to the same judge with a renegotiated plea would tend to increase the likelihood of his becoming, in practical effect, a party to the negotiations.

A plea negotiation is fundamentally a negotiation about the correctional disposition of a case and is, therefore, a matter of moment to the community as well as to the defendant. If the offense is a serious one, a plea bargain should be founded on the kind of information, fully shared between the parties, that probation departments develop for presentence reports. In the District of Columbia the defender's office has an experimental project, in many respects resembling a probation service, for evaluating defendants and developing correctional plans for them. Such a service might well be one means of securing the full information that is needed in order to dispose of serious offenders effectively, as well as a means for developing the less complete information that would be adequate for arriving at dispositional decisions about minor offenders.

At the same time subtle and difficult questions are presented in some cases by an approach calling for full sharing of information. Defense counsel may well possess information adverse to his client, and the prosecutor may have erroneous information which defense counsel knows paints an unjustifiably favorable picture of his client. For example, an apparent conflict exists between the need for a frank exchange of information with the prosecutor and counsel's obligation to act only in ways favorable to his client. Obviously all exchanges in information must be explicitly authorized by the defendant, and if conflicts are likely, the problem is one to be considered by defendant and counsel before consent is given. While the consent of the client simplifies some aspects of this problem, it is clear that the expansion of discovery and the sharing of information early in the case will create new professional responsibilities for both prosecutors and defense counsel. Experience may provide guides for some of the problems presented, other norms may be provided by such efforts as those of the American Bar Association redefinition of the canons of professional ethics or the consideration of the role of counsel by the ABA Special Project on Minimum Standards for the Administration of Criminal Justice.

§ 3.7 Court proceedings

The cases decided at trial are only a small fraction of the total of cases, but they are most important to the process because they set standards for the conduct of all cases. The trial decides the hard legal issues, and reviews and rules on claims of official abuse. Trial procedures have evolved over centuries and in general have proven that they can resolve disputed cases effectively.

Unlike the administrative proceedings in the pretrial stage, court proceedings are continually being studied by lawyers and are now receiving intensive scrutiny from other groups. The Judicial Conference of the United States sponsors continuing studies of the Federal Rules of Criminal Procedure, proposed rules of evidence in criminal cases in the federal courts, and the habeas corpus jurisdiction of those courts. The American Bar Association, through its sections on criminal law and judicial administration and its Special Project on Minimum Standards for the Administration of Criminal Justice, is conducting broadly based studies that relate to many major areas of interest in the criminal law and court administration. The American Law Institute has sponsored intensive studies that have produced the Model Penal Code and a draft of a Model Code of Pre-Arraignment Procedure. The National Conference of Commissioners on Uniform State Laws has drafted several model state statutes dealing with problems of criminal administration.

§ 3.8   —The news media

Newspaper, television, and radio reporting are essential to the administration of justice. Reporting maintains the public knowledge, review, and support so necessary for the proper functioning of the courts. Critical inquiry and reports by the media on the operation of the courts can prevent abuses and promote improvements in the administration of justice. On the other hand, a fair jury trial can be held only if the evidence is presented in the courtroom, not in the press, and jurors do not come to their task prejudiced by publicity.

Two recent cases decided by the Supreme Court have dramatized how prejudicial publicity can endanger a fair trail. In the *Sheppard* case a murder trial was turned into what one court described as a "Roman circus" by an overzealous press and an overtolerant judge. In the *Estes* case the Court found that the presence of television and still cameras in the courtroom during trial destroyed the "judicial serenity and calm" necessary for a fair trial.

While unrestrained newsgathering in the courtroom can prejudice the actual conduct of a trial, a more serious threat to fairness is release to the press by police, prosecutors, or defense counsel of inaccurate or legally inadmissible information. Increasing attention has been given to regulation by law enforcement agencies and the courts of such statements. The Department of Justice and the New York City Police Department, among others, have issued regulations and standards identifying types of information that should not be disclosed to the press in pretrial statements by law enforcement officers. Thoughtful and constructive studies by a committee of the American Bar Association Project on Minimum Standards for

Criminal Justice and by the American Newspaper Publishers Association have identified the issues that must be faced in placing limitations on statements to the press.

The guarantees of both free press and fair trial must be scrupulously preserved and that indeed each sustains the other in a most fundamental sense. To avoid abuses which might affect fair trial adversely, reasonable regulations with respect to release of information should be adopted and enforced by administrative discipline within police departments, by professional discipline with respect to prosecutors and defense counsel, and in limited instances by the courts. In addition, courts should firmly control or prohibit those news gathering activities in the courthouse that detract from the dignity of a judicial proceeding or threaten to prejudice the fairness of a trial, while permitting legitimate, nondisruptive newsgathering.

§ 3.9   —Judicially supervised discovery

The relatively informal exchanges of information between the prosecution and the defense proposed earlier in this chapter are intended primarily for the case that will be disposed of before trial, although their usefulness for the fully litigated case is apparent. In addition to such procedures, there has been, in recent years, increasing interest in and expansion of the procedures for formal discovery of evidence before trial. Over the past generation broad discovery, by examination of witnesses and evidence, has become commonplace in civil cases, but its utilization in criminal cases has been slowed by fears that pretrial disclosure of the Government's case would lead to perjury and threats to witnesses, and that undue disclosure of confidential criminal files would impede ongoing investigations. The defendant's privilege against testifying forecloses the full mutuality of discovery by both sides that exists in civil cases and could place an unfair additional burden on the prosecution.

Several states, particularly California and Minnesota, have been experimenting with expanded discovery in criminal cases. Within the year the federal courts have adopted new rules providing freer disclosure to a defendant of his own statements; his testimony before a grand jury; medical, scientific, and expert witness reports; and tangible evidence in the possession of the Government. In California the defendant also may obtain the names and statements of witnesses upon application. In many jurisdictions, however, the right of discovery in criminal cases is extremely restricted or nonexistent.

There also has been expansion within constitutional limits of the prosecution's right to discovery of the defendant's evidence. In a number of states the defendant, by statute or rule, must disclose in advance whether he will assert particular defenses, such as insanity or an alibi, what witnesses he will call, and what physical evidence he will present. The Government in Great Britain is seeking legislation requiring the defendant to give notice of alibi defenses. Under the revised federal rules the court may make the defendant's discovery of the Government's case conditional upon his own disclosure of physical evidence and scientific reports.

After a case has begun, neither the prosecutor nor defense counsel has legal power to compel the appearance of witnesses for pretrial examination. In civil cases depositions and other examinations of witnesses before trial have been widely and successfully used, but in criminal cases their use has been limited in most jurisdictions to situations in which a witness may be unavailable to testify at trial and his testimony must be preserved. Prosecutors frequently can convince witnesses to cooperate by assertion of the prestige of their office, although in some places subpeonas and grand jury process are used for these purposes without legal authority. Expanded availability of depositions would provide for both sides a legitimate method to make these examinations which are so important to proper trial preparation.

§ *3.10   —Habeas corpus and finality*

There has been a rapid growth in the number of petitions for habeas corpus and similar relief filed in the federal courts between the 1940's, when a few hundred petitions were filed each year, and 1965 when 5,786 reached the courts. Our system is unique in the extent to which a person convicted at trial can continue to challenge his conviction in a series of appeals and collateral attacks in the nature of habeas corpus in the state and federal courts. Frequently this procedure is the only way he can obtain judicial consideration of substantial constitutional infirmities in the process by which he was convicted. The availability of such a remedy is embodied in the Constitution and is basic to our system of law.

The vast increase in the number of petitions, including a large proportion of frivolous petitions; public exasperation about cases in which punishment is postponed, sometimes for many years, because of successive hearings; the resulting sense of friction between the state and federal courts—all have reinforced the need for reevaluation of the use and administration of the writ. A result has been new federal legislation and extensive studies by the Judicial Conference of the United States, the National Conference of Commissioners on Uniform State Laws, and a committee of the American Bar Association Project on Minimum Standards for Criminal Justice.

The issues raised are complex and highly technical in several respects. In large part the increase in the number of petitions for habeas corpus is a reflection of the expanding interpretation the courts have given to constitutional standards applied to the criminal process. As standards change, the number of cases in which these issues can be raised by habeas corpus grows apace. In addition, the court rules governing such petitions have been liberalized to permit greater recourse to the writ.

Finality, the conclusive end of a case, is desirable, but so is providing a man in prison or under sentence of death every opportunity to press his claim that he is wrongfully held. This is complicated by the nature of the federal system, which in certain circumstances makes it possible for a single federal district judge to sit in review of state court actions and decisions that have been considered and approved by the full supreme court of a state.

A partial answer to the great number of habeas corpus proceedings is the improvement of trials. This means not only insuring that constitutional rights are protected but that the protection is fully documented on the record. Judges should take pains to insure that constitutional issues present in the case are confronted and decided.

A more important partial solution lies in the improvement of state procedures for dealing with postconviction claims. Much of the criticism of current practice is based on the sense that federal courts are becoming involved to an excessive degree in state criminal proceedings. But frequently when the federal district court holds a hearing on such a petition, it is because there is no available procedure through which the prisoner can obtain relief in the state courts. Far fewer than half of the states now have satisfactory postconviction procedures by statute or judicial rule. Most of the remainder rely on a faulty and antiquated system of ill-defined common law remedies that fall far short of the protection available in federal courts and of that which is constitutionally required. In a recent Supreme Court decision, Mr. Justice Brennan, after noting the considerable drop in federal applications from state prisoners in a state that enacted a modern postconviction relief act, described succinctly the attributes of such a law:

> The procedure should be swift and simple and easily invoked. It should be sufficiently comprehensive to embrace all federal constitutional claims. . . . It should eschew rigid and technical doctrines of forfeiture, waiver, or default. . . . It should provide for full fact hearings to resolve disputed factual issues, and for compilation of a record to enable federal courts to determine the sufficiency of those hearings. . . . It should provide for decisions supported by opinions, or factfindings and conclusions of law, which disclose the grounds of decision and the resolution of disputed facts. Case v. Nebraska, 381 U.S. 336,346 (1965).

Another pressing need is the more frequent provision of legal counsel to prisoners seeking release on habeas corpus. Legal assistance and advice for all prisoners seeking them should be supplemented by the assignment of counsel for prisoners with substantial claims to present to the court. The assignment of counsel in appropriate cases would tend to curtail worthless petitions, since petitions an attorney refused to sign would carry less weight in court. It would also unearth worthy claims that now are not presented or clearly articulated because of the ignorance of the inmate. Programs in Kansas, Wyoming, and Pennsylvania offer models for providing legal advice in prisons through law professors and students, as well as through practicing lawyers.

§ 3.11 —Appeals by the prosecution

In every jurisdiction in this country the right of the prosecution to appeal from an adverse ruling by a court is more limited than the comparable right of the defendant. The argument against retrying a man who has convinced a court of the merit of his cause has led to double jeopardy clauses in the Federal Constitution and the constitutions of 45 states. The same argument inhibits appeals that, if successful, would result in just such a retrial. But in most states and the federal system these considerations do not forbid all appeals by the prosecution, particularly those from pretrial rulings that are made before jeopardy attaches in the constitutional sense. Developments in the law, particularly the growth of search and seizure law and exclusionary rules governing confessions, call for a reexamination of the adequacy of the prosecution's right to appeal.

Under common practice motions for the suppression of evidence are required to be made before trial when possible. These motions are likely to become more frequent as a result of recent court decisions, and in an increased number of cases the prosecution will be blocked by a pretrial order suppressing evidence or a statement. Frequently the prosecution cannot successfully proceed to trial without the suppressed evidence. Yet in only a few states does the prosecution have the right to appeal from the grant of such orders, and in the federal courts the right to appeal applies only to narcotics cases.

Not only does the absence of a right of appeal preclude successful prosecution in many cases, including important cases involving organized crime, narcotics, and major thefts, but it has distinctly undesirable effects upon the development of law and practice. The law of search and seizure and confessions today is highly uncertain. This uncertainty is compounded by lower court rulings that restrict police conduct yet cannot be tested on appeal, and by inconsistent lower court decisions that can be resolved only on an appeal sought by the defendant.

When the prosecution is not permitted an appeal, law enforcement officers faced with restrictive rulings they feel are erroneous have available two courses, each of which is undesirable: They can follow the lower court decision and abandon the practice, in which case an authoritative decision by an appellate court never can be obtained; or they can continue the practice, hoping that in a future case a trial court will sustain it and that a defendant by appealing will give the higher court an opportunity to resolve the point. The first choice is undesirable because it results in the abandonment of what may be legitimate police practice merely because there is no way of testing it in the appellate courts. The second choice is equally undesirable for it puts the police in the position of deciding which court decisions they will accept and which they will not.

A more general right of the prosecution to appeal from adverse pretrial rulings is desirable. Controls may be needed to insure that appeals are taken only from rulings of significant importance and that the accused's right to a speedy trial is preserved by requirements of diligent processing of such appeals.

§ 3.12 —Immunity

A grand jury subpoena can compel the attendance of a witness and the production of books and records, but the grand jury has no power to compel a witness to testify or to inspect private books and records if their owner demurs. However, it is constitutionally permissible under proper conditions to displace a witness's privilege against self-incrimination with a grant of immunity from criminal prosecution. On the federal level immunity is available only in prosecutions under specific statues, such as those dealing with narcotics, antitrust, and Communications Act violations. Some states follow a similar pattern, while others have enacted general immunity statues permitting the prosecution to grant immunity in any criminal case.

Immunity provisions are particularly necessary to secure testimony in cases of official corruption, and the special need for the power to grant immunity in organized crime cases is readily apparent.

One serious danger, in the light of court decisions with respect to the application of immunity given by one jurisdiction to prosecutions in other jurisdictions, is that the grant of immunity to a witness in one proceeding will interfere with investigations elsewhere. Since facilities for communication between elements of the federal government are better developed than those at state and local levels, the problem is greater in state courts and grand jury investigations. The creation of interagency communication procedures where none now exist and the improvement of existing procedures are most important if grants of immunity are to be intelligently made. The Attorney General or other chief law enforcement officer must be in a position to ascertain whether other investigations are pending if he is to have the perspective necessary for him to choose which investigation is most important to the overall administration of justice.

Filing with the court a notice of the grant of immunity would reduce the possibility of abuse of authority by prosecutors as well as the danger of hidden immunization for corrupt purposes.

§ 3.13 —Perjury

The criminal law must offer more effective deterrents against false statements. The integrity of the trial depends on the power to compel truthful testimony and to punish falsehood. Immunity can be an effective prosecutive weapon only if the immunized witness then testifies truthfully. Perjury statutes provide criminal penalties for false testimony under oath, but the infrequency of their use and the idfficulty of securing convictions in perjury cases has limited the effectiveness of this criminal sanction.

Perjury has always been widespread; according to Pollock and Maitland's standard history of English law, "our ancestors perjured themselves with impunity." The requirements for proof in perjury cases are complicated by special common law rules of evidence, particularly the two-witness rule and its corollary, the direct evidence rule. In essence the former requires that the falsity of the testimony of the defendant charged with perjury be established by more than the uncorroborated oath of one witness, and the latter that circumstantial evidence, no matter how persuasive, will not alone support a conviction for perjury. There are, in addition to the direct evidence rule, decisions which hold that contradictory statements under oath may not be the subject matter of a perjury prosecution without additional proof of the falsity of one of the statements. Dissatisfaction has led to changes by statute in some jurisdictions; however, the common law rule prevails in federal proceedings and in a number of states. These restrictive evidentiary rules are an unwarranted obstacle to securing legitimate perjury convictions.

There is no apparent reason for the distinction between perjury and other crimes. Sound prosecutive discretion, proof beyond a reasonable doubt to a judge and jury, and the other traditional safeguards applicable to every criminal case provide adequate protection against the unwarranted charge and conviction of perjury.

II.   ADJUDICATION AND THE COURTS

SOURCE: Clarence Schrag *Crime and Justice: American Style* National Institute of Mental Health Washington, U.S. Government Printing Office, 1971, pp. 157-186.

Americans traditionally take pride in the idea that their society operates under the rule of law. But there is much controversy over what the rule of law means. Even the experts are far from reaching any agreement.

Some extremists, for example, contend that the law is nothing more than a system of rules governing the use of coercive methods by agents of authority. Court officials are seen as the community's authorized decision makers on legal matters. They speak for the people. Their decisions are the law. In making decisions, moreover, their only constraints are those they impose upon themselves. If a decision is overturned, the law is changed. However, legal changes can be accomplished only by officials having higher authority than the initial decision makers. Thus authority lends its power to the law. Individuals are not only obligated but also compelled to conform. Too much nonconformity therefore implies a weakness in law enforcement.

In this view social order is construed as a hierarchy of official positions, a kind of legitimate pecking order. From the top of the order to the bottom, an individual of any given rank has authority over those beneath him. This is intended to make certain that the strong will prevail over the weak. Except for the transition from physical prowess to legal authority, therefore, the rule of law is much like the law of the jungle.

Another extreme view is that the law should merely codify the basic desires of the people. More fundamental than any written laws, in this view, is the conventional moral order. Moral order consists of precepts and practices, often unspoken and adhered to without conscious effort, which grow out of custom and tradition.

Relationships among friends and close associates are allegedly governed by moral norms, as are the primary institutions of the family, the neighborhood, and the community. Written laws, by contrast, deal mainly with voluntary associations, contractual agreements, and relations among strangers. These laws may be needed to produce order when individuals do not share the same values and interests. Yet there is always the danger that laws will create barriers between people and in this way tend to weaken the underlying moral order.

Many laws are therefore considered unnecessary. Some are not viable. Unless they have a foundation in public sentiments and attitudes, there can be no assurance that people will conform. Nor does conformity to the law guarantee that a legitimate social order will be the result. A few laws are actually destructive of order. They require people to engage in immoral conduct. Examples cited by proponents of this view are the Nazi attempt to exterminate the Jews, the war in Vietnam, the execution of lawbreakers, the racist policies of many American institutions, and numerous other legal demands that receive strong opposition from various groups and organizations.

Hence the existence of a law is no criterion of its legitimacy. To be legitimate, it must gain willing compliance. Too much nonconformity implies a weakness in the law's substance rather than in its enforcement procedures. Indeed, if conformity requires the use of coercion, this is often regarded as sufficient evidence of the law's moral and practical inadequacy. It is argued that good laws have enough moral support to make forced compliance an infrequent event.

One of the problems with this view, of course, is that it overestimates the amount of moral consensus in modern societies. Conceptions of morality vary in time, place, and circumstance. Where conflicts occur, it is doubtful that laws can be written so as to meet the implied criteria of legitimacy. And if people are allowed to make individual judgments regarding their relationship to the law, perhaps there can be no legal system. Too much emphasis on moral values confuses the law with public sentiment and makes social order equivalent to the expression of a group's will.

By focusing on different aspects of the legal system—practices versus values—the above models arrive at diametrically opposed conclusions concerning the use of force. The first model says the law is what the court does. Coercion is therefore justified whenever it is necessary to carry out the orders of the court. The second model says the law is what the people determine it should be. Forced compliance, accordingly, is never justified unless it has the endorsement of a majority of the people. A more moderate viewpoint, asserted by John Stuart Mill and other libertarians, holds that the only purpose for which the power of the state can legitimately be exercised against an individual, contrary to his will, is to prevent harm to others. However, none of these views is consistent with present judicial procedure.

Neither an official's decision nor a vote of the people justifies the use of force under the rule of law. Both tyranny and mass action are regarded as inimical to democratic process. In theory, at least, officials and citizens are held together by normative checks and balances that prevent one from gaining dominance over another. Court officials are under the constraints of legal precedent and statutory enactments, while the people's interests are likewise expressed through authorized channels. If the legal system works according to its design, it should weed out capricious decisions, mob actions, unnecessary use of force, and other injustices.

However, justice under the law is an ideal towards which people are ever striving. Instead of describing current practices, it serves as a guide to future developments. Yet certain minimum conditions can be stated for the attainment of the ideal. First, the members of a society must consider its laws equitable. Second, the members must ordinarily conduct themselves by voluntarily applying to their own behavior the laws that are prescribed for everyone. Where official force is required to obtain conformity, the rule of law gives way to the rule of might. Third, the agents of authority, in responding to the legal transgressions that are bound to occur, must conform to official rules of procedure. Some discretion may be permitted, but it is always limited by the law and subject to judicial review. It is clear from even a cursory inspection that none of these conditions can be met in contemporary society.

How well the legal system appears to work may therefore depend in part upon one's perspective. But there also are more objective criteria for assessing its operation. One method, for example, is to measure the amount of public support for laws and judicial procedures. Another is to compare the system's prescriptions with its performances. Still another is to determine if its means are well adapted to its ends. Any significant trends in the information gathered by such methods should tell us the direction in which the system is moving.

Before attempting to make an interpretation of the available evidence, it may be helpful to examine the system's skeletal structure. Official versions of justice are encoded in substantive and procedural laws. Substantive laws spell out behavioral prescriptions and specify the penalties for any violations. These laws are ordinarily gathered together in a criminal code, and the actions of criminal courts are restricted to matters contained therein. Hence one of the maxims of criminal law is that the courts cannot legislate new

categories of crime, nor can they declare an act to be a crime unless
it is included within the code.

Substantive laws are of three kinds: universals, alternatives, and
specialties. Universals are binding on all members of the community.
Certain acts or omissions—murder, assault, robbery, or the failure to
wear clothing, for instance—are defined as criminal. Alternatives
designate a set of activities having equal status before the law. While
it may be against the law for a person to appear in public without
clothing, for example, many different styles of dress and adornment
are permitted. Specialties identify certain categories of people to
whom particular regulations are applied—doctors, employers,
brokers, landlords, and so on. By standardizing the relationships
between doctor and patient, lawyer and client, or landlord and
tenants, these regulations facilitate the division of labor that
characterizes modern societies.

It is generally assumed that a person who flouts the law should not
be treated the same as one who willingly accepts its restraints.
Penalties are therefore provided as an incentive for obeying the law.
Rewards for conformity, of course, would serve the same purpose.
But the administration of rewards may be more costly, especially if
violations are infrequent. Furthermore, the supply of rewards—
particularly those of a pecuniary variety—is often severely limited,
whereas punitive measures can be found in relative abundance.

In earlier times penalties were commonly graded according to the
status of the offender—nearly always to the advantage of the wealthy
and the powerful. More recent legal reforms have stressed the
universality of punitive measures, so that penalties are prescribed
without regard for an offender's age, sex, religion, race, or other
extraneous characteristics. However, universality applies mainly to
the written law. In practice, both the frequency and the severity of
punishment are known to vary in terms of the offender's background, his demeanor, and several other factors.

Practices of the courts, the police, and other authorities are
regulated by procedural laws. These laws outline the methods that
may be legitimately employed in handling alleged violations of the
substantive law. Procedural laws, then, place constraints on the
authorities in the same manner that substantive laws place constraints on the entire community.

American criminal procedure is conspicuous for the rights and protections accorded individuals suspected of having committed a crime. An accused person is entitled to a speedy and public trial. His innocence is presumed until guilt is established beyond reasonable doubt by evidence lawfully admitted in court. He is protected against self-incrimination or unreasonable search and seizure. He has the right to confront his accusers and to cross-examine them, to investigate the state's evidence, and to indicate any circumstances that might mitigate his guilt or responsibility. He is assured of legal counsel. If he cannot afford to employ an attorney, one must be provided for him at public expense. These rules are set forth in the federal constitution and the laws of the states. They attempt to make certain that official reactions to violations of the substantive law are confined to lawful procedures and to penalties prescribed by the substantive law itself.

Modern criminal procedures developed largely as a reaction against the star chamber methods employed by courts in the past. The inquisitorial courts, for example, held their sessions in secret. Cases were tried by a single person or a small group. The roles of judge, prosecutor, and defense counsel were combined into one. Torture and threats were employed in obtaining confessions, and the objective of most trials was to gain a confession of guilt. The innocent, as a consequence, were often convicted.

Yet it was not the secrecy or the conviction of innocent persons that caused the inquisition to fail. It was more a lack of public confidence and the system's inability to demonstrate that all evidence was impartially considered. Reforms therefore were not aimed only at improving the quality of official decisions. The development of public faith in the system was considered equally important.

In order to build public support, it was necessary to separate the roles of court officials, to make each serve as a check on the others, and to establish a coherent regimen for arriving at decisions. The adversary procedures were instituted to insure the independence of police, courts, prosecution, and defense. The criminal trial was divided into an orderly sequence of presentations by the prosecution and the defense. Provisions were made for appealing to higher authorities if the court's decision was improperly determined. Gradually the judicial process evolved to its present stage of development.

Law is not essential to social order. Order can sometimes be achieved by force and fraud without the benefit of law. Nor is a legal order equivalent to the rule of law. It can sometimes be established without public support if the authorities have sufficient power and integrity. But the rule of law can be attained only if people endorse both the law and its means of enforcement. The rule of law implies willing compliance. It presumes that the laws intended for all are employed by each individual in regulating his own conduct, and that the agents of authority—in responding to law violations—are acknowledged to be in conformity with the rules of criminal procedure. This, in the final analysis, is the essence of law and order.

§ 3.14   Criminal procedure

If human behavior is to be brought under the control of official regulations, provisions must be made so that laws can be proposed, formulated, enacted, interpreted, applied, and enforced. These activities involve numerous organizations that are themselves under procedural controls.

Agencies of the legal system can be arranged in a hierarchy of functions. At the top of the pyramid are venerable documents such as the Federal Constitution, the Bill of Rights, and the constitutions of the several states. Next in line are the legislative bodies which decide on definitions of crime and on appropriate punishments. Below the legislatures are the courts, where laws are applied to individual cases and questions of fact are resolved. At the bottom are the police and other enforcement agencies. These receive complaints, investigate alleged offenses, bring cases before the courts, and conduct programs of surveillance and crime prevention. Each level of the hierarchy has its distinctive functions to perform. Any encroachment of one agency on the prerogatives of another may destroy the integrity of the whole system.

In recent years the rapid growth of government has produced another kind of legal organization. Administrative agencies, mostly under political domination, have become prominent in fields such as housing, health, welfare, race relations, education, and the like. Here bureaucratic officials formulate rules and regulations, apply them in specific instances, and make a variety of discretionary decisions. Becuase they frequently deal with social problems and aberrant behavior, their decisions are important to crime control. While the decisions, in principle, are subject to judicial review, they are sheltered somewhat by executive authority. Administrative agencies have already enabled the executive branch of government to assume many of the functions previously performed by the legislature and the judiciary. Indications are that the scope and significance of these agencies will continue to grow, at least in the immediate future.

The processing of conventional crimes, however, continues to fall primarily under the jurisdiction of the courts. Most important in this connection are the trial courts. These are of two kinds. First are the courts of limited jurisdiction—justice courts, municipal courts, misdemeanant courts, traffic courts, and a variety of special tribunals. Such courts make decisions on minor offenses and handle felony proceedings through the preliminary hearing. Courts of general jurisdiction, by contrast, have much wider authority. They are empowered to hear felony cases, adjudicate them, and sentence the convicted offenders. As a consequence, general courts are ordinarily much better equipped in personnel and other resources.

In addition there are appellate courts which review cases on appeal following trial. Usually the grounds for appeal are that the original trial was not properly conducted, that a violation of the defendant's rights occurred prior to trial, that new evidence has come to light, or that the law under which the initial decision was made is unconstitutional. These courts, like the trial courts, are operated by the states as well as the federal government. Examples of courts that handle cases mainly on appeal are the Federal Courts of Appeal and the United States Supreme Court. The latter nevertheless has original jurisdiction over a few types of cases specified by the federal constitution.

Appellate courts have the highest status among the different kinds of tribunals. In most cases their judges have better training and experience, their libraries are superior, and there are more clerks, reporters, and other employees. At the bottom of the list are the courts of limited jurisdiction. This is reflected in judicial salaries, reaching as high as $60,000 for justices of the supreme court ($2500 more for the chief justice). State courts of appeals pay from $19,000 in Mississippi and Wyoming to more than $40,000 in New York, New Jersey, and California. Courts of general jurisdiction have an average salary of $23,345. Mississippi's $16,000 is again the minimum. Seventeen other states pay less then $20,000, while eight pay more than $30,000. Salaries are considerably lower in most courts of limited jurisdiction, with their magistrates receiving less than $10,000 in about 15 states. Sometimes the justice of the peace is paid by fees.

Most criminal proceedings begin in courts of limited jurisdiction. They are technically initiated against a suspected offender at the time he is arrested by the police. Sometimes an arrest is preceded by a warrant from the court. But the police have authority to arrest without warrant if there is probable cause to believe that the suspect has committed a felony. Misdemeanor arrests often require a warrant unless the offense is committed in the officer's presence. Hence there is some legal basis for the preference of the police to treat questionable cases as felonies. This preference is also supported by pragmatic considerations, since felons are more likely to be tried than misdemeanants and their conviction usually keeps them off the streets longer.

Following apprehension the suspect is taken to a police station where the arrest is reviewed by a supervising officer. Some cases are for various reasons terminated at this time. Others are assigned to detectives for further investigation. The remainder are prepared for presentation to the prosecuting attorney.

Unless it is decided to release the suspect, his case is booked in the police files by making notations regarding his identity, the circumstances of the offense, and the charges against him. Most of the individuals booked are lodged in jail, though the law frequently allows a magistrate to release suspects on bail or on their promise to appear in court. Confinement prior is sometimes used to facilitate the interrogation of a suspect, to impede his defense, or as a form of punishment. It is doubtful that any other step in the judicial process is attended by as much controversy.

The law stipulates that information supporting an arrest shall be promptly submitted to the prosecuting attorney. When he receives information concerning an alleged offense, whatever its source, it is the prosecutor's responsibility to determine if further proceedings are justified. In addition to deciding whether the evidence is sufficient for conviction, he may consider a wide range of alternatives to prosecution. Among these are *nolle prosequi* (decision not to prosecute) in order to protect an offender on his promise to compensate the victim, and civil commitment for narcotics offenders, alcoholics, sexual deviants, or the mentally ill. The prosecutor's role is not simply to obtain convictions but to judge the merits of each case in terms of the public interest and to arrive at a just disposition. Since the decisions made informally at this time have such low visibility, it is often difficult to hold the prosecuting attorney accountable for his discretionary judgments.

If the decision is to proceed towards a trial, the prosecutor prepares a formal complaint identifying the defendant, specifying the charges against him, and requesting the court to issue a warrant of arrest.

The complaint and petition for a warrant are ordinarily presented to a magistrate in a court of limited jurisdiction. Here the magistrate may refuse to issue an arrest warrant on the grounds that the complaint is insufficient or otherwise inadequate. In some states the magistrate actually decides on the charges to be made, if any. Other states allow the prosecutor to make these decisions, as already suggested. Especially in the latter states, the court makes only a perfunctory examination of the complaint. Since the defendant, in most cases, is already under police arrest and in custody, the court's response to the prosecutor's request is hardly more than a ritual.

Very soon after the warrant is issued, it is expected that the defendant will be taken before the magistrate for his initial appearance. Although the defendant technically has a right to counsel from the time of his interrogation by the police, it is mandatory in felony cases that a defense attorney be appointed for him at this appearance if one has not previously been employed. The appointment of counsel is also fairly common in certain misdemeanor cases, excluding minor traffic offenses.

Procedures are truncated in misdemeanor cases, and the defendant is usually requested to enter a plea at the intital appearance. If he pleads guilty, as the vast majority do, he may be sentenced immediately. Even if he pleads not guilty, he may be tried without delay in cases where the arresting officer and complainant are present in court. Otherwise, the trial, normally conducted by the magistrate without a jury, is scheduled for a later date. Court records show that defendants represented by counsel are more likely to demand trial or to have sentencing postponed in the event of a guilty plea. The threat of a costly or time consuming trial and the postponement of sentencing are often used by the defense for leverage against the prosecution in subsequent negotiations.

In felony cases the initial appearance is only one of the intermediate steps leading to trial. At this time the defendant is informed of the precise charges against him. He may renegotiate his bail, or try to make bail if held in jail. He also decides whether or not to have a preliminary hearing. Unless the hearing is waived by the defendant, it is usually scheduled for a few weeks after the initial appearance.

Scores or even hundreds of preliminary hearings may be held in a single court on a given day. A deputy prosecutor hurriedly tries to convince the magistrate that there is "probable cause" to believe a crime was committed and that the defendant committed it. He presents the minimum amount of evidence necessary to establish probable cause, at the same time trying not to reveal to the defense the strengths and weaknesses of the state's case. Since little can ordinarily be learned by the defense, perhaps the main advantage it can gain is in using the hearing to delay the trial. In most cases, however, the defendant waives the preliminary hearing, a trend that seems to be growing in popularity.

If the prosecution should fail to demonstrate probable cause at the preliminary hearing, the case is dismissed. But if probable cause is established, a formal accusation against the defendant is prepared for submittal to a court of general jurisdiction. Sometimes a grand jury of citizens hears evidence on the accusation in secret and returns an "indictment," while in other cases the prosecutor prepares the accusation and supporting evidence—called an "information"— without recourse to a grand jury. The grand jury is a costly and time consuming procedure that adds little to the quality of justice. Its deliberations are largely a reenactment of the preliminary hearing, except that the defendant is commonly excluded. The jury's task is to evaluate the state's evidence and determine if a trial is justified. Although a grand jury indictment is still mandatory for felony cases in the federal system and about half of the states, the trend is towards greater use of information. Some states make information optional, while others are turning to it almost exclusively. In many places, therefore, the grand jury is no longer employed to screen out unwarranted prosecutions. It survives in these areas mainly because of its occasional use as an investigative agency.

Information, when used in lieu of indictment, tends to speed up the charging process. It usually can be filed a week or two after the preliminary hearing, whereas the grand jury may take several months. It also seems to encourage negotiations leading to the settlement of cases without trial. When both prosecution and defense are willing to make some concessions, the initial charges are often reduced in return for a plea of guilty. In this way it is possible to minimize costs, risks, and perhaps harmful publicity. The extent of such negotiations may be partly reflected by the number of guilty pleas, which account for more than three-fourths of all criminal convictions, as many as 95 percent in some areas. This, of course, greatly decreases the actual number of court trials as compared with the potential amount.

In some jurisdictions justice by negotiation has received further encouragement from the recent development of "discovery" procedures. Discovery refers to the mutual exchange of relevant evidence by prosecution and defense prior to trial. The prosecution, for example, may make available for inspection the names of its witnesses, any statements made by witnesses or the accused, the testimony of its experts, its physical materials or exhibits, and the minutes of the grand jury. In return the defendant agrees to appear in a line-up, to speak for identification by witnesses to the crime, to be fingerprinted, to pose for photographs, to furnish specimens of material under his fingernails or on other parts of his body, to give samples of his handwriting, and so on. Although used extensively in civil cases, discovery has been limited in its application to crime. Its application in this area requires some modification of conventional views regarding the adversary process. Yet there is growing acceptance of pretrial discovery in several states. It appears to make better use of evidence, to speed up and simplify judicial procedures, and to lend greater finality to the court's dispositions. Moreover, it seems to be in line with recent Supreme Court Rulings, including the requirement that after a witness has given testimony at a trial the prosecution must turn over to the defense any statements made by that witness before trial (Jencks v. United States, 1957), or that the prosecution must disclose evidence in its possession favorable to the defense (Brady v. Maryland, 1963).

If all efforts at negotiation fail, however, the felony case is eventually tried in court. The last step prior to trial is arraignment of the offender in a trial court. Here again the defendant is read the information, or indictment, and asked how he pleads. If he professes innocence, his case is tried by a judge or a petit jury. In more than half of the cases, the accused waives his right to a jury trial. This means that the judge who presides at the trial is also the one who renders a verdict. In addition, the sentence is normally imposed by the judge before whom guilt was established.

Judges are known to differ from one another both in their proneness to convict and in their sentencing habits. Accordingly, the prosecution and the defense are much concerned about the previous records of judges who handle their cases. They play a game of maneuvers to get the right judge. Whoever wins the game has a decided advantage in the struggle for a favorable disposition. Rather than risk a trial before a hostile judge, for example, the losing side may be willing to make important concessions in order to settle by plea. Negotiations may continue beyond the date set for trial or even after the trial has begun. Both sides are always mindful of the merits of a negotiated disposition as compared with the probable outcome of a trial. Most of the uncertainty is in the trial. By giving evidence of likely court actions, therefore, the few cases that are tried have a determining influence over many that are not. They have an impact on justice far greater than their numbers would suggest.

In practice, American justice is largely a matter of negotiations. In theory, however, justice is the outcome of adversary procedures. Adversary methods are a form of institutionalized skepticism. They assume that the tribunal before which trials are held, whether judge or jury, has no prior knowledge relevant to any particular case. Hence the trial consists of competitive demonstrations in which prosecution and defense alternate in presenting the evidence most favorable to one side and then the other. The adversaries have the responsibility of establishing beyond reasonable doubt both the legal grounds and the factual basis for a decision. Each side is also expected to reveal any infirmities in the argument of the opponent. The result is often two contradictory interpretations of the same set of facts. Until the interpretations are fully developed, the tribunal is merely a passive observer. Then it is called upon to select the interpretation it finds most convincing.

If neither interpretation is compelling, the court may come up with a decision fitted to the individual case. It may acquit a defendant who, so far as the revealed facts are concerned, appears to be guilty. Or it may find him guilty, only to suspend his sentence or otherwise to circumvent the penalty prescribed by law. It may likewise convict an offender and treat him harshly for reasons having little connection with the evidence—to instill fear of the law, for instance, or to make a public exemplar of one who has committed a heinous crime. Thus the courts can ameliorate the law by making lenient dispositions, or they can, in effect, resurrect ancient ordinances, put teeth in them, and "throw the book" at offenders who previously, though technically in violation of the law, went unpunished. Few agencies other than trial courts and prosecutors have such power to manipulate the law for their own purposes.

Where such discretionary authority exists, there is always the possibility of privilege and favoritism, on the one hand, or cruel and unusual punishment, on the other. But the effects of unfettered discretion are not limited to individual cases. Without reliable assessments or public accountability, discretion also leads to many mixtures of policy and to many different procedural arrangements. Some legal jurisdictions, for example, use public defenders, others assigned counsel; some forego the preliminary hearing, others the grand jury; some emphasize negotiated justice, others conceal them; some try many cases, others very few; some try mostly by jury, others rely more on bench trials. Such procedural alternatives appear to a staggering array of combinations and permutations. Yet there have been only rare and piecemeal efforts to compare their effects by research and experimentation.

Lacking much guidance from research or tradition, the courts are left largely alone to handle their affairs. Such things as calendar arrangements, assignment of cases to judges, and other procedural details are usually decided by the individual courts. Although there is much diversity and flexibility in the overall picture, the procedures in specific courts are often rigid and arbitrary. Patterns accepted as legitimate, or even essential, in one court are viewed with suspicion in another. Each judge rules his own court in his own way, and most court workers tend to go along with him. Instead of having a unified court or an organized judiciary, therefore, we have many different courts and many different styles of judicial administration. To the extent that the courts function as autonomous units, of course, there can be no such thing as an American system of justice.

§ *3.15　Problems in the administration of justice*

Courts are the most formal and the most highly institutionalized parts of the justice system. They play a leading role in the process by which society—in reacting to criminal violations—identifies offenders, labels them, and administers punishment. They regulate and provide legitimation for many of the activities of the police and the correctional agencies. More important, they stand nearly alone in enforcing the procedural laws that protect citizens against mistreatment by the authorities. Inadequate performance by the courts is therefore a threat to both procedural and substantive laws. No other element of the justice system—or nonsystem, if that term is preferred—has greater significance for the rule of law.

Yet there is little reliable information on court activities, much less than on the other agencies of justice. Several states maintain fairly adequate court records, but national data are not available. The only national compilations of court statistics were made by the Bureau of the Census from 1932 to 1945. During those years, even though numerous attempts were made to standardize court records, the number of states involved in the reporting system was never greater than thirty-two. Judges were often resistant or diffident, and the effort was eventually abandoned. The result is that national estimates of court actions are mainly extrapolations based on data from a variety of sources, some of questionable reliability.

§ *3.16   —Overcrowding*

Exact information may not be necessary, however, for sketching the major problems. Overload is a good example. In spite of the constitution's promise of a speedy trial, court calendars are crowded and disposition are delayed to such an extent that this problem is obvious. Moreover, delays and overcrowding are getting worse rather than better, since current resources are continually swamped by the rising tide of criminal litigations.

About 10,000 judges are sitting in the courts of America—7,000 state or county judges, 2,000 city judges, and 1,000 federal judges. How many of these handle criminal cases is unknown. But it is certain that the number of cases handled runs into millions each year. In 1966, for example, court dispositions made in Los Angeles County were employed in estimating the number of prosecutions for the entire country: a half million felony cases, considerably more than a half million offenses involving juveniles, five million misdemeanors, and forty million traffic offenses, excluding parking violations.[1] No doubt these estimates would be much higher today.

The time needed for processing a criminal case depends upon the seriousness of the charge, whether or not a trial is held, and numerous other considerations. Some felony cases remain in session for months or even years. Many run for several weeks. The vast majority, however, are disposed of much more quickly.

This is evidenced by the Los Angeles data for 1966. To handle the workload in that county, every criminal court judge disposed of nearly seven hundred felony cases during the year, an average of more than three cases per day. Juvenile cases moved somewhat more rapidly. Assisted by referees, each juvenile court judge handled about a dozen offenders per day. Yet the volume of decisions was much greater in courts of limited jurisdiction. Here each judge handled about ten misdemeanor dispositions and preliminary hearings on felony charges plus eighty traffic cases per day. In the limited courts, eighty judges handled 25,000 preliminary hearings, 185,000 misdemeanor dispositions, and 1,500,000 traffic cases (exclusive of parking violations) during the year. This amounts to more than 21,000 cases per judge.

Nor is the Los Angeles story unique. One year a Detroit judge for instance, handled 20,000 nontraffic misdemeanors and petty offenses. Three judges in Atlanta disposed of more than 70,000 cases. Four judges in the District of Columbia processed 1,500 felony cases through the preliminary hearing, made final dispositions of 7,500 serious misdemeanors, and heard 38,000 petty offenses along with an equal number of traffic violations.[2] Assuming that a judge spends around 210 days per year in the courtroom, and assuming further that his time is approximately equally divided between the bench and his chambers, it appears that the average misdemeanor case is disposed of in about two or three minutes.

Even swifter justice occurs in some specialized courts. Traffic courts, for example, may arraign a defendant, hear his plea, and impose a sentence in an average of fifty-one seconds.[3] It hardly seems possible that justice can be dispensed with any greater dispatch. To achieve such rapidity, however, the courts must employ assembly line procedures.

Assembly line justice processes defendants by the batch. A batch is comprised of the defendants who appear in court on any given day. The members of a batch are gathered in a group and advised of their rights. Then they are herded by bailiffs into the aisles of the courtroom, arranged in line according to the order of their scheduled appearances before the judge, and moved forward step by step as names are called and cases adjudicated. Witnesses and attorneys wait in court until called. Nothing is permitted to disrupt the smooth flow of the line. Stragglers are promptly prodded into action by both the authorities and the mass of defendants. Once a case gets to the head of the line, everything is done to dispose of it quickly. The quickest disposition, of course, is a guilty plea followed immediately by sentencing. Sentences, to save time, are usually made by formula. A machine could be programmed to exercise as much discretion as is reflected in the decisions of some judges.

Many defendants plan initially to contest their cases, but very few follow through with these plans. Most are overwhelmed by the tacit norms and other pressures that keep the line moving. They are reluctant to ask questions, make comments, or do anything that might disrupt the routine. Contempt citations are issued often enough to make them aware of the power of the court. By the time the defendant reaches the judge, his sole interest is in getting out of the courtroom as fast as possible. The vast majority plead guilty, more than ninety percent in many traffic courts and other special tribunals having limited jurisdiction. But it is difficult, under the circumstances, to determine if such pleas reflect an acknowledgement of the charges or if they are more the result of conditions prevailing in the courtroom.

This is the kind of justice with which most minor offenders are familiar. They experience it first-hand. Although it may tend to shock the sensibilities of unsophisticated observers, the assembly line adjudicates more cases of law violation than the other judicial procedures combined. It is in some respects the cornerstone of American justice.

However, assembly line justice may work to the advantage of career criminals and other recidivists. Experienced defendants, knowing the pressures under which the courts operate, are frequently able to maneuver the system to their own advantage. They commonly gain concessions from the prosecution, for instance, by threatening to demand a trial or by otherwise convincing the prosecutor that a trial would not be in his interest. Concessions ordinarily entail reduced charges, elimination of some allegations, or the promise of light sentences. Many veteran offenders believe that, even if no specific concessions are involved, guilty pleas generally result in lighter sentences than those imposed after trial. Moreover, this view is consistent with much of the evidence on sentencing, especially in courts of limited jurisdiction. Most of this evidence suggests that defendants who plead guilty do in fact tend to get preferential treatment.[4]

Preferential treatment is not surprising if we consider the importance of guilty pleas in controlling the workloads of the courts. Most courts—especially trial courts—have such a backlog of unfinished cases that delays are inevitable. Some authorities fear that any appreciable increase in trials may force the courts into a dilemma where they have to choose between interminable delays and rejection of the adversary system. In their view, then, assembly line justice may be necessary to preserve access to trials in selected cases.

By manufacturing pleas of guilt, assembly line justice holds down the number of court trials. It should be realized that slight variations in the proportion of cases disposed of by plea have a great influence on the number of trials. Assume, for example, that in a certain court the proportion of pleas were to be reduced from, say, 85 percent to 75 percent. If the total number of cases remained constant, such a reduction would produce a 67 percent increase in the number of trials. Specifically, the proportion of trials would be increased to 25 percent from the original 15 percent. On this basis alone, it is reasonable to expect that the court may view with alarm any procedural changes designed to lessen the amount of pleading.

Hence the assembly line seems likely to survive. Its elimination would require either a tremendous enlargement of court personnel or the development of substitute procedures and other innovations that do not add to the court's workload. Yet, if official personnel were in adequate supply, they would perhaps place severe limitations on any innovative efforts. This further illustrates the disorganization of the system of justice. Although the system prescribes trials and adversary procedures, its survival demands the continued expansion of practices such as the assembly line and other forms of negotiated justice.

Increased emphasis on negotiations tends to enhance the power of the prosecutor while limiting that of the judge. It also tends to conceal judicial procedures from public view, thereby making it more difficult to hold the authorities accountable for many of their decisions. Moreover, negotiated decisions are often justified in terms of the system's needs, rather than the merits of the individual case. What the system needs, in the view of its agents, is greater efficiency in case processing—efficiency as measured in volume of cases per unit of time. Hoping to improve efficiency, some states have enacted statutes requiring that criminal trials be held within a specified time after the filing of an indictment or information. California, for instance, has a limit of sixty days. Unless the defendant consents to a delay, failure of the prosecution to meet the deadline results in dismissal of the case.

§ 3.17   —Delay

In spite of efforts to speed up the trial process, however, delays in most places have been increasing. Data from the federal court in the District of Columbia illustrate some of the trends. In 1966 the median amount of time between filing and termination of cases convicted by a jury was 6.3 months. For all criminal cases, whether tried or not, the median interval of time from filing to termination was 4.8 months. By comparison, the interval in 1962 was 3.0 months; in 1956, 2.4 months; and in 1950 it was only 1.2 months. This indicates that between 1950 and 1966 the time required for disposing of criminal cases increased fourfold. During these years approximately 70 percent of all felony prosecutions occurred without trial. The number of cases filed in this court was about 30 percent lower in 1966 than in 1950, while the proportion of cases pending at the end of the year increased from 25 percent in 1950 to 44 percent in 1966.

Similar conditions are found in state and local courts. At the end of 1969, for example, New York City's criminal courts had a backlog of more than 520,000 nontraffic cases, enough untried defendants to populate a medium sized city. About 177,000 of the defendants could not be located—itself an indication of inefficiency. The remaining 343,000 alleged offenders were experiencing around a year's delay between indictment and trial. Nearly 2,000 of these had been held from three to twelve months in jail without trial; 202 from one to two years, and 11 for more than two years.[5] Under such circumstances, recent congressional action with respect to preventive detention may serve mainly to legitimate practices that apparently are already prevalent.

Delays are a complex problem. They have a feedback effect on one another that tends to escalate their frequency and duration. They reduce the relevance of any punitive reactions. They impede justice by making it harder to preserve evidence, to locate witnesses, or to keep the complainants interested in assisting the prosecution. For these reasons delays aid the guilty far more than the innocent.

Yet delays seem to be increasing everywhere—even where reductions have occurred in the number of cases brought before the court, in the number of trials, and in the rate of convictions. Nor are they prevented by increasing the number of court officials. For instance, in 1961, after a 25 percent augmentation of the judicial manpower in federal district courts, delays continued to grow while criminal dispositions increased by only 5 percent.

No doubt the recent development of public interest in judicial matters is a factor. Judges are more often required to justify their court records. Records consume time both in their preparation and their use. To illustrate, the Los Angeles County courts of limited jurisdiction produce around 1.7 million sheets of records in a year.[6] In addition, the clerk's file on felony cases runs from about five to twenty pages, with exceptional cases consuming several hundred pages. Since felony dispositions amount to more than 19,000 per year in this county, their records probably include more than 200,000 sheets of information. This amounts to a total of around two million sheets. Assuming that these could be read at a rate of two sheets per minute, it would take a person two thousand days to read the materials produced in one year. Eight social workers; researchers, or legal reporters would be employed full time merely to read the materials. Digesting the information, analyzing it, and preparing it for public consumption would probably take them another year. Such work is nevertheless a necessary first step if the community is really to be informed regarding court operations. Hence there is obvious need for a judicial information system utilizing microfilm and magnetic tape along with computerized storage, retrieval and processing if this task is to be performed. The same system would also provide the documentation needed to evaluate the effectiveness of court procedures.

Reflecting the growing interest in judicial affairs are many appellate decisions and legislative enactments that regulate the conduct of courts and protect the rights of defendants. These have undoubtedly increased the amount of time required to process a criminal case. Federal rules of procedure, for example, demand a pretrial hearing on motions to suppress evidence, and they allow for the renewal of such motions at the time of trial. Many states have similar rules. Among the most important court decisions are those in the cases of Durham, Jencks, Brady, Mallory, Miranda and Escobedo. Durham resulted in a substantial increase in the number of mental examinations relating to the defendant's culpability. Jencks and Mallory pertain mainly to the admissibility of evidence. When a confession is challenged under the Mallory rule, the court must hold a hearing in the absence of the jury to determine if the confession can be admitted. Under the Jencks ruling, time is consumed during trial while the court decides if certain witnesses for the prosecution must be produced for examination by the defense counsel. Miranda and Escobedo hold the court responsible for determining the legitimacy of investigations conducted by the police. These rulings, and others like them, may tend to delay disposition even though their primary intent is to insure a fair trial.

Delays that occur for the above reasons are partly a matter of logistics. They could be greatly reduced by better staffing, scheduling and case processing. Information systems should go far towards alleviating problems of schedule and procedure, while additions to court personnel should also be helpful.

Many other delays, however, seem to have a different motivation. For instance, the cases of defendants released on bail are processed much slower than those of persons held in jail. The previously mentioned District of Columbia study shows that in 1950 the jailed defendants were sentenced or discharged in an average of 62 days, compared with 104 days for those granted bail. Both groups, of course, took longer in 1965—116 days for jailees and 142 days for bailees. In addition, the jailed suspects have a decidedly higher rate of convictions. Thus, defendants with adequate financial resources are able to remain out of jail prior to trial and to delay their convictions longer. They also have a much better chance of avoiding conviction.

Other delays that appear to work to the advantage of selected defendants are related to the filing of motions, continuances and appeals. Motions may be made for the discovery of information, mental examinations, suppression of certain evidence, severance of the cases of codefendants, post conviction remedies, and so on. Such motions are being filed with increasing frequency. In the federal court of the District of Columbia, for example, the number of motions filed was more than 60 percent greater in 1965 than in 1950 despite a reduction in the number of cases brought before the court. The greater the number of motions, the longer the lapse of time between indictment and disposition. When no motions were filed, the 1965 cases were disposed of in 74 days. By contrast, 153 days were needed for cases having two or more motions. The time lag is also influenced by the type of motion. Thus, mental examinations, which are called for in 10 or 15 percent of the felony trials, usually suspend court proceedings for at least 60 days.

Continuances are increasing even more rapidly. According to the District of Columbia data, their number grew between 1950 and 1965 by more than 300 percent. Furthermore, the average time per continuance increased from 29 days in 1950 to 94 days in 1965. In the latter year, nearly 70 percent of the continuances were requested by the litigants, about 45 percent by the defense and 25 percent by the prosecution. The remaining 30 percent were necessary for the court to solve problems of scheduling due to overcrowded calendars or insufficient time to terminate preceding cases.

Appeals also are increasing. The average time consumed by an appeal is approximately one year, though this varies from six months in some courts to more than two years in others. A number of courts, especially those in the federal system, are reducing this interval by weeding out the appeals that can be disposed of without oral argument. It is contemplated that such screening methods may result in the handling of most appeals in about six months. The greater use of appellate procedures, however, will continue to delay final dispositions even if the process is considerably accelerated.

Perhaps it is the case that delay has evolved into a strategy of crime control. Both the prosecution and the defense use it in achieving goals that might be jeopardized by the expeditious processing of criminal cases. The prosecution, by tactical delays, can sometimes confine offenders longer in jail without trial than they would be likely to serve if convicted. The defense, likewise, can employ the tactics of delay in its own interest. If it exploits all opportunities for motion, appeals, and the like, official action may be deferred until community interest in the case has diminished and the defendant has had a chance to set his affairs in order.

Nor are more strenuous measures unknown. Stories may be planted in the mass media so as to make a change of venue inevitable. Officials and witnesses may be bribed, threatened, or otherwise influenced illegally. Evidence may be misplaced or mishandled. Occasionally a judge is deliberately goaded into errors that provide grounds for appeal or dismissal. Even after conviction there are ways in which the execution of a sentence may be put off almost indefinitely. Nearly everyone is familiar with cases of entertainers, athletes, or other famous persons who have remained at large for years following arrest or conviction.

§ 3.18   —Discrimination

When it comes to delays and other strategies of negotiated justice, rich defendants have a great advantage over poor ones. Poor defendants are unable to employ their own attorneys. Instead, they have access to public defenders or to counsel assigned by the court. For minor offenses they usually have no lawyer at all. Unable to make bail, they are held in jail before trial. They plead guilty more often than defendants who retain their own counsel; they are more frequently sentenced to prison; and they are less inclined to use legal remedies.[7] Indeed, the vast majority of poor people never utilize the services of an attorney, whereas most middleclass citizens do so. Lacking the resources and know-how for legal negotiations, the poor are more likely to rely on extra-legal devices.

However, the lack of resources is only one of the problems. The law itself often works to the disadvantage of the poor. Some offenses, such as vagrancy or "the lack of visible means of support," are clearly oriented towards the lower classes. While the means of support are hardly more visible among some of the wealthy, the latter rarely come under the purview of these laws. Poverty and crime are often intermixed in the law. Mothers of illegitimate children have been prosecuted under otherwise unenforced adultery and fornication laws. Mothers receiving support for needy children have had their homes subjected to night raids without search warrants in order for the authorities to discover if there were "a man in the house." Continued residence in an area has sometimes been established as a precondition for the receipt of welfare benefits. People have been evicted from their homes for violation of welfare regulations. At least one state has attempted to reduce medical care for indigents. These are some illustrations of how the law discriminates against the disadvantaged.

The agencies of justice, too, are involved in discrimination. In the Detroit riots of 1967, for example, a total of 7,200 persons were arrested. Nearly all of those arrested were black, indigents, or of low income. Subsequently 4,260 of these individuals were brought before the criminal court, three-fourths of them (3,230) charged with looting, a felony calling for a five-year sentence. This charge laid the foundation for high bail and for extended delay in processing the cases. In all of the felony cases the prosecutor demanded, and the judges, nearly without exception, imposed bail ranging from $10,000 to $20,000. Few of the defendants, of course, could make bail. For a week, until the amount of bail was reduced, many people found themselves separated from families and jobs, incarcerated in jail, and out of contact with attorneys or other resources. A University of Michigan Law School report charged that the judges had adopted a policy of expediency, abandoning their judicial roles and acting as an arm of executive government in an effort to help quell the disorder. In the end it was determined that, of the more than three thousand felony defendants, only nine had been found guilty of charges serious enough to warrant imprisonment.

Similar treatment was accorded more than 21,000 other riot defendants in Watts, Newark, Chicago, Washington and Baltimore.[8] In Chicago, for instance, the cases of rioters arrested for felonies were processed differently from other felony cases. One out of five riot felonies was dismissed at the preliminary hearing on the prosecutor's motion or because the magistrate found no probable cause for holding the defendant. An additional case in every twenty was disposed of at this hearing, either by discharge or by conviction after the charges were reduced. The remainder—nearly three-fourths of the cases—were presented to the grand jury for indictment (Criminal Justice in Estremis, 1969). By contrast, a study of non-riot felonies in Chicago shows that four-fifths of these cases are disposed of at preliminary hearings, leaving only one in five for presentation to the grand jury.[9] Hence it seems clear that the rioters were treated more harshly than other defendants charged with the same crimes.

§ *3.19* *—Sentencing*

Another judicial problem is disparity in the sentencing of convicted offenders. In most jurisdictions the judge is responsible for sentencing. Yet there is little in his training or experience that prepares him for this task. Partly for this reason the judge is often assisted by probation officers who prepare presentence investigations covering the offender's personal and social background, his criminal history, his physical condition, his attitudes and emotional characteristics, and culminating the probation department's recommendations to the judge. Studies show that, where presentence reports are available, the judges comply with the recommendations in more than 90 percent of the cases.[10]

The sentence imposed by a judge must fall within limits set by the law. Criminal codes provide an elaborate classification of crimes with penalties corresponding to their perceived seriousness. Within each category of offenses, however, a variety of sentencing alternatives are specified—fine, probation, imprisonment, and so on. The judge ordinarily may choose among these alternatives according to his discretionary judgment. Such discretion permits discrepancies to occur, especially in the frequency with which probation is granted and in the duration of imprisonment. Since the judge is usually the final arbiter in matters of sentencing, there is little the offender can do if he gets an unfair decision.

Several proposals have therefore been made to promote more rational sentencing policies. One proposal is to have sentences set by an administrative board comprised of specialists in human behavior. Boards of this kind have much merit, and they exist in several states. But they have been hampered at times by the political appointment of their members, by severe limitations on their authority, and by the lack of reliable information on which to base their decisions. Another proposal would have judges discuss with one another any planned sentences before they are imposed. Still another proposal would enable an offender to bring his case before an appellate court empowered to affirm the sentence, reduce it, or order further proceedings required under the circumstances. None of these proposals, perhaps excepting the first mentioned, has gained widespread support, and their use is largely restricted to a few jurisdictions.

In spite of growing concern over sentencing disparities, the lack of rationality and of uniformity continues. Some illustrative data come from the federal district courts. The federal courts, in 1958, meted out prison sentences averaging from a low of 9 months in Vermont to a high of 58 months in an Iowa district. Variations by type of crime are just as prevalent. In 1966 narcotics offenders in one district served an average of 33 months in prison, as compared with 74 months in another district. Average sentences for forgers ranged from 14 to 36 months. District averages varied from 4 to 26 months for liquor law violators, from 25 to 41 months for auto thieves, and 24 to 53 months for other offenders. By 1968 the national average for narcotics offenders had increased to 74 months, with a high average of 12¼ years in one district and a low of 7½ months in another.

The same discrepancies are found in other courts. A study of sentencing in Philadelphia, covering nearly 1500 cases in 1956-57, revealed that the nature of the offense was the main factor influencing the severity of sentences, and that other influences included the degree of contact between offender and victim, the amount of bodily injury, the number of criminal acts covered by the charges, and the number of previous convictions.[11] It appeared that, in general, female offenders were given preferential treatment over males, youths over adults, and whites over blacks. Some consistency was shown in the sentences of the least serious and the most serious cases, but wide variations occurred in the disposition of intermediate cases.

There is convincing evidence of discrimination against Negro offenders. National prison statistics between 1930 and 1964 show that 89 percent of the individuals executed for rape were negroes. In 1965 it was estimated that 63 percent of the courthouses in southern and border states had segregated courtrooms. During a twelve months period ending in June, 1962, more than 2,000 persons served terms in Georgia's prison system because of their inability to pay small fines. Seventy percent of these offenders were black. A more recent investigation of sentences in seven southern states reported average terms of confinement of 16.8 years for negroes and 12.1 for whites.[12] In Arkansas, the average sentences were 14.4 and 7.5 years, respectively, a difference of nearly 2 to 1.

Other studies add to the evidence of disparity, much of it non-racial in nature. In a single state court, one judge sentenced only

34 percent. One judge granted probation nearly twice as frequently as the other. A further illustration involves the separate cases of two men who were convicted of forgery in amounts under $100. Each of the offenders was in dire financial straits and had substantially no prior criminal record. The penalty in one case was 30 days in jail; in the other, 15 years in prison.

Frequently it is the experienced criminal who gets the favored treatment. This is evidenced in the account of two gamblers, one a professional and the other a novice. The professional had a criminal record going back 30 years. He was arrested for managing a $4,000 per day gambling enterprise. The novice, who had no previous arrests, was apprehended for having lottery tickets in his possession. Yet the novice was sent to prison for two years, whereas the professional gambler received probation.[13]

These examples are by no means rare. Comparable inequities probably can be found in the files of most courts. Unless the discrepancies are explained to the community's satisfaction, their effect is likely to be a lessening of public confidence in the system of justice.

Practices such as those mentioned are of little assistance in controlling crime. They may indirectly encourage criminal behavior. Their survival therefore suggests that they serve other social functions. For example, they are certainly effective in maintaining the subordinate status of poor people, especially those labeled as criminals. Although studies of criminal victimization and self-reported offenses show little connection between law violations and social status, the cases processed through our courts come mainly from the ranks of the poor and the disadvantaged.

Conditions are not getting better. In spite of continued increases in average family income, there nevertheless have been only small gains in the financial status of the lower classes. Moreover, the rate at which poverty was being ameliorated has slowed down considerably during the past decade or so. With nearly 6 million unemployed and 25 million living in what is officially defined as a condition of poverty, it would take an outlay of more than 10 billion dollars to raise these incomes above the poverty level. Hence it is doubtful that financial subsidies and other welfare measures can ever solve the problems of justice for the poor.

§ 3.20   Rejuvenating the system

The system of justice in practice often bears little resemblance to the model prescribed by law. Nearly all of the rights and protections promised defendants are regularly circumvented, frequently with the complicity of the defendant or his counsel. This poses a problem for those who advocate greater respect for the law as a solution to criminality. Is respect for the legal model their objective? Or is it respect for conventional practices? Since precept and practice do not coincide, support for one implies opposition to the other.

National policy on this matter seems to vacillate between one viewpoint and the other. Under the leadership of former Chief Justice Earl Warren, the Supreme Court stressed constitutional requirements and worked for their implementation. For this the court was so severely criticized that it became an important political issue in the Presidential campaign of 1968. More recently a reorganized court has toned down some of the earlier decisions. Congress also has championed the strengthening of conventional practices, especially in the field of law enforcement. It legalized preventive detention, gave the police wider latitude in criminal investigation, and established the Law Enforcement Assistance Administration.

LEAA distributes federal funds to state and local agencies in an effort to facilitate crime control. Thus far most of the funds have been spent for training personnel, developing computerized records, coordinating communications, and modernizing equipment or hardware. Other proposals include reducing the size of juries in noncriminal cases, using lay experts to assist in holding trials, in sentencing, or in working with probationers, and bringing up-to-date business techniques into court management. More funds also are being expended in jail construction and in upgrading correctional treatment. Prisons are coming under closer public scrutiny. Following the exposure of corruption and inmate abuses, for example, a major state prison was declared unconstitutional and threatened with closure.

The objective of these programs is apparently to increase the efficiency of the justice system. However, most of the programs are aimed at the official apparatus of justice, with informal measures getting comparatively little attention. This reveals a weakness in the current approach. Much of the evidence on crime control suggests that offenders processed informally do better after discharge than those who are officially labeled and stigmatized. Formal procedures may therefore be a means of criminalization. And if efficiency is defined so as to encourage the use of formal procedures, it is not clear that greater efficiency will curb crime. A more rational approach would be to assess programs and procedures, whether official or not, in terms of their impact.

§ 3.22 —Inadequate laws

Another reason for slow progress in justice is the recalcitrance of the law. The language of law is itself a specialty that is sometimes so obscure as to be unintelligible to any except members of the legal priesthood. Even lawyers may have to wait for court decisions before they can speak with authority regarding the law's content. An example is the following statement from an official taxpayer's guide issued in 1971:

> Bribes and kickbacks to nongovernmental officials are deductible unless the individual has been convicted of making the bribe or has entered a plea of guilty or nolo contendere.

Although the substance of this statement seems clear enough, a person preparing his income tax may have questions about its intent or its use by the authorities. On occasion a law's logic may be defective, as in the case of an old statute which provided that: "Two locomotives, when meeting at an intersection, shall come to a complete stop, and neither shall move forward until the other has passed through."

Greater difficulties, no doubt, are produced by laws passed without any intent of enforcement. By enacting such statutes, legislators are able to dodge wearisome political issues. One faction of voters is appeased by their enactment, while another faction is satisfied by their nonenforcement. The "blue laws" and laws against the sale of contraceptives are some examples. In most places these are openly violated without fear of reprisal. It is also a striking fact that the people who insist on retaining such laws are often among the last to assist in their prosecution.

Different from nonenforcement is selective enforcement of the law. Many laws specify extreme penalties for minor offenses. In such cases it is not expected that the penalties will be invoked with any regularity. Rather, they are used by the prosecutor as a club in obtaining confessions. In this respect the law becomes the instrument of its own enforcement, relieving the police and prosecution of the necessity of more conventional investigations. Among laws intended for selective enforcement are those providing for the lifetime imprisonment of persons convicted of two or more felonies. Such "habitual criminal" laws are found in several states. They are used primarily as a threat against recidivists who are given a choice of pleading guilty to specific charges or running a risk of conviction as habitual criminals. Technical regulations governing the conduct of probationers and parolees are sometimes employed in a similar manner. These offenders can be returned to prison—or to court in the cases of probationers—for noncriminal violations instead of being tried on new charges.

There is still another branch of criminal law where the integrity of enforcement seems inclined to deteriorate. This deals with laws covering morality, including prostitution, gambling, narcotics traffic, homosexuality, and the like. Such "crimes without victims" require a willing participant who is averse to assisting the police in preventing his own exploitation. Selective or sporadic enforcement is an almost inevitable consequence of the difficulties involved in detecting these offenses. Frequently the police have to use entrapment, paid or protected informants, and other unsavory methods. Sometimes the tactics of the authorities are as offensive, and possibly as illegal, as the crimes they are intended to suppress.

Many authorities nevertheless advocate the perpetuation of these laws. Severe penalties, even though rarely used, are also seen as an advantage, since they simplify the problem of enforcement as mentioned above. In addition, the management of vice is a highly profitable enterprise. It therefore seems likely to survive in spite of any attempts to eliminate it.

For these reasons some legislators are beginning to look to the so-called vices, especially gambling, as a source of public funds. By legalizing off-track betting, for example, New York officials have estimated that 200 million dollars can be added annually to the state's treasury. Recent surveys suggest that such a profit would require a betting volume of 2.5 billion—assuming that gambling salons handled betting on sports other than racing, that winnings were tax-free, and that the minimum bet were lowered to one dollar. The planned gambling enterprise is designed for its appeal to low income customers. Since winnings are presumably proportional to the amount contributed in bets made, it is not clear that the legalization of gambling will increase the financial status of the poor. However, the promise of a big pay-off may make their plight much more palatable. And their losses will no doubt replenish the state's financial coffers, in this way helping to solve its tax problems. It is not clear that justice is served by the expedient of legalization, nor is there any certainty about the superiority of present laws.

§ 3.23 —Court policy

The same questions can also be raised about judicial procedures. Judicial activities, like most other social enterprises, are controlled by both formal and informal norms. In the courtroom, for instance, events are regulated by a vast array of formal prescriptions. Laws and other official rules govern the roles played by judges, attorneys, court aids, defendants, witnesses, and spectators; they specify the criteria for granting a law degree or a litigation; and they spell out the rights and responsibilities of the litigants, their representatives, and other participants.

Informal expectations generally cover matters of speech, dress, and conduct, though these things are also subject to some formal constraints. Despite the contentiousness of many of the proceedings, it is expected that mutual expressions of courtesy and an attitude of dignity will prevail in court. The judge is officially required to rule on legal questions; he is informally expected to learn his subject well, to be objective and impartial in his rulings, and to maintain the integrity of the judicial process. Attorneys are required to proceed in a lawful and orderly manner, and it is expected that they will present forceful and concise arguments in serving the interests of their clients. Other participants have their particular assignments, each of which is regarded as essential to the legal process.

The implicit assumption behind legal procedures is that if everyone involved plays his role properly the result will be a true and just decision. This indeed is the main goal of the proceedings. However, a true decision and a just decision are not always the same thing. An empirically true decision is one that agrees with the facts in the case, whereas a just decision, in legal terms, is one obtained in accord with the rules of procedure and of evidence. Court officials may therefore face a dilemma demanding a choice between goals and norms. In such cases the legal ritual seems often to place a higher value on procedures than on the factual adequacy of the substantive decisions.

For example, a major consideration in assessing the performance of judges is the number of instances in which their rulings have been overturned by higher authorities. Since procedural errors furnish the chief grounds for appeal to higher courts, it is not surprising if many judges are particularly attentive to such matters. Yet personal bias and selective perception may be more important than procedural error in determining the empirical correctness of court decisions. Studies show that judges, in spite of their honest efforts to avoid bias, are not very consistent in their decisions, especially in their sentencing of criminal offenders. The decisions are more often evaluated by their legal fitness than by their empirical consequences.

Prosecutors and defense attorneys face the same dilemma. Thus, a prosecutor who goes to court with everyone he believes guilty of crime may do well to get convictions in half of his cases. But if he tries only those whose conviction is almost certain, he may increase the conviction rate to about 95 percent. While the latter policy may be politically the more expedient, it no doubt reduces the number of impirically correct decisions. The defense attorney must also decide how to handle prospective clients he believes to be guilty. By refusing these cases, he forces them to find another defender, probably a professional competitor, and he runs the risk of reducing his income. By defending them to the best of his ability, he may come to feel responsible for acquitting a number of his clients who are in fact guilty.

There are no easy solutions to such problems of role conflict. Training, experience and ideology, however, may tend to alleviate the sense of personal responsibility by encouraging lawyers to think in terms of their client's legal vulnerability, rather than his factual guilt or innocence. Some lawyers argue, for example, that a person is innocent until proved guilty in court. An attorney therefore cannot really know a client's guilt prior to the court verdict. Although he may be suspicious of some of his client's testimony, it is the jury's responsibility to determine its validity. And the rules of the adversary system, such as the obligation of confidentiality between lawyer and client, make this kind of argument feasible except in obvious cases. Moreover, a good attorney does not gain his reputation by handling the obvious cases. He gains more in winning the questionable ones.

Consistent with the ideology of many lawyers, the rules and procedures used in arriving at a court decision are also the ones used in justifying that decision. Such circularity makes the court the final arbiter in questions of truth and justice. But if truth and justice are whatever the courts declare them to be, if there are no criteria of consequence other than court procedures, then the maintenance of procedural patterns becomes the major function of the court system. The energies of officials, accordingly, are devoted primarily to norm formation and norm enforcement.

Such ritualism and extreme emphasis on pattern maintenance are likely to occur whenever the norms dominate the other elements of any social system. But they do not help in achieving the objectives for which the system was established. It is typical of ritualistic organizations that the stronger the opposition they encounter the more they rely on traditional procedures. Instead of developing new policies better suited to goal attainment—or modifying old ones to the same end—they can think of nothing but preserving their orderly operations. Hence the system of justice may soon have to decide whether it is better to preserve the arrest→conviction→punishment model or to formulate new models hopefully more proficient in crime control and prevention. In view of the prevalence of diversions from the traditional model, it might seem that this decision has already been made. But the diversionary model has not been officially acknowledged, nor is it receiving the attention it deserves in the current movement towards judicial reform.

Notes

1. R.C.F. Hayden, "Problems in the Management of Criminal Courts for Which Science May Offer Solutions," pp. 97-108 in *National Symposium on Science and Criminal Justice*, Government Printing Office, 1966.

2. The President's Commission on Law Enforcement and Administration of Justice, *Task Force Report: The Courts*, Washington, D.C.: U.S. Government Printing Office, 1967.

3. Ralph Nutter, "The Quality of Justice in Misdemeanor Arraignment Courts," *Journal of Criminal Law, Criminology and Police Science*, 53, 1962, pp. 215-219.

4. Donald J. Newman, "Pleading Guilty for Considerations: A Study of

Bargain Justice," *Journal of Criminal Law, Criminology and Police Science*, 46, 1956, pp. 780-790.

5. Irving R. Kaufman, "The Judicial Crisis, Court Delay and the Para-Judge," *Judicature*, 54, 1970, pp. 145-148.

6. Hayden, *op. cit.*

7. Lee Silverstein, "Manpower Requirements in the Administration of Justice," Appendix D, in *The Courts*, Government Printing Office, 1967. See also, Jerome Carlin, Jan Howard and Sheldon L. Messinger, *Civil Justice and the Poor: Issues for Sociological Research*, Russell Sage, 1968.

8. Jerome H. Skolnick, "Social Control in the Adversary System," *Journal of Conflict Resolutions*, Volume II, 1967, pp. 52-70.

9. Donald M. McIntyre, *Law Enforcement in the Metropolis*, American Bar Foundation, 1967.

10. Robert M. Carter, and L.T. Wilkins, "Some Factors in Sentencing Policy," *Journal of Criminal Law, Criminology and Police Science*, Volume 58, 1967, pp. 503-514. See also: Robert M. Carter, "The Presentence Report and the Decision-Making Process," *Journal of Research in Crime and Delinquency*, Volume 4, 1967, pp. 203-211. and Robert O. Dawson, *Sentencing: The Decision as to Type, Length and Conditions of Sentence*, Little and Brown, 1969.

11. Edward Green, *Judicial Attitudes in Sentencing*, Macmillan, 1961.

12. Charles Morgan, "Dual Justice in the South," *Judicature*, Volume 53, 1970, pp. 379-384.

13. Joseph Tydings, "Ensuring Rational Sentences," *Judicature*, Volume 53, 1966, pp. 68-73.

III. FUTURE ROLES OF JUDGES, PROSECUTORS AND DEFENDERS

SOURCE: Ernest C. Friesen, Jr., "Future Roles of Judges, Prosecutors and Defenders," *Future Roles of Criminal Justice Personnel: Position Papers*, Project STAR, American Justice Institute, Marina del Rey, California, 1971, pp. 1-62.

Trends in the development of the justice system as a whole will have substantial impact on the role of all components of the system. These trends and their consequences should first be considered together in predicting the roles of judges, prosecutors and defense attorneys of the future.

The basic nature of the adversary system will change perceptibly but not dramatically. The culture of the courts which for years accepted ambush and surprise as basic tools of prosecution and defense is slowly changing to reject these devices. More and more full disclosure of the factual case on each side is the rule and surprise the exception. Within the past several years appellate opinions have announced a right for the defendant to know the facts in the prosecutor's file. By the same measure, short of violating standards of self-incrimination, the prosecution has a right to know the theory on which the defendant will defend.

The role of each of the functionaries changes as more of the facts are discoverable before the trial. Preparation of the case for the trial becomes more important than skill in the trial. The prosecutor must build a stronger case. The defender must know how to discover in inexpensive ways and the judge must be prepared to supervise this process both to insure its effectiveness and to prevent delays.

Greater preparation based upon a more thorough knowledge of the facts will require a higher degree of inter-personal skills in the attorneys. Witnesses will need to be thoroughly interrogated in advance of trial. The technology of crime will need to be mastered. More time will be needed and therefore, for the same number of cases, more judges, prosecutors and defenders.

A major change in the adversary process will be an increased and more sophisticated use of settlement procedures. Negotiations rather than advocacy will be the tool. The judge will play the mediator rather than the decider. Plea Bargaining as it is known today will disappear. Open negotiation with a discussion of the facts as asserted by each side will take place on the record. Attempts will be made to fit the guilty defendant into an appropriate treatment or reform process. All parties will need to know the alternatives and their effectiveness when applied to persons from widely differing backgrounds.

The most significant alternative in the justice system will be the slow reduction of political consideration in the selection process. Judges and prosecutors, now selected through political processes in a majority of jurisdictions, will be selected for their abilities. This trend is slow but the growing awareness in the people of the adverse effects of political selection is leading to merit systems for judges in many states. The logic will eventually carry over to the selection of prosecutors.

In part the receding emphasis on politics is the result of size and not of reform. In many large cities a cadre of professional prosecutors and defenders has developed due largely to the necessity of providing continuity and experience in these offices. The working level attorneys often stay on after the change of political administrations. This trend has many consequences which will be considered separately below.

Continuing legal education has become an accepted fact throughout the legal profession. Schools for judges and prosecutors are over subscribed and with adequate funding the new school for defenders will have an excess of applicants.

The legal aspects of the judges, prosecutors and defenders' roles will find adequate perhaps even excessive programs. An analysis of the legal training needs may show significant redundancy and little attempt to recognize the actual need for training. The expansion of criminal law and procedure has been rapid. There is some evidence that a period of stabilization will occur when new developments will come less rapidly and the need for new development courses will subside.

Education in related fields such as negotiations, counseling, and inter-personal relations generally is not readily accepted among judges and lawyers. With the growing recognition of these special skills by the populations, it may be anticipated that the law will follow—not more than the usual ten years behind the trend.

Careers in judging which start shortly after graduation from law school are not likely. Careers in prosecution and defense may well become the rule rather than the exception within the next twenty years. The trend toward specialization is well on its way in the legal profession. As more law students accept careers in the public service—a clear trend—careers in prosecution and defense will become socially acceptable and pursued.

The growth of large offices and large courts will lead to specialization in all three areas. Courtroom teams which include judges, prosecutors and defenders will emerge out of this increase in specialization. This will result in part from administrative necessity and in part from the desire of the specialists to excel. Countering this trend will be the growth of administrative expertise which will rotate personnel among specialties to avoid organizational dry-rot.

The growth of management capacity will be one of the major changes of the next decade. Though presently non-existent the art of justice management is being discovered. Once a cadre of managers are trained and active in the field, even the smaller offices will seek out people who can help their organizations to function effectively. Government generally is seeking out experienced and trained administrators. This trend is now reaching the several components of the judicial prosecutional and defender organizations.

The law is authoritarian. Unless specific efforts are made to counteract the tendency, the legal institutions will adopt authoritarian models for management with its consequent regulations, orders and bosses. Engrafted on political selection and professional needs the model will be disastrous. Boundaries between the courts, prosecutors and defenders which are now dysfunctional will become bureaucratic fiefdoms. Arguments over authority, responsibility and who's-to-blame will lead to greater delays than are now experienced under basically uncoordinated ad hoc operational systems.

Public personnel systems with their abhorrence of lateral entry, rigid job descriptions and lock step promotion standards will be imposed where patronage once reigned supreme.

Courts will centralize administrative authority within the states while the prosecutors and defenders will be county officials. There is a slight trend toward statewide control of prosecutors by the Attorney General. This will come—but very slowly. With it will come a regionalization of supervision and a further development of careers as prosecutors. Size of operations being the principal force for this trend.

More modern management techniques will follow the failure of the authoritarian systems. Both an increase in inter-personal skills and an awareness of management information will come as a result of intelligent people trying to make the system work. Effectiveness measures will be established after ten years of floundering and goal identification. When these measures are discovered, methods of operation and priorities will be changed. A new concept of effective prosecution, judging and defense will emerge.

Workloads will change as more of the victimless crimes are diverted into other channels. Traffic offenses which are sanctioned to preserve order will be taken from the courts. Some traffic related offenses such as drunken driving will probably remain. Narcotics offenses will be diverted from trials but the diversion will in most cases be subject to court supervision. The role of the judge, prosecutor and defender will not be basically adversary.

New technology in crime detection and law enforcement will increase the need for competence and for thorough preparation. Judges will need to anticipate technical evidence and have time to study the technology. Pre-trial procedures will include a review of the evidence by all three participants so that learning delays, based on technological knowledge gaps can be anticipated.

The trial will become less and less important as more and more is known about a case in advance of trial.

Judicial manpower will lag behind the workloads imposed by these trends toward more complex cases and procedures. After some stress the use of para-judicial personnel will come into vogue. Referees, Commissioners, Magistrates and Assistant Judges will be called for and given tasks which at first the judges deem demeaning. Later the judges will give more complex tasts to these persons until judges will be used only for the most complex matters. After many years the para-judicial will develop as trainees for judges and the trend toward a specialty of judging will be complete.

The tripartite interdependence of the three basic parts, judicial, prosecution, and defense will continue. Each, however, will become more closely identified with the court working in part for justice rather than victory. The adversary system will be ameliorated but not abandoned.

§ 3.24   Judges

The clearest trend in the world of judges is an increasing awareness that they are responsible for the movement of a case through the courts. The scheduling of cases will be a judicial function with judges taking a firm stand against all forms of dilatory tactics.

Workloads will continue to go up requiring an increase in total judicial manpower. Even though auto personal injury cases will decline with the adoption of no-fault insurance plans, other, perhaps more important litigation will take its place. Litigation is a product of lawyer time. As the supply of lawyers increases with population (or perhaps at a greater rate) litigation will increase. Pollution, consumer rights, poverty law all bring new actions to the courts. If in fact only 30% or 40% of crimes are now detected the diversion of large numbers of crimes out of the courts will only release prosecutors to pursue other matters not now pursued.

The long-term trend is to resolve the more complex disputes out of court. This trend may well be reversed as courts become more competent to deal with them. The decision to resolve a dispute out of court is often made on the basis that the judges (and juries) are not to be trusted. As the courts begin to manage and decide the complex cases more competently, the courts will get more of them to decide.

Juries will be used less and less as personal injuries are eliminated from the court workloads. Non-personal injury cases are seldom tried before juries today. The judge will find himslef, therefore, hearing more cases in which he must give the facts his full attention and in which he will not be able to hide behind a "standard" instruction on the law.

In the criminal area it is difficult to foresee the effects of the changing court function on the judge. Hopefully he will accept the new role and act as a sort of team leader to find an effective disposition for a convicted person. When the effectiveness of alternative is more accurately predictable than it is today and when there are more alternatives, the adversary process with judges as referees will have to yield to a much more active role.

Judicare, a shorthand name for legal fee insurance, is on its way. The forgotten man in litigation has always been the person who is too poor to litigate a claim and too wealthy to get help from legal aid. Legal fee insurance will bring many cases within the economic range which were not otherwise there. An increase in family disputes, neighbor disputes and the like may be the result. In all probability the variety of cases will increase with judicare requiring the judges to be more broadly informed than is now the case.

Many functions will be the same as in the past with new emphasis. Divorce will not be based on fault but child custody cases will be just as difficult as in the past. There will be more knowledge available about the consequences of custody decisions, more counseling within the court on the better decision and hopefully more consistent results.

Specialization will continue but not along Civil-Criminal lines. Judges will specialize for one or two years at a time and rotate in assignments. Separate criminal courts will be abolished (as will separate Family, Juvenile, Traffic, etc.). Courts, under proper management, will fix assignments by skill and necessity and remain flexible in the use of manpower.

Policy matters in courts will be resolved by the full court or by committees. In large courts committees will work on most of the major areas of administration with the help of trained administrators.

Every court of six or more judges will have a trained administrator whose role will be defined by the judges.

Judges, as the principal managers, will need to understand modern management techniques and tools.

The substantive and procedural law will undergo constant change. Changes in societal relationships, enactment of complex regulatory legislation, and the urbanization of society will create a need for self-renewing people as judges. Certainty in the law will have to accept a new time frame consistent with a changing world.

§ 3.25   Prosecutors

Prosecutors will undergo the greatest role change within the justice system. It will not be rapid.

As the central screening authority in the justice system the prosecutor will be handed the role of diverter from the system. If he is afraid or refuses to accept the role the diversion systems now being designed will never take effect.

Professionalization of the prosecutor's office will take place as the offices grow larger and come under more state control. Many states will adopt a Department of Justice System with the State Attorney General at its head. District prosecutors will be appointed by the Attorney General and will continue to be political. Their staff deputies will be career men who hold their positions an average of five or more years.

Salaries and fringe benefits will parallel those of lawyers in corporate practice. Turnover will be caused by the existence of better opportunities rather than by political change.

The criminal law will become more complex as legislatures continue to make criminal all types of behavior they wish to disavow. Increased sophistication in the detection of crime will make the job of presenting and explaining police work to judges and juries more difficult. An increase in the numbers of fraud related cases will increase the time for preparation and presentation of cases.

Experts will be used in almost all cases of the future. Their expert knowledge will range across a very wide spectrum of skills. Specialization in the prosecutors office will more often be by background in expert areas rather than in particular crimes.

Prosecutors will continue to specialize in crimes which involve multiple defendants and conspiracies. Whether or not this activity is carried under the label "organized crime" there will be a growing need for prosecutors to head teams of investigators aimed at concerted criminal activity.

Computer information systems will provide background information on potential witnesses, defendants, experts and many other matters. An understanding of the use and abuse of computerized information will need to be in the skills of all prosecutors. Fairness interpretations will make all information available to the prosecutor also available to the defense attorney. Thorough preparation rather than surprise will be the only reliable technique of the prosecutor. Walking into a courtroom to read the file for the first time will end in all but the most routine cases.

§ 3.26 Defenders

The trend is definitely toward an increase in the number of public defenders. Multi-county defender districts will have to be created to make this movement feasible. The success of large city defender offices will lead to the establishment of regional or district offices coterminous with court administrative areas.

The public defender movement, as a new concept which is relatively free from politics, presents an opportunity to develop a legal specialty and a rewarding career. At present this has not happened. Most of the assistant public defenders who carry the burden of defense are recent law graduates thrown into the courtroom with little more than a perfunctory orientation on top of a few hours of criminal and constitutional law. The specialty career will follow the development of training competence.

Much of the defense function will continue to be performed by individually assigned counsel. Where a good public defender system exists, conflicts of interest will force the assignment of outside counsel. The persons assigned will be drawn from the less experienced part of the bar. They will continue to be compensated at hourly rates which are unrealistic. They will not voluntarily participate in training programs that require long absences from their offices.

As more treatment alternatives become available the experienced defender will participate as much in the selection of an appropriate treatment program as he does now in the attempt to free the defendant. Specialists in "sentencing" will develop in the larger offices so that the defendant may be represented by a different person after conviction. Diversion of defendants from the criminal justice process in preconviction proceedings will result in teams of defenders considering the defense from a legal point of view, as well as from the view of a possible diversion.

The automation of information about defendants and their backgrounds will increase the sophistication with which the defense lawyers can handle their cases.

Pressures will be high on the defender to play a different role from the one now advocated. It is presently popular to argue that each defendant is entitled to all of the tricks, delaying tactics, administrative pressures and unsupported appeals that might be brought to bear by an unethical lawyer representing a wealthy client. The defense attorney of the future, whether client selected or court-appointed, will fall under a new set of ethical norms. He will be required to expedite his case at all times and to advance no argument or position that he does not believe has merit. The future will see the wealthy client represented ethically rather than permitting the indigent the equivalent representation of the few who operate unethically.

PART 4

CORRECTIONS

213

§ 4.1 Introduction

The American system of corrections is comprised of a variety of penal institutions, correctional facilities, and treatment programs administered by federal, state, county, and municipal levels of government. On any given day the system handles about 1.3 million convicted lawbreakers. It receives more than 2.5 million offenders per year. Its annual budget for operations is well over a billion dollars.[1]

About two-thirds of the convicted offenders are under supervision in the community, while the remaining one-third are confined in institutions. Of the more than 420,000 individuals confined, 220,000 are felons, 140,000 are misdemenants, and over 60,000 are juvenile delinquents. The cost of operating the correctional institutions exceeded 800 million dollars in 1965: an average of $2,000 for each felon, $1,000 for each misdemeanant, and $3,500 for each juvenile offender.

An additional 850,000 offenders are in the community on probation or parole. These programs are operated at an annual cost of around 200 million dollars. Since it costs only one-tenth as much to supervise an offender in the community as it does to confine him in an institution, the use of probation and parole has been growing much more rapidly than prison confinement. Moreover, these alternatives to incarceration, if properly managed, do not seem to involve any increased risk to the community.

The main problem in corrections is the ineffectiveness of the traditional prison. Maximum security prisons, such as the one recently abandoned on Alcatraz Island, neither protect society nor reform the offender. In spite of the lip service given to rehabilitation and to the successful reintegration of the offender into civilian life, the fact remains that many prisoners live under conditions that encourage patterns of immorality, dependency, manipulation, irresponsibility and destructiveness.

Many prisons, especially the oldest and the largest ones, are only warehouses for storing human outcasts. They are obviously more adapted to control and containment than to correction and reintegration. If reintegration were truly the goal of society, these vast warehouses would soon be consigned to a museum along with the scaffold, the rack, the ball and chain, the scarlet letter and other relics of the war that man has waged against himself in the interest of social order.

The choices confronting society are to reform the outmoded prisons or to replace them with more effective programs of correction. Reform is difficult because of the large size of these institutions, their unwieldly construction, their isolation from the community, their reliance on force and punitive measures, and their traditions of inmate regimentation and subordination. The federal experience with Alcatraz suggests that it may be easier to develop alternative facilities than to reform a tired, worn-out institution.

Replacement of the prison is also hard to achieve, however. One obstacle is the huge public investment in resources—funds, physical plant, equipment, personnel, statutes, and administrative machinery—already committed to maintaining these institutions. Another factor is the people's faith in punishment and repression as methods of crime control. This often challenges the legitimacy of measures other than incarceration. Even more important, perhaps, is the prison's heritage as a charitable institution. Imprisonment was adopted less than two centuries ago as a humane substitute for the much harsher physical punishment given law violators at that time.

Evidence of the ineffectiveness of prison treatment has encouraged the development of alternatives to confinement. Some alternatives are employed early in the judicial process, even before a criminal conviction has occurred. Others are adopted after conviction but before prison commitment. Still others take place after the offender has been admitted to prison. Parole is an illustration of the last mentioned variety.

It is not clear that the extensive use of parole has reduced the amount of time offenders spend in prison. Nor is it clear that it reduces the recidivism rate.[2] Just the opposite may be the case. Parole rules have been increasing in number and complexity, making it harder for parolees to avoid technical infractions.[3] And it appears that the greater the intensity of parole supervision, the greater the proportion of a noncriminal kind.[4] Hence the number of parole rules, the amount of time officers have to spend with their clients, and recidivism rates may have important interrelationships.

This means that current trends towards smaller caseloads might be a misdirection of resources. Although small caseloads seem to increase the number of technical violations, they do not appear to have any significant influence on the number of crimes committed by parolees.[5] If return to prison for technical violations prevented subsequent infractions of a more serious kind, small caseloads could perhaps be justified on this account. Whether more serious offenses are prevented has not been fully investigated, but present indications are that crime prevention is not achieved by the enforcement of technical rules. Unless preventive effects can be demonstrated, it seems unlikely that the interest of justice is served by returning parolees to prison for activities that are condoned in the rest of the population. It is certain that many are returned for noncriminal reasons, though the extent to which this occurs is presently unknown.

Instead of having a double standard, it would be better in the long run to set caseloads according to the requirements of crime prevention. Some parolees no doubt require more supervision than others. Caseloads should therefore be flexible, depending upon the degree of crime-risk presented by the parolees. And the rules should be aimed at making criminal activities visible, not at enforcing multiple standards of morality.

California's parole work unit program is a step in the direction of greater flexibility. Parolees are classified as requiring minimal, average, or maximal supervision. A standard caseload is comprised of about 120 minimum supervision cases, or 40 average cases, or 25 requiring maximum supervision. Some officers have mixed caseloads, while others specialize in handling parolees of a certain kind. After several years of experience with this program, the California authorities decided that many offenders formerly held in prison can be kept in the community under varying degrees of supervision. The financial cost is much less than that of imprisonment, and there is no increase in recidivism.[6] Partly as a result of the conditional success of parole, many states are beginning to release prisoners while technically serving their sentences. More than half of the states have statutory provisions for work or training release, and about 22 of them have operational programs.[7] Inmates are released during the day to attend school or to hold jobs in the community. Some spend the night in halfway houses or jail annexes instead of returning to prison. In most places the number of participating inmates is very small, reaching as many as a thousand only in North Carolina.

Preliminary reports on these programs are nevertheless favorable.[8]

Inmates on work release in North Carolina earn an average of about $3,400 per year, approximately $250 more than they made prior to commitment. Their average stay in the program is a little more than ten months. Around 16 percent are retained by their employers after discharge from prison, and this proportion seems to be increasing.

The firms involved typically employ about four or five prisoners at a time, with an average of twenty-four per firm during a five-year period. Most employers are supportive of the program. Ninety-two percent state a preference for hiring ex-prisoners with experience in work release over those serving their entire sentences within the institution. Expansion of the job market for ex-prisoners may therefore be one of the program's unanticipated consequences.

Prisoner furloughs are also being used with increasing frequency. Furloughs differ from the previously mentioned release programs. They are temporary leaves granted for purposes such as preparing parole plans, locating employment or housing, consulting advisors and handling personal affairs, strengthening family ties, and so on. Experience to date suggests that prisoners ordinarily use the leaves for the purposes intended, and that law violations or failures to return on schedule are infrequent.[9]

These are some of the ways in which the criminalizing effects of imprisonment may eventually be alleviated. Thus far their direct influence on criminality has been minimal. They do not seem to produce any great reduction in recidivism, in time served, or in the rate of prison admissions. But they may tend to soften the abrupt transition from prison to the community, to lessen the prison's isolation, to modify its architecture and its policies regarding community contacts, and to discourage the construction of massive close-custody institutions.

More important, no doubt, are the programs' indirect effects. Among these are the freer exchange of information about prison life and its consequences, the greater involvement of civilians and ex-offenders in prison affairs, and the growing recognition of community influences—employment, housing discrimination, public finance, civil rights, opportunity structures, social ties, etc.—in matters of crime control. Through these programs we are learning that recidivism and crime prevention are more community problems that prison problems.

Better results are generally reported, however, when the alternatives to confinement are employed prior to incarceration. Probation disrupts people's lives less seriously than does imprisonment. The probationer's contacts with the community are not completely severed. The process of stigmatization is less pervasive. And the probationers do not have to contend with the criminogenic environment of the prison. Otherwise, the probationers and the paroled prisoners seem quite similar, although the relative proportions of high-risk and low-risk cases vary according to statutes and official policies. But the probationers, as a group, do much better than the parolees. They have a lower incidence of arrests, better employment records, and more social ties of a legitimate kind. While much of the difference is probably due to case selection at the time of sentencing, it is not likely that this is the whole story.

In 1964 the federal probation system in San Francisco experimented with random assignment of probationers to caseloads of different sizes. The objective was to assess the effects of variation in the degree of supervision. Officers having small caseloads were able to give their probationers about 14 times as much attention as those with large caseloads. Except for the lower violation rates, the findings nearly parallelled those mentioned previously for parolees. Serious infractions were about equal in large and small caseloads. But the overall violations were much more frequently in small caseloads than in large ones—38 percent versus 24 percent, respectively. Hence the main difference was in the proportion of official reactions to minor offenses, mostly transgressions of technical rules. The researchers concluded that technical violations are a function of the amount of time officers can devote to case supervision and that the incidence of criminality remains unaffected.[10]

It is often difficult to partial out the influence of variations in supervision because the size of caseloads may be related to other factors such as staff training, degree of professionalization, and efficiency of management. Several studies conducted in Los Angeles County illustrate these relationships.[11] In 1957 probation caseloads were reduced by about one-third and the officers were given special training in case management. Within two years there was an appreciable decrease in the amount of time probationers spent in detention, in the average time the cases remained active, and in the number of court hearings. There was also a significant increase in the use of informal services and in referrals to other agencies. Whether these differences resulted from the special training or the smaller caseloads could not be determined. However, the county continued to expand its training programs while holding caseloads at the same size.

Several years later the county instituted a work unit program similar to the one adopted by the state department of corrections. Instead of relying primarily on supervision as a means of control, more attention was focused on treatment—casework, group counseling, halfway houses, family assistance, forest camps, and the like—and on the delivery of social services. Again there was a reduction in the amount of time probationers spent in detention or other forms of supervision, along with a considerable increase in the speed and efficiency with which law violations and rule infractions were handled. There was also some indication that certain types of offenders performed best under intensive interaction with their agents, while others were more successful when contracts were minimal. Although this finding is reported in numerous studies, there is yet no clear identification of the relevant characteristics of the offender types. Even if the assignments have to be made on a trial and error basis, however, it appears that a better articulation of caseloads with client requirements is more appropriate than an across-the-board increase in the amount of supervision.

Still later it was demonstrated that delinquent boys who were ordinarily sent to forest camps could be retained in the community on probation with no increase in recidivism and at one-third the cost of the camp program. In either case, however, the recidivism rates were distinctly lower than for boys released from state correctional institutions. Many other comparisons of graduates from institutional and noninstitutional programs suggest that the latter are more successful, especially for juvenile offenders.[12] These findings support the contention that intensity of supervision is less of a factor in determining the success of correctional treatment than are things such as the degree of official stigmatization, the extent to which offenders are involved in planning their treatment programs, and the amount of community acceptance of ex-offenders who are trying to make good.

Energies devoted to the enforcement of technical rules could probably be better spent in providing needed services, building the offender's ties with the community, and creating an atmosphere in which self-respect can be restored. The Essexfields project in New Jersey, for example, attempts to create prosocial norms and traditions of mutual assistance among groups of delinquent boys. Offenders under treatment and those who have graduated from the program are regarded as change agents and treatment resources. The boys live at home overnight and on weekends, but they work together during the day and their evenings are spent in group interaction sessions. These sessions are aimed at getting the boys to disassociate themselves from antisocial pressures and to participate in the formation of constructive peer group influences. Staff members view the sessions as a means of making the boys responsible for the informal norms that comprise a major part of the program through the boys' own initiative.[13]

Other related projects, including Collegefields and Southfields, have evolved out of experience at Highfields, a residential treatment center established more than 20 years ago as an alternative to conventional confinement. Offenders selected for these projects have consistently performed better than those discharged from more traditional institutions. Although evaluative efforts have suffered from problems of research design, it does not appear that case selection alone accounts for the differences.

Another program attracting much attention is the Community Treatment Project operated since 1961 by California's youth authority.[14] Offenders received at the state's reception center were randomly assigned to "control" and "experimental" groups. Controls were confined in an institution and released on parole in the usual manner. Experimental subjects were immediately returned to the community for intensive treatment in caseloads of about 10 (caseloads for paroled controls were around 55). Treatment given the experimental subjects was mainly determined by tests of their interpersonal maturity, but it included individual and group counseling, family assistance, academic and vocational training, employment services, and a variety of other devices. A series of follow-up studies has shown a uniform and statistically significant advantage for the experimental cases over the controls. By 1966 it was assumed that more than three-fourths of the offenders committed to the youth authority could be handled in community treatment programs, and about 600 youths were by then already involved. Savings in operational expenditures were estimated at nearly a million dollars, and this does not include the 7 or 8 million dollars, it would cost to construct an institution for 600 residents.

Criticisms have been directed against the evaluative studies, however. It was found that two-thirds of the failures among control subjects were for technical violations, while less than one-third of the experimental cases were classified as failures for this reason. Serious violations were classified as failures in both groups, of course. But the controls were clearly more likely to be handled as failures for minor offenses than were the experimentals. At the same time, the experimental subjects had a larger number of known infractions than did the controls. The latter finding may result from more intensive contacts that occurred between staff members and experimental cases, whereas the former seems to reflect a distinctive difference in policy. Community treatment apparently shelters its clients from the double standard, previously described, that allows many parolees to be returned to institutions for reasons other than criminal behavior. Whether society would be better protected if community treatment adopted the more conventional policy is open to question.

Information needed to make a reliable assessment of these programs is not available. We know that about half of the offenders released from correctional institutions are rearrested within five years. What we do not know is the comparative rate of arrests in sections of the community from which offenders ordinarily come. There is some evidence that the two rates may be quite similar. For example, a recent cohort study of 10,000 Philadelphia boys born in 1945 shows that at least 35 percent were delinquent by the age of 18. Records of delinquency were found for nearly 30 percent of the white subjects and for more than half of the nonwhites. If these data are indicative of general trends, it may be that crime rates in urban communities are equally as high as among parolees or probationers. Ghettos and other disadvantaged areas may be expected to have even higher rates. So long as we cannot be fairly certain about differences between ex-offenders and the rest of the population, it is obvious that the assesssment of treatment variations will have to be less than convincing.

All of the programs mentioned involve the offical labeling of the offender. Potentially more important are programs that circumvent the labeling process. Diversion from the system of justice prior to conviction occurs in the vast majority of law violations. For various reasons people refuse to report offenses, police refuse to arrest, prosecutors refuse to prosecute, and courts refuse to convict. Efforts are often made, presumably in the community's interest, to minimize the publicity on diverted cases. It sometimes appears as though the unofficial procedures are not really considered legitimate. The offenders are accordingly handled by informal methods having low visibility. Yet the resources available for informal treatment are far more extensive than those used in official cases. Literally hundreds of agencies and thousands of individuals, officials and private citizens alike, are involved. Through these resources jobs are preserved, families are kept intact, academic and vocational training are continued, and ties between the offender and the community are revitalized. How many crime-damaged lives are salvaged is not known.

We have, in effect, two competing models of correctional treatment. One is official and based on the concept of punishment. Arrest leads to conviction and punitive reactions. The other is unofficial, founded on a philosophy of supportive services. Information regarding an offense is collated; a diagnosis is made; the problem is referred to an appropriate agency; and corrective measures are taken with little concern for stigma or punishment.

Notes

1. Clarence Schrag, *Crime and Justice: American Style*, National Institute of Mental Health, Washington, Government Printing Office, 1971, pp. 187-188 and 213-220.

2. Paul Mueller, *Advanced Releases to Parole*, California Department of Corrections, 1965.

3. Nat R. Arluke, "A Summary of Parole Rules: Thirteen Years Later," *Crime and Delinquency*, Volume 15, 1969, pp. 267-274.

4. James Robinson, and Marinette Kevorkian, *Intensive Treatment Project: Parole Outcome*, California Department of Corrections, 1967.

5. Joan Havel, *The Parole Outcome Study*, California Department of Corrections, 1965.

6. James Robinson and Gerald Smith, "The Effectiveness of Correctional Programs," *Crime and Delinquency*, Volume 17, 1971, pp. 67-80.

7. Elmer H. Johnson, "Report on an Innovation—State Work-Release Programs," *Crime and Delinquency*, Volume 16, 1970, pp. 417-426.

8. W.S. Cooper, "Employers and Employees in the Work-Release Program in North Carolina," *Crime and Delinquency*, Volume 16, 1970, pp. 427-433.

9. Narman Holt and Rudy Renteria, "Prerelease Program Evaluation: Some Implications of Negative Findings," *Federal Probation*, Volume 33, 1969, pp. 40-45.

10. Joseph D. Lohman, et al., *The San Francisco Project: Classification Criteria for Establishing Caseload Models*, University of California, 1967.

11. Stuart Adams, et al., *Parole Performance Trends Among Community Treatment Center Releasees*, District of Columbia Corrections Department, 1968.

12. LaMar T. Empey and Steven G. Lubeck, *The Silverlake Experiment*, Aldine, 1971.

13. Saul Pilnick, Albert Elias and Neale Clapp, "The Essexfields Concept: A New Approach to the Social Treatment of Juvenile Delinquents," *Journal of Applied Behavioral Science*, Volume 2, 1966, pp. 109-124.

14. Marguerite Q. Warren, "The Case for Differential Treatment of Delinquents." *Annals of the American Academy of Political and Social Science*, Volume 381, 1969, pp. 47-59.

I. CORRECTIONS AS A SYSTEM

SOURCE: Robert E. Keldgord, *Coordinated California Corrections: The System*, Sacramento, Board of Corrections, State of California, 1971, pp. 23-54.

As a total system, what is the state of affairs of corrections today? Possibly the most striking feature of the correctional system is that it is *not* a system. It is a "non-system." The system is composed of separately operating agencies and organizations having a functional relationship one to the other, but taken separately, or as broad categories, lacking the characteristics of a system. Although all of the agencies or organizations maintain a working relationship with each other, they have not been ordered within a common rubric of intent or control. Most frequently the sense of purpose, the philosophy of operation, the style of action, the programs offered, and the operational decisions made by each correctional agency tend to develop in isolation from, and without coordination with, the other segments of corrections.

The absence of a "system framework" is one of the fundamental weaknesses of corrections today. Inevitably it means that corrections is less effective and less efficient than it should be, and reflects the continuing problems of relationship between state and local government, as well as between institutions and field service programs. It also reflects the differences in sense of goal and purpose, operational philosophy, use of knowledge at hand, and public concern and support. It is, in the end, a reflection of the weaknesses and too few of the strengths of what can, and should be, the outstanding system of corrections in American society.

The magnitude of crime dictates that states can no longer afford the luxury of corrections being a non-system. In the last analysis, it is the state which stands responsible for defining crime, adjudicating individuals as offenders, and delivering a correctional program for those who are adjudicated. It is clear that states have a responsibility in addressing themselves to this basic condition of corrections.

§ 4.2   Goals

It follows from the comments made above that one would not expect to find a uniform sense of goals where one finds that a system is, in fact, a "non-system." A review of numerous studies graphically describes the fact that there is no agreement as to the general goal of corrections, and little agreement as to the goals of the specific components of the correctional system. There is no dearth of documentation in this regard. Frequent references are to be found to such terms as rehabilitation, incapacitation, retribution, treatment, punishment, vengeance, revenge, prevention, and even reintegrating the offender into society. The lexicon of corrections is rich with suggestions, and consequently offers to any agency or individual a rich opportunity for choice. Unfortunately, the richness of choice creates a situation in which the work and intent of one goal too frequently defeats the work and intent of another.

Too few correctional organizations have given explicit attention to this fundamental question. What is the mission and purpose of this organization and how does it fit in with the general mission of corrections?

There is an immediate need for the systematic examination of the question of goals for a system of corrections in each state. A clearer sense of goal is an essential condition for the construction of a coordinated and effective system of corrections.

The only tenable position is that the goal of corrections, and all of the component parts thereof, is the protection of society through actions calculated to minimize the probability of future illegal conduct by present offenders.

§ 4.3   Intake

It is the intake process which accounts for the definition of the subjects of correctional responsibility. It is through the intake process that individuals become defined as criminal law violators and remanded to the responsibility of the correctional system for handling.

A cursory examination of the present intake process, as it operates reveals that the process defines and brings forward to corrections a curious mixture of persons. On the one hand, the intake process defines and labels a group of individuals as criminals who have engaged in behavior which violates criminal law according to the classic definition. That is, the behavior is held to have resulted in social harms. On the other hand, it also defines a large category of individuals who have engaged in behavior which again has been found to be in violation of criminal law, but in this case the behavior does not result in social harm; rather it is offensive to the sensibilities of the social order and possibly detrimental to the welfare of the person. Such behavior involves a wide variety of conduct ranging from behavior which is referred to as "delinquent tendencies" to common drunkenness. In general, such diverse forms of social conduct appear to have in common certain characteristics that are perceived as social problems which society feels must be handled in some way. The vehicle of response currently employed in dealing with these social problems is the use of criminal law, and consequently the use of corrections.

As a result of this situation, intake provides corrections with a potpourri of behavior problems. In addition to criminal behavior, corrections becomes a "dumping ground" for those forms of problem behavior which are not handled elsewhere at the present time. At best, corrections is ill-equipped to respond positively to the demands that are placed upon it in respect to criminal offenders. It is even less well-equipped to respond effectively to the additional forms of problem behavior. It is highly questionable that a correctional system can ever be designed with a coherent philosophy and set of operational techniques which can respond effectively to both groups of clients. All of the available evidence indicates that a correctional response is, without doubt, a costly response. That is, it appears on the surface that alternative program operations would at the least offer the exciting advantage of being more economical.[1]

Additional problems of considerable importance develop during the intake phase of the correctional process. The practices of arrest, booking, bail, holding, the use of citations, release on own recognizance, and similar aspects all have profound consequences for corrections. The expectations, program, and operational problems of juvenile halls and jails are obviously affected by these practices. Equally affected are the operations of probation and subsequently all of the correctional components.

In this regard, the important factor to note is that there is little coordination and understanding among those who participate and are affected. At its worst, there is no coordination or understanding among these agencies and operators of the correctional process. As a consequence, there exists a continuing tug and haul, thrust and parry, characteristic of the intake process's interfacings with the remaining portion of corrections. Needless to say, the offender becomes the first victim. Finally, it is the public who is victimized by the loss of effectiveness and the inevitable loss of efficiency.

Each state should immediatley undertake a study of the intake process in the entire correctional system. Included in such a study should be the intake process involving both adults and juveniles, the use of citations, bail and O.R. (i.e. release of persons on their own recognizance), housing of unsentenced offenders, and the need for diverting certain categories of behavior out of the correctional system into some other more appropriate system.

The recommendation made above does not, of course, necessarily address or provide a solution to one aspect of the problem previously identified. This is the lack of coordination among the component parts of the criminal justice system. It is self-evident that the actions and responsibilities of the police, the courts, the probation department, the jails, the juvenile halls, the juvenile institutions and camps, and the other agencies not mentioned are inextricably and necessarily related one to the other. The policy and actions of the police have dramatic consequences for the courts and the defense and prosecuting systems. In turn, the policies of the courts have important consequences for the jails. Whether it is operatively recognized or not, all of the components of criminal justice live in a precarious, uneasy relationship with one another. Too little coordination, or an absence of coordination, among these components of criminal justice brings a toll of heavy costs and low effectiveness.

The case for coordination need not be argued extensively. None of this study's evaluations have indicated that there is a tolerable level of coordination extant today at any level. The need is clearly there and it must be met.

§ 4.4　Classification

Corrections has understood for many decades that classification is an essential function to be performed if any organization or the corrections system as a whole is in fact to be correctional. The function of classification is diagnosis and prescription. The essential problem is to develop an understanding of the individual as he has behaved and is likely to behave within the free community. The study of his past pattern of conduct and lifestyle and the factors which affect or account for these acts and lifestyles comprise essentially the diagnostic function. A fairly rich literature exists which describes alternative theoretical approaches and alternative methodologies for accomplishing this task. Once the diagnostic function has been carried out, the remaining task of classification is to make predictive and prescriptive statements which attempt to fit programs of treatment or strategies for effecting the probability of future illegal conduct on the part of that person. Both of these elements of classification, namely, diagnosis or study and program planning, must be part of an ongoing evaluative process. In brief, classification is a continual, progressive function, not a static one.

As indicated above, corrections has long understood that it is essential to have a classification capability at each and every point from initial intake through the entire continuum of corrections. If such a capability does not exist, corrections cannot be a rational system designed to reduce the probability of future illegal conduct. Instead, it would at best be a system for holding and moving offenders for an unspecified period of time.

Some components and agencies already have fairly good capability and are delivering valuable classification materials. Many components have a very modest classification capability which provide limited information. For example, many institutions classify their clients only on the basis of custodial requirements. Such reports do not indicate what needs to be or can be done to insure the minimum probability of a new offense. Some components have, for all practical purposes, no classification capability whatsoever. Too frequently, even where classification exists and provides what appears to be useful information, this information is not transmitted and used in the actual program operation of the component.[2]

When classification does not exist, is too limited, or not used, the ability to carry out a correctional effort is at the outset improbable if not impossible. A minimum level of classification is essential if we are to say that every offender is to be provided an equitable opportunity to receive correctional service.

It is essential that a uniform and minimal capability exists in every component of corrections and throughout that component. It is essential that this capability use sophisticated tools of diagnosis in its operation. At the present time, too few components use any of the variety of sophisticated diagnostic tools which are available, e.g., I-Level, typologies, behavior modification, or transactional analysis.

Each state should have a Department of Correctional Services and it should be given the responsibility to carry out a systematic evaluation of the classification programs offered within each component of corrections. Further, the Department of Correctional Services should be given the responsibility to develop statements of minimal standards regarding the needed classification capability in all agencies of each correctional component.

§ *4.5   Programs and treatment*

A few states have long been noted for their willingness to pioneer in the development of an experimentation with new programs for the treatment of offenders. In many ways, this reputation is well-deserved. Recent studies, however, indicate that much about this reputation camouflages the reality. In spite of this reputation, when corrections is examined as a whole, the overwhelming impression is that of programs which are conventional for a correctional system. It is a picture of correctional programs in which far too much of what occurs involves merely the managing, movement, and shuffling of offenders into, around, and then out of the system.

Dividing the current programs of corrections into the conventional categories of institutional and field programs, the following observations generally apply. Characteristic of institutional programs is that they are very limited and very conventional. Too little in the way of alternatives exists in the vast majority of institutions, and in a great many there is little which can properly be labeled as treatment programs. Probably most important is that offenders are confined for considerably longer periods of time than program capability or effect warrants. A study of juvenile institutions indicates that there is apparently little value in holding a youth in custody for a period longer than six months. A study of prisons points out that almost all treatment effect can be accomplished in the institution in a period no longer that 24 months and that continued confinement beyond these time limits leads to disguised idleness and deterioration on the part of the inmate. A jail study indicates that there is so little program available in institutions that confinement in institutions for the purpose of treatment is in most instances a hoax. Further, numerous surveys agree that the connection between institutional programs and later field programs (i.e. parole) are fragile at best and non-existent most of the time.

No doubt it will be necessary to continue to confine a certain number of individuals in institutions. However, it is clearly the responsibility of society to insure that confinement in an institution means more than simple incapacitation or holding of the person, that confinement of the individual is meaningful for the inmate, and that confinement contributes to the minimizing of future illegal conduct. This means that all institutions, and most particularly county jails, must have an adequate program capability to meet the service and treatment problems posed by the offender population there confined. As one study pointed out, it is necessary in each institution to establish a "climate for learning."

Finally, the literature on jails and correctional institutions and, more especially, recent research dealing with these institutions, confirm that the single most important problem is that institutions *qua* institutions tend to be very unreal places in which people live, work, and change. Institutions tend to have too little which replicates the demands and responsibilities of ordinary life-situations in the free community. Institutions are too dissimilar from real-life situations. If corrections recognizes that it is ultimately responsible for the return of the offender to free society and that, in turn, it has the responsibility to do everything to minimize the probability of future illegal conduct, the atmosphere of an institution must approximate the atmosphere of the outside "real" world. Further, the transition from the institution into that outside world must be planned in such a way that it is helpful to the purposes of corrections and helpful to the individual involved, not merely one more instance of shuffling a body from one point to another.

Turning to those programs of corrections which are conventionally referred to as field programs, when looked at as a whole, the modal characteristic of field programs is that they are "paper programs." That is, most of what is done in many of the programs is to deal with and move paper, interspersed with brief moments of contact with individual offenders. It is recognized that available evidence suggests that, for a significant number of offenders, it would appear that such "paper programs" and those which are incident thereto are sufficient. For these offenders, no greater program capability appears to be needed to insure the minimization of future crime. However, the evidence further suggests that, for many offenders, such paper programs are inadequate for the task to be performed. Too little differentiation or classification of offenders is done. There is too little differentiation in the type of programs planned and offered which might meet the problems to be confronted. A notable exception is probation subsidy. The subsidized program in probation clearly is an important development in the modification of the general malaise.

However, even with further extension and elaboration of the current subsidized probation program, a sizeable portion of the field services will remain untouched. There is great need to plan new programs and variants to existing programs which will meet the differential needs of the offender population. Significant gaps in program development for particular types of offenders are noticeably apparent. Programs for girls and women, violent offenders, and the mentally distrubed, must be developed. Attention must be given to these areas of need if corrections is to claim that it is making a real effort to provide correctional service.

Another striking feature of field programs is that they tend to be almost exclusively confined to one general strategy for minimizing future illegal conduct. This strategy is described as "individual intervention." That is, the strategy utilized is to provide casework-oriented treatment services aimed at the individual offender, to motivate and hopefully correct something characteristic of the behavior pattern of that person. Only rarely are other strategies employed. A few programs appear to be utilizing what was earlier referred to as "sociological-institutional strategies." A few "community-treatment" programs exist in which an effort is made to support, modify, and motivate individual patterns of conduct through strategies aimed at changing, modifying, improving and supporting collective, organizational, and/or institutional entities.

Little if any attention is given to the other strategies such as "political-legal-administrative" and "technological."

Finally, it is clear that there exists a richer program resource in the community than is currently being employed. Even where these resources are recognized as existing, too little use is made of them. Probably the most significant reason for this under-utilization is the lack of organizational encouragement or organizational capability for such utilization. Each field service component should assess the extent to which additional and much needed program capability could be obtained without the further development and expansion of the agency itself, but through contracting with existing agencies, groups and persons. Contracting of program services has several immediate advantages to recommend it. First, the costs of program planning are reduced, particularly as related to the specifics of the program plan. Second, the need for the development and training of staff capability to carry out the program is reduced, if not eliminated. Finally, the need for extension of facilities and other support capability would be reduced. Thus, in general, it appears that such contracting offers the opportunity to expand and extend program services in a most economical way.

Research empirically confirms the view held by specialists in the field that the greatest need at the present moment in corrections is to develop programs which emphasize the reintegration of the offender into the community, the maintenance of the offender in the community, and the correctional capability for environmental manipulation, in addition to the conventional "individual intervention" programs. This needed new emphasis throughout corrections will place greater stress on the ability of professional correctional workers to organize, manage and deliver programs rather than being the "treaters." Correctional workers, or at least some of them, must develop the ability to view the community as their treatment resource, to design ways of utilizing the program potential of the community in achieving the goal of the system, to maximize the collective motivation for legal conduct, to minimize the opportunities for engaging in illegal acts, and to bring equitable treatment with justice to all those touched by the criminal justice system.

The single most important conclusion of this study is that programs best calculated to meet the objective of correction are those which are offered and carried out in the community. It was in the community that the behavioral act occurred which brought the individual into the criminal justice system. It is in the community where behavior will or will not recur, and may constitute the basis for finding the existence of a new offense. Violation of the norms of a correctional organization should not be the real interest of corrections. Far too much attention is given to the violations of institutional rules, probation and parole regulations, and normative expectations of the correctional worker. Although correctional norms are important within a limited context, they do not constitute the real measure of the correctional objective. Much greater attention and emphasis than necessary continues to be given to the violation of such norms—by correctional workers themselves and by those who would judge correctional effectiveness utilizing measures which reflect these considerations. The most effective programs currently carried out are those which operate essentially within a community context.

Basically, all correctional programs should be placed within the communities of the state and responsibility for their development and operation should also be given to the community (county or other arrangement of a sub-unit of a community or collections of communities.) The state should offer a few highly specialized programs, implemented in small institutions for the limited number of offenders requiring maximum security for a relatively extensive period of time, i.e. longer than one year. Additionally, the state will need to operate institutions of essentially a medical-psychiatric variety for a limited number of offenders requiring security and intensive modes of medical-psychiatric treatment. The primary role, however, for the state is to assume full and complete responsibility for the organization and support of the correctional effort. Essentially this role involves (1) planning, (2) coordination, (3) standard-setting, (4) training, (5) consultation, (6) funding support and (7) research and development. The President's Commission on Law Enforcement and Administration of Justice pointed out in this regard:

> The variety among correctional administrative structures in the country makes it difficult to determine how the new community programs can best be administered. The limited history of the prototypes indicates that the state itself will have to play a major and continuing role in order to coordinate services.[3]

It is felt that the state could best deliver these needed services by pooling and coordinating its resources in a combined department, a major division of which would be assigned to supply community services.

The community should be responsible for both institutional and non-institutional programs operated in the community, by the community, utilizing its agencies, talents, and resources. The community has the only real capability for delivering effective correctional programs and must accept its responsibility and be joined and supported by the state in organizing itself to do this job. All aspects of the community must accept this responsibility and be involved. As the President's Task Force on Corrections pointed out:

> Whatever the administrative arrangement, it is essential that all elements of corrections should be involved. Special community programs must be perceived by all parts of the correctional apparatus as legitimate and integral parts of the system to push forward with its own existing programs. . . .Failure to involve important elements of the correctional community can jeopardize not only the creation of new community programs but the survival of those which prove successful. . . . It is clear that new community programs must be integrated into the main line of corrections if they are to succeed and survive.[4]

Too frequently, staff of correctional agencies are reluctant to seek out and accept the involvement of other social agencies and elements of the community. If a community correctional program is to be developed and is to be effective, local and state professional correctional workers must accept the responsibility to solicit and develop the support and involvement of public and private agencies within the community, and ultimately, the community itself. As the President's Task Force on Corrections has indicated:

> Finally one of the most critical problems in developing new community programs is to secure the involvement and participation of the community itself. Too often promising programs such as halfway houses have failed simply because the community was not prepared to tolerate them. Thus it is essential that the public be brought into planning early and that the correctional managers make intense efforts to insure citizen understanding and support.[5]

To achieve the objective of community understanding, involvement, and participation, one of the essential tasks to be taken on and effectively met is the task of public education. Keldgord makes the case, in "The Choice for Corrections—To Stand Up, Speak Up, or Shut Up,"[6] that the pattern of action on the part of corrections is one of inconsistency, indifference, and nonperformance. He points out that corrections is obliged to operate ongoing education programs if it is to expect the public to support programs about which they currently know little if anything. There is always the danger of "overkill" in programs of public education, and suggests that such public education efforts can create illusions regarding the potential effectiveness of any given program. This caveat is well-taken but does not detract from the clear general need for programs of public education as requisite to insuring public support and involvement in what is the responsibility and business of the public.

Movement of programs to the community level should provide the opportunity to overcome the conservatism characteristic of most contemporary correctional programs. Undoubtedly, part of the reason for their essentially conservative or traditional character is to be explained by the character of the administrative organization and the administrative styles of these organizations.

Hence, one of the clear responsibilities assumed by the state would be the role of correctional gadfly, critic, motivator, and in general, prodder of local correctional organizations, to be willing to assume some risk in the development of its programs. Local program administrators must be supported in summoning courage to embark upon untried programs which could result in negative repercussions within the local community. If the correctional program is to meet the challenge of crime, it is clear from this study that new and innovative programs are a *sine qua non*. Through its varying roles and responsibilities, the state must provide support to the local administration willing to embark upon the tenuous path of new and innovative programming.

§ *4.6 Organizational structure, administration, and decision-making*

The general organizational structure which typifies many correctional components is what most organizational theorists call the bureaucratic model. This model places emphasis upon several concepts which include:

(1) Structured Hierarchy—a principle which suggests that an office or

individual be supervised and controlled by a higher one.

(2) Task Specialization—Within the totality of any organization, the employees are chosen on the basis of merit and ability to perform specialized tasks.

(3) Specialized Field of Competence—The specialized tasks performed within any organization remain the sole responsibility of the specialist; job descriptions are constructed as an application of this requirement.

(4) Standards of Conduct—Organizational life should be predictable and the implementation of organizational stability should be accomplished by individual compliance with policy statements.

(5) Records—The organization should record all administrative acts, decisions, policies, and rules as a method of maintaining a stability within the organization's boundaries.

In general, a bureaucracy is a chain of command, structured along the lines of a pyramid. It is a typical structure and one which coordinates and controls the business of almost every human organization known to man—industrial, governmental, educational, investigatory, military, religious, and voluntary. It contains a well-defined chain of command; a system of procedures and rules for dealing with all contingencies relating to work activities; a division of labor based upon specialization; promotion and selection predicated upon technical competence, personality, and human relations. The bureaucratic model was developed as a reaction against personal subjugation, cruelty, and the capriciousness of subjective judgments which emerged from managerial practices of the early days of the industrial revolution. Bureaucracy has emerged out of organizations' need for order and precision and the workers' demands for impartial treatment.[7]

The concept of a bureaucratic model is not negative in nature, but the question remains about its suitability for today's correctional organization. Four general problems can be noted which indicate a need for a modification of the classic bureaucratic model used in corrections:

(1) Rapid and Unexpected Change—Bureaucracy's strength lies in its capacity to manage efficiently the routine and predictable events in human affairs. Bureaucracy, with its clearly defined chain of command, rules, and rigidities, is ill-adapted to rapid change and increasing demands.

(2) Growth in Size—In theory there appears to be no height and breadth

which bureaucracy cannot attain. However, the complexity of centralized control becomes an overwhelming menace to the effectiveness of the organization. The movement of corrections away from a few large units to a larger number of small units makes the problem of growth doubly difficult to administer within standard bureaucratic operating procedures.

(3) Increasing Diversity—In today's organization and particularly the organization of the future, the type of tasks to be performed will be of a varied nature. It will either require the advent of a new organizational "generalist" specialist or the management of today's specialists in such a way that they become effective entities within this new organizational structure.

(4) Change in Managerial Behavior—Increasingly in our society, conceptions of man as a worker are based on notions that workers have an increasing fund of knowledge; a new concept of power relationships based on collaboration and reasoning, replacing a model of power based on coercion and threat; and a new concept of organizational values based on humanistic democratic values, replacing the depersonalized, mechanistic systems. Managers today are having to shake off the old prejudices about the eggheads and long haired intellectuals, for these are the very individuals who make up part of the new organization.[8]

This is a period of intense organizational growth and upheaval. This phenomenon is evident in corrections and must be examined. It is something to which the future correctional organization must be able to adapt, identify, and work with. Today, due primarily to the growth of science, technology, research, and developmental activities, the organization's environment is rapidly changing. It is a turbulent environment—not a placid, predictable one.

The situation is further complicated by the fact that organizational complexity and diversity lead to different orientations within sub-systems, so that goals that may be clearly identified in one part of the organization may be dysfunctional in another or, at best, only vagely understood by others in the organization.

"Most organizations have a structure that was designed to solve problems that no longer exist."[9] Much of what any bureaucratic organization accomplishes after it reaches its initial plateau stability is the promotion of its own internal quest for organizational harmony. This is not an ill of correctional organizations, rather it is a reflection upon Weber's "idealized formal bureaucratic organization."

The modern organizational theorist has raised many questions about the direction of change and its impact on organizations of the future.

> Bureaucracy, with its 'surplus repression,' was a monumental discovery for harnessing muscle power via guilt and instinctual renunciation. In today's world, it is a prosthetic device, no longer useful. For we now require organic-adaptive systems as structures of freedom to permit the expression of play and imagination and to exploit the new pleasure of work.[10]

Unfortunately, most correctional organizations are currently either tradition bound or encumbered by a transitional period which is filled with anxiety and frustration. The transitional values, at the base of much of the new frustration, include an emphasis on human needs, a sense of community, consumer rights, personal expression and meaningful work, non-material objects, research and education, and a new emphasis on existential values. These values suggest a new personal responsibility and integrity, a personal identity and shift from an organizational identity, and a new area of self-directed choice.

The traditional organization encumbered by internal preservation, rigidity, non-communications, inflexibility, and a lack of creativity is no longer an acceptable model for the future. This kind of organization often forgets that people are human beings and unique, and that the organization must adapt to meet the individual client's needs. Corrections deals with people, many of whom cannot be dealt with efficiently. Besides, efficiency many times consists of doing an irrelevant thing well. The question posed here is whether the correctional organization of today which is rigid and, with reason, somewhat efficient, can exist in an era when not only the public but the professional in the organization are more socially conscious and concerned. The public as well as some public officials are beginning to question why an organization cannot maintain a flexible, adaptive posture. Organizationally, this is the dilemma that corrections faces today. This is an era of organizational change for corrections.

> The general direction which organizational change will take is toward less rigidly structured relationships both within the work unit and between superior and subordinate. It can be predicted that administrative and management practices will move toward a results orientation. This means that corrections will shift from a reliance on task and job descriptions; and

on bureaus, divisions, sections, and the like to an organizational form more
related to the client and his progress toward some sort of goal.[11]

An imperative for the future organizational development of
corrections is a flattened hierarchial structure. The long lines of
communication and command are dysfunctional and disruptive for
an effective new correctional organization. In most correctional
organizations, the director of that organization tends to become
encapsulated at the top of the structure. In turn, this affects his
capacity to make decisions based on the best set of information.
That information does not flow smoothly and unrestricted is an
inherent problem with all hierarchially-arranged organizations. Therefore, it is imperative that a new organizational model be developed to
handle the problem of communicative interference which occurs
between levels of the organization. To reduce organizational "noise"
between the working levels and the policy levels, the new structure
must reduce the distance and provide for a greater degree of
integration between them.

All correctional organizations should follow the general principle
of flattening the structure. If the bulk of the correctional operations
were transferred to the local or community level, it would become
possible to flatten the overarching state organization to a minimum
number of line relationships. At the statewide level the preponderant
number of units would become staff units operating through the
director of a new State Department of Correctional Services. It is
essential that this occur in order to have clear and effective
interaction between community and state.

Research indicates that worker morale in many correctional
agencies studied is generally low; staff rate the quality of communications as being poor, and perceive a significant problem in the
general organization of corrections. Many employees perceive an
inherent conflict existing in the organization which on the one hand
is purportedly oriented to the client, his needs and problems, and on
the other hand exhibits an authoritarian administration and style
which appear to be more concerned with the problems of the
organization's maintenance and survival.

The typical organization of lines of communication and decision-
making procedures are seen as reflecting this problem. Communication tends to be organized in a way that factual information flows up

and decisions and control directives flow down. The consequence of this type of organization results in a curious inversion of the original problem about which decision-making would appear to occur. The fundamental problems of correctional organization are seen as those relating to the question of what should be done for, with or to the offender. This form of organization tends to make a decision on the offender's problems not where he is located, but several points removed in the organizational hierarchy. In general, the more important the problems are perceived to be, the higher up the hierarchy the decision is made. Removal of the decision from the locale of its origin is inevitably accompanied by an attendant loss of ability to review that decision and be held accountable for the results of the decision. Among the most critical decisions made relating to institutionalized offenders is the decision regarding their release from the institution. That decision characteristically is carried out through a process which calls for the flow of information from the level of inmate and workers who are in immediate contact with the inmate through the hierarchy to a paroling authority far removed. The information which is transported through the communications system is sometimes modified, lost and interpreted in the process. The decisions which are reached, although possibly correct, are frequently difficult to interpret in the original context within which the decisions are to be implemented.[12]

In the opinion of many correctional workers the organization produces a situation where staff become people manipulators (e.g. "cooling-out" clients; "slanting" reports, etc.) rather than treatment agents. Further, it results in the appearance that the organization is run for the convenience of staff rather than for the needs of the clients.

With a flattened organizational structure, it should become possible to develop lines of communication which are bilateral and encourage interaction. Supervisor or manager would be close to worker and client, resulting in the operation of decision-making processes nearest to the point of relevance. In turn, this would allow for the input and almost immediate feedback or reaction to it on the part of each person relevently related to that decision. With such an organizational structure and style, it would be much easier to exercise accountability and relate accountability to the productiveness or consequences of decisions rather than to the exercise of control and authority.

§ 4.7   Facilities

Much of the current correctional program is carried out within some type of correctional facility. One general conclusion emerges from extensive research in one state which showed that correctional facilities are too large and poorly located.

Correctional institutions represent the best example of the conclusion stated above. As a general rule, they are too large; difficult if not impossible to manage; and too far removed from the real world of people, problems, and real life styles. Frequently, the location of correctional institutions has been politically motivated; rarely does their location or design reflect any correctional philosophy. The unreality that size and location bring to the institution, becomes an inherent obstacle to the eventual reintegration of the offender back into the community and the attendant use of the community resources for that reintegration.

To a lesser extent, but generally true, the location and size of field service facilities also tend to be poor and too large. An example of this is graphically presented in the City of San Francisco. Although the city is only seven miles by seven miles in size, the distance between Hunter's Point (an area of high delinquency referrals) and the Youth Guidance Center in the world of social reality is probably nearer seven thousand miles.

Even when facilities are reasonably located and of tolerable size, most of them are in great need of modernization. Buildings and equipment are frequently fifty or more years old. Humane and effective treatment in such facilities is difficult, if not impossible, to achieve.

Correctional programs moved to the community level would allow the state, in partnership with each community, the opportunity to overcome this problem. It would offer the opportunity to develop small, decentralized, and community-based facilities. These facilities should provide institutionalization as required, day care operations, work furlough programs, specialized treatment centers, probation and parole programs, and all of the other of the range of correctional programs which require a facility as a condition of their operation. The general objective should be to develop or modify facilities in such a way that the facility serves to deliver the program rather than having the program fitted to the character of the facility.

§ 4.8   Staff

Correctional manpower and staffing needs are similar, nationwide. Many states face a shortage of professionally qualified treatment staff workers. The acute needs are in such areas as community probation and parole workers as well as psychiatrists, psychologists, social workers, and teachers.

These shortages have occurred for a variety of reasons in an era when employment opportunities in the field of corrections should be tight. Admittedly salaries are low, but growing. The working conditions are viewed as intolerable in some instances and few institutions or correctional facilities are located near population centers. The public generally has little knowledge about corrections and, hence, often does not hold a career in corrections in high esteem. This factor, combined with organizational and administrative rigidity, does not provide strong inducements for employees or potential employees to seek a career in corrections.

Manpower needs in the areas of more traditionally-oriented custody functions are in better condition, due in large part to lower job requirements. There are, however, a series of questions raised about the quality and need for increasing numbers of staff members to fulfill the custodial requirements of state correctional programs. It is in the area of conventional treatment and helping programs that corrections is particularly understaffed and poorly organized. Seldom are the more traditional programs of rehabilitation and reintegration generously staffed.

One of the major sources of the staffing problems in many state correctional organizations is quite frankly and simply that there are too many administrators. Corrections is blessed with an abundance of functional specialists in managerial and supervisory positions who frankly should be paid what they are worth, but who are not trained to carry out the activities of correctional administration. The result of this hierarchical promotional activity has left the field of corrections with an over elaborated administrative structure filled with too few competent administrators. At the same time, this process has removed a large number of competent "treaters" from their area of greatest competence by pushing them into the administrative ranks in order to be promoted.

A common complaint voiced within the correctional system is that line personnel are seldom involved in the decision-making process. Frequently, these complaints are directed toward staff specialists, such as personnel and budget analysts, who are often seen as the controlling and decision-making agents within the organization. Similarly, there are complaints voiced against the supportive functions of research and planning which are seldom available to deal with the relevant or action issues.

A final comment about the current state of correctional staffing patterns is the issue of minority employment practices. While some efforts do exist to eradicate the past inequities of minority employment and staff utilization, they are much too limited and should be vigorously expanded.

The organizational change suggested earlier is dynamic and will be viewed by some as a traumatic exercise in organizational development. Administration and management as a process for getting things accomplished within an organizational structure and staffing patterns and staff development are the vehicles permitting or restricting the dynamics of administration and management to move toward organizational goals and objectives.

The staffing and personnel management problems facing corrections today are to some extent the result of rigidity brought about by civil service reforms which were designed to clean up an era of "spoils" within the public sector. Those reforms were a vital necessity for the 1920's and they have served their purpose well. However, corrections as well as other segments of public service are entering a dynamic new era of public administration, one requiring creativity and flexibility. The concept that organizations are designed to fulfill an unending responsibility in certain functional areas is quickly giving way to a deeper understanding that rigid function and functional specialist categories can no longer meet the changing personnel needs of corrections. There is a critical need to develop new personnel classification formats which would provide flexibility within role performance and job specifications, job and career mobility, and to include para-professionals and volunteers as legitimate staff in the correctional scheme. Organizational needs are changing and with those changes will come a need to change the format of personnel administration for corrections.

The task for corrections is to modify its personnel administration in ways which will accommodate large numbers of workers, occupying a large number of work roles, which overlap and depend upon close integration of effort. Correctional administration will need to develop the capability to put together correctional teams composed of professionally trained, para-professional, and volunteer workers. Such teams will have program or project responsibilities to fulfill.

If an interest in program or project management is developed, then most assuredly staffing patterns will have to change. The traditional hierarchical model will have to be modified and the need for many layers of supervisory roles will be reduced. The traditional ideas of "span of control" and "one-man-one-boss" will vanish and in their place will develop a new concept of participative or team management for corrections. This approach has both economic and manpower advantages. Economically, it makes resource utilization more flexible and, on a manpower basis, it not only increases personnel utilization but through contractual arrangement widens the present scope of the personnel market.

If there is an acceptance of program management for corrections, then the traditional functions of the "staff" personnel will have to change as well. No longer will staff functions be allowed to operate in a posture of opposition to those of line workers. Rather specialized staff will be required to serve as part of a team with line workers in the common pursuit of the system's goal of protecting society.

The team approach will have a significant impact on the traditional barriers between correctional agencies. The achievement of more flexible civil service regulation will at long last permit interagency transfers, at all levels of service, between the counties and the state.

The greater flexibility in civil service requirements, the advent of a team approach to management, as well as a new understanding of the role of corrections in society will hopefully break down the "professionalism syndrome" which currently restricts the para-professional and the volunteer from taking an appropriate place on the correctional manpower team.

The utilization of volunteers and para-professionals in program development in the field of corrections is one of the most effective means of helping meet the goals and challenging needs of today's correctional administrator. Traditionally, some of the problems which have plagued corrections since it became a profession are at long last being faced with an adequate solutional base.

Corrections has long lacked (in members) the totally professional staff it had needed to meet its clients' requests for better service. The position taken by this study regarding the development of community correctional programs is that it will require the advent and widespread utilization of the volunteer and para-professional. Supervisor, professional, para-professional, and volunteer must be welded together in a correctional service team.

§ 4.9 Training

The current status of training within the correctional system varies tremendously. The range of programs is from sophisticated to nonexistent. Generally, training is a function which is relegated to the status of correctional stepchild. It is of vital importance to most correctional organizations until the squeeze of a limited budget casts it aside for some other function deemed more important.

The training programs of various probation departments throughout the nation vary from a high level of sophistication to virtual nonexistence. Of the sixty probation departments in California, approximately 11 maintain full-time training officers while 7 others employ part-time training assistance.[13] Most smaller departments depend upon the State Youth Authority to supply the bulk of their training needs. The advent of probation subvention in 1966 has clearly had the greatest impact on upgrading the level of probation training in specialized supervision units, as well as creating a salutory spillover to other units. However, many of the problems cited below still apply.

The 1968 California Task Force on Correctional Manpower and Training pointed out four training areas of particular concern: pre-service, orientation, in-service, and cultural programs.[14]

(1) Pre-Service—Currently California needs approximately 2,200 new correctional personnel each year. The pre-service training program at the community and four year college level meets only about one quarter of the current manpower needs. However even most graduates of these academic programs need further correctional training before they can assume responsibilities in their respective agencies. There is a serious question about the quality and relevance of this needed training.

(2) Orientation—The Department of Corrections and the Youth Authority both have programs for institutional and field service positions. However, there are no programs for the advanced ranks of these divisions. Only a few counties have orientation programs and for the most part county employees step into existing positions or caseloads and "learn by doing."

(3) In-Service—There is a general lack of coordination of training efforts, knowledge, and resources both within California's correctional system and between subsystems. Few departments have their own training officer or planned training program. The bulk of probation training is handled by the Youth Authority, but it is a "boot strap" operation lacking adequate funding, training, coordination and resource support.

(4) Cultural—Minority groups are represented in large numbers as correctional clients in all parts of the system and there is anticipation that these groups will constitute over 50% of all correctional clients within the next decade. Yet, there is almost a complete lack of training programs and content centering around cultural problems; this void exists in the form of lack of resources, personnel, and programs. Except for a very select few Community Colleges and four-year colleges, this knowledge component is not developed or available.

Training within California's correctional system is of an insignificant proportion. Less than 1 percent of the current budget is spent by either the Department of Corrections or the Youth Authority on training programs throughout the state.

Deficiencies with California's training efforts for corrections pointed out by Phase II of the California Correctional Training Project in 1970 include the following:[15]

(1) There is no formal, underlying plan for training activities within most agencies.

(2) There is no consensus between administrators as to how training is to be made available—for example, where and by whom.

(3) There is little evidence that any concepts have been formulated upon which to design programs or stage specific activities.

(4) Within individual agencies, training resources are not evenly distributed. Most of the available training is for field personnel. Investigative, institutional, and clerical employees are generally neglected.

(5) There is little provision for personnel to receive special training in advance of assuming new and greater responsibilities. This is particularly true of supervisors.

(6) Training officers also generally lack special preparation.

(7) Agency administrators and training officers tend to conceive of training in limited terms usually orienting new employees and stressing procedural matters.

(8) Since training is often seen as a luxury rather than a necessity, sufficient funds are generally lacking.

(9) There is a serious need for some agency or authority to become the focal point for organizing training on an inter-departmental basis.

(10) Effective training programs need not only money but a whole chain of factors from administrative commitments, to management direction, to staff study and planning, to the development of program concepts which should be the core for developing training.

The Correctional System Study confirmed the deficiencies pointed out by the California Correctional Training Project and has arranged those findings into a coordinated resolution which suggests that California corrections develop a posture predicated upon four areas of concern: agency commitment, increased planning, expansion of resources, and statewide coordination.

The first requisite for improvement of training in any department is a strong administrative commitment to the value of that process. The commitment is meaningless if it is little more than "lip service." The administrative structure of any department must provide the necessary resources for effective training programs and permit, indeed encourage, staff participation.

Generally, correctional training efforts are meager at best. They are by tradition very similar and often are the result of a crisis situation which necessitated them, but which makes their perpetuation absurd. Breaking the cycle of mediocrity may be realized through the following strategies: (1) the formulation of general training goals and policies congruent with the goals of the agency, (2) the development of an understanding for staff needs in relationship to those training goals, (3) the development of specific training programs and resources to meet the needs expressed, and (4) the development of a "measurability" capacity to assess degrees of expected outcomes in a process of continuing evaluation and modification.

The major indices of effective training programs are that they be relevant, individualized, ongoing, and flexible. First of all, any training should be appropriate to the responsibilities and duties of those individuals receiving it. Lack of adherence to this principle was found in field and institutional units where staff was trained, at considerable time and cost, in I-level theory and techniques when they had workloads that almost totally prohibited the implementation of this system. Another example is the training of supervisors in sophisticated therapeutic techniques such as psychodrama when they neither use these techniques with clients nor teach them to other staff. Secondly, to maximize the investment in the professional development of each worker, training must be individualized, i.e. based on his training needs rather than those of an overall group of workers. The most frequent abuse of this occurs when large groups of employees are "processed" through the same program with the primary consideration being, not individual needs and capacities, but available space in a particular program. Third, just as no one ever reaches the zenith of knowledge, so no correctional worker ever achieves, let alone maintains, his maximum capability; professional development is a never-ending endeavor. Fourth, a repetitious or unmodified training program quickly develops *rigor mortis*. Any effective effort at professional development must be malleable and flexible so that it can be adopted to new and changing needs and techniques.

Trainers and training are at a premium in corrections. To acquire a greater share of existing resources or to develop new ones will necessitate both a greater budgetary commitment and a sharpened resourcefulness. Obviously, these are both largely dependent on overall agency commitment and careful planning.

Some agencies have progressed rather far in this regard, while others have barely begun to tap available resources. The first and most important source of training potential is within each individual agency. The most recent study of training, referred to above, stressed two priority targets:[16] the development of specialized trainers in each agency and the motivation and enabling of first line supervisors to carry out their role as training agents in their organizations. While large agencies are or should be able to provide most of their own training, the state needs to play an increasingly stronger role in providing basic training for small departments and more specialized programs for all who need them. Cooperative or contractual arrangements with other correctional, or non-correctional agencies with similar needs (e.g. welfare, mental health, or law enforcement agencies), could provide an increased sharing of training resources. Similarly, contracts with private agencies or individuals could make expert assistance readily available. Colleges and universities have been a traditional pre-employment aid if not *sine qua non* for corrections. However, only minimal use has been made of the potential for graduate or specialized training. Departments should not only allow but should actively encourage and enable their staff to participate in advanced educational programs.

The fourth system-wide need is the coordination of training activities and resources throughout the state. This responsibility should be assigned to a special unit within a Department of Correctional Services, generally following the principles and guidelines of the CO-ACT concept, a design developed by the California Correctional Training Project in the document Training for Tomorrow.[17] The model suggests:

(1) The creation of a training unit which would be part of the Department of Correctional Services and serve as a single staff arm for manpower and training for California's State and county correctional agencies.

(2) The informal consolidation of all specialist training personnel employed by and/or assigned to service correctional agencies into a structured association or network.

(3) The activation of a partnership between the training network system and the state training unit by appropriate means, such that each partner will serve the other to the advantage of the total correctional system. The state training unit and its accompanying statewide network would exist to:

a. Serve as a coordination point for correctional manpower development planning.

b. Constitute a seat of authority and expertise by which corrections can interact with other segments of the criminal justice system and with the spokesmen of higher education relative to matters of manpower development and training.

c. Provide about 35 probation departments (too small to support their own formal manpower development programs) a complete array of orientation, initial basic, and on-going in-service training.

d. Assume responsibility for providing, upon the request and with the assistance of a particular agency, specialist, supervisory, and management training and other manpower development services to that agency.

e. Develop and make available to network personnel an extensive inventory of information, expertise, equipment, material, and other resources.

f. Request, receive, and disburse funds for the use of individual correctional agencies to enable them to initiate and/or augment their own training programs.

g. The nature of this unit should be temporary and flexible. Its concern should be with distribution of service not with self-perpetuation.

(4) The formation of an advisory body of representatives from local criminal justice, correctional, and educational agencies, as well as other appropriate persons, to assist in the accomplishment of all the above.

In addition, it is recommended that this central training coordination unit assume the responsibility, together with its agency network and their advisory body, for developing and operating a *certification* program for correctional personnel. Certification, long urged by many correctional practitioners, should assure uniform minimum requirements for employees, lead to higher and more uniform quality of performance by staff, provide the basis for greater flexibility and mobility of workers between agencies, increase the correctional worker's self-image as a recognized professional, and promote the image of corrections as a profession in the public's eye. The various types or levels of certification, the requirements for each, and other details of administering the program need to be worked out by the Department of Correctional Services. It is suggested that the minimum requirements include an appropriate level of academic achievement and the completion of an on-the-job "internship" during which a satisfactory level of competence is demonstrated.

§ *4.10   Funding*

Funding has always been critical in corrections, and data from one state clearly reflects this problem. The total correctional population consisted of some 274,000 offenders. Of this number, approximately 53,000 or 18% are institutionalized. Some 80% of the offender population is handled by field services.

The fiscal data available indicate that in support of these correctional programs the state spent in excess of $220,000,000. An analysis of the expenditure of these funds reveals the very striking facts that (1) approximately 67% of the funds were spent on the 18% of the population who were in institutions, whereas (2) only approximately 33% of the funds were expended on the 80% of the offender population who were handled in field programs.

An inescapable observation emerges from this analysis. In the most gross terms, the state is presently expending a disproportionate amount of its correctional dollar on programs with the smallest number of clients, and which currently appear to have the smallest payoff. Crudely put, it appears that the state is wagering too heavily on the wrong horse.

Additional analysis reveals that the burden of these funds is inequitably distributed. Probation supervision which handles the largest proportion of the population, is paid for primarily by the county with some help from the state. The same is true in the funding of juvenile camps, ranches and schools. County jails, including work furlough programs, are funded totally by local government. The state assumes fiscal responsibility for the operation of prisons and juvenile state institutions with very little reimbursement paid to it by counties.

As indicated earlier, in the last analysis the state must assume the ultimate responsibility for crime, criminals and their correction. It is the state which has the responsibility to insure that the funding for corrections is sufficient, and that it is equitably and effectively distributed.

The state corrections subsidy should establish priorities. Among these priorities are the following:

(1) Probation supervision and investigation, including probation-operated day care centers. These should be subsidized by the state at 75% of the operational cost.
(2) Local "open" institutions, which provide residents with almost daily contact with the community. These should be subsidized by the state at 60% of the operational cost.
(3) Local "closed" institutions, which are short-term (i.e. maximum confinement not greater than six months) and community-based (i.e. located in or adjacent to the communities which they purport to serve and involve a high degree of interaction with the community.) These should be subsidized by the state at 40% of the operational cost.
(4) Other local institutions, which are not short-term or community-based. These should be subsidized by the state at 25% of the operational cost.

Additionally, it is recommended that county correctional operations which find it necessary to seek commitment of offenders to state operated institutions be required to reimburse the state for 75%

of the "career cost" for such commitments, to include institutional care and parole supervision, unless the county wishes to contract with the state for county provision of the parole supervision.

Further, it is recommended that counties be allowed to invite the state to provide probation services. When such a request is made of the state and found to be appropriate, it should be possible for the county to contract with the state for such services. The county should then pay the state 25% of the operational cost.

This new subsidy program should be reviewed annually and revised as necessary. The state, in cooperation with the counties, should develop minimal standards for the operation of the local correctional program and require adherence to such standards as a requirement for receiving the subsidy. The state should have the obligation to enforce these standards.

It is anticipated that commitments to state institutions would continue to decline. This would allow the state the opportunity to close existing facilities that are old and poorly situated, with consequent savings developing therefrom. It is strongly recommended that the savings realized be sequestered for the use of correction. Additionally, it is recommended that the proceeds resulting from the sale of any institutions which are closed also be sequestered for the use of corrections.

Finally, it is recommended that the state seek appropriate federal funds to augment the state's correctional budget during the first year of the operation of this new correction subsidy program.

§ *4.11 Standard setting*

The concept of the state having responsibility to set and enforce standards for the operation of correctional service is not new. At the present time, some states have such provisions regarding certain correctional agencies.

For example, the California Board of Corrections is presently charged with the responsibility for approving all plans for jail construction and, in addition, is charged with the responsibility for inspecting jails. It does not, however, have any authority to close those jails which it finds to be substandard. The laws which define this responsibility and which grant the existing authority are inconsistent and, in terms of the intent, are patently ineffective. This situation continues to exist in spite of the fact that evidence available indicates that virtually all the sheriffs who operate these jails are in favor of mandatory and enforced state standards for jail operations.

The state must discharge this responsibility in a way which is creditable to the local correction operation; the state does not necessarily have a history of credibility along these lines. For example, the state currently insists that no county operated juvenile institution can house more than 100 youths. At the same time, the California Youth Authority operates juvenile facilities with capacities up to 1,200.

The standards developed by the state must not only be credible but realistic. Endemic to the field of corrections today are a host of correctional "myths" which masquerade as correctional standards. An example of such a correctional myth is the arbitrary figure of 50 as the standard maximum caseload size for probation and parole. Carter and Wilkins assert:

> The fifty unit workload as a standard for probation and parole supervision is an example of one of the myths. Where did this number come from? On what empirical data is it based? Is it an appropriate limitation of caseload size? If it is not appropriate, what should be the workload for corrections? A search of the literature dates the fifty unit concept back to at least 1922, when Charles L. Chute, then President of the National Probation Association, observed: 'To this end fifty cases is as many as any probation officer ought to carry.' The fifty unit concept found its way into the prestigious academic literature . . .
>
> The institutionalization of the fifty unit concept is now firmly entrenched. Budget for operating agencies, testimony before legislative bodies, standards of practice, and the projection for future operational needs all center about this number. There is no evidence of any empirical justification for fifty, nor for that matter, any other number.[18]

The setting of standards which are realistic and related to the task to be carried out presents both a conceptual and empirical problem. It is suggested that the crucial determining variables revolve around client and staff needs, resources and capabilities. It is also necessary that the state be provided with the capability essential to the accomplishment of setting realistic and effective standards, namely an evaluative and research capability.

§ 4.12   Research and evaluation

The most conspicuous problems in corrections today are lack of knowledge and unsystematic approach to the development of programs and techniques. Changes in correctional treatment have been guided primarily by what Wright calls 'intuitive opportunism,' a kind of goal-oriented guessing.[19]

The President's Crime Commission's description accurately portrays the current state in California corrections. It may seem curious that this is the case when the state of California is internationally respected for its correctional research.

If the correctional system is to operate as a system, it must have the capability to count and describe its actions, evaluate those actions and feed back those evaluations, and project and evaluate new forms or styles of correctional action. At the present time, most components at best have only a minimal capability of feeding back even this elementary information. Only in a limited portion of the various correctional components is there any capability for providing more adequate description; capability for evaluating the outcomes and feeding back that information to the practitioner is even more limited.

A clear need exists to have a research and evaluative capability extant at all levels of corrections and integrated together into a statewide research system. It is the position of the System Task Force that the state has the responsibility for the creation of such a capability. The state must devise a research and evaluation system which would provide to the program unit information regarding that program unit *per se* and additionally information regarding the nature and activity level of other closely related units. Such a system should bring to the practitioner timely descriptive information and reasonably current analytical evaluations. It should provide the practitioner with information for decision-making, a capability which does not exist at the present time.

It is envisioned that such a system would allow corrections to assume an orientation consistent with its goal. It would allow corrections to be "outcome" oriented. The system as a whole and components within could make determinations regarding the continuation or modification of programs based upon an analysis of their outcomes. It is the position of this study that programs should live or die on the basis of results and not mere historical inertia.

It is essential that the research and evaluation system be integrated into the organizational structure of the correctional system and that it be part of the communicative linkage. If it is to serve its purpose, research must be close to each practitioner. The practitioner must not only be in a position to receive informational output from the research operation but additionally be in a position to input questions, hypotheses, and theoretical perspectives. Where research capabilities currently exist, too frequently they tend to stand and operate in isolation from the practitioners. Thus, the results are often seen as curious and irrelevant to the decisions which must be made by a program administrator. Also, they are frequently viewed as providing answers to the wrong questions. Further, they are frequently viewed as impoverished in conceptual or theoretical equipment which could be gained from the minds of the correctional practitioner.

The current absence of an evaluative capability throughout the entire system aids and abets the continuation of discontinuities within the correctional enterprise. It allows program decisions to reflect current fads and fashions, prejudice and hunch, rather than rational determination and planning.

Notes

1. In this regard, the recent reports of one of the communities in California are informative with regard to the problems of intake, the problem of cost, and the problem of effective treatment. The recent reports of The San Francisco Committee on Crime dealing with "non-victim crime in San Francisco" provide an excellent analysis of the problem under discussion.

2. In this regard, see the companion Task Force Report on Juvenile Institutions for an excellent discussion of these problems.

3. President's Commission on Law Enforcement and Administration of Justice, *Task Force Report: Corrections*, (Washington: U.S. Government Printing Office, 1967), p. 44.

4. *Ibid.*

5. *Ibid.*

6. Robert E. Keldgord, "The Choice for Corrections—To Stand Up, Speak Up, or Shut Up," in *Corrections, the Public and You*, Frank Dell'Apa and Charles Weller (editors) Boulder: Western Interstate Commission for Higher Education, June 1968, p. 16.

7. Warren G. Bennis and Philip E. Slater, *The Temporary Society*, New York: Harper & Row Publishers, 1969, p. 54.

8. Warren G. Bennis, *Organization Development: Its Nature, Origins, and Prospects*, Reading: Addison-Wesley Publishing Co. 1969, p. 20.

9. John Gardner, *No Easy Victories*, New York: Harper & Row Publishers, 1969, p. 44.

10. Warren G. Bennis, *Changing Organization*, New York: McGraw-Hill, Inc., 1966, p. 14.

11. Marshal Fels, "Specialized Manpower in a Changing Correctional Climate" in *Perspectives on Correctional Manpower and Training,* Staff Report of Joint Commission on Correctional Manpower and Training, Lebanon: Sowers Printing Company, 1970, p. 48.

12. For a discussion of the general problem, see Clarence Schrag, "Some Foundations For a Theory of Correction," in *The Prison*, Donald R. Gressey, Editor, New York: Holt, Rinehart and Winston, Inc., 1961, pp. 309-357.

13. Department of Youth Authority, *Training For Tomorrow*, State of California, Sacramento, July 1970, p. 36.

14. California Task Force on Correctional Manpower and Training, *Mobilizing Correctional Manpower for California*, Sacramento, 1968, pp. 67-81.

15. Department of Youth Authority, *Training For Tomorrow*, op. cit., pp. 44-49.

16. *Ibid.*, pp. 81-83.

17. *Ibid.*, pp. 2-3.

18. Robert Carter and Leslie Wilkins, "Some Factors in Sentencing Policy," *Journal of Criminal Law, Criminology and Police Science*, Volume 58, No. 4, 1967, pp. 503-504.

19. President's Commission on Law Enforcement and Administration of Justice, *op. cit.*, p. 13.

II.   CHANGES IN CORRECTIONS DURING THE NEXT TWENTY YEARS

SOURCE: Daniel Glaser, "Changes in Corrections During the Next Twenty Years," *Future Roles of Criminal Justice Personnel: Position Papers*, Project STAR, American Justice Institute, Marina del Rey, California, 1971, pp. 1-62.

In anticipating trends in corrections during the next twenty years one must project current developments, both in corrections and in society as a whole. This will suggest that: (1) some change will occur in the characteristics of the offenders committed to correctional agencies; (2) there will be considerable shift in the location and type of service and control provided for them; (3) there will be much alteration in the offenders' relationships to correction staff and in their incentives for program participation; (4) there will be major modifications of the manner in which decisions are made on an individual's correction.

§ *4.13   Changes in correctional population*

Any forecast of correctional change in the next twenty years would be grossly deficient if it neglected one of the most crucial determinants of policy for corrections, the size and characteristics of its population input. Two important trends should be taken into account in correctional manpower recruitment and training plans: decriminalization of more and more behavior by changes in the law, and changes in the attributes of those committed to correctional agencies for behavior still regarded as criminal.

(1) Elimination of Victimless Crimes

One conspicuous change in American criminal codes which is slowly beginning and will probably accelerate in the next two decades, is a shift from prohibition to regulation or to nearly complete toleration of private vices. These actual or alleged abuses of one's self-interest, the victimizing of oneself rather than of others, will either be fully permitted (as perhaps not so damaging after all, or as the concern only of those involved), or they will be regulated by a licensing system. When licensing is established, criminal penalties are imposed only for violation of certain stipulations, such as a restriction on the age or other characteristics of the persons involved in the regulated activity, or a limitation of the locations where this activity may be pursued, and such violations generally are viewed as misdemeanors. Such changes in government reactions to private vices now are developing rapidly with respect to gambling, homosexuality and public intoxication, but only the latter creates a large correctional population, which is usually restricted to jails. These changes will affect prisons, probation and parole primarily in the control of drug use.

That a change in our marijuana laws is inevitable can be inferred simply by projecting age statistics. Polls reveal that about half the 18-to-20 year-old population use marijuana, large proportions of those in their twenties use it, but its use is known to relatively few in the age ranges above that, including less than 5 percent of those aged 40 and over. Marijuana use now is distributed through all social class strata, and is more common at colleges and universities, especially at the elite higher educational institutions, and particularly among those in fraternities and sororities. In twenty years today's young users will predominate among this country's policy-makers. Changes in our drug laws, prodded especially by this growing proportion of the electorate, will probably occur long before twenty years elapse.

Although proponents of present prohibitions against marijuana argue that research is needed before policy can be determined, sufficient knowledge already exists to establish clearly that marijuana is not as disabling as alcohol. But chemical effects were not the main factors determining passage or repeal of the Eighteenth Amendment, and repeal of the current marijuana prohibitions is as certain now as repeal of the Eighteenth Amendment was certain when gin parties prevailed among the college elite in the 1920s. When most or a very large fraction of the influential population have regular habits of consumption which may somewhat impair their behavior—whether the substances consumed are alcoholic beverages or marijuana—one cannot effectively impose severe criminal penalties against them. Furthermore, as society becomes more differentiated and mixed in occupations and life styles, tolerance of diversity in behavior increases, provided the behavior does not injure others. Also, consistently and completely enforcing laws against private and widespread behavior is so difficult, that corruption and inequity in law enforcement, and an overload for administration of justice frequently result. Therefore, many who find the illegal behavior objectionable nevertheless question the wisdom of declaring it criminal, in terms of the economic and social costs of enforcement efforts.

In recent years one city or state after another has ceased to employ correctional facilities for persons whose only misconduct is public intoxication, several have legalized gambling, and moves to reduce penalties for marijuana, or for its complete legalization, gain support from year to year. Changes in government reaction to use of opiates also are in progress which doubtless will accelerate in the coming decade. The purely repressive approach against marijuana and opiate use was intensified in the 1950s, but its failure became so manifest by the end of that decade that a civil commitment and psychotherapeutic treatment approach was substituted in the 1960s in the states with the highest concentration of addicts. The repressive approach was naive from the standpoint of psychology and economics, in assuming that the law could suppress private use and traffic of highly compact substances, especially drugs such as opiates which create physiological dependence in users and hence an inelastic demand. The civil commitment approach was sociologically naive in assuming that drug users concentrated involuntarily in institutions would lose rather than intensify their preoccupation with drugs, and their internalization of the connoisseur-like drug-appreciation values of their subculture.

Licensing of opiate use, by facilitating the addicts' oral intake of the least disabling opiates, methadone and acetylmethadol, is the pattern to which the United States and Britain are increasingly converging. This is supplemented by encouragement of ex-addict organizations that promote abstinence, such as Synanon and its scores of imitators. The dramatic advantage of these policies over their predecessors in this country can already be demonstrated so clearly, in terms of crime and cost reduction, that they make inevitable a rapid shift from a criminal to a public health approach to opiate addiction.

Implications for corrections of these changes from repression to regulation of marijuana and opiate use are readily apparent in recent trends. By 1970 narcotic offenses ranked just behind theft and burglary in frequency as the basis for a felony arrest in the United States. A very large fraction of the metropolitan theft and burglary arrests were for property offenses committed by addicts to pay for opiates. If drug possession or sale is either legal or a misdemeanor, and if drugs are cheap when legal, a large proportion of their effect on the correctional input will be eliminated. Of course, drug induced crimes of various sorts may still occur, but these are not likely to approach in frequency the currently alcohol-related majority of homicide; assault, rape and forgery convictions. If marijuana replaces alcohol as the social drug of preference in the United States, total arrests for crimes committed due to an intoxicated condition from one substance or another should decline simply because marijuana does not impair motor controls and moral inhibitions as much as alcohol does.

The other vices rapidly being legalized, notably off-track gambling, probably will not affect the correctional population greatly, as few gambling law violators now are arrested and convicted. Some increase in impulsive non-professional property offenses committed in desperation to recoup gambling losses may follow legalization of gambling, but those who commit these offenses are never likely to be a major part of our correctional burden. This is partly because persons involved in such offenses due to stress usually are better correctional risks than offenders who more routinely seek their income from property crimes instead of from legitimate employment.

(2) Changes in the Attributes of Those Committed to Correctional Agencies

A striking feature of correctional populations in the past two decades, especially in prisons, has been the higher-than-ever proportions who are from minority groups. These are primarily the poor minority groups, but now as ever, poverty is correlated with commitment to correctional agencies independent of ethnicity. In most correctional systems there have also been marked increases in the proportion of the clientele who are youthful, as well as in the number who are female. Since these trends reflect multiple causal processes, the task of forecasting their future direction raises complex considerations. They will be addressed here under the headings of age, ethnicity, poverty, and sex.

Age. It is characteristic of technological development in advanced industrial societies that the period of transition between complete economic dependence as a child and complete self-sufficiency as an adult takes longer and longer, and involves greater segregation of age groups than ever before. In less developed countries today, or in the United States only a few decades ago, most youth terminated their education at age 16 or earlier and began full-time employment. Even when still in school their part-time employment was required in household chores and in family farms or shops. Today most youth finish high school and enter some subsequent educational institution. When they are not in school their services at home or in family enterprises are less often required than formerly, and indeed, the prospects are greater than ever before that both parents will be at work when the children are not at school. Furthermore, affluence and urbanism increase the extent to which leisure activities for each age group occur away from home. The net result is that youth spend a larger percentage of their lives than ever before in an age-segregated world, with persons of about the same age as they are.

The transition from childhood dependence to adult self-sufficiency in our society is mainly structured by schooling and by employment. A third way exists for females only, that of marriage and becoming a housewife, but this is a full-time and secure preoccupation for a decreasing proportion of our female population and for a decreasing duration.

A fundamental law of sociology and anthropology is that social separation produces cultural differentiation. As a consequence of age segregation, youth today more than ever before differ from adults in their customs of speech, dress and behavior, including their standards of right and wrong. This is most dramatically illustrated by the figures already cited on marijuana use, an experience accepted and shared by most Americans in their late teen years today but still completely eschewed by over nine-tenths of those over 40 years old.

Superimposed on this greater age segregation is the longer period of schooling necessary before a youth can achieve economic self-sufficiency legitimately, in addition to his longer period of potential conflict with adults over his style of life. As a consequence of these trends, for the average person growing up in our society, there is a higher probability than ever before that at some time before he achieves autonomy by a legitimate economic self-sufficiency he will be in conflict with the law.

As a result of these trends the percent of total arrests reported to the FBI which were of persons under 18 increased from 4 percent in 1950 to 15 percent in 1960 and 24 percent in 1970. The extent to which this statistical trend reflects shifts in the completeness of reporting by age group we do not know, but one can think of reasons for believing that some shift occurred towards not reporting arrests of younger persons as well as some opposite shifts.

The causes of these trends which are creating a younger population input to corrections are primarily the technological changes, such as more home appliances and larger scale organization of enterprise, in corporations and government, which reduce the extent of parent-child contact in the family. These trends are likely to continue; therefore, it is probable that *the average age of first conflict with the law* will continue to decline somewhat. Whether the average age of correctional populations will also decline, however, will be determined by trends in the birth rate and in police and court decisions affecting assignment of offenders to correctional agencies and the duration of their retention by these agencies.

The birth rate trends are the most difficult to predict with confidence, but current indications are that the United States birth rate is declining. Because of this, the proportion of total population in the juvenile and youthful offender age range will decline within the next two decades, somewhat offsetting any decline in the average age of first conflict with the law. Police and judicial decisions affecting the age input to corrections, and the various factors affecting the duration of an offender's stay under correctional control, will be discussed later in this paper.

Ethnicity. For at least a century, and perhaps longer, the segments of our population most over-represented in the intake of American correctional agencies have been the children of those unskilled laborers who were the newest migrants from rural areas to our cities. In the late 19th century these were children of Irish and German peasant immigrants. In the first third of the 20th century they were children of Italian and Polish peasant immigrants. In the second third of this century they were children of Black, Puerto Rican and Mexican migrants to our cities.

Each of these ethnic shifts has been significant for correctional manpower recruitment and training because a major impediment to correctional effectiveness has been the ethnic prejudice and cultural conflict between correctional staff and their clientele. Anticipating changes in this problem in the next twenty years probably is the most difficult forecasting problem of this paper, but the current salience of this ethnic factor in correctional effectiveness is so great that an effort to reason out what its future may be seems worthwhile.

At present, in the early 1970s, limited data and general impressions suggest that Black, Puerto Rican and Mexican offenders predominate in correctional institutions more than ever before. The annual increase in the percentage of arrests that were non-white, however, had ceased by 1970, and a slight decline was indicated. Nevertheless, for some years, both in and out of prison, we have been in a period of high intensity of conflict between persons of Black, Puerto Rican, or Mexican descent and the ethnic segments of the population with greatest current status and power, those who are of White European descent. Projecting recent trends and applying sociological laws on the consequences of heightened intergroup conflict, however, leads one to predict that we are beginning a period of transition.

A fundamental law of sociology, unfortunately difficult to formulate with high precision, is that conflict within a group leads to a reduction of the causes of conflict, and hence ultimately increases the cohesion of the group. This must be qualified with the provision that this conflict is not over values so basic to the group's existence that it disintegrates the group. Interethnic conflict has repeatedly stimulated ethnic secessionist and revolutionary movements in most of the history of long-established countries. When previously subordinate groups do not achieve clear dominance or independence by these means, however, intergroup conflict ultimately is resolved by the minority group's achievement of more attractive statuses in the country's social, economic and political life, and eventually, by much fusion of ethnic groups.

Expansion of an underprivileged ethnic group's opportunities at first increases their discontent, for they become most aware of their relative deprivation only when they begin to view it as changeable. This is the current condition of America's Black and Spanish-speaking minorities. The rate of progress of members of these groups in achieving more prestigious, influential and rewarding social positions in the United States is increasing, however, and in the next twenty years they will probably become much more dispersed and assimilated in our social structure. While prejudice and ethnic militancy in the life of currently low achieving minorities will not disappear, the mobility of members of these groups to higher social, economic and political statuses should make ethnicity a less pronounced correlate of correctional commitment twenty years from now than it is currently. Already the proportion of non-Whites among arrestees for the FBI's Index Offenses appears to have reached a plateau at about 38 percent during the past five years. Non-Whites are an even higher—though in recent years declining—percentage of opiate crime arrestees (these are not Index Offenses). Decriminalization of opiate use by methadone programs should reduce this source of non-White correctional caseloads.

Immigration policies of the United States now restrict entrance of the unskilled. Puerto Rico probably will continue to send some rural unskilled persons to the mainland's urban slums, and legal or illegal entry of the unskilled from Mexico and other Latin American areas will continue as long as the difference in Gross National Product per Capita between the U.S. and these countries remains large. Immigration from elsewhere will probably continue to be limited by government controls primarily to more skilled or affluent persons.

As the current U.S. population of Latin American descent gains political and economic status, the discrimination problems encountered by newly migrant Latin American poor people probably will diminish. Even more important for them and for our poorest Black population is our next topic of discussion here, the fact that some of the most criminogenic features of the lives of all poor people in the United States probably will soon begin to change. These trends should reduce from its current peak the ethnic contrast of correctional and non-correctional populations.

Poverty. A major factor in many criminal careers is poverty. In our society there are tremendous pressures today to own an automobile and certain other possessions, such as a television set, in addition to having a satisfactory income. Most crime which results in prolonged commitment to correctional agencies involves an effort to obtain money or an automobile illegally. Recidivism frequently reflects a continued inability to earn much income. Persistent serious juvenile offenses are associated with two frequent correlates of poverty, the fatherless home and the concentration of multi-problem welfare families in certain parts of the city, especially in public housing projects. It is not suggested here that these conditions alone cause delinquency or crime, but that they increase its probability. A full discussion of the complexities of criminal etiology is beyond the scope of this paper.

As of this writing the most drastic revision of American welfare legislation principles since the Social Security Act has twice passed the U.S. House of Representatives and will doubtless become the law of the land either just before or after the 1972 elections. This is currently designated the Family Assistance Plan, and its variants have been dubbed "negative income tax" or "work incentive welfare" programs. Most of the remaining opposition to such proposals in Congress is over initial levels of subsidy, and perhaps over which party shall get credit for passing it, rather than opposition to it in principle. Most now seem to recognize that economic assistance for poor people in the United States for nearly four decades has had, more or less completely, the following problem-generating features:

a. Continuous welfare payments to those who are not physically handicapped or of old age is based primarily on their being mothers of dependent children. The presence of an employed father in the household renders the mother ineligible for aid-to-dependent children, regardless of the level of the father's earning. Therefore, many families of low-earning males gain income if the father is not in the household and does not officially support them.

b.   When members of a family on welfare earn some money or are given financial assistance by an absent father or other relative, they are expected to report this, and if they do, it will be deducted from their welfare payments. They are thereby subjected to a 100 percent tax on such income, and thus discouraged from seeking part-time or low-paying work, or encouraged only to work at tasks of which welfare officials will not be informed. Illegal earnings are the easiest to hide, as they involve no social security deductions.

c.   Those on welfare are expected to live within an approved budget, which usually means that they must have low cost housing. They have priority in public housing. Therefore, they tend to be concentrated in certain parts of the community where generations are reared and multiply accepting welfare as the normal way of life.

d.   Federal welfare contributions are, in part, proportional to state contributions, and in part independent, and net welfare payment rates vary greatly. Therefore, migration from the poorer states, such as Mississippi and Alabama, to high welfare payment states, such as New York and California, is encouraged. The courts have now barred lengthy state residence requirements as a precondition for welfare eligibility.

Some of these problems from welfare administration already have been alleviated by state and federal actions, but all would be corrected by the "Family Assistance Plan" now before Congress as H.R.1, and by alternate bills that have been proposed. The principal features of these measures are:

(a)   Payment is the same to all households according to their total earnings, the number of people in the household, and their ages, regardless of sex and marital status. This eliminates the economic incentives to not having a father in the household, and greatly expands the number of families in the "working poor" who are eligible for welfare. Some states already have initiated this feature to some extent.

(b)   Payments to those who work is on a sliding scale, over a wide range of earned income, so that all of an increase in earnings is not offset by a decrease in welfare payments. To suggest hypothetical figures, for example, it might be that if a family of four had only $2,000 in earnings thay would get $2,000 in welfare for a total income of $4,000; if they earned $3,000 they could receive $1,500 in welfare for a total income of $4,500; if they earned $4,000 they might receive $1,000 in welfare for a total income of $5,000, and only as their earning approached $6,000 would welfare payments dwindle to zero. This would mean that more families would be eligible for welfare initially than under current policies, but one could get off welfare safely and gradually.

(c)   As originally proposed, the payments would come entirely from federal funds and would be identical in all states. This was a stumbling block in Congress and has been compromised so that wealthier states have some matching fund arrangements for higher rates than the poorest states, and so that spokesmen for the poor may be alleviated of their fears that, under the new bill, payments to welfare families in wealthy states would diminish.

(d)   Welfare payments for those not working would be conditional on their participation in education or training programs, if they are not handicapped, and child care centers for working mothers would be expanded. These measures already are widely initiated under separate state and federal legislation.

The net effect of all these trends should be to diminish the importance of poverty in the determination of criminal careers, especially be diminishing the effect of welfare in expanding family problems, and concentrating the problem families in limited areas. It may reduce rural to urban migration of the poor, especially if welfare payments among states are equalized. Therefore, it would increase somewhat the proportion of the correctional population whose offenses reflect mainly subcultural variations, intergenerational conflict, and psychological stress apart from poverty.

Sex. Women's liberation, though still far from complete, has come furthest in this century. Consequently, women engage increasingly in all occupations traditionally restricted to males, and they also resemble males increasingly in their avocational pursuits, their social independence and their responsibilities. This means that to a growing extent they also engage in vocational, avocational or assaultive types of crime previously restricted to males. Therefore, the percentage of females among all arrestees reported to the FBI has slowly risen, from 10 percent in 1950 to 15 percent in 1970. With women's liberation now accelerating one can expect this percentage also to increase more rapidly in the next than in the past twenty years, perhaps doubling.

The increase of women in correctional populations will not be only in total proportion, but also in distribution by offense categories. In 1950 the proportion of male arrests that were for auto theft was about five times the proportion for this offense in female arrests; by 1970 this ratio was only three. In 1950 the proportion of male arrests that were for narcotics offenses was twice the proportion for these offenses in female arrests; by 1970 narcotics arrest comprised 5.2 percent of male arrests and 5.7 percent of female arrests. In general, the percentages in various offense categories should become more similar for the two sexes just as their percentage distributions in various occupations become similar.

Summary of Changes Expected in
Correctional Populations

For reasons set forth above, we can expect a correctional population in twenty years that will differ from that now received by correctional agencies, in being younger at first contact with corrections, but less contrasting with the general population in other attributes, such as ethnicity, poverty and sex. Accordingly, inter-generational, interpersonal and intra-personal conflicts will be even more prominent in the etiology of crime and delinquency, while economic handicaps will be less pronounced as causal influences in the future than now.

§ 4.14   Changes in location and types of correctional service

The only highly comprehensive survey yet undertaken of the distribution of correctional services in the United States was conducted during 1966 by the National Council on Crime and Delinquency for the President's Commission on Law Enforcement and the Administration of Justice; it is published as Appendix A to the Commission's *Task Force Report: Corrections,* in addition to being published separately by the Council.

The 1966 survey found the average daily population of corrections in the United States to be about 1¼ million, with two-thirds in the community and one third in institutions. About 28 percent were juveniles, of whom only 18 percent were in institutions; among the adults, 39 percent were in institutions. They estimated total expenditures for corrections as almost one billion dollars, with 80 percent spent for institutions despite their holding only a third of the people in correctional care.

Slightly less than a third of the population in correctional care during the 1966 survey were under state or federal authorities, in institutions or on parole. The remainder were under correctional agencies of local government. It was believed that this two-thirds under local authorities represented an increase from earlier times, since it was well known that locally administered probation and juvenile detention facilities had increased greatly since World War II (in large part due to efforts of the surveying agency, the National Council on Crime and Delinquency, originally the National Probation Association). Analysis of current developments suggests a continued localization of corrections through three processes: probation expansion and differentiation, growth of informal community corrections, and dispersion of state correctional operations. Jail use, however, may well decline.

(1) Probation Expansion and Differentiation

In California, and in other states to a lesser extent, dramatic increases of local predominance in correctional responsibilities have occurred since the 1966 survey. The major impetus for this in California was the initiation in 1966 of the Probation Subsidy Program under which the state pays each county for increasing the proportion of its youthful offenders whom it places under local probation instead of committing to state institutions; the state pays the counties some of the monies it saves from not institutionalizing these youth cases, but these monies must be employed by the counties to improve the rehabilitative services provided for probationers. Part of the probation expansion in lieu of commitment to state institutions has been accomplished by split sentences, with the first portion in jail, and the last on probation, thus increasing jail populations. The split sentence increase is presumed temporary.

While there currently are some administrative quarrels regarding the determination of probation subsidy payment rates, the overall program is regarded as a ringing success. It seems likely to continue, even if modified, and to be extended to all age ranges. In addition, the U.S. Law Enforcement Assistance Administration, in its funding and its publications, is fostering the development of local correctional services.

In the course of this expansion, probation is being differentiated in several ways. One way, long established in the two largest probation agencies, those of Los Angeles County and New York City, is that of separating the presentence investigation from the probationer supervision function of probation staff. Probation officers there, and increasingly elsewhere, are either presentence investigators or case supervisors, not both. This split was necessary because, despite the rhetoric of social workers in probation on the need to build relationships between officers and clientele, an officer is much more immediately and powerfully motivated to prepare investigation reports for the judge than to build rehabilitative relationships with clientele. Reports are tangible creations, are used and assessed by the officer's superiors, and have deadlines, none of which can be said of the officer's relationships with clientele, so the proportion of time spent on presentence work almost invariably expands at the expense of services for probationers.

A second type of differentiation likely to grow in probation offices is the administration of pretrial release on recognizance. Since the Manhattan Bail Project of the Vera Foundation in the early 1960s there has been increased support for release of defendants without monetary bail, provided they have been stable in residence and employment, and have other characteristics indicating that if released they probably will report to court voluntarily and on schedule. Administering such a program well requires a special staff to interview and investigate defendants in order to advise the court on the risk in releasing them without bail. In New York City this task now is performed by a special section of the Office of Probation. Opposition to release on recognizance has come mainly from the bonding companies who lose business from it and so impede change through major contributions to the political campaigns of those who oppose change, and from "hard-line" law enforcement officials or others who advocate pretrial "preventive detention." Despite these objections, the obvious moral, economic and rehabilitative advantages of release on recognizance over bail or jail, and the successful experience with this mode of release, will doubtless foster its growth during the next twenty years. Nevertheless, continual objection to it will create pressure for careful investigations and research in conjunction with such release, and hence continuous need for appropriately trained recognizance investigators and researchers.

A third type of special function likely to be administered through probation offices is conditional release to employment or training. This might be considered a type of probationary release on recognizance. The Manhattan Court Employment Project of the Vera Foundation, as well as Operation Crossroads in the Washington, D.C. courts, and several other experimental programs financed by the U.S. Department of Labor, involve pretrial release of persons who are not employed and hence could not meet normal requirements for recognizance. This kind of release is granted on their agreement to report regularly to an office which tries to place them in vocational training programs, often with a stipend, or helps them procure employment. If they fail to cooperate in these efforts the court is notified, and the court also receives a report on their training and employment progress whenever their case is ready for trial. Frequently, this pretrial record renders them safe risks for probation or even moves the judge to dismiss charges against them, whereas without the program they would be in jail before trial and probably would not be considered a good probation risk if convicted. The rehabilitative and economic advantages of such programs over traditional court procedures makes it probable that they will grow and will require appropriately trained administrative personnel.

The fourth function for probation offices which can be expected to increase is the collection of fines. Research has repeatedly indicated that employed persons are markedly deterred from a considerable variety of crime if they are merely fined. This penalty is less conducive to crime, and less penalizing to the families of offenders than is imprisonment. Experience in Britain, Scandinavia and elsewhere, as well as obvious principles of equity and psychology, suggest that fines should have two features usually absent when they are imposed in the United States:

a. Fines should be fixed as a fraction of the offender's annual income rather than being the same for all persons regardless of their income.

b. Fines should be payable in installments, if necessary, rather than being automatically replaced by jail confinement if the convicted person does not have the required funds immediately.
This means that the court must investigate the income of offenders and must operate as a collection agency, which in turn requires that it recruit and train special administrative personnel.

All of these changes in the functions of probation offices are resisted by many social work-trained probation officials as incompatible with the psychotherapeutic role they recommend for a probation officer. Whether this psychotherapeutic role is a realistic description or a myth in most cases can be debated. Regardless, specialized personnel for presentence and recognizance investigation, and for administration of pretrial employment and the collection of fines, are needed in the interest of justice and rehabilitation. These services need not be administered entirely or at all by social work-trained probation officers, but they should be undertaken by someone in the Probation Office or in some other court agency. Regardless of which agency does them, these new duties will increasingly create new and special types of personnel recruitment and training requirements during the next twenty years. Some additional features of probation service changes will be discussed in later sections.

(2) Growth of Informal Community Corrections

Broadly construed, corrections encompasses every action taken to alter the behavior of a person accused of delinquency or crime, if it is directed at reducing the probability that he will commit further offenses. It follows that much police and court action prior to trial or in determination of sentences may have a correctional component. Determination of guilt and efforts to rehabilitate presumably should occur in succession, but in most police and court action informal admission of complicity (if not guilty as charged) precedes formal finding of guilt. Increasingly correctional plans or actions are initiated following informal admission or presumption of guilt.

The Anglo-American police system, which evolved from the 18th century one of privately employed watchmen, often persists, as James Q. Wilson has observed, in a watchman's style of operation. This style involves extensive informal contacts of police with politicians and other influential persons in the neighborhood and much informal handling of offenses without bringing the cases into court when the accused are from the neighborhood, especially if charges are not pressed. It also involved corruption. In the immediate post-World War decades a legalistic or militaristic style of policing developed, emphasizing formal training and discipline, impersonal enforcement of the law and referral of all cases to court. More recently, however, starting in suburbs and increasingly extended to central cities, a "service" style of police work has developed. This combines much of the decentralization and public relations concern of the watchman's style with the higher standards of professionalism, impartiality and freedom from corruption more characteristic of the legalistic style.

The service style in city policing is expecially extensive in handling juveniles, where patrolmen refer young arrestees to special police juvenile officers who investigate the possibilities of handling these cases outside the courtroom. If they refer a child to the probation officer of the juvenile court, they now have already handled much of the social investigation that was traditionally initiated only by the probation officer. Frequently there is much police disposition of these cases without referral to the courts, and this often involves unofficial probation, that certain behavioral requirements are laid down by the police officer to the juvenile or to his parents. Sometimes these conditions include regular reporting to the police, with the proviso that non-cooperation will result in referring the case to court.

In Los Angeles and elsewhere this service style of policing is rapidly being extended to adults with what Los Angeles calls the "Basic Car Plan," whereby one patrol car and its staff on all shifts are assigned to a given area of the city. They hold monthly public meetings and make many other efforts to know all residents in their area as well as possible. This increases the prospect that they will negotiate many criminal complaints of victims against offenders in a mutually agreed manner without referral to courts. With this service style of policing also comes the conception of police functions as comprising much more than law enforcement. The police are available for a large variety of emergency services and have a strong interest in delinquency and crime prevention. If, as seems probable, the service approach to police work increases, many commitments of offenders to correctional agencies will diminish, especially for juveniles.

One additional consequence of the service style of policing will be greater use of the summons instead of arrest in lesser offenses, to assure court appearance or to impose fines which the offender can elect to pay without appearing in court, as now is done for lesser traffic offenses. This will be the standard policy for a variety of misdemeanors by adults, especially where the police officer establishes that the offender is a local resident. This is a widespread practice in Britain and has been successfully pioneered in New York.

A second aspect of informal correctional service in the community involves the public defender's office. A correctional service before trial is justified if it is recognized that in most criminal cases the issue of guilt or innocence is really not in question, and that pretrial negotiation between the prosecution and the defense on the sentence that will result if defendant pleads guilty is the usual method for disposing of cases in the United States. Where this is accepted, it follows that the ultimate disposition of the case will be in the best interest of society if the rehabilitative needs of the accused are taken into account in the negotiations. Otherwise, the outcome of plea bargaining is determined only by the time requirements and uncertainty of results facing a prosecutor if he presses for conviction. A pretrial concern for rehabilitative needs often is shared by prosecutor and defense, but its effective reflection in their negotiations requires a staff to advise them of the offender's background, character and prospective circumstances under alternative sentences.

Supported by a grant from the Law Enforcement Assistance Administration, a program of *Rehabilitative Services for the Criminal Defense* was completed in the District of Columbia in 1967-70, on which a report with that title was widely distributed by LEAA. This controlled experiment employed a staff of both college-trained personnel and exoffenders of limited education. They investigated the backgrounds of accused persons in order to recommend to defense and prosecution lawyers before trial a disposition that would be optimum for the defendant's rehabilitation. The defense lawyer could then seek to obtain this disposition as a condition for his client's pleading guilty. The randomly selected experimental group of defendants whose lawyers received this service were acquitted or granted probation, or, if incarcerated, received short sentences, more frequently than did the control group, whose lawyers received no such service. Yet at a followup date the experimental group were found to have less recidivism than the control group, despite the fact that the average member of the experimental group had been free in the community longer, and thus had more opportunity to recidivate, than the average member of the control group. Savings in confinement costs more than paid for the rehabilitative services.

All of these developments will create new kinds of correctional manpower needs, in police and court agencies not usually conceived as part of corrections. If effective, as seems probable, they may reduce the number of cases handled by traditional correctional agencies, possibly creating a pressure for manpower reduction at traditional agencies.

(3)   Changes in Jails

The developments described above will diminish the use of jails for pretrial confinement. Recurrent scandals of homosexual rapes and other aggression by inmate cliques will evoke a reduction in the present utilization of group cells for pretrial offenders in jails. This will make some of our most modern jail structures (such as the Central Jail in Los Angeles and the Orange County Jail at Santa Ana) obsolete for their present functions.

Jails will increasingly be small structures near the courts, with a separate room regarded as a right of those pretrial prisoners who desire it. There will be more educational, organized recreation and work programs for sentenced jail prisoners, with pay incentives. These programs also will be available on a voluntary basis for unsentenced prisoners, if compatible with custodial requirements dictated by their record and the gravity of charges against them.

Work release and night-only confinement will increase. In total, jail sentences of continuous confinement for a full term will diminish as community correctional programs replace confinement of offenders, where their adjustment should and can be facilitated in the community immediately. Those whose record warrants more complete removal will be the residual requiring longer duration confinement in a prison, for protection of society from their serious predations.

All of these trends will change the character of jail employees, making more of them in civil service status as treatment specialists, and fewer deputy sheriffs dependent on appointment by elected sheriffs, and hence on political patronage.

(4)   Dispersion of State Correctional Operations

Prisons in the United States are located primarily in rural areas remote from the metropolitan slums from which most of their inmates come. Their locations reflect especially the malapportionment of representation in state legislatures prior to the One-man-One-vote decisions of the Supreme Court a decade ago. Legislators from rural counties, many of which were losing population due to the mechanization of agriculture, insisted that the state spend money for institutions in their counties as a condition for their supporting appropriations or legislation desired by metropolitan areas. That is why such anomalies occur as the Attica State Penitentiary in New York where 85 percent of the inmates are Blacks and Puerto Ricans, primarily from New York City, and all of the staff are White, predominantly from the rural areas around the institution. Continued politicking by institutional area residents, and by correctional employees' unions, have in some cases helped to preserve these maldistributions, notably in New York.

Correctional officials have long advocated smaller penal facilities near the metropolitan areas from which offenders come. They could establish many such centers only with the growth of work furlough and similar programs for continuous release of prisoners during the day to seek or to hold employment. This is usually permitted only during the few months immediately preceding the inmates' prospective date of parole, although in North Carolina it can be initiated when as little as 15 percent of a sentence has been served, and some other states have also permitted such release to occur soon after the sentence begins.

Special facilities for such programs were pioneered by the Federal Bureau of Prisons in the early 1960s, using units in major cities, each having a capacity of only 20 to 30 residents. Frequently these units were just a leased floor of a large YMCA or of a private hotel in the heart of the city. These special housing units were quite successful from an administrative, rehabilitative and diagnostic standpoint. Escapes were not appreciable, services could be seen as greatly relevant to the releasees' problems within the community, and where the resident's behavior indicated that he would not be a safe risk for parole, this risk could more quickly be known and acted upon than under traditional parole supervision.

Such centers have increased in the federal system and are now growing in several state systems. One of the better examples is the Central City Correctional Center in Los Angeles which now holds 60 inmates and may soon be expanded to accommodate 90, including both sexes. Residents arrive at the center when up to six months remain before their prospective parole dates. The District of Columbia has opened eight such centers in three years, several operated under contract by private agencies, including some under an organization of ex-convicts. It is clear that this trend creates a new location and a new set of qualifications for correctional institution employment.

It should be added that many residential homes are being provided for probationers and for parolees, especially for juveniles. The California Youth Authority's Community Treatment Program, the Wisconsin and New Jersey Departments of Corrections, the cities of Provo, Utah and Los Angeles, are among the units of government which now have many years of carefully researched experience with such "half-way in" houses. They are intended for selected types of offenders not requiring secure custody confinement if intensively serviced in the community, but with home situations which preclude a satisfactory adjustment if released immediately to live at home.

Summary of Changes Expected
in Location and Type of Correctional Services

Developments described above can be expected to locate correctional service more than ever before in the communities from which the offenders come. This service will consist much more of probation than of institutionalization, and probation or other court-administered offices will acquire new functions, such as investigating eligibility for release on recognizance, supervising pretrial employment, providing pretrial advice on rehabilitative needs to defense and prosecution lawyers, investigating offender's wealth or income as a basis for advising on appropriate fines, and collecting fines paid on an installment basis. In addition, the pre-sentence investigation and post-sentence supervision of probationers will increasingly become specialties performed by different staff. Also, much informal correctional action, such as unofficial probation, will be undertaken by police departments. For misdemeanors by adults the police will increasingly use a summons rather than arrest. Finally, more state and federal residences for imprisoned offenders near their parole date will be established in major cities, and such homes will also be used for some probationers.

§ 4.15   Changes in offender-staff relationships and in progress participation incentives

Preoccupation with punishment, with custody, or simply with efficient mass handling of large numbers of people, leads to treating people as objects, to be moved about with maximum social distance between them and staff. Interest in changing the ·characteristics and capabilities of offenders requires a different kind of relationship. Increasingly, it has become evident that people behave according to their past learning, current social relationships, and anticipated rewards. Therefore, rehabilitation requires an effort to change the offender's experience and his or her view of others. Four consequences of this perspective are evident as trends in corrections are likely to continue during the next twenty years. The first is a collaborative style of correctional institution management; the second is use of programmed instruction and "token" economies, to structure the relationship between rewards and performance; the third is recruitment of ex-offenders to correctional staff; the fourth is expansion of correctional clientele, so that it includes not just offenders but also, their families and their friends.

(1)   Collaborative Corrections

In a statement on correctional institutions which I prepared for the Corrections Task Force of the President's Commission on Law Enforcement and the Administration of Justice, I distinguished between the "traditional institution" and the "collaborative institution." The traditional institution keeps its inmates highly dependent on staff decisions as to when they should get up, what they should eat and what work they should do. The prison management tries to keep the inmates isolated from staff and from the community. This has the perhaps unintended effect of giving more influence among inmates to those few inmate politicians who know how to manipulate the prison situation most effectively; inmates must rely on advice from other inmates rather than from staff. In a traditional institution the staff necessarily controls inmates largely through key inmates whom they trust in jobs close to top officials. They rely on inmate informants for knowledge about other inmates, and accordingly, inmates do not trust each other or staff. Pressure against communication with staff puts the inmates on their own with respect to conducting or protecting themselves from aggression of inmates against other inmates. The vitality of an inmate subculture founded on violence and corruption is directly correlated with the social distance between inmates and staff.

Contrastingly, in the collaborative institution there is an effort to reduce mass handling of prisoners and to increase their individual responsibility for their own activities and schedules. In the optimum institution this has meant increased participation of line officers and work supervisors in consultation with inmates on classification and parole decisions, through replacement of central classification committees by unit classification teams. It has also involved more unit control of discipline, in part as an inmate group responsibility, and has fostered inmate participation in work, menu, safety, recreation, and other management planning. This model probably has been most developed in the federal correctional system, and perhaps least in New York, among larger states, for there all correctional officers still carry clubs and are highly autonomous at each institution.

Despite the shallow proposal to build superrepressive institutions, preferred by some New York State officials after the Attica riot, progress of collaborative approaches in the federal prisons, in the prisons of the State of Washington, and elsewhere, should influence American corrections most in the next twenty years. This will be somewhat impeded, but by no means terminated, from the effects of expanded probation and parole in making the offenders still in institutions more exclusively those who have been highly committed to crime, violent or intractable. Concentrating "trouble-making" inmates increases their social distance from staff, bases their treatment on the self-fulfilling assumption that they will be trouble-makers, and thus fosters their greater orientation to making trouble. Dispersing them where they can be fewer at one point, hence more readily controlled by staff and by other inmates, and giving them continuous opportunities to better their lot in prison by their own performance, can make almost all of them both more controllable and perhaps less oriented to crime after release. The prospect of a more collaborative approach growing in institution management will be enhanced by other types of rehabilitation program, discussed below, which also increase inmate responsibility and reduce distance between inmates and staff.

(2) Programmed Instruction, Token Economies
and Monetary Incentives

A revolution in applied psychology has developed over the past two decades from the demonstrated success of Skinner's operant conditioning frame of reference in coping with many types of learning deficiency and deviant behavior. Behavioral psychologists, guided by his frame of reference, have revealed subtle ways in which differences in reward for alternative types of conduct cause people to reject officially approved modes of conduct, become increasingly retarded in school, and acquire alternative types of learning and behavior, even extreme psychotic withdrawal or catatonia. They have also demonstrated that a radical metamorphosis can be achieved by close control of the frustrations and rewards which a person encounters.

Programmed instruction means breaking up learning tasks to simple components which are just difficult enough to offer some challenge to the student, but will neither frustrate him nor bore him. Only as he masters one unit does he go on to the next one. This is done on an individual basis by programmed texts or by teaching machines. It contrasts with traditional classroom methods of instruction, where a student who gets behind the class in one lesson unit is increasingly retarded as the class moves on to other lessons which require mastery of the unit in which he failed. Programmed instruction gives students the experience of continuous success, whether they go rapidly or slowly. It is especially relevant to the major fraction of correctional clientele who have had conflicts with school authorities early in their educational experience that impaired their learning, and who thereafter found school a progressively more frustrating and humiliating experience. In addition to being useful for most academic subjects, programmed instruction is highly effective for teaching many types of skilled trade.

The most effective uses of programmed instruction in corrections and other settings involves some combination of group and individual methods, and payments for lessons completed with token funds that can be used to purchase improved housing, food, recreation or other desiderata—even furloughs. In the Federal Youth Center at Morgantown, West Virginia and at the Draper Correctional Center at Elmore, Alabama, these methods have perhaps been most advanced. Inmates there have a diverse mixture of group and individual responsibilities and rewards, the provisions being dependent partly on personality differences among inmates. Dramatic changes in inmate achievement and behavior have been clearly demonstrated with these procedures. They already are being adopted by many institutions, particularly for juvenile and youthful offenders, and will doubtless become more widespread in correctional institutions, as they have in the armed forces and in industry. They require teachers and other staff with special training in behavioral psychology, and ideally, trained by an internship period at institutions where these methods are well-established.

The reduction of this nation's Gross National Product by suppression of prison industries during the Great Depression, from which prison work programs have nowhere fully recovered, will finally be recognized as not in the public interest. With a better managed economy and welfare programs which establish a floor on family income regardless of employment circumstances, there will be more willingness to introduce commercial manufacturing operations into prisons. These will be geared to training for job opportunities in the community. This will involve care to see that it is not exploitative, and that its pay does not compete with attractions in education and training programs. This will be achieved by providing comparable monetary incentives to achievement in all assignments, and by having educational and training progress requirements for more remunerative jobs. While prison pay rates will compare more favorably than they do at present with outside pay rates, there will be charges to working inmates for room, board, clothing and other supplies and services. Budget counseling will thus occur in prison, as well as savings, payments to dependents and even some credit. This will require more bookkeeping supervision staff and electronic bookkeeping equipment.

(3) Ex-Offenders as Correctional Staff

A major problem in relationships between offenders and staff is the difference in their backgrounds. Not only are the staff required to be free of criminal record, but the location of correctional institutions and the educational requirements for probation and parole officers usually result in correctional employees being very different in ethnic and economic background from most offenders. This probably impairs the staff's capacity to understand the

,offender, and it also makes it difficult for the offenders to have confidence that the staff member is capable of advising them soundly, or even that the staff members are trustworthy.

A growing development in the past decade, especially in the past few years, has been the supplementation of correctional staff by persons of a background similar to that of the correctional clientele. Not only are they similar ethnically, but they are often from the same neighborhood, had similar educational and vocational handicaps at one time and even have a criminal record.

The use of such paraprofessionals who once had the same problems as the clients has been extensive with alcoholics and drug addicts, following Alcoholics Anonymous and Synanon leadership. This model has now been extended to offenders without these addiction problems. Among the most dramatic examples is the RODEO project in Los Angeles, where each probation officer has two assistants called "community workers" that are from the neighborhood and often are themselves former probationers. All three share a single caseload, so that one or another is available at almost any time for crisis intervention. This program was used initially for juvenile offenders who would otherwise have been committed to probation camps. By saving this expense it has more than paid for itself, from an economy standpoint, in addition to coping more effectively with the needs of the subjects in the community.

The RODEO model has now been extended to adults in the Model Cities Program area of Los Angeles, in a project with the Swahili name HARAMBEE. Similar programs employing persons of ex-offender status as counsellors, or even as regular correctional officers, have been initiated in several other institution, probation and parole systems in the United States. They seem to be working well, and are likely to expand in the next two decades, increasing the job market for so-called "New Careerists."

(4)   The Offender's Social Circle
as Correctional Clientele

Although our law commits to correctional control only those individuals actually found to have engaged in delinquency or crime, we recognize that their behavior in the free community after their release will be very much affected by their families, friends, and other associates. In diverse ways some correctional programs are taking this into account.

Concern with the prison inmate's family has long been recognized in prison visitation programs. In Mississippi provision has long been made for conjugal visiting, partly on the assumption that it would preserve marriages, but perhaps mainly as an incentive to good behavior by inmates on farm assignments. In California conjugal visits have been more appropriately introduced as part of a family visitation program; it consists not just of two hours in which a man and his wife are alone in a shack, as in Mississippi, but involves all-day and overnight visits by an entire family in a cottage-like structure on the prison grounds. As frequently happens, this program was better understood and received by the public than by many correctional staff. Despite the fears of some officials, it has been successful in California, where it now is being expanded and probably will be adopted in most correctional systems within the next twenty years.

In probation and parole services, especially for juveniles, it has long been recognized that one must work with the families or even through the families to help an offender. In the RODEO and HARAMBEE projects this has been extended to specify that not just the offender's problems, but the entire family's problems, are the concern of the offender's probation officer and community workers. If the staff infers that the mother has difficulty in supervising her children because of her health problems, home management deficiencies, or economic difficulties, they concentrate on trying to help her solve these problems. The offices for these programs are small and located in the communities they serve. Offices include some recreation and coffee lounge space, so that they may be something of a community center or hangout, through which staff may become familiar with the associates of their clientele. In this way they learn much more about the probationers, and thus can be more effective in both controlling or assisting them, as circumstances require. The logic of this approach is so much sounder than that which employs only a downtown office to which only the client must report, that this decentralized approach and targeting on more than the client, is likely to increase in the next twenty years.

*Summary of Changes Expected in Offender-Staff Relations
and Program Participation Incentives*

For reasons elaborated above, correctional institutions can be expected to move towards closer collaboration between inmates and staff in those aspects of the management of institutions which do not involve custody decisions. This will occur in conjunction with decentralization of much classification and discipline responsibility to residential or work unit staff within the institution, working in close consultation with inmates. Programmed instruction and token economies will enhance inmate motivation to participate in rehabilitation programs, and their consequent achievement there. Employment of ex-offenders as staff, especially in community correction centers and in probation offices, should further reduce social distance between correctional clients and staff. Finally, directing efforts at assistance not just to offenders, but to all those to whom they are close in the community, should increase the crime prevention effectiveness of correctional efforts in the coming decades.

§ *4.16   Changes in decision-making processes for fixing the turning
points of correctional experience*

In most of the 19th century the duration and condition of a prisoner's confinement was determined almost entirely by one person and at one moment in time. When he sentenced a person to prison the judge specified the particular institution, the exact period of incarceration, and even some of the conditions, such as hard labor or solitary confinement. Of course, he was limited in this by the legislature, through its criminal statutes. With the introduction of probation the judge made a decision based on advice from a probation officer, and subject to change later if warranted by the subsequent behavior of the offender.

With parole the decision on duration was not only deferred, but responsibility for it was in large part transferred from the judge to a separate administrative agency. Good time laws also defer decision on duration of confinement and they give prison authorities some control over the release date, in addition to the control over an inmate's place and condition of confinement which they received, mainly in the 1930s, from prisoner classification laws. There have been many complaints about the incompetence with which decisions are made as to how long a man should be confined; whether these decisions are made by judges, prison wardens or parole boards. Important developments, however, can improve these decisions, and are likely to result in a shift in the location and basis of initiative for determining the turning points of a criminal career.

(1)   Deferral of Decision and Graduation of Release

One of the most dramatic changes in correctional administration has been the delegation to prison staff of authority to determine when an inmate may be permitted to leave the institution daily in order to work or attend school in the community. As indicated earlier, this not only applies in work release from traditional institutions to the adjacent community, but in assignment of inmates to community correctional residences within metropolitan areas. While this practice has been praised for its treatment advantages, it should be stressed again that it is also a diagnostic device. These are forms of trial release. They help staff determine more accurately than they could be observation in the institution alone whether an offender can safely be granted full release.

The knowledge which community correction officials acquire on the community adjustment problems of their wards often have a salutory effect in making traditional institution programs more relevant to the needs of offenders. It also improves the ability of administrators to judge the differential risk in releasing various individuals, confirming once again the repeatedly demonstrated fact that adjustment to prison life is a poor predictor of post-release adjustment, especially for older offenders.

The growing expertise, of correctional administrators in release risk assessment, contrasts sharply with the ineptness of traditional parole board members; particularly those who have no training relevant to correctional work and are political appointees. They make decisions of tremendous impact on the lives of prisoners on the basis of limited contact with each offender, of frequently irrelevant or inadequate information, and without systematic feedback as to the consequences of their decisions. The community corrections officials are each involved with only a few score men at one time. They know, immediately and daily, of the adjustment of those men whom they allow to go into the community. Contrastingly, a parole board deals with hundreds of offenders whose release does not occur until several months after its authorization by the board, and without close followup and analysis of the relevance of post-release behavior to the basis for release decisions.

Dissatisfaction with indeterminate sentences because of callous and incompetent administration by nonprofessional parole boards, and dissatisfaction with definite sentences because of the diversity and frequent incompetence of sentencing decisions by separate judges, continually creates pressures for new alternatives in determining the turning points of criminal careers. In Wisconsin and in Michigan this has been partially solved by civil service parole boards, whose members have experience in both the institution and the field services of the state correctional system. In the federal government and increasingly in states which make extensive use of community corrections, the parole boards are largely leaving decisions on work or study release to correctional administrators, then accepting parole recommendations on the basis of the offender's record during such graduated release. These two patterns are likely to expand in the coming decades, as they make more sense than those which are traditional.

Systematic learning from experience requires statistical record-keeping that is oriented to evaluating experience in a manner which provides policy guidance. This is done in business with profit and loss statements and with cost analyses. Corrections is slowly moving in this direction, but it has been greatly handicapped by conceiving of such a task as the separate province of a luxury called research, rather than as an integral part of management record-keeping.

(2)   The Fusion of Operational and
Research Record-Keeping and Accounting

In order to learn from experience one must know what that experience has been. In correctional operations the information and observations deemed noteworthy are recorded in operational records of many types, on each offender. These records include jacket face sheet summaries, detailed case histories, lists of institution assignments and disciplinary infractions, logs of casework staff contacts and actions, investigation reports and recommendations, written parole or probation reports submitted by the offenders, criminal record "rap sheets," and so forth. These are only partially standardized; the forms vary from system to system, there are often variations from one agency to another within a system, and officers vary in the completeness or style of their entries on the forms. Some officers who provide good correctional service keep poor records, and some officers who provide minimal service keep excellent records and write beautiful reports.

In general, correctional records are most likely to be prepared in a careful and complete manner if they are to be used by colleagues or superiors of the person who prepares them. They are most often filled out carelessly if they are used only by the person who prepares them, or if they are sent to a distant office from which there will be no feedback regardless of how carelessly the reports are completed. The latter situation has been a major impediment to guidance of correctional policy by research.

Presumably the information which is recorded for operations purposes is that which is deemed relevant to case management decisions. Because research and operations are poorly integrated in corrections, information for research is either collected expensively by research staff from operation records and special interviews with staff or offenders, or it is collected by operations staff on special forms they send to a research office. Either system of research data collection is prone to much error because the researcher is a stranger to the situation where he endeavors to collect data or because there is inadequate feedback to those who collect it for him if their entries are made carelessly or if they are made with misunderstanding of the instructions. In any case, operational decisions are guided by operations records and research analyses are based on research records, each frequently collecting different information or recording it differently.

Two persistent problems in operations are, first, uncertainty as to the relevance of the information recorded to the decisions which it is hoped the records may guide, and secondly, the time and expense of collecting a continually expanding variety and volume of records. Required operations report forms tend to expand because some item of information seems relevant on some case and officials then ask that this information be collected on all cases. There is much reliance on narrative accounts in correctional reports because officials wish to capture the complexities and uniqueness of each case, although narrative reports make it difficult to find answers to specific questions as compared to the ease of finding it on forms where there is a specific section for the answer to that question. Caseworkers in institutions, and probation or parole officers are especially burdened by demands for narrative reports, and they tend to divert time from casework to writing reports because only their reports are visible to their superiors, and because the reports are more tangible products of their work than are most of their observations or actions in casework.

In a few scattered correctional agencies it is beginning to be recognized that one of the research operations most useful to correctional administration and policy guidance is research on the record system used for routine operations. This research begins with a tabulation of the types of information collected in operations and the manner in which it is collected. Such an analysis usually reveals considerable duplication on some items of information, incompleteness on others, and diversity in the way the same kind of information is formulated on different forms. Analysis of evaluations and ratings that are in standardized categories reveal that each rater uses the categories differently; some call most people "excellent" while others call most "good" or "average," some usually make unfavorable judgments, others usually are favorable, and still others refuse to be very definite in any assessments.

The second step is to draft standardized forms in which all entries are to be made by checking precoded alternative categories under specific headings. These are based upon studies of which items of information are used most in making decisions, which are most correlated with variations in recidivism or other performance rates, and what formulations of the categories will be used in the most standard manner by staff (e.g., "top third, middle third and lower third" instead of "above average, average and below average" or "good, fair and poor"). Any such form should have some space for narrative comments on every page, to be used as a supplement whenever a staff member feels he should explain why his forced choice of a particular entry on the form should be qualified or when he thinks a special feature should be noted in a particular case.

The third step in developing such a form is to test it extensively, getting reactions of staff at all levels in using it, and perhaps having several staff complete the forms independently on the same cases, so that a check can be made on the items on which they disagree and the forms revised to reduce disagreement. Any form should require no separate instructions, if possible, or only minimal instructions, for if care in studying and remembering separate instructions is necessary for reliable entries it is likely that the quality of entries will deteriorate quickly in practice. This deterioration occurs because people forget instructions after initially studying them and they do not again refer to them (often they are unaware that they have deviated from the instructions). In addition, new staff later will start using the forms without referring to the instructions.

The forms to which reference is made here are just about all that are used in correctional operations: presentence, preparole or classification case summaries, parole or probation violation reports, work, education and other assignment records, disciplinary reports, and so forth. No system need revise all forms in this fashion at once, but all benefit with each form revised in this manner, and one revision usually generates requests for others. A narrative supplement can regularly be appended to these precoded forms if desired, but once an efficient precoded form is introduced one finds that most use is made of its short entries rather than the narrative; one can find the information one desires more efficiently from the short entries that are standardized and tested for optimum style, content and location. When the forms are prepared by one staff member for use by his colleagues or superiors, they are especially likely to be filled out completely and accurately, for staff members will be "called down" if there are gaps or errors in their entries. Staff soon prefer these "check off forms" to traditional forms because they are so much more efficiently prepared and used.

While these forms should be designed to meet operational needs, they can also be planned for efficient statistical tabulation of their entries. Ideally, they can be designed for direct conversion to computer card or tape records by an optical scanning machine, but where this is not feasible they can be keypunched. For many forms, including case summaries, those offenders who are literate can be asked to fill out the form, then the caseworker will check each entry with them and with other sources of information where possible, and correct it or, if he desires, take notes for use in preparation of a narrative supplement. This use of the offender is time-saving, increases accuracy, and makes part of the record not a mystery to them, thus promoting trust. With modern duplicating machinery or through multiple copy forms initially, one copy of every operational form can go to the research office for tabulation.

There are tremendous advantages in such an integration of research and operational records. Research staff can continually make cross-tabulations to see which information collected by operations, and presumed by them to be a useful guide in their decisions, is actually correlated with criteria of performance, such as parole violation, disciplinary problems, escapes, post-release earnings, recidivism, and so forth. Optimally, performance will be tabulated for similar types of offenders in different programs, to determine which programs are most effective for each type of offender. Because the same categories are used in operational descriptions of persons, assignment, and performances as in research tabulations on these matters, the relevance of research tabulations to operational considerations is more immediately evident than when research uses one language and operations another. Finally, because operations officials know what information is on their forms and, therefore, on computer tapes, they can decide on the tabulations they desire in connection with any questions which may arise in their deliberations, and the tabulation can be quickly provided. Their ability to assess experience and to justify alterations in policy is tremendously enhanced by such records improvements; it can make all programs and officials much more accountable.

Unfortunately, neither researchers nor operations staff are usually aware of the potential advantages for each that such integration of their records can provide. Nevertheless, scattered experience in such records integration, expansion of electronic data processing resources, and increased pressure for program performance budgeting in corrections should accelerate these improvements in the next two decades. Especially relevant is the ready utilization of such records for costs-benefits analysis.

It should not be concluded that all operations and research data requirements will be permanently satisfied by these precoded records. Special questions will arise requiring supplementary data collections, but these can be linked with the standardized data. Furthermore, the integrated record system should be continually monitored, so that the least useful items may be deleted, and persistently required supplementary information can be added to that which is routinely recorded. Finally, the optimum method for evaluation in many situations will still be controlled experimentation with new measures, and these usually will require special types of data collection to be linked with the standard data.

There obviously will be a need in the next two decades for research staff more oriented than most university Ph.D.s to correctional operations and policy needs. Unfortunately, correctionally experienced persons with higher degrees assigned to research tend to be clinicians whose training is not geared to statistical assessment of policies, and who often are not sensitized to non-clinical policy issues in corrections. Conversely, academically trained persons without experience in correctional administration often are oriented more to abstract issues, excessively complex statistics, and global appraisals than to the provision of guidance on immediate issues on which decisions must be made. Well-designed scientific evaluation studies for policy guidance are increasing, however, often by contracting private or non-profit research firms and institutes, and government officials are becoming more sophisticated in assessing and appreciating research. Therefore, it can be assumed that recruitment and training of research personnel for corrections will improve in the coming decades, guided by consultation with the small number of persons who have successfully completed much useful correctional research.

Summary of Changes in Decision-Making

For the reasons indicated, it is anticipated that changes in the next twenty years will expand the role of administrators in determining the turning points of correctional careers. The release turning point, however, will become less abrupt, because extended trial release via community correctional facilities will become the most prevalent procedure in determining readiness for release from confinement, as well as in reducing uncertainties as to whether probation or commitment to an institution is appropriate. The influence of judges and parole boards in case management will then diminish to the setting of outer limits and policy guidelines for administrative discretion. Policy guidance will be facilitated in all aspects of corrections by an integration of operations and research records to make forms and reports more standardized, and more relevant to decisions, as well as more readily converted by computers to statistical guidance data in policy-making.

§ 4.17   Conclusions

In the next twenty years the population input to all correctional endeavors will gradually change. There will be a lower average age at first conflict with the law, but this will be offset in its effect on the total correctional population, by a decline in the birth rate creating a smaller proportion of United States residents in the juvenile and youthful age ranges. It will also be offset in its effects on traditional correctional agencies by more informal police and court action to divert offenders, especially juveniles, from formal adjudication and commitment to correctional agencies. The net consequence of these trends will be an average age of the correctional population older than it is at present, just as the average age of the total United States population will be higher in the future than now.

In twenty years, more complete equality of opportunity for occupational achievement by today's repressed ethnic minorities, and their greater representation in prestigious political and social positions, will make the ethnic characteristics of the correctional population more like those of the general population than they are at present. This trend will be facilitated by welfare reforms currently proposed which will put a more uniform national floor on family income and reduce the current welfare law's encouragement of fatherless households, permanent complete dependence on welfare, and neighborhood concentration of multi-problem families.

Just as the progress of women's liberation in the next twenty years will distribute the sexes more equally than they are at present in various occupations, the proportion of females in the correctional population probably will increase, perhaps doubling.

Probation will continue to expand and institutional population decline. The presentence investigation and probationer supervision components of the probation officer's job will increasingly become separate specialties. Probation or other court offices will assume the tasks of investigating eligibility for release on recognizance, and checking the income or wealth relevant to fixing the rate of fines. They will also supervise conditional pretrial release to special employment training or placement programs, and will handle the installment collection of fines. Jails will seldom be employed as a means of "collecting" fines.

Informal disposition of delinquent or criminal complaints through mediation and warning by police will become more frequent. Adult misdemeanants will more frequently receive a summons instead of being arrested. Also, rehabilitation information will be provided by special court staff investigators to both defense and prosecution lawyers, to make consensus on rehabilitation needs a factor in their pretrial negotiations, if guilt is admitted.

New correctional institutions will consist primarily of small correctional centers in the community for graduated release from other institutions, or as group homes for community treatment of those without satisfactory home conditions, particularly juveniles. These community correction centers will be in regular residential structures, such as family-type houses, or in part or all of hotels and roominghouses, rather than specially constructed security type edifices. Use of jails will diminish, rehabilitation programs in jails will nevertheless expand for those who are confined there, and group confinement of pretrial prisoners in jails will markedly diminish.

Within institutions there will be more collaboration of inmates and staff in management, hence more inmate responsibility and less social distance between staff and inmates. Classification and discipline decision-making will be decentralized, and the concentration of "troublemakers" in particular units will be avoided. Progress in education and training while in prison will be accelerated by programmed instruction. There will be greater monetary incentives for achievement and conformity, including more opportunities for commercial involvement in prison industry by private firms, but under restrictions which will gear their activities to all program participation incentives in the institution, and to post-release job placement in the community.

An aspect of the reduction of social distance between correctional staff and their clientele will be more use of ex-offenders in corrections, especially in the community. This will be in conjunction with an expansion of the target of treatment, especially for juveniles, of not just the offender but his entire family. Such developments will involve a dispersion of probation offices to the neighborhoods where the probationers reside.

Transition from custody to community life will become more gradual for most offenders. This will shift responsibility for case decisions on the turning points in correctional careers from judges and parole boards to administrators; the courts and boards will only set outer limits and guidelines for administrative discretion.

This shift in the focus of decision-making will be facilitated by achieving a more scientific basis for decisions through closer integration of correctional operations and research. A major factor in this integration will be the fusion of operational and research records, to make the records more relevant and useful for both individual case management and statistical assessment of programs and policies.

III. RECYCLING HUMAN BEINGS

SOURCE: Edward Peoples, *Why We Are Failing to Recycle Our Most Valuable Resource–Human Beings,* Paper presented at the Congress of the National Recreation and Park Association, October, 1972.

It is vogue in many quarters today to cry out against the American correctional system and to demand its reform. For many, who are seeking an issue from which they might gain public or political recognition, it has become a new and popular theme to exploit for personal advantage. For others, the few who have had a sincere concern for their fellow man, it has become a new variation on a time-worn theme they have espoused in vain for years.

For some then, it is a personal opportunity to advance their own careers, with possible penal reform coming as a by-product of their efforts. For others, it is a rare opportunity to be heard, and possibly, to influence the civilizing of our society. In either case, it is unfortunate that unless a new approach to solving the problem is taken, their efforts will fail.

Their efforts will fail because they do not recognize that the direct source of our correctional problem lies not within the prison walls, but in the contractual relationship between the general public and those hired to administer all the parts of our system of criminal justice: the judges, defense and prosecuting attorneys, probation and parole officers, and institutional personnel.

§ *4.18 Accountability*

The key to understanding this relationship is one word, accountability. The public does not require it of those hired to administer the criminal justice system, and those in the system do not seem to believe they should be required to give it to the public. And neither, certainly, feels the need to be accountable to the offender. This relationship has developed over the years to the point where our correctional system now is assumed to be an autonomous service organization, tax supported, yet free to direct its own affairs toward goals which it defines for itself. It measures its failures in nebulous terms which lend themselves to easy manipulation, but in no way does it assume the responsibility for those failures. It lauds its successes before state legislators, yet those successes are measured against standards which are set from within the system.

In order that we might consider the full implications that this has, let us set aside for a moment the service organization model imposed on us by the system and imagine a business organization model. We can then view the entire situation more objectively and place it within a contemporary and more meaningful context—social ecology.

Think of it this way. We, the general public, have formed a gigantic recycling company called the administration of criminal justice in which each of us holds an equal share of stock. We have established three divisions within the company to handle production: law enforcement, the courts and corrections. And, we have hired managers to run the various branch plants. However, unlike other publicly owned companies, our recycling company is one of the few which has been able to remain in business without yielding a measurable return on investment.

Let us examine the operations of our company and the relationship between management and the stockholders in an attempt to understand some of the reasons for our failure to recycle your most valuable resource, human beings. To understand why, instead of returning a socialized, creative human being who will enhance our environment, we continue to return products that pollute it, and why we, in turn, blame the product completely for its problems upon re-entry to the environment.

Those in the police division are hired to detect and remove the products on the market who have developed behavioral flaws, as defined by the stockholders, to the point where some pollution of our environment by them is suspected. Relative to other divisions, the police share little of the blame for our company's failure. They are the one plant division operating today from which we do demand some accountability.

The court division is another matter. It is there that the actual recycling process begins, and begins to break down. True, of those working in that division—judges, defense and prosecuting attorneys—many are sincerely concerned about our human ecological problems and appreciate the weight of responsibility carried by their positions. Occasionally, one of them will cry out in the wilderness to improve our social environment. Unfortunately, too often their cries are either ignored or branded as nefarious by one extreme or another. However, there are others of that ilk working in our various court plants who hold themselves in high esteem as champions of justice, but who are in reality the *bête noir* of human ecology.

They are the defense attorneys who use the court room as a forum to advance self-serving ideas, and have no feeling of responsibility toward the company, or its stockholders, and who, in fact, seek personal glory by exploiting the very product they were hired to help, the offender. They are the district attorneys who sup at the public trough, obstensibly representing directly the stockholder's interests, while actually self-serving in their efforts. Those who seek political careers via inquisition or statistical conviction record, for example. Or, those who seek either to please a judge or become one, again at the expense of our human resources, the offender.

And, when these two meet in court as protagonists and, rather than seek some semblance of truth, they play Hotspur vs. Hal, or stage one of their Gilbert and Sullivan productions, or when they play games over the fate of the offender by using him as a pawn in their back room plea-bargaining sessions, are they concerned about our human resources or our social environment? I think not! I really think not!

And judges; we cannot overlook the role of the judges in our recycling process. Fortunately, most of them are qualified to determine whether or not a flaw in our product does exist, as defined by law. But that is where their qualifications end, and that is where their function in our company should end. They are not trained to determine the true nature and extent of the flaws our product might have. They know of recycling *places,* but not of recycling *processes;* and their thinking should not be the determining factor in the process prescribed for our products—in sentencing the offender.

§ 4.19 *Recycling*

This brings us to the third, and most important component of our company, the recycling plants, themselves, the corrections division. Corrections operates three types of processing subdivisions: probation, the institutions, and parole. Usually, those are further subdivided into juvenile and adult operations.

In theory our juvenile divisions operate differently than do the adult. Their original management philosophy was designed to represent the interests of the product and to protect him from being polluted by the environment. This division intervened in a juvenile situation as a substitute parent and gently recycled the product in his own behalf, while at the same time modifying the environment to better accomodate the needs of the product. This theory was fine; it still is. But for some reason the application has often failed to achieve the stated goals.

The juvenile court hearing to determine if flaws exist, once informal and civil, has evolved to a formal proceeding just short of an adult criminal trial. In many instances the court has brought this shift upon itself. The rhetoric spoke of methods "on behalf of," "in the interests of," or "for the protection of" the product, when anyone who has seen the process knows that far too often the juvenile has received full blame for his defects, was recycled just as severely as the adult, and had to accept the full responsibility for failing in the market place. If those working for the company did not realize this, the product did, and still does.

Many of our juvenile probation divisions report an increasing number of young defective products being referred to them for recycling rather than to institutions. In many cases their annual reports to the stockholders shows a sizeable return of those products to our environment as recycled—corrected—rehabilitated—cured.

This would be considered good business if it were not for the fact that most of those products were never defective in the first place. Their normal behavior to both normal and abnormal situations was deviant merely as the result of a definition imposed on them by the powers that be. Often they were brought into the community recycling division just to serve organizational goals. Call it a need for company growth. I call it probation colonizing.

I suppose that stockholders should feel grateful for this reported success. In truth, they are lucky that so many naturally wholesome young products made it through the process in spite of the recycling. There are some, however, not quite so fortunate, for they are on the verge of becoming defective. With the proper direction they can learn to guide themselves out of that position. But no, they become engulfed in the system and soon find themselves before a corrections worker who substitutes policies, procedures and rules for compassion and understanding, and knowledge for wisdom. By the time that worker leaves the case he will have found a defect in the product if he has to put one there himself. As time goes on other workers will spread the defect until the product actually does pollute the environment and has to be removed from it. All this is done "in behalf of" the product. And, all done in the public interest.

All this is not to say that we have no juvenile products in need of recycling. Indeed, we have many that are polluting our environment and need to be removed from it, for their sake as well as ours. Once removed, however, their defects should be defined honestly and treated honestly by workers trained in human ecology, not in management games.

Our community corrections divisions for adults are usually in worse condition than those for juveniles. They get less attention, receive fewer resources and often are staffed by less qualified (though more cynical) workers. In many of these divisions little recycling is attempted beyond surveillance, and immediate perfection in all behavior is expected of the product. Some products make it through this process unscathed; again, in spite of the system. They did not need company help in the first place. Others have their defects compounded and are then ordered into one of our institutional plants for an extensive recycling job.

Once a product is delivered to one of our 400, or so, massive stone plants, he is stripped of what self-respect, creative thought, dignity and independence he had left. He is told that he will be released when his defects have been corrected, and that when released he will be expected to return to a normal life. Unfortunately, many of those administrative functionaries (parole board members) who determine the degree of recycling necessary have no understanding of human ecology. Receiving their jobs through political patronage, they equate recycling with repayment in years of one's life. Their training does not provide them with alternative standards.

If the stockholders required the prison plants to return a profit in human output, those plants would have been closed years ago. The recycling process used molds the product into a dependent, unproductive, frustrated and hostile human being whose ability to adjust when returned to the environment so often has been totally destroyed. This is not surprising when one considers that 90% of the $1.5 billion spent annually on our prison plants goes for custody. The 10% spent on actual recycling often goes for methods outdated and meaningless in contemporary life.

I am cynical, I suppose, because I am confident that most of the general public will be unimpressed by the fact that our institutions fail to correct human defects, but instead force the products into an anti-social organizational relationship among themselves in order to survive. That the whole experience is brutalizing, de-humanizing and counter-productive in providing a meaningful way of life for the offender has rarely moved the public conscience. The fact that both the stockholders and the company managers have a moral obligation to provide true correction of human defects, and to allow the product to participate in his own correction has never received significant concern from them. The situation in most juvenile institutions is no better. Visit any juvenile reformatory, correctional facility, training school, or what ever name they go by, and talk to one of the wards about why he was sent there and what he thinks is the criteria for his release. He will tell you that he is serving time; that he must pay back society for a crime he committed with years from his young life.

A dedicated reformer, hearing this presented rather coldly as a recycling process might well ask "Aren't you merely stating in mechanical terms what I have been saying in human terms for years?" No! Not quite! Again, the reformer does not understand the relationship between the public and the system, nor does he recognize the basic approach needed to gain meaningful public support to change that relationship.

The majority of individuals who make up what we call our American society have for generations been motivated into action for a variety of reasons. Seldom has the honest concern for the dignity and welfare of others defined by them as deviant, been one of them. The pursuit of pleasure, profit and safety are those factors considered by most of us when directing our energies into action. The sincere reformers who have sought public support, thinking their cause was good, have tried to impose their own motives upon the public conscience. The usual results have been public apathy, an occasional token reform implemented by some administration as hush-money, and frustration for the reformer, all at the expense of both the offender and the public.

Occasionally, someone from the communications media has presented a documentary or an editorial vividly describing some of the de-humanizing, de-basing treatment rendered delinquent or criminal offenders placed in our "correctional" institutions. Often, and particularly in light of recent events at Attica, Soledad and San Quentin, this has aroused public indignation. We can expect that feeling to last about three days if it is over the treatment of adults, and possibly a week if it is over the treatment of juveniles. When the heat of the moment cools, the average good citizen turns his attention back to the immediate concerns of his own life.

The average citizen does not want to become involved in problems which he believes do not concern him. Why should he worry about some poor deviant whom he does not know, with whom he cannot identify, and whose treatment or condition he believes will never effect his own life? "Rehabilitate the offender? Sure," he will say. "That's a fine idea, but do it somewhere else, not near my neighborhood. He needs a rural setting, and don't expect me to pay out my hard earned money just to make his life more meaningful."

Protection is his primary concern, and he believes that the best protection he can receive is by having the offender removed from his immediate environment, forever if possible. A secondary consideration is the public's desire for revenge. The non-offender does not feel better if the offender is treated as a human being, for that makes the offender his equal. He feels better if the offender is punished, for that makes his own law abiding behavior worth the effort.

The solution, then, is fairly easy to comprehend. We merely need to use the public's own motivations to gain their support in bringing needed changes to our system of administering criminal justice. If the public is made to realize that they are not well kept by the system, but have allowed themselves to be used in an incestious relationship to satisfy the desires of their keepers, they will seek other arrangements. It is a simple matter to show that our correctional system fails to correct. The rub lies in convincing the public that *only* through the complete rehabilitation of the offender will they truly be protected, and free to pursue, and even increase their pleasure and profit. Only when the defective products have been fully recycled will they stop polluting our environment and instead, contribute to it. If the public and the managers hired to run our plants fail to revolutionize their processing methods, a revolution will be forced upon them by that element they fear most, the offenders themselves. They will have no other way of giving meaning to their lives.

When all the rhetoric of "correct," "rehabilitate," "re-train," "re-socialize," or "cure" is peeled off and the cold reality of the process is laid bare, we do not recycle the offender. We put him in a warehouse and prescribe time for his cure. We place him on a shelf where all his living is programmed. All decisions are made for him—when to rise, when and what to eat, and when and where and even how to sleep. As if he were a thing, we take a vital, living, feeling human being and recycle him with less concern than we have for a returned beer can. And worst of all, we do it on our terms. We define his defects, and by what process and in what form we want him to return to society, and never do we ask him to participate in the decisions by which that process and that form are determined. When we, or rather our plant managers decide that the process is complete, we relabel the product and push him out the door. And then we say, "be independent and responsible, and make it on your own, and do these restrictions much more demanding than we ourselves are willing to live by. If you fail, it is your fault, not ours."

Upon his return to the environment, we put the product under the re-entry processing plant, parole, wherein workers are hired to watch for any signs of cracks or flaws. When problems do occur in re-entry, rather than aiding the offender in working them out, many of those workers are all too quick to return him to the plant for additional recycling.

The stated company policy says to "re-socialize" the offender, but our plants operate to "de-socialize" him. If all this sounds too critical or too cynical, it is done deliberately in order to dramatize the issue. Gloom, despair and regression does not pervade the entire system for we have made some progress, particularly in federal corrections and in some states such as California, New York, Texas, Michigan and Georgia, and others. But to paraphrase a line by Robert Frost, "We have miles to go before we sleep."

Aside from self-protection, the public shows little concern for the problems of the offender while in the plant or during that period of adjustment upon his return. After the company managers re-label him as cured, the public denies his economic, social, moral and legal re-entry. He is the bastard child from the illicit relationship of which I spoke. Disinherited, yet condemned again if he soils the family name. It is time that what we refer to as the offenders' problems be considered more honestly as environmental problems.

If the public is made aware of the fact that 90% of the imprisoned offenders are returned to our environment, ready or not, they might re-evaluate their relationship with the company and recognize that they have a vested interest in the company's production and profit. The public now holds business and industry accountable for any polluting of our waters, our earth and our air. If ecology is as important as the public leads us to believe, it seems reasonable that they should want to hold the criminal justice system accountable for any polluting of our social environment. It seems logical to think that the public would want to say to those they hired to administer the company, "Look, that is not your company it is ours. You work for us. You are not in business for yourself. You *will* manage the plants by methods that we determine to be in our interests, not yours. You *will* use processes which actually recycle our products, and not just re-label them, for they are of us and will return to us. And, if you don't we will hire someone else who will. Those products are our most valuable resource, human beings."

PART 5

THE PUBLIC

§ 5.1 Introduction

Citizen involvement in crime prevention efforts is not merely desirable but necessary. The reports of the President's Commission on Law Enforcement and Administration of Justice emphasize the need for direct citizen action to improve law enforcement and for crime prevention to become the business of every American. Police and other specialists alone cannot control crime; they need "all the help the community can give them"[1]

Similarly, a task force of the National Commission on the Causes and Prevention of Violence noted:

> Government programs for the control of crime are unlikely to succeed all alone. Informed private citizens, playing a variety of roles, can make a decisive difference in the prevention, detection and prosecution of crime, the fair administration of justice, and the restoration of offenders to the community.[2]

These and other pleas for citizen action are heeded by too few. Most citizens agree that crime prevention is everybody's business, but too many fail to accept crime prevention as everybody's duty. "There are simply too many important aspects of the private citizen's duty to expect local government to solve the crime problem by itself."[3]

Crime prevention as each citizen's duty is not a new idea. In the early days of law enforcement, well over a thousand years ago, the peacekeeping system encouraged the concept of mutual responsibility. Each individual was responsible not only for his actions but for those of his neighbors. A citizen observing a crime had the duty to rouse his neighbors and pursue the criminal. Peace was kept, for the most part, not by officials but by the whole community.

With the rise of specialization, citizens began to delegate their personal law enforcement responsibilities by paying others to assume peacekeeping duties. Law enforcement evolved into a multifaceted specialty as citizens relinquished more of their crime prevention activities. But the benefits of specialization are not unlimited. Criminal justice professionals readily and repeatedly admit that, in the absence of citizen assistance, neither more manpower, nor improved technology, nor additional money will enable law enforcement to shoulder the monumental burden of combating crime in America.   303

The need today is for a more balanced allocation of law enforcement duties between specialists and citizenry—for citizens to reassume many of their discarded crime prevention responsibilities.

> Community leadership appears all too willing to delegate (or default) its responsibility for dealing with antisocial behavior. Eventaully that responsibility is assumed by large, public agencies . . . (The extremely expensive services of these agencies) never seem to catch up with the need. They come too late to be "preventive" in the most desirable sense of the word. Moreover, the policies are controlled from political and administrative centers far removed from the "grass roots" . . . where delinquency and crime originate through obscure and complex processes.[4]

In its report, State-Local Relations in the Criminal Justice System, the Advisory Commission on Intergovernmental Relations noted that:

> The distance between city hall or county courthouse and neighborhoods is often considerable. As a result, the delivery of services may be slow, communications channels may be cumbersome, and policy-makers may be unaware of the real needs of neighborhood areas. Moreover, highly centralized decision-making may deter citizens from participating in crime prevention efforts.[5]

Many crime prevention authorities believe that, for some anticrime programs, the responsibility for planning, decision, and action should be placed at the lowest level consistent with sound decision-making— that is, in the neighborhood with the individual citizen.

Some authorities advocate that neighborhoods receive government financial and technical assistance to spur grassroots citizen involvement. One authority in the field of juvenile delinquency programs suggested that federal program guidelines "might require minimum levels of community involvement in a program before it can receive federal funds . . ."

As a result of recommendations for government decentralization issued by the Advisory Commission on Intergovernmental Relations, the National Advisory Commission on Civil Disorders, and the National Commission on Urban Problems, many people are advocating the establishment of neighborhood citizen councils that would exercise substantial control over the delivery of certain services, including those related to crime prevention. In 1972, for example, the Indiana Legislature passed an act that will permit first-class cities to create a system of citizen councils beginning in 1974.

The National Commission on Criminal Justice Standards and Goals believes that government sharing of authority with neighborhood organizations, as recommended by the above-mentioned commissions and adopted by the Indiana Legislature, is a logical and essential element of community crime prevention.

This is not an inflexible, all-purpose prescription for citizen action. To the contrary, it presents concepts, suggestions, and possible approaches with an acute awareness of what is not known about crime and its causes. Incomplete knowledge does not justify inaction; it mandates that crime prevention programs be tailored to local conditions, not merely mimicked because of alleged effectiveness elsewhere.

The first aspect of citizen action, treated below pertains to the many levels at which the public may pursue a crime reduction effort. For example, a citizen may help ex-offenders find employment in his capacity as an employee or employer, as well as in his capacity as a member of a private organization established for that purpose alone. Included next are brief descriptions of the many types of crime prevention activities available to citizens, followed by a discussion of basic organizational and managerial questions that almost any citizen group must face during the course of its formation and operational life.

The typical citizen response to the crime problem is a demand for greater action by the police, courts, correctional institutions, and other government agencies. The citizen asks too infrequently what he can do himself. And when the public does decide to act, its activities often are short-lived, sporadic outbursts in response to a particularly heinous crime or one that occurred too close to home.

Fortunately, this limited and frequently counter-productive type of citizen action shows signs of yielding to more informed citizen involvement in crime prevention efforts. Today the public is beginning to heed the advice of the President's Commission on Law Enforcement and Administration of Justice: "Every American can translate his concern about, or fear of, crime into positive action. Every American should." Each citizen can exert his crime prevention leverage through each person with whom he is acquainted and through each organization with which he is affiliated.

But before an individual takes positive action, he should be cognizant of the many avenues of approach to any given problem. For example, an individual may help prevent illicit gambling in his community by insuring that his family and neighbors know that the proceeds from such activities are a principal source of income for organized crime and thus help finance the importation of hard drugs.

A citizen's antigambling efforts also may be pursued through a block or neighborhood crime prevention organization. In one instance, members of a neighborhood association followed numbers runners in order to determine the neighborhood gambling network. This information then was turned over to local police.

Members of a church, social club, fraternal group, or civic association can exert pressure on the organization's officers and other members to discontinue limited and informal but nonetheless illegal gambling that occurs on the premises. The slot machine, sports pool slip, and punch board may provide enjoyment for a club's membership, but they also may supply funds to criminal elements.

In his capacity as an employer or employee, a citizen can be alert for signs of inplant gambling. As recommended in 1972 by the Committee for Economic Development, "Individually, businessmen can clean their own houses. Organized gambling need not be tolerated on business premises . . . ."[6] Members of a regional or national crime prevention organization can insure that illegal gambling receives its share of attention.

Other organizations through which citizens can encourage crime prevention efforts include trade associations, educational institutions, political parties, unions, charities, foundations, and professional societies. Several years ago the executive vice president of the American Institute of Certified Public Accountants issued this call to action to his profession:

> There are already cases on record where publicly traded companies have become dominated by hoodlums. A CPA should be watchful of changes in ownership and management of his clients.
>
> If he finds a once solid company taken over or influenced by unsavory elements, he may have to make a difficult decision. He may decide to withdraw from the engagement or he may feel obligated to remain on the scene to protect innocent investors and creditors.
>
> The auditor is expected to have absolute integrity. Any evidence of organized crime coming his way should trigger prompt and drastic action to discharge his professional responsibilities. It should also bring forth cooperation with authorities to discharge his civic duties.[7]

No one is asking an organization to make extraordinary sacrifices on behalf of crime prevention. What is suggested is that decisions relating to daily operations be reviewed in terms of their crime prevention impact as well as other criteria. Does personnel policy permit the hiring of ex-offenders? Are crimes that come to the attention of the organization reported to the police? Do community crime prevention efforts receive adequate consideration in terms of the organization's charitable donations? Is time off for jury duty or court testimony granted grudgingly? Are management controls so loose that they invite crime?

Although crime prevention may not be the main purpose of an organization, crime prevention opportunities still may exist therein. Such opportunities need not focus directly on specific crimes. Tenant patrols may help prevent burglaries in apartment buildings, and cargo security councils formed and supported by local transportation companies may reduce the incidence of cargo theft. But so will programs geared to increasing the employability of the jobless, furthering the education of the dropout, supplying adequate medical treatment for the alcoholic and drug addict, and providing adequate recreational and other constructive activities for youth.

Almost any organization can support and engage in the latter type of crime prevention activities, which in the long run are far more important than tenant patrols or cargo security councils. Studies reveal that more than 80 percent of those in prisons are school dropouts, and that the majority of inmates in many correctional facilities are functional illiterates.[8] Research indicates a high correlation between unemployment and crime, and that a substantial portion of convicted offenders do not have salable job skills. In some penal institutions, as many as 40 percent of the inmates are without previous sustained work experience. There is also a high correlation between drug addiction and robbery. And, according to the estimates of the Federal Bureau of Investigation's Uniform Crime Reports, over 50 percent of the murders in the Nation are committed by persons under the influence of alcohol.

Collective efforts by citizens may be directed at strengthening the crime prevention activities of government agencies (e.g., courts, corrections, and law enforcement agencies), or at bolstering anti-crime measures undertaken exclusively within the private sector. For instance, the focus of a block crime prevention association is often on self-help measures designed to increase the safety of persons and property over and above the protection afforded by local police. Other citizen groups, such as local chambers of commerce, may concentrate on the criminal justice system by sponsoring surveys of police effectiveness, proposing more effective methods of selecting judges, or promoting support for community-based corrections facilities.

Citizens may participate in the crime prevention efforts of government agencies by attending community relations meetings conducted by the local police department, working as volunteers in a probation program administered by the city court, donating time as parole volunteers under the supervision of a state parole commission, or volunteering to help a municipal social or rehabilitative agency improve the delivery of its services.

Voluntary service by citizens within the context of government agencies can occur at several levels. First, the citizen volunteer may act at the direction and under the close supervision of the agency. At another level, the citizen may be involved in an advisory capacity, his role being essentially one of reacting to plans and decisions made by the agency. Finally, citizen participation may involve sharing planning and decisionmaking powers with the agency.

Many organizations play important crime prevention roles as a result of the initiative taken by individuals who comprise them. Organized efforts to reduce crime do not replace individual action; they result from it. Organizations do not relieve a citizen of his crime prevention duty; they offer excellent reasons and opportunities for him to exercise it.

Important as it is, individual action independent of the efforts of others is not enough. Our society is built upon the premise that each person is responsible for himself and for the general welfare of others. Exclusive reliance on a self- or family-oriented approach to crime prevention causes individuals and family units to become isolated from one another. The result is that the crime prevention effectiveness of the community as a whole becomes considerably less than that of the sum of its parts.

Indeed, with each citizen looking out for himself only, there is no community, no strength in numbers, but rather a fragmentation that can serve only to embolden criminal elements. The burglar, for example, is encouraged if he knows that he need not contend with the eyes and ears of an entire neighborhood, but only with the obstacles in the apartment or house he intends to enter.

An overly self-centered approach to crime prevention results in individuals transforming their residences into stronger and stronger fortresses, which, in turn, increases social isolation and the inability of the block or neighborhood to present a united front against crime. As a result, there may be citizen involvement in crime prevention but not community involvement.

Without a sense of community, the crime prevention potential of mutual aid and mutual responsibility is unfulfilled. As noted by one authority on juvenile delinquency:

> Although little systematic research has been done in this area, the reported incidences of communities getting "together" suggest that active "community involvement" in fighting the problems may well be an effective way, and perhaps *the* most effective way, to prevent and reduce crime and delinquency.[9]

For example, in 1971 a rash of burglaries occurred in an economically depressed suburban ghetto on the West Coast. "Outraged by the frequency and prevalence of burglaries, neighborhood residents and store owners got together and forced the local 'fences' out of business . . . and the burglary rate dropped to almost zero."

Noting that a typical response to crime had been the call for more police protection, for extra locks on doors, and for watchdogs, guns, burglar alarms, etc., a group of concerned West Philadelphia, Pa., residents recognized the potential of joining together in a positive program of mutual aid and community development. The rationale for such a program deserves careful consideration by all citizens:

> We have been about the task of organizing ourselves into block meetings for the purpose of strengthening our sense of community and making our neighborhood a better and safer place to live in. As parents and homeowners, we have been particularly concerned to seek out solutions to our problems which avoid racial, class and age polarization, and the quick-draw answers to reactive hardware. It seems clear to us that we do not well serve our children or our community by fostering a "barricade mentality" which would increase our dependence upon locks, guns, data banks and other commercial gimmicks and agencies whose interests may not meet our real needs. Instead, we have tried to encourage our friends and neighbors to come back out onto the streets and begin to share more of our cares and resources in positive community-building

activities which recognize the protective and corrective value of greater neighborhood togetherness.

In order to provide some coordination and mutual assistance in this effort, we have recently gathered our blocks into a Neighborhood Block Safety Program.[10]

When frayed by the rise of specialization and professionalism, or eroded by the availability of an overpowering and, perhaps, overprotective institutional structure of urban life, the fibers of mutual assistance and neighborliness that bind citizens to a sense of community have grown precariously thin. Citizen involvement in crime prevention, at all levels, must take care to reinforce, not sever, those fibers.

Notes

1. President's Commission on Law Enforcement and Administration of Justice, *Task Force Report: The Police,* Washington: U.S. Government Printing Office, 1967, pp. 221, 228. See also the Commissions's *The Challenge of Crime in a Free Soceity,* Washington: U.S. Government Printing Office, 1967, p. 288

2. National Commission on the Causes and Prevention of Violence, *Law and Order Reconsidered,* Washington: U.S. Government Printing Office, 1969, p. 278.

3. *Ibid.,* p. 281.

4. E.K. Nelson, quoted in Kenneth Polk, *Non-Metropolitan Delinquency*—An active Program, Washington: U.S. Government Printing Office, Department of Health, Education, and Welfare, 1969, p. 11.

5. Advisory Commission on Intergovernmental Relations, *State—Local Relations in the Criminal Justice System,* Washington: U.S. Government Printing Office, 1971, p. 269.

6. Committee for Economic Development, *Reducing Crime and Assuring Justice,* New York: CED, 1972, p. 62.

7. Leonard M. Savoie, "What Issues Will Challenge CPA's in the 1970's?" Paper delivered before the convention of the Ohio Society of CPA's, 1969.

8. Chamber of Commerce of the United States, *Marshaling Citizen Power Against Crime,* Washington: Chamber of Commerce, 1970, p. 62.

9. Ruby B. Yaryan, "The Community Role in Juvenile Delinquency Programs" (paper prepared for the Fourth National Symposium on Law Enforcement, Science and Technology), 1972.

10. Block Association of West Philadelphia, "Neighborhood Block Safety Program" (mimeographed handout), 1972.

I.   PUBLIC'S ROLE IN LAW ENFORCEMENT

SOURCE: Advisory Committee on Intergovernmental Relations, *State-Local Relations in the Criminal Justice System*, Washington, Advisory Commission on Intergovernmental Relations, 1971, pp. 261-271.

The emergence of the "law and order" issue as a focal point of national concern beginning in the mid 1960's reflects the growing politicization of the crime issue. Linked with this is the popular belief that law enforcement is primarily the responsibility of elected public officials as well as policemen, judges, prosecutors, and corrections officers. Successful law enforcement obviously depends heavily upon the actions of these professionals and on the support they receive from political leaders. Yet, centering attention on the efforts of only these groups obscures and downgrades the role of the ordinary citizen in crime prevention and control.

The purpose of this section is to explore the ways in which the public can participate in crime reduction. This involves the various types of action that can be taken by individuals or citizens' groups on their own. Moreover, the discussion includes steps that cities and counties can take to stimulate greater citizen involvement in anticrime efforts and develop better relationships between law enforcement agencies and the communities they serve.

§ 5.2   *The roles of citizens in law enforcement*

In order to be effective, law enforcement must be a joint effort. In other words, the entry and movement of an offender through the criminal justice process, his return to society, and his inclination to recidivate are dependent on not only law enforcement agencies and professionals, but also on the general public. The capacity of police to detect and apprehend suspected offenders, for example, is conditioned by the extent citizens cooperate by reporting violations of the law and suspicious incidents or persons. The prosecution of an alleged offender depends on the willingness of persons to provide information, to testify in court, and to serve on jury duty. And the rehabilitation of offenders and their successful re-entry into society are closely linked to the community's acceptance of ex-convicts.

Clearly, then, "law enforcement is not a game of cops and robbers in which the citizens play the trees."[1] Instead, citizens have a basic responsibility to assist law enforcement agencies in preventing as well as controlling crime. Moreover, the public's role here extends well beyond facilitating crime reduction through informing, testifying, and other cooperative approaches. Citizens can and should play an action role in reforming and revitalizing the components of our criminal justice system.

§ 5.3 Organizing citizen participation for crime prevention

Citizens often serve on the policy-making boards of voluntary community organizations providing services designed to prevent crime and delinquency. These include: boys clubs, family and child welfare, mental health, education, prisoner aid, labor, and religious groups; and national organizations such as the National Council on Crime and Delinquency (NCCD). Not to be overlooked, of course, is the financial support these groups receive from the public. It is estimated that more than 100,000 non-governmental agencies currently exist, each of which to varying degrees, is involved in preventing crime.[2]

Another type of organized public involvement in crime reduction is service on the policy boards of state and regional law enforcement planning agencies. Public members of such boards sit as co-equals with state and local police, court, corrections, and prosecution professionals and with elected public officials. They participate in decision-making in connection with the contents of comprehensive law enforcement plans and action projects to help prevent crime. Advisory Commission on Intergovernmental Relations staff surveys indicate that as of the end of 1969, 17 percent of the members of the 50 State Planning Agencies supervisory boards were public representatives.[3] With respect to the regional policy boards, of 291 substate regions listed in the 1970 comprehensive plans of 31 states, 27 percent of the membership were citizens.

A third approach is through membership on criminal justice committees or task forces of local chambers of commerce, leagues of women voters, urban coalitions, and other "good government" organizations. These groups are usually funded by the business community, private foundations, or individual contributions. They conduct a wide range of crime prevention activities, including fact-finding, information dissemination, promotion of improved street lighting, operation of programs such as court watching and corrections volunteers, and development of improved legislation. Often, public officials serve on these bodies in an advisory capacity.[4]

§ 5.4   Types of citizen action

In several cities in the nation, citizen-sponsored crime reduction programs have been operating successfully. The types of agencies vary widely in accordance with such factors as the personnel and financial resources of the group, the severity of the crime problem, and the responsiveness of law enforcement agencies and public officials. Listed below are a number of typical citizen-initiated efforts in the police, courts, and correctional areas.[5]

§ 5.5   Police-related activities

Some citizens' groups have set up programs to educate citizens concerning the importance of the procedures for reporting information to the police in connection with suspected criminal activity and the ways to better protect themselves from crime. Many are tied in with the establishment of a special fast-response police telephone number. These programs—called "crime check," "crime alert," "crime stop," or the like—rely heavily on the public media, billboards, window decals, bumper stickers, and bulletin boards to convey their message.

Closely related to crime check programs are citizen preventive patrols. One such effort is community radio watch in which business firms equip their vehicles with two-way radios to be used to report crimes or other emergencies to their dispatchers, who in turn report the incident to the police. Operators of these vehicles do not make arrests or perform other police responsibilities. Another approach is civilian police reserve units which, in cooperation with regular police officers, patrol recreation areas, assist in handling crowds during special events, direct traffic, and help in search and rescue missions.[6] Youth patrols also have been formed to serve as a watch-dog for crime in the neighborhood areas.

Several cities have provided better lighting of streets and buildings at the urging of citizen groups. Often these groups assist in identifying suitable locations or in generating support for increased funds for this purpose. The U.S. Chamber of Commerce reports that improved illumination has resulted in a 60 to 90 percent decrease in certain categories of crime.

Many citizens' organizations have prepared and distributed booklets dealing with the prevention of shoplifting and some have set up chain-call warning systems for merchants to use in alerting one another about shoplifters and bad check passers. Another common information service is the dissemination of facts regarding drug abuse and addiction, particularly in the schools.

Finally, some citizens' groups have assisted in police recruitment, such as setting up police cadet and minority officer programs. A few also have provided financial and technical support for in-service training and educational programs for policemen or have worked with colleges and universities to set up such programs. Citizen organizations often campaign on behalf of pay raises for police.

§ 5.6   Court-related activities

Many citizens' groups conduct court watcher efforts, where individuals sit in courts daily and identify weaknesses in the judicial process. Data sheets are often used to record such information as the names of the judge, defendant, and prosecuting and defense attorneys, the race and age of the offender, and the charge, plea, finding, and sentence. The U.S. Chamber of Commerce study found that court watching in Indianapolis resulted in the following improvements ". . . nonappearance of arresting officers is less frequent; most judges appear in court on time; fewer pro tem judges; fewer delays; absence of police witnesses occurs less often; prosecutors prepare cases more thoroughly."[7]

Some citizens' groups have provided financial support for court reorganization studies and analyses of case-scheduling problems. Another common activity involves improvement of the administration of jury service.

Several groups and individual citizens provide volunteer services to the courts. It has been estimated that in 1969 volunteers contributed three million hours of service to the 1,000 courts where they were at work.[8] Between 15 and 25 percent of the juvenile courts make use of this manpower source. The availability of trained volunteers is particularly helpful in the probation area and the types of tasks they perform range from record-keeping to actual casework.

§ 5.7   Corrections-related activities

Several citizens' organizations have sponsored volunteer efforts in the corrections field, including counseling inmates, involvement in work-release programs, aiding with educational and vocational training, and performing clerical tasks. Other types of citizen action include support for reform legislation, promotion of detention and foster homes, financial aid for academic and vocational courses for institutional personnel, advice to corrections officials concerning the relevance of prison education and training programs, and provision of job opportunities for released offenders. For example, California's 70 Management-Labor Advisory Committees, which perform most of the above functions, consist of over 1,000 citizens.[9]

In some states, citizens still serve on the boards of directors of state correctional institutions and local jails. In recent years, however, the administrative responsibilities of these boards have been assumed by state correctional agencies.[10]

Finally, some national organizations have attempted to mobilize citizen support for new legislation, increased appropriations, better administration, higher personnel standards, and other correctional improvements. The National Council on Crime and Delinquency for example, has set up Citizen Councils in 21 states composed of representatives from business, labor, news media, religion, agriculture, civic associations, and the general public to spearhead this movement. It also has created Citizen Action Committees in 130 cities to undertake special crime and delinquency prevention projects.[11]

§ 5.8   *The responsibilities of state and local governments*

The willingness of citizens to become involved in crime prevention and control efforts, as well as the extent and effectiveness of their participation, depend a great deal on the status of law enforcement and criminal justice agencies in the community's eyes. If they are viewed as being corrupt, as a means of minority suppression, or as tools of a political machine, then many citizens will not become involved. Yet, the fact that many times such views are based on hearsay rather than on fact underscores the information gap that often exists between law enforcement agencies and the communities they serve. The task of developing closer ties between these parties should be a top priority item if public participation in this area is to be meaningful. The alternative may be continued distrust, alienation, and apathy on the part of key sectors of the citizenry.

§ 5.9   Police-community relations

Friction between police and segments of the public hinders the citizen cooperation and involvement so necessary for both curbing crime before it begins and apprehending those suspected of committing offenses. Most law enforcement officials readily concede they cannot do the job alone. Not only is crime prevention rendered ineffective by the absence of cooperative citizen action, but bad community feeling toward the police actually stimulates crime for a number of reasons:[12]

(1) Violations of the law and suspicious incidents or persons are not reported;
(2) Witnesses refuse to testify or provide information;
(3) Actions against police occur which, in turn, may result in an improper police response that sets off widespread rioting;
(4) Fearing citizen charges against them, police may become reluctant to enforce the law in hostile neighborhoods or against certain individuals.

These factors underscore the conclusion of the President's Crime Commission that, "No lasting improvement in law enforcement is likely in this country unless police-community relations are substantially improved."[13]

§ 5.10   Basic problems

The police-community relations problem is not an entirely new phenomenon in this country. Historically, many Americans have been distrustful of the police.[14] Prior to the 1840's, there was no police organization as we know it today. And the establishment of organized forces in larger cities was not an easy matter. The typical police officer was paid very little and usually was not highly respected.

The fairly low status of the police in the community in the mid-nineteenth century is highlighted by the reaction to a suggestion made in 1865 that police wear uniforms. They objected to the idea for fear that if they could be recognized they might become objects of attack.[15]

Moreover, in 19th century New England, members of the force were often viewed as agents of an unfamiliar governmental system and of ascendant economic and Yankee interests. At the same time, however, the heavy reliance on the recently arrived did much to bridge attitudinal, ethnic, and other barriers in municipalities caught in the great tide of immigration beginning in the 1840's.

Much has changed during the course of the last 130 years—new immigrants replacing old, civil service reformers battling spoilsism, professionalism contending with amateurism, declining political machines and ward organizations, and growing reliance on personality and mass communications techniques. In light of these developments, police departments face new pressures and problems, as well as some old ones that in many respects resemble those they confronted at their inception: distrust on the part of some of the municipal citizenry, lack of widespread consensus on social and institutional goals, and assumption by the police of roles outside the strictly law enforcement area.

It should come as no surprise, then, to learn that attitudes regarding police vary from jurisdiction to jurisdiction and within jurisdictions. Opinion studies reveal that, overall, a majority of citizens have a high regard for police work. Yet, a survey conducted by Louis Harris Associates in 1969 found that nearly one-fifth of the white and four-fifths of the black respondents believed there were discriminatory patterns in police-minority group relations.[16] Some lower income whites, some "liberals," and some young also have similar complaints against the police. Some studies, for example, indicate that adolescents from both lower and middle class families tend to be extremely hostile toward police, possibly in part because of the belief that police are preservers of the status quo.[17] Moreover, the recent surge in demands for the establishment of civilian review boards to handle citizens' complaints against the police or for the creation of citizens' crime commissions to investigate the operation of police departments also highlights the mutual distrust existing between police and some sectors of the community.

A Harris poll published in the March 8, 1971 edition of *Newsweek* supports some of the earlier survey findings. Almost two-thirds of the white respondents indicated skepticism about danger of police brutality, but over half of the blacks believed that such allegations are more times than not likely to be true. Whites, unlike blacks, tend to accept the notion of a conspiracy to kill policemen. Seventy-two percent of the whites approved preventive detention, but no more than 44% of the blacks concurred.

Community opposition to the police, however, is only one side of the coin. The police also hold attitudes toward the community which adversely affect their relationship with citizens. The roots of these feelings were revealed by William V. Turner in his book, *The Police Establishment:*

> I know of no period in recent history when the police have been the subject of so many unjustified charges of brutality, harrassment, and ineptness.
> It almost seems that the better we do our job of enforcing the law the more we are attacked. The more professional we become and the more effective we are, the more we impinge upon the misbehavior of society.[18]

In a 1969 opinion poll, the International Association of Chiefs of Police (IACP) probed the attitudes of policemen in 286 state and local departments across the country.[19]

Eighty-three percent of the experienced policemen felt that many people looked upon a policeman as an impersonal cog in the governmental machinery rather than as a fellow human being. Only half of the officers indicated that public support for the police was improving, while approximately three-fifths of the administrators stated it was getting better. At the same time, nearly three-fourths of the experienced police officers polled thought that they were not receiving enough support from the political power structure in their city.

IACP's survey also showed that a substantial majority of policemen usually are in agreement on questions concerning civil disobedience, civilian review boards, and community relations efforts. With respect to the first issue, nine out of ten respondents disagreed with the proposition that laws should be deliberately disobeyed if they were considered unjust. A comparable proportion indicated that persons who violate an "unjust" law to attract attention to their cause should be handled as any other violator; 93 percent of the white officers concurred here, while 83 percent of the black officers agreed.

Turning to the public role in law enforcement generally and to civilian review boards in particular, almost two-thirds of the police officers agreed with the following statement: "Since ours is a government 'of the people, by the people, and for the people,' the public has a right to pass judgment on the way the police are doing their jobs." Sixty-nine percent of the white respondents and 74 percent of the blacks concurred. Nevertheless, 62 percent of the policemen still opposed the idea of civilian review boards.

In the area of community relations, 69 percent of the officers felt that programs of this type were important ways for their department to open lines of communication, build respect, and gain citizen cooperation. Sixty-eight percent of the whites and 82 percent of the blacks adhered to this favorable position.

§ 5.11   Nature, extent, and objectives

The major goal of a police-community relations program is to foster better relationships between the policeman and the public, especially residents of high crime neighborhoods. The police and citizen representatives together should develop programs for involving all segments of the community in meaningful activity that will produce (as a by-product) mutual trust, greater confidence, and better understanding. Possible approaches include junior police or safe driving clubs, neighborhood "rap" sessions, and similar types of programs geared to involving more citizens in a crime prevention and control partnership.

St. Louis, Missouri, set up one of the first police-community relations programs in the United States and several other efforts have been modeled after it. The program is organized around a district committee composed of both police officers and citizens representatives located in every police district. Each committee has eight subcommittees, which are assigned certain continuing functions as well as special projects involving specific local problems. Responsibilities of these committees include juvenile delinquency, public relations, automobile theft, traffic, sanitations, and voluntary citizen action. They do not formulate policy, but instead polices are decided by an independent body of private citizens. Thus, although the police department provides the manpower, the committee is not its tool. Most of the major segments of the community are involved in the action-oriented programs sponsored by the committee to not only improve police-community relations but also to upgrade certain neighborhood areas.[20]

Prior to the 1960's, little effort was made to formulate programs to achieve better communication between police and the community. But the last decade witnessed the growth of a "new breed" of law breakers who were not the traditional "criminal types." These persons were protesting the social ills of our society and they had to be dealt with somewhat differently, such as civil disorders strike forces. After a number of failures, several cities followed the lead of St. Louis and established a division in their police department to handle relationships with the community. At the same time, many changed their basic departmental orientation from the control to the prevention of crime. As part of this new approach, these departments developed innovative police training and education programs, broadened their recruitment base, formulated standards and procedures, improved testing and screening of applicants, and tightened internal and external control over individual officers.

The following case studies illustrate some of the types of programs that have been attempted recently. Their effectiveness in terms of building a close police-citizen relationship, however, has varied considerably:[21]

(1) Chicago's police community relations program found major problems in the areas of police training and communication with minorities, youth, and non-English speaking residents of the city. As a result, an intensive effort was launched to retrain many officers in new techniques for handling riots and methods for preventing riotous situations. A number of community-wide programs were created to close the communications gap, including "ride in" programs, youth-police workshops, and school visitation.[22]

(2) In Berkeley, California, policemen meet with residents on a door-to-door basis to increase community support for their department.

(3) In Pittsburgh, the Commission on Human Relations handles each complaint. Due to its excellent relationship with the police department, it has been effective in acting on the citizen's behalf.

(4) In Grand Rapids, Michigan, the police department initiated a sensitivity training program geared toward developing a more workable relationship between citizens and police. Small groups of citizens and policemen meet for 15 day periods to help break down racial barriers, establish greater rapport, and consider reform in police-community relations problem areas.

(5) In Detroit, a sensitivity training program brings police and citizens together for purposes of mutual understanding. The police department cites this program as a major contributing factor to the absence of major disturbances in the city in recent years.

(6) In Riverside County, California, policemen are required to know and become known by the citizens in their patrol area. In-service training is conducted informally during off-duty hours at a resident's home or a local church.

Despite recent progress, many cities still have not established police-community relations programs. In a 1967 survey, the International City Management Association (ICMA) found that 20 percent of the responding cities had a police-community relations program. A survey conducted three years later, however, still revealed that only 44 percent of 650 reporting cities had such a program.[23]

As might be expected, police-community relations programs were more frequently found in the larger cities. All but one of the cities over 250,000 population reporting to the 1970 poll, for example, indicated they had such a program. This contrasts with the 22 percent in the 10,000 to 25,000 population group that were making an effort on this front.

Seventy-one percent of the central cities but only 24 percent of those in the smaller independent categories had a program. More western cities were involved than those in other regions. Northeastern municipalities were least likely to have police-community relations programs.

With respect to police community-relations training, this was provided by 475 of 654 respondents to a 1969 ICMA survey of the nation's police departments. Half of the participating cities with no such training had less than 25,000 population. The findings indicate that the larger cities' "box score" was much better, with 90 percent of the central city policemen receiving community relations training.

The content of police-community relations training varied in different localities, but generally the larger cities had more comprehensive programs. The teaching methods also were more diversified in these municipalities.

§ 5.12   Use of federal funds

Despite the fairly large number of participating cities, relatively little federal money has been used for police-community relations purposes. Only 17 percent of the cities reporting to the International City Managers Association survey received federal funds to support any of their police-community relations plans or programs. Moreover, ACIR's report *Making the Safe Streets Act Work: An Intergovernmental Challenge* indicated that a meager $1,518,001 or 5.4 percent of the $27,857,319 allocated as subgrants to state and local jurisdictions by February 28, 1970, was used for community relations purposes. [24]

According to ICMA, larger central cities received the bulk of the federal funds that have been allotted for police-community relations. Although Western municipalities are most often involved in such programs, only six percent relied on federal financial support.

Typically, cities have set up special units to deal with police-community relations, although this is not necessarily the case in smaller municipalities. Criteria of effectiveness for these community relations units include:

(1) *Proper objectives.* Focusing on the actual improvement of relations between police and citizens, not merely presenting a good police image.

(2) *Proper scope of activity.* Providing services to the police as well as to the people with whom it works.

(3) *Proper work load.* Varying the unit's activities in accordance with specific local problems and the unit's capacity to do its job well.

(4) *Adequate authority.* Involving the unit in department policy-making and establishing direct communications channels with the chief of police.

(5) *Adequate prestige.* Giving the unit relatively high status, as reflected in the size, pay, and rank of its personnel.

(6) *Adequate facilities.* Furnishing the unit with adequate office space and equipment, competent secretaries and other office personnel, a systematic filing and reporting system, and sufficient vehicles.

(7) *Proper intradepartmental relationships.* Informing the rest of the department of the unit's operations and accomplishments through regular intradepartmental communications, and encouraging the unit to perform as many services for the rest of the department as possible.[25]

Some authorities have contended that formal "outside" procedures are needed to ensure equity and impartiality in the handling of complaints concerning police activities. They assert that internal procedures for monitoring compliance with departmental policies and for investigating alleged misconduct often fail to convince many citizens, particularly low-income and minority groups, that the police "system" is handling their grievances fairly. Two major proposals that have been advanced are the ombudsman and the community service officer.

§ *5.13   The ombudsman*

The Scandinavian ombudsman concept has been suggested as a

model for investigating complaints against law enforcement and criminal justice agencies in this country. In Sweden, Finland, Denmark, and Norway, the ombudsman, or "citizen's defender" as he is often called, receives written complaints, regardless of whether the complainant first contacted the appropriate administrative agency. He then requests relevant information and an explanation from the agency. If more data are needed, he may ask the police to investigate. The ombudsman may initiate investigations or hold hearings on his own, even if a complaint has not been filed. He is assisted in performing his responsibilities by a professional staff who are usually lawyers. The ombudsman is not authorized to order administrative officials to take action, although he may order prosecutions or issue public reprimands or criticisms. He also helps individuals obtain compensation for damages.[26]

To date, the ombudsman idea has not been well received in the United States. Several state and local governments, as well as the U.S. Congress, have considered this approach. But resistance from the legislative body and bureaucracy, cost considerations, existence of complaint handling machinery, and other political and economic factors have prevented the adoption of the true Scandinavian variety of ombudsman. Currently, two counties have set up Ombudsman-type systems—King County (Washington) has an Office of Citizens Complaints that investigates complaints, subpoenas witnesses, and makes recommendations; and the Montgomery County (Maryland) School Board ombudsman who looks into complaints independent of action by school administrators.

Some American cities and counties have established citizen complaint machinery that partially incorporates the ombudsman concept. The Nassau County (New York) Commissioner of Accounts, the Buffalo Citizens Administrative Service, and the Savannah (Georgia) Community Service Officer, for example, investigate complaints in connection with police as well as other public services. As a result of their efforts, administrative errors have been corrected, interagency communications channels have been improved, and coordination has been increased.[27]

Some experts have proposed creation of the position of community service officer (CSO) as a means of better sensitizing police departments to ghetto problems, of ensuring the provision of adequate police services in high crime and low income areas, and of increasing the number of minority police personnel. In its task force report on the police, the President's Crime Commission recommended that CSO's be employed by urban police departments. They would be young, minority group persons recruited from neighborhoods like those in which they would be assigned.

The CSO in effect would serve as an apprentice policeman; he would not carry a gun, nor have full law enforcement powers. His prime responsibilities would be to assist precinct line officers in their patrol and investigative work and to improve communication-channels between the police department and neighborhood areas. Typical CSO functions would include working with juvenile delinquents, referring citizen complaints to administrative agencies, investigating minor crimes, aiding families with domestic problems, organizing community meetings, handling service calls, and working with police-community relations units.

The President's Crime Commission also suggested that to offset the isolating effects of precinct consolidation, small neighborhood offices be established in deprived communities from which CSO's would operate.[28] It indicated the importance of the CSO's work in terms of police-community understanding.

The very presence of the CSO in the neighborhood would symbolize a closer relationship between the police and the community . . . They would help to inform the officers with whom they work of the culture and attitudes of the community and, conversely, would help to inform the community of the officer's concerns.[29]

§ 5.14 Civilian review boards and citizens' advisory committees

Popular demands for greater scrutiny of police affairs have resulted in the establishment of civilian review boards and citizens' advisory committees to police departments. Proponents of these approaches point out impartial treatment of the individual by law enforcement agencies. Safeguarding individual rights and guaranteeing that suspected offenders will receive a "fair shake," they contend, will generate more citizen respect and confidence in police departments and greater public knowledge of and support for their operations.

In response to the dissatisfaction voiced by some citizen groups—particularly civil rights organizations—concerning police internal review procedures, a few cities have set up civilian review boards.

These include Chicago, Washington, D.C., Philadelphia, Minneapolis, Rochester (New York) and New York City. Boards of this type have been abolished or rendered inoperative in Rochester, Philadelphia, Minneapolis, and New York City.

Although the civilian review boards vary in organization and procedures, they share certain basic features. Their members are non-uniformed employees of the police department, and consequently they are by no means truly independent. All boards are purely advisory in nature with no authority to make decisions in connection with cases that come before them. Most have the power to investigate complaints, usually in cooperation with the police department. The most common types of charges that come before them are brutality, illegal entry and search, harassment, and false arrest. After receiving a complaint, the board may provide for an informal settlement, conduct hearings, and recommend either the convening of a police trial board or punishment.[30]

Several problems have hindered the operation of civilian review boards. The President's Crime Commission reports that many citizens have been unfamiliar with board procedures and that complaint forms have been difficult to obtain. Moreover, typically several months have been required for the boards to make a determination, mainly because they lack adequate staff support and often do not receive full cooperation from police departments. Some critics also contend that the boards should be completely independent of the police department.[31]

Despite these problems, some successes have been achieved. While often not enthusiastic in their assessment of review board operations, minority group leaders state that some improvements in police-community relationships have resulted from the establishment of this machinery. The boards also have caused some police departments to re-evaluate their own internal review procedures and make necessary changes on them. Although rank-and-file officers generally oppose boards, top echelon officials tend to have a more positive view and work closely with the board to settle complaints quickly and informally, often without a hearing.[32]

Some cities have organized neighborhood, precinct, or city-wide advisory committees as a means of maintaining open communication channels with citizens, particularly minority groups. A recent survey sponsored by the International Association of Chiefs of Police and the U.S. Conference of Mayors found that of the 165 reporting municipalities (all over 100,000 population, or between 30,000 and 100,000 with more than five percent non-white population), only eight percent had precinct committees and 19 percent had a city-wide committee.[33] Since that time, a number of cities have adopted this approach.

Generally, the former type of committee is formed under the auspices of the police department. It is composed of citizen representatives who meet periodically to discuss police policies and practices and the complaints and needs of neighborhood residents. Precinct committees serve only in an advisory capacity vis-a-vis department officials. City-wide committees bring the heads of the police department together with civic leaders to discuss police policy issues of importance to the community as a whole and to coordinate the activities of precinct committees. Often, neighborhood committees are represented on the city-wide body.[34]

Another survey by Michigan State University showed serious deficiencies in the operation of these committees. Several were not adequately representative of neighborhood residents. Business, civic, and religious leaders tended to dominate the membership rolls while minorities and residents of high crime areas were underrepresented. Low-income individuals and those who were hostile to the police usually did not belong, a matter that suggested board members would have difficulty understanding citizen grievances. As a result of these factors, according to the study's committee, deliberations were dominated by the police and controversial matters—including use of discretion and such enforcement practices as the use of dogs, stop-and-frisk procedures, and saturation patrols—were usually not considered. At the same time, the survey revealed lack of support for the committees on the part of district and precinct commanders, failure of lower-ranking officers to participate, and poor police staff assistance.[35]

In light of these deficiencies, it is not surprising that many of these committees have not materially improved police departments relationships with residents of high crime areas, minorities, and low-income groups. If such bodies are to realize their potential, they should be representative and willing to tackle tough, controversial issues. They also need full and continuing police support.

§ 5.15　 Decentralization of services

One reason for public non-involvement in crime reduction efforts is the geographic and political remoteness of law enforcement and criminal justice agencies from the areas in which services are delivered. Especially in larger jurisdictions, the distance between city hall or county court house and neighborhoods is often considerable. As a result, the delivery of services may be slow, communication channels may be cumbersome, and policy-makers may be unaware of the real needs of neighborhood areas. Moreover, highly centralized decision-making may deter citizens from participating in crime prevention efforts.

In response to this situation, some authorities have urged that the delivery of municipal and county services should be decentralized to neighborhoods and that citizen involvement in policy-making in connection with these services should be encouraged. They argue that existing complaint handling machinery—such as special bureaus, mayor's assistants, and telephone numbers—do not go far enough in bringing services "closer to the people." Decentralization, they contend, would promote efficiency and responsiveness, and would facilitate public support for anti-crime programs.

Others advocate "community control" of decentralized services. A referendum in Berkeley, California, for instance, decided that the city would not be divided into "black," "white," and "campus" communities, each having a police council under citizen control responsible for all police activities within its jurisdiction.

The devices, which have been proposed to implement these administrative decentralization and citizen participation objectives, vary widely in terms of the numbers of citizens involved, the extent of their "control," and the types of services affected. Most observers agree, however, that in order to increase efficiency and effectiveness in delivering services and to encourage citizen participation, formal decentralization machinery should be established.

§ 5.16　 "Little city halls"

"Little city halls" and multi-service centers, some assert, are the most feasible ways to expedite the administration of public services in neighborhood areas.[36] A recent survey conducted by the Center for Governmental Studies, Washington, D.C. and the International

City Management Association sheds light on the purposes and extent of use of these devices. Of the 106 urban counties and cities over 50,000 population reporting some decentralization of services, 21 had "little city halls" and 50 had multi-service centers. The principal distinction between the two is that the former serve mainly as branch offices for the chief executive officer and provide services similar to those available at the main city hall or county court house, while the latter serve mainly as branch offices for a public or private agency and provide two or more government-type services. Many of these units have full-time professional staff and some have advisory boards composed of area residents. Most "little city halls" and multi-service centers are located in economically depressed neighborhoods or in minority neighborhoods. Their major services include furnishing information, providing referrals, receiving and acting on complaints, helping cut "red-tape," acting as an advocate for citizens, and providing interagency coordination.

With respect to law enforcement, over half of the respondents had decentralized police services. Twelve cities and three counties reported police affairs as a function dealt with at "little city halls," and in 17 cities and five counties multiservice centers handled police matters. None of the respondents, however, indicated that corrections, prosecution, or court related services had been decentralized to neighborhoods through these devices.

§ 5.17   Neighborhood sub-units of government

In its 1967 report *Fiscal Balance in the American Federal System,* CACIR recommended that states authorize large cities and counties to establish, on the petition of affected residents, neighborhood councils. These sub-units would be responsible for providing supplemental public services in neighborhood areas and would have authority to levy taxes—such as a fractional millage on the local property tax or a per capita tax—in order to finance these special services. Neighborhood sub-units could be dissolved unilaterally by the city or county if they became nonviable.[37]

This approach offers several advantages not found in "little city halls" and multi-service centers. Neighborhood sub-units seek to achieve political as well as administrative decentralization. They could help revitalize political life in the neighborhood. They would have advisory or delegated substantive authority in connection with crime and juvenile delinquency prevention and control programs, as well as other local services. Instead of further fragmenting local governmental structure, the election of neighborhood councils would help ensure both responsiveness and accountability. Moreover, their representative nature would help overcome the distrust and apathy with which "little city halls" and multi-service centers sometimes have been viewed. Neighborhood sub-units would not be creatures of the "system" which minority and low-income groups frequently believe has been unmindful of pressing community needs. Rather, they offer real political and economic power to disadvantaged groups and a basis for both healthy competition and cooperation with city officials. Adoption of this approach, then, could go a long way in making city and county governments more responsive and responsible and in curbing citizens disillusionment and alienation.

To date, only a few local governments have considered adopting the sub-unit device. A July 1969 proposal by the Los Angeles City Charter Commission to create sub-units of government was not approved by the city council for inclusion in the ballot.[38]

§ 5.18   Crime compensation boards

A few states have responded to the urging of some observers, that government should recognize that it has a financial obligation to the innocent victim of crime stemming from its failure to protect him. Since 1967, five states—California, Hawaii, Maryland, Massachusetts, and New York—have established crime compensation boards modeled after those which have been used in Sweden, England, New Zealand, and some Canadian Provinces. A sixth state—Delaware—collects fines from criminal offenders and remits them to their victims.

For the most part, existing compensation boards are small, independent units. The members are appointed by the Governor and typically have a legal background. Board staff investigate claims and if the victim can demonstrate financial hardship, except in Hawaii where no such "need" factor is called for, he is eligible to receive an award up to a specific amount. In each state with a board, except Hawaii, compensation is available for personal injury but not for property loss. Apprehension of the offender is not a condition for receipt of an award, and criminals or their relatives are ineligible for compensation.[39]

Proponents claim that this approach recognizes that the victim deserves as much attention as the offender. Compensation can cover the costs of medical treatment for injuries sustained during the crime, and to help pay the bills if the victim is temporarily unable to return to work. This financial assistance is particularly important in light of the difficulty in obtaining civil remedies, and the fact that disadvantaged people generally have limited or no medical insurance or workmen's compensation coverage. Although opponents of compensation boards are concerned about high costs, some suggest that the expense of compensation awards could stimulate greater public cooperation in law enforcement efforts. Moreover, spreading the costs of crime throughout the population of a state would be more equitable than concentrating them in high crime areas, usually low-income or minority neighborhoods.

Thus, there are a variety of devices and methods which can be used by citizens to become more involved in crime reduction; and there are actions that state and local governments can take to develop a working partnership with the community in the criminal justice effort. It is important to recognize, however, that there is no "one best way" as far as the public's role in law enforcement is concerned. Instead, the nature and extent of citizen involvement will depend upon such factors as the severity of the crime problem, the adequacy of law enforcement and criminal justice agencies, the activism of "good government" and similar types of citizen groups, and the history of police-community relationships. For many jurisdictions, "trial and error" experimentation might be the best way to achieve meaningful public participation.

At the same time, the critical importance of public involvement in law enforcement cannot be overemphasized. The stakes in crime prevention and control in terms of the quality of life and the viability of the federal system are too high to make this matter solely the responsibility of public officials. Crime reduction is everybody's responsibility. As Chief Justice Warren E. Burger has stated: "If we do not solve what you call the problems of criminal justice, will anything else matter very much?"[40]

Notes

1. U.S. Chamber of Commerce, *Marshaling Citizen Power Against Crime*, Washington, D.C.: The Chamber, 1970, p. 11.

2. United Nations, *Administration of Justice in a Changing Society: A Report on Development in the United States, 1965-1970.* Prepared for the Fourth United Nations Congress on the Prevention of Crime and Treatment of Offenders, Kyoto, Japan: August, 1970, pp. 78-79.

3. Advisory Commission on Intergovernmental Relations, *Making the Safe Streets Act Work: An Intergovernmental Challenge,* Washington, D.C.: U.S. Government Printing Office, September 1970, p. 25.

4. U.S. Chamber of Commerce, *op. cit.,* pp. 78-81.

5. Except where otherwise noted, this description relies heavily on Chapter VIII of the U.S. Chamber of Commerce report, *Marshaling Citizen Power Against Crime.*

6. President's Crime Commission *Task Force Report: Police,* Washington, D.C.: U.S. Government Printing Office, 1967, p. 223.

7. U.S. Chamber of Commerce, *op. cit.,* p. 113.

8. United Nations, *op. cit.,* p. 79.

9. *Ibid.,* p. 81.

10. *Ibid.,* p. 80.

11. *Ibid.,* p. 82.

12. President's Crime Commission, *op. cit.,* p. 144.

13. *Ibid.*

14. See Oscar Handlin, "Community Organization as a Solution to Police-Community Problem," *Police and the Changing Community: Selected Readings,* Nelson A. Watson, ed., Washington, D.C.: International Association of Chiefs of Police, 1965, p. 107.

15. Alan A. Altschuler, *Community Control: The Black Demand for Participation in Large American Cites,* New York: Pegasus, 1970, p. 17.

16. National Council on Crime and Delinquency, "Problems in Police-Community Relations," *Information Review on Crime and Delinquency,* Vol. 1, No. 5, February, 1969, p. 4.

17. U.S. Commission on Law Enforcement and Administration of Justice, *A Naitonal Survey on Police and Community Relations,* Washington, D.C.: U.S. Government Printing Office, 1967, p. 14.

18. William V. Turner, *The Police Establishment,* New York: G. P. Putnam's and Son, 1968, p. 44.

19. Nelson A. Watson and James W. Sterling, *Police and Their Opinions,* Washington, D.C.: International Association of Chiefs of Police, 1969, p. 55.

20. Handlin, *op. cit.,* p. 115.

21. With the exception of Chicago, the other case studies are cited in: District of Columbia, *Report of the City Council Public Safety Committee on Police-Community Relations,* Washington, D.C.: The Committee, August 20, 1968, p. 19.

22. City of Chicago, Citizens' Committee to Study Police-Community Relations, *Police and Public—A Critique and a Program: Final Report,* Chicago: The Committee, May 22, 1967.

23. International City Management Association, "Recent Trends in Police-Community Relations." *Urban Data Service,* Vol. 2, No. 3, March, 1970, pp. 10-11.

24. U.S. Advisory Commission on Intergovernmental Relations, *op. cit.*, p. 53.

25. ICMA, *op. cit.*, pp. 4-5.

26. President's Crime Commission, *op. cit.*, p. 202. See also The American Assembly, *Ombudsmen For American Government?* Stanley V. Anderson, editor, Englewood Cliffs, N.J.: Prentice-Hall, Inc., 1968; Walter Gellhorn, *When Americans Complain: Governmental Grievance Procedures*, Cambridge: Harvard University Press, 1966; Institute of Governmental Studies, *Buffalo Citizens Administrative Service: An Ombudsman Demonstration Project*, Berkeley: the Institue, 1970.

27. International City Management Association, "The Ombudsman: The Citizens' Advocate," *Management Information Service*, Volume 1, No. 1-10, October 1969, pp. 6-14.

28. President's Crime Commission *op. cit.*, pp. 123-124, 166-167.

29. *Ibid.*, p. 166.

30. *Ibid.*, pp. 200-201.

31. *Ibid.*, p. 201.

32. *Ibid.*, p. 202.

33. *Ibid.*, p. 156.

34. *Ibid.*, pp. 157-158.

35. *Ibid.*

36. Joseph F. Zimmerman, "Heading Off City-Hall Neighborhood Wars," *Nation's Cities*, November 1970, pp. 18-21, 39.

37. Advisory Commission on Intergovernmental Relations, *Fiscal Balance in the American Federal System: Volume 2, Metropolitan Fiscal Disparities*, Washington, D.C.: U.S. Government Printing Office, October 1967, pp. 16-17.

38. Zimmerman, *op. cit.*, p. 20.

39. Gilbert Geis and Herbert Sigurdson, "State Aid to Victims of Violent Crime," *State Government*, LVIII, No. 1, Winter 1970, pp. 16-20.

40. Chamber of Commerce, *op. cit.*, p. 2.

II. CITIZEN INVOLVEMENT IN LAW ENFORCEMENT

SOURCE: Judith Toth, "Citizen Involvement in Law Enforcement," National Commission on the Causes and Prevention of Violence, *Law and Order Reconsidered*, Washington, U.S. Government Printing Office, 1969, pp. 411, 426.

When discussing the crime problem, people turn to the police, the government, and the courts and ask "Why don't they do more?" Rarely do they ask "What can I do?" Individual activity against crime usually reveals itself in sporadic bursts of indignant response to a specific act or a series of acts of crime, to the sensational, or to the crime that got a little too close to home this time.

Nonetheless, the citizen can do a great deal to help not only the police and the community, but also himself. In fact, there is a *need* for citizen involvement in crime prevention and law enforcement, as some communities have shown by their active cooperation.

§ 5.19 The Indianapolis experience

In October 1961, an elderly retired psychologist, Dr. Margaret Marshall, was fatally beaten by a teenage purse snatcher on her way home from church in Indianapolis. In the wake of the attack, police and local newspapers were peppered with phone calls and letters from women, demanding that "something be done" to make the streets safe after dark.

It occurred to Eugene S. Pulliam, assistant publisher of *The Indianapolis News,* that the women themselves might have some valuable ideas, so he asked Mrs. Margaret Moore of the paper's public-relations department to look into the matter. Mrs. Moore called together 30 leaders of Indianapolis women's clubs for a brainstorming luncheon. Counting on their clubs for fund raising and as reservoirs of volunteers (together they represented some 50,000 Indianapolis women), the leaders mapped out several committees, each to tackle a specific factor the women felt to be contributing to the city's overall crime pattern. Thus, the Indianapolis Women's Anti-Crime Crusade was born.[1]

During this period, retail stores, service stations, banks and other places of business had been frequent victims of burglary and armed robbery. All business people were faced with the threat of higher insurance costs because of increased frequency and greater severity of crimes. The Indianapolis Chamber of Commerce began to take an active role in upgrading law enforcement. It solicited emergency funds from private firms and formed the Special Committee on Law Enforcement. This committee, in turn, was made up of task forces on the various aspects of crime control—uniformed police, the investigative division (principally the Detective Division), courts and prosecution, public information, and legislation. The Chamber of Commerce and the city government jointly financed a study on police reform by the Indiana University for Police Administration that led to substantial reforms in police operational techniques and organization during 1963-1964.[2]

Other organizations have subsequently participated in the Indianapolis anticrime movement. One such group is the Citizens Forum. Formed in 1967 for a clean-up and beautification campaign, it has since that time organized a large number of block clubs and has broadened its activities to include self-help and crime-awareness programs.

Numerous church and social clubs have similar programs; organizations attack the social and economic causes of crime. The Volunteer Advisory Council and Citizens Against Poverty, for example, have focused on the problem of unemployment in Indianapolis.

In 1967, *The Indianapolis Star* initiated a program called "Crime Alert." A special police department number was publicized with the help of the Chamber of Commerce and the local merchants. Citizens could call this number to report not only crimes but also suspicious situations or persons. Police response was guaranteed even if the caller chose to remain anonymous.

The citizen involvement campaign has contributed to a slowdown in the growth of the overall crime rate in the Indianapolis metropolitan area. In particular, these programs, especially the Crime Alert Program, have discouraged the commission of crimes of burglary and robbery. Groups like the Volunteer Advisory Council and Citizens Against Poverty have, at the same time, fought unemployment in Indianapolis, recognizing that an increase in employment and the decrease in crime are more than casually related. Also, among other things, a vigorous city administration has kept playgrounds open and youth occupied, thus contributing to a decrease in delinquency.

For all the success that the anticrime campaign has had in Indianapolis, it has nevertheless been subjected to some criticism. These groups, many feel, deal not with the causes of crime but with acts of violence per se, and therefore offer only short range solutions to the problem of crime in their city. Moreover, say the critics, some groups are repressively paternalistic and their fervor to "clean up their city" has vigilante undertones.

There is, however, reason to be optimistic about the idea of citizen involvement in law enforcement after studying the example of Indianapolis. In many cases, these groups have had good liaison with the police force, which respects their judgement and helps them to solve community problems. Experiments and pilot projects in other cities have been equally encouraging,[3] leading to the conclusion that citizen participation in law enforcement has a promising future.

§ 5.20   The danger of vigilantism

Citizen action in crime control is nothing new in the United States. Prior to 1833, no paid, professional police forces existed in this country. Sheriffs and constables had responsibility for law enforcement, and nightwatchmen patrolled towns and villages. Extremely violent disorders were dealt with by the military. Direct dealing with the criminal by the citizens was common, as was ad hoc community enforcement. The result was often chaotic, and justice was often roughly served because of the vigilante nature of most of the citizen crime control groups.[4]

From our national experience, two major dangers apply to citizen participation in law enforcement: first, vigilantism—volunteers exercising full police powers with no police disciplines and few legal constraints—and, second, the anti-police patrol—a community organization created independently of and in opposition to the police and serving as a roving check on its behavior.[5] Vigilantism will inevitably produce oppressive and unfair practices, while anti-police patrol will worsen police-citizen relations by bringing the two groups into organized conflict.[6] Because of these dangers, therefore, individuals and groups should participate in the fight against crime in conjunction with officially sanctioned programs. Independent, unofficial action directs itself toward fighting the deeply rooted causes of crime like poverty and discrimination, and toward assuming personal responsibility for reducing the temptation to commit crime.

§ 5.21   The informed citizen

The single most important ingredient of improved citizen participation in the law enforcement process is improved understanding of the law and of its enforcers, the police. This can come about only through programs of education. Too few people really know their rights and responsibilities under the law, and fewer still understand the "twilight zones" between dissent and civil disobedience, liberty and license, legitimate protest and anarchy.

Most elementary and high school teachers have not been trained to teach about the interrelationship of law, government, and society. The old discipline of "civics" has largely disappeared from many schools. Many communities now make up for this gap by sponsoring in-school programs that provide speakers on law and law enforcement and issue publications geared to inform the teenager of those aspects of the law that most directly affect him. Police departments, as part of their developing community relations programs, send personnel into the schools to explain such concepts as safety, crime prevention, and drug abuse to the young.

Similar programs are being conducted with adult groups and by adult groups in an increasing number of cities. The most common education program currently in effect is the distribution of pamphlets on a wide variety of subjects dealing with crime prevention, and with the response to and the reporting of crime. Local citizens groups consider the war on crime as part of their overall programs, like beautification and recreation. Citizens with an interest in the upkeep and value of their property are now more aware than ever of what crime in the community means to their pocketbooks.

Such organizations as the American Association of Federated Women's Clubs and the National Auto Theft Bureau have conducted auto theft prevention campaigns in several cities by accompanying the police on their rounds, by leaving pamphlets in unlocked cars, and by attaching warnings to parking meters on the dangers of leaving keys in the ignition.[7] Several cities, under the auspices of the Department of Justice, have initiated educational programs to inform the public about what it can do to fight crime. Newspapers, television, and radio have taken upon themselves a responsible community service role by constantly reminding people of what they can do when faced by crime.

The Oakland, California police department initiated in March of 1969 an education program called "Operation Involvement." This project is a controlled experiment, financed and manned by the department itself, that attempts to reach every homeowner, resident, and businessman in defined geographical areas to explain the crime problem and the problems of the police, to urge citizens to report crime, to teach citizens how to prevent crime, and to restore a sense of community and mutual reliance in the neighborhood. This umbrella program will eventually expand to the entire city. To date, it has already effectively cut home burglaries and car thefts in the experimental areas.

Citizen involvement programs sanctioned by, and often directed and funded by, the police have been tried with varying degrees of success in cities throughout the country. Such programs could help many communities where, according to needs and capabilities, they can be combined, adapted, or rejected.

§ 5.22   Citizen auxiliaries

Crime has dropped 40 percent since the fall of 1968 in the 107th Precinct in Queens, N.Y., for example, because of the efforts of 120 male residents of the Electchester Housing Project who have volunteered their time to the New York City Police Auxiliary. The auxiliary, under the command of Captain Amile Racine, is the largest volunteer police force in the world with about 3,700 active men and women participants.

Candidates are carefully screened, then enrolled in 40 hours of course work. An auxiliary policeman is considered active when he contributes 20 hours of volunteer time per quarter. The volunteer must buy his own uniform and equipment, but he does not wear a gun unless licensed to do so for other reasons. The auxiliary police generally patrol in pairs in or near the precinct where they live.

The New York Auxiliary Police assist in preventing major racial outbreaks, substitute for regular police during civil disorders, participate in traffic and crowd control, in locating witnesses, and in other police chores—thus relieving the professional of time-consuming jobs which often keep him from performing his primary law-enforcement function.

Similar, although smaller, auxiliary forces exist in other cities throughout the country. The one in Indianapolis is one more cog in the crime-fighting mechanism which has contributed to that city's success. Cities like Denver, Colorado have volunteer reserve squads trained in crowd control and traffic control, in the use of firearms (which they generally do not carry), and in disaster response. These men often patrol as observers in police cars with regular officers, and they have responded to natural disasters, such as floods, by contributing the additional necessary personnel to patrol and to safeguard the city.

Auxiliaries put more sets of eyes and ears on to the street to detect crimes and summon the police; they thus deter criminals. James Q. Wilson has recently described citizen auxiliaries as perhaps "the single most effective addition to police practice," and he has urged that the President of the United States use his office and prestige to enlist citizen interest and action in such programs.[8]

Citizen auxiliaries could be greatly improved if they could reimburse volunteers for or provide them with their uniforms and equipment, as well as compensate them for services in many cities where there is a shortage of police manpower. Their most valuable contribution may be relieving the regular police from activities not directly associated with crime, such as traffic and crowd control.[9] Short of creating a separate agency for these functions, this may prove the most effective means of freeing well-trained and badly needed personnel for normal police activities.[10] Also, citizen auxiliaries, especially the women volunteers, could provide relief at the precinct houses from the volume of paper work that must be handled by regular police.

§ 5.23   Youth patrols

Youth patrols have become increasingly common in our cities in recent years. Most began as riot control units when local citizens insisted that, if left alone, they could bring their communities under control. A notable example is the young men in Tampa, Florida, who are called "White Hats" because of their distinguishing helmets. The White Hats, during the summer disorders of 1967, were decisive in quieting the city. Instead of disbanding afterwards, they continued by acting as advisors to the Commission on Human Relations on the problems of the people who live in Negro slums, and by maintaining their unarmed patrols.[11]

Like many other cities, Atlanta, Georgia initiated an experimental Junior Deputy Program in the summer of 1968 that was so successful that it continued in the summer of 1969. In addition, the police department has a general youth program involving some 2,000 young people in recreational programs. The Junior Deputy Program is designed to improve community relations. Each young man (minimum age 17) is called a Community Service Officer and he patrols his neighborhood.

So successful have the Youth Patrols been, throughout the country, that cities that have not yet organized them have, for the most part, put them under serious consideration. In March of 1968, New York conducted a one-week experiment to study the feasibility of maintaining such a group on a permanent basis. This idea of having young men from New York City ghetto areas patrol the areas in which they live in an effort to bring services directly to the people and help combat crime was, considering the short period allotted for the experiment, very successful. The 22 young volunteers, found through community groups, churches, and word of mouth, were assigned in platoons to beats in the areas between Fifth and Seventh Avenues and 110th and 127th Streets. They were equipped with walkie-talkies, and wore "uniforms" of tan and brown jackets. During their 11 a.m. to 2 a.m. duty, they broke up fights, reported suspicious situations, escorted women from work to home, and reported such things as potentially dangerous uncollected refuse, unsecured vacant buildings, defective trash barrels, pot holes, and abandoned refrigerators with doors that had not been removed. The success of the experiment was indicated by the favorable response of the community to their many services and by the enthusiasm of the participants for the program.[12] The city of New York is now seriously planning to make the program permanent.

The most important aspect of having youth patrols is that the police department has, out on the street, agents who can communicate with their contemporaries. Crime has risen most in the 16-25 age group, and many of these young people are out of reach of not only the police, but of older people in general. Giving members of this age group their own "Mod Squad.' or patrol, may help to restore their trust in the police and to break down the ever-growing barriers between them.

§ 5.24   Volunteer receptionists

New York City precinct stations receive more than five million calls for help a year, a large percentage of which are not related to the law enforcement function of the police. In December 1967 the Department began a pilot program in which twenty housewives and other women volunteers living in the 23rd Precinct worked on Friday and Saturday nights at the station on 104th Street, learning the needs and listening to the requests of local residents. The Ford Foundation subsequently granted funds to the Police Department for expansion of the program to two more precincts.

The receptionists' duties include greeting visitors, providing information, or putting the inquirer in touch with the appropriate official in the station or in a city agency. Police Commissioner

Howard R. Leary has expressed the hope that this program will reduce the friction between his men and the community by "humanizing the police," while at the same time permitting the station houses to provide greater service to the people living in the slums by offering advice and counsel on their health, housing, education, and welfare programs.

§ 5.25 Community centers

Programs such as the Community Action Center in Washington, D.C., are being conducted throughout the United States by urban police departments. The purpose is like that of the volunteer receptionists—to bridge the gap between the citizenry and the police in order to make the "system" a little more responsive to the people while at the same time facilitating the work of the police in law enforcement. The pilot project in the 13th Precinct in Washington is to engage paid resident workers in satellite centers to provide around-the-clock assistance to citizens referred by police on patrol as well as to those who walk in off the street.

Denver's Police Department has an on-going community relations program in which citizens meet every Wednesday evening at the precinct stations to voice their grievances. This program has met with varying degrees of success depending on the precinct and, as has been the experience in Washington and other cities, the meetings often deteriorate into shouting matches where everyone gets "off his chest" what has been bothering him about the police or the public during the previous week. Chaotic as these meetings may sound, they have often been constructive in restoring communications within the community between the police and the people and in giving both sides a channel for expression.[13] As one community relations director explained, "I would rather have them shout at me there than to have them ignore me or hate me out on the street when I really need them."

Experience has shown, however, that programs like these are extremely fragile and that failure may preclude additional programs for some time to come. Care must be taken at the outset to fully understand and outline the boundaries of and barriers to action in the community.

§ 5.26 Improved crime reporting

Generally, when one wants to call the police, the number must be

Jooked up. Most people still do not keep emergency numbers handy and many do not know who to call, especially in the case of overlapping jurisdictions (city, state, park police, etc.). In some cities, several numbers are listed for the same police department. Precincts often have different telephone numbers from one another. In an emergency, this becomes an impossible situation for most people. Frequently, people dial the operator, explain the situation and trust her to get response from the proper authorities.

Information campaigns, publicizing one emergency number, have been successful in a number of cities. Programs such as Crime Alert in Indianapolis, Chec-Mate in Saginaw, Michigan, Crime Check[14] in Omaha, Nebraska, to name a few, facilitate the reporting of crime and of suspicious situations.

Under these programs, a central switchboard emergency number is well publicized, and calls are immediately put through to a dispatcher. In some cases, the caller need not identify himself or become "involved" beyond making the phone call.

In Omaha, in the two weeks after official announcement of Crime Check, the call load went up 11 percent, a considerable increase. In the first seven months of the Indianapolis program, police dispatchers received 63,547 additional calls, and 1,041 more arrests were made than in the corresponding period in 1966.

In all cases where rapid telephone crime reporting has been effective, the program has had the complete support of local businessmen, the press, the government, and police, as well as of the general public. Sustained interest in and promotion of this program seems to be its most essential ingredient.

Some cities have simplified reporting even further by recently installing a special short telephone number, "911." Pay phones have been converted to give a free dial tone so that the operator can be dialed without the usual dime. Strong arguments support a nationwide, universal telephone number such as "911" similar to the programs which now exist in Belgium, Denmark, Sweden, and England.[15] The best reason is the speed with which one obtains the proper authority in an emergency. Secondly, response time, especially in crimes of violence, is extremely important to "hot" apprehensions. Catching a criminal on or near the scene of the crime is possible only if the policeman is on the spot or called in immediately. Rapid response may save the police department hours, even days, of investigation and pursuit in the apprehension of a criminal.[16]

Another method of crime reporting that is catching on is the telephone chain. In this case, citizens, especially businessmen, are urged to keep in touch with one another and with the police and to keep an eye out for the others' property. If they see a suspicious circumstance, they immediately call the police and one another. The Neighborhood Crime Prevention Council in Seattle, Washington, sponsors a program of this type, as does the Harbor Division of the Los Angeles Police Department.

More and more police departments are also urging citizens to let them know about anything going on in the community that would affect their work. In Portland, Oregon for example, the Sheriff's Officer has been passing out leaflets that say "Do you know something that the sheriff of Multnomah County should know? By addressing a letter to me and marking 'Personal' on the envelope you can be sure that I will personally read your letter. P.S. You may remain anonymous if you wish." This technique does bring in an expected number of crank letters, but occasionally it yields information about a pending or past crime that makes the program worthwhile.

In addition to these crime-reporting programs, Motorola Communications and Electronics, Inc., has sponsored over the past two years a Community Radio Watch program, which has been formally adopted by nearly 700 American cities and towns. Each city enlists the cooperation of individuals and companies with two-way radio equipped vehicles, asking each driver to act as additional "eyes and ears" for the police. Typical calls by observant drivers include highway accidents, gang fights, burglaries, medical emergencies and fires. As a public service, Motorola makes available all the necessary materials in any quantity to any community, free of charge. (Community Radio Watch, 1301 East Algonquin Road, Schaumburg, Illinois, 60172).

§ 5.27 Block mothers

A program which is becoming popular throughout the nation is the block mother, or "helping hands," program. Responsible women are trained by social welfare and police officials to care for and supervise children and to interview adolescents and older youths. The program is designed to prevent the isolated problem of child molesting and also to provide emergency babysitting or supervision of older youngsters. Any threatened, frightened or run-away child can seek refuge in the home of a block mother who displays a "clasped hands" sign in the front window. This program is especially effective in urban ghettos where large numbers of children are concentrated in a small area.

§ 5.28   *Preventive patrols*

The neighborhood patrol is perhaps the oldest form of law enforcement. It is generally set up by assigning evening shifts to pairs of volunteers within a defined community who drive or walk around keeping their eyes open for lingering strangers or anything out of the usual. Given enough willing volunteers, this can effectively deter burglars and vandals, and it adds the extra eyes to the neighborhood after dark which the police need.

§ 5.29   *Youth activities*

The best deterrent from crime for the young is to keep them busy in constructive activity. To this end, it is the responsibility of not only the family and the government, but the community at large, to provide the activities and facilities necessary to attract young people. Citizens groups should urge more parks with better equipment and club houses. After-school and summer programs should offer variety and challenge. Young people should be urged to join organizations like the Y.M.C.A., Boy Scouts, and the local Boys' Club. Gangs should be engaged in constructive activities. Teen-age boys can be involved in educational as well as financially rewarding activities. Employers should be encouraged to give part-time employment as a viable alternative to "hanging out" and looking for excitement in the form of criminal activity.[17]

The problem today seems to be a shortage of adults willing to donate their time and energy to youth activities. Many are too busy or too tired after work to pitch in the few extra hours of volunteer time necessary to assure the success of a program. This seems to be the malaise of parents and adults in general these days. Yet, in order to get at the problem of juvenile delinquency, the community has to meet the young people half-way in terms of commitment by providing the large number of volunteers required.

§ 5.30   Citizen pressure groups

Citizen groups have been very active in promoting anti-crime educational programs. Yet they have another role of equal importance, that of actively participating in community planning and in pressuring the government at the local level to provide recreational facilities, well-lit streets, and adequate police forces. Also, like the Chamber of Commerce in Indianapolis, they can form study groups or task forces in order to better understand the system and to operate as informed pressure groups. Most important for the citizens group is getting attention focused on the deeply-rooted economic and social causes of crime.

§ 5.31   Anticrime organizations

The National Council on Crime and Delinquency is perhaps one of the oldest organizations in this country with the singular purpose of reducing crime. Similar groups are being established throughout the country as public awareness of the burgeoning crime rate has increased. These organizations conduct research into the causes and prevention of crime, as well as programs designed to improve police methods, court procedures, the corrections system, and citizen involvement. They depend primarily on individual citizens, companies, and foundations for financial support. Groups of this type, when broad-based, can be very effective through their programs and should receive more support from federal, state and local governments. They should be discouraged only when they take on political overtones or adopt an extreme ideological approach to crime.

§ 5.32   The involvement of the individual

Perhaps the most effective role against crime the individual can take is getting out and actively pursuing solutions with his neighbors. Through civic associations, block organizations, church groups, and direct action groups the individual can participate. He can volunteer his time and/or money to programs designed to improve the material and human resources of the community. He can attack some of the underlying causes of crime such as poverty or lack of education, or he can deal directly with juveniles, ex-convicts, and dope addicts to prevent crime. In any respect, commitment and involvement are a solution—far better, more extensive and beneficial to society than arming oneself and hiding behind locked doors waiting for *them* (the government, the police, the courts, the elected representatives) to do it all.

The individual also has the opportunity on a day-to-day basis to prevent crime by reducing the opportunity to commit it. Many crimes would not be committed, indeed many criminal careers would not begin, if there were fewer opportunities for crime. The victim is often an unconscious accessory to the crime through neglect, ignorance or naiveté. The individual should take action in this respect by educating himself with regard to protection of property and making a conscious effort to remove temptation to crime.

Crime is made attractive and easy by the citizen who leaves his newspapers on the doorstep when he is away. The most blatant example of citizen negligence is auto theft. According to F.B.I. statistics, the key had been left in the ignition or the ignition had been left unlocked in 42 percent of all stolen cars.

Homeowners and apartment dwellers are also careless. One-fifth of the burglaries were made easier for thieves because residents left the doors or windows unlocked. Other burglaries can be traced to giving keys to unknown repairmen—and allowing newspapers to pile up, or similar acts tipping off the burglar that the family is away.

Many crimes would not occur if individuals had proper locks on their doors and windows and enough lighting to discourage prowlers. Simply leaving a light on inside the house while absent may be enough to keep a prospective burglar away. Businessmen are also careless and need to be better informed about locks, lights, and alarm systems to protect their property.[18]

Obviously, the individual can do much to combat crime. Since people neither want to be the victims of crime nor to live in fear of crime, and since they care about crime, why are they not more motivated to do something about the apparently spiralling crime rate?

A survey by the President's Commission on Law Enforcement and Administration of Justice asked people whether they had ever "gotten together with other people around here or has any group or organization you belong to met and discussed the problem of crime or taken some sort of action to combat crime?"[19] Only 12 percent answered yes, although the question was quite broad and included any kind of group meeting or discussion. Also most persons did not believe that they as individuals could do anything about crime in their neighborhoods; just over 17 percent thought that they could do something about the situation. Yet, there are more than one million independent volunteer organizations in the United States; 320,000 churches with more than 100 million members, 2,000 united funds and community chests, 35,000 voluntary welfare organizations, 36 million Americans in fraternal and service organizations. A nation-wide poll estimates that sixty-one million adult Americans would, if asked, contribute 245 million man-hours every week to voluntary activities.[20]

The problem of non-involvement goes even deeper than failure to participate in crime prevention programs, however. In recent years, the media have been filled with stories of passive bystanders, remaining aloof and inactive although witnessing a crime which could be forestalled or interrupted by an action as simple as a telephone call.

Psychologists John M. Darley and Bibb Latane have made an experimental study of why bystanders do not respond during the actual commission of a crime or other crisis. They conclude:

> It is our impression that nonintervening subjects had not decided *not* to respond. Rather, they were still in a state of indecision and conflict concerning whether to respond or not. The emotional behavior of these nonresponding subjects was a sign of their continuing conflict, a conflict that other people resolved by responding. The distinction seems an academic one for the victim, since he gets no help in either case, but it is an extremely important one for arriving at an understanding of why bystanders fail to help.
>
> Thus, the stereotype of the unconcerned, depersonalized *homo urbanis* blandly watching the misfortunes of others proved inaccurate. Instead, we find a bystander to an emergency is an anguished individual in genuine doubt, concerned to do the right thing but compelled to make complex decisions under pressure of stress and fear. His reactions are shaped by the actions of others and all too frequently by their inaction.[21]

As this study simply points out, the individual, when faced with immediate crisis, has to make a series of decisions, all of which are influenced by the presence of other people around him. He must first *notice* that something is happening. He must then *interpret* that event as an emergency, and then he must decide that he has *personal responsibility* to intervene. If he fails to notice an emergency, or if he concludes that he is not personally responsible for acting, he will then leave the victim unhelped.

Group behavior is quite different from individual behavior. Darley and Latane use this illustration, among others:

> If your car breaks down on a busy highway, hundreds of drivers whiz by without anyone's stopping to help; if you are stuck on a nearby deserted country road, whoever passes you first is apt to stop. The personal responsibility that a passerby feels makes the difference.
>
> A driver on a lonely road knows that if he doesn't stop to help, the person will not get help; the same individual on the crowded highway feels that he personally is no more responsible than any of a hundred other drivers.[22]

The individual, then, can decide that when he next confronts a fellow citizen in apparent danger or distress he will take some action, on the chance that the other fellow does in fact need his help; he will stop at the next gas station and report the plight, he will pick up the telephone and call the police, he will ask the other fellow if he needs help.

At the community level, leaders are needed who can mobilize individual citizens into action against crime. These citizens are not usually inactive out of apathy, but because so many others are inactive, and because personal responsibility has been so effectively diluted. Appropriate leadership can tap these resources.

The entire social fabric of our urban areas is being altered by the changing patterns of conduct of our "law-abiding citizens." The single most damaging of the effects of violent crime is fear, and that fear must not be belittled.[23] This fear, according to the President's Commission on Law Enforcement and Administration of Justice, "has greatly impoverished the lives of many Americans, especially those who live in high-crime neighborhoods in large cities. People stay behind locked doors of their homes rather than risk walking in the streets at night. Poor people spend money on taxis because they are afraid to walk or to use public transportion. Sociable people are afraid to talk to those they do not know."[24]

America is slowly becoming a fortress society—each man standing alone in fearful defense against his fellow man. We are losing the valuable traditions of community cooperation and personal responsibility for the welfare of the whole. This trend must be reversed by citizen involvement.

Notes

1. Medford S. Evans and Margaret Moore, *The Lawbreakers*, New York: Arlington House, 1968.

2. Chamber of Commerce of the United States, "Indianapolis Chamber Leads in Upgrading Police Quality," *Urban Action Clearing House*, Washington, D.C.: Oct. 1968.

3. At this writing, every major city in the Untied States has some type of citizen involvement program in operation.

4. See the President's Commission on Law Enforcement and Administration of Justice, *Task Force Report: The Police*, Washington, D.C.: Government Printing Office, 1967, for a history of law enforcement in the United States.

5. An example of an anti-police patrol is the "Better Berkeley Council" which was mustering some 20 persons every Friday and Saturday nights to check on the operation of police patrolling Telegraph Avenue in Berkeley, California. See San Francisco Chronical, October 7, 1968, p. 5.

6. This is not to say that the citizen should not concern himself with police ineptness, corruption, or brutality. Rather, he should confine his means of protest to channels other than indiscriminate harassment of the "cop on the beat." This can be counterproductive by simply lowering the morale of the police and resulting in an even less effective police force. There are many legitimate means of registering concern open to citizens.

7. Task Force Report, The Police, *op. cit.*, p. 222.

8. James Q. Wilson, "Crime and Law Enforcement," *Agenda for the Nation*, edited by Kermit Gordon, Washington, D.C.: Brookings Institution, 1968, pp. 186, 206.

9. Except control of protest parades and similar demonstrations, which should be handled by highly-trained, well-disciplined police regulars.

10. Oakland, California is initiating a program with LEAA funds that will start with ten "police representatives" who are not required to have the training of full-fledged police officers, but can more than adequately perform many police functions such as traffic and crowd control. This program has caught on in other areas with varying degrees of success.

11. See for complete background Terry Ann Knopf, *Youth Patrols: An Experiment in Community Participation*, Waltham, Massachusetts: Brandeis U., The Lemberg Center for the Study of Violence, 1969.

12. George Nash, *The Community Patrol Corps: A Descriptive Evaluation of the One-Week Experiment*, New York: Columbia University, Bureau of Applied Social Research, May 1968.

13. Eleanor Harlow, "Problems in Police-Community Relations, A Review of the Literature," *Information Review on Crime and Delinquency*, vol. 1, No. 5, New York: National Council on Crime and Delinquency, February, 1969.

14. Crime Check is a nationwide project of the International Association of Chiefs of Police, Inc.

15. Roger W. Reinke, "A Universal Police Telephone Number," *The Police*

Chief, Washington, D.C.: International Association of Chiefs of Police, February 1968, pp. 10-16.

16. Challenge of Crime in a Free Society, *op. cit.*, p. 97.

17. Pride, Inc. in Washington, D.C. (and expanding into other major U.S. cities) is a prime example of entrepreneurial involvement of young people who might otherwise become delinquents.

18. See U.S., Congress, Senate, Crime Against Small Business: A Report of the Small Business Administration Transmitted to the Select Committee on Small Business, S. Doc. 91-94, 91st Cong., 1st session, 1969.

19. Task Force Report: Crime and its Impact—An Assessment, *op. cit.*, p. 91.

20. From address by John N. Mitchell, Attorney General of the United States, before the Conference on Crime and the Urban Crisis of the National Emergency Committee of the National Council on Crime and Delinquency, Fairmont Hotel, San Francisco, California, February 3, 1969.

21. John M. Darley and Bibb Latane, "Are Passive Bystanders Really Guilty?" *Psychology Today*, reprinted in Washington Post, January 12, 1960, p. B-4.

22. *Id.*

23. Challenge of Crime in a Free Society, *op. cit.*, p. 3.

24. *Ibid.*, p. 52.

INDEX